Cambridge Studies in Comparative Politics

General Editor

Margaret Levi *University of Washington, Seattle*

Assistant General Editors

Kathleen Thelen *Massachusetts Institute of Technology*
Erik Wibbels *Duke University*

Associate Editors

Robert H. Bates *Harvard University*
Stephen Hanson *University of Washington, Seattle*
Torben Iversen *Harvard University*
Stathis Kalyvas *Yale University*
Peter Lange *Duke University*
Helen Milner *Princeton University*
Frances Rosenbluth *Yale University*
Susan Stokes *Yale University*
Sidney Tarrow *Cornell University*

Other Books in the Series

David Austen-Smith, Jeffry A. Frieden, Miriam A. Golden, Karl Ove Moene, and Adam Przeworski, eds., *Selected Works of Michael Wallerstein: The Political Economy of Inequality, Unions, and Social Democracy*

Andy Baker, *The Market and the Masses in Latin America: Policy Reform and Consumption in Liberalizing Economies*

Lisa Baldez, *Why Women Protest? Women's Movements in Chile*

Stefano Bartolini, *The Political Mobilization of the European Left, 1860–1980: The Class Cleavage*

Robert Bates, *When Things Fell Apart: State Failure in Late-Century Africa*

Series list continues following the Index.

Waves of War

Nationalism, State Formation, and
Ethnic Exclusion in the Modern World

Andreas Wimmer

CAMBRIDGE
UNIVERSITY PRESS

CAMBRIDGE
UNIVERSITY PRESS

University Printing House, Cambridge CB2 8BS, United Kingdom

Published in the United States of America by Cambridge University Press, New York

Cambridge University Press is part of the University of Cambridge.

It furthers the University's mission by disseminating knowledge in the pursuit of
education, learning and research at the highest international levels of excellence.

www.cambridge.org
Information on this title: www.cambridge.org/9781107673243

First published 2013
4th printing 2014

Printed in the United Kingdom by Clays, St Ives plc

A catalogue record for this publication is available from the British Library

Library of Congress Cataloguing in Publication data
Wimmer, Andreas.
  Waves of war : nationalism, state formation, and ethnic exclusion in the modern
  world / Andreas Wimmer.
     p.   cm. – (Cambridge studies in comparative politics)
  Includes bibliographical references and index.
  ISBN 978-1-107-02555-4 (hardback) – ISBN 978-1-107-67324-3 (paperback)
  1. Nationalism–History–20th century.   2. Nation-state–History–20th
  century.   3. Ethnic groups–Political activity–History–20th century.   I. Title.
  JC311.W469 2013
     925409′04–dc23   2012016081

ISBN 978-1-107-02555-4 Hardback
ISBN 978-1-107-67324-3 Paperback

Contents

Figures

Tables

Acknowledgments

Many colleagues have helped to shape and sharpen the arguments that run through the chapters of this book with their suggestions, criticisms, and encouragements. Many more labored on the different datasets they analyzed, so many, in fact, that acknowledging them needs to be relegated to the first footnotes of each chapter. Here, I would like to thank the coauthors of the various journal articles on which four of these chapters are based.

I had the pleasure to work with Brian Min, formerly a graduate student in political science at UCLA and now assistant professor at the University of Michigan, over the first seven years after we had both moved to the City of Angels. During our intense collaboration on the two projects that resulted in Chapters 4 and 5, he patiently, politely, and good-humoredly introduced me to the secrets of quantitative research and data management. Lars-Erik Cederman, professor of political science at the ETH Zurich, initiated our collaboration on the dataset analyzed in Chapter 5. This allowed us to test my argument that ethno-political inequality is a key factor in explaining contemporary conflict processes. Clemens Kroneberg recently received his PhD in sociology from the University of Mannheim and is now assistant professor there. Five years ago, he approached me with the idea to formally model aspects of the theory of ethnic boundary making I was working on, which eventually led us to write Chapter 2. Yuval Feinstein is a PhD student in the department of sociology at UCLA and soon to be assistant professor at the University of Haifa. He has suffered with me through the pains of building a dataset, analyzed in Chapter 3, on territories for which no data exist, and shared the joys of an analysis full of surprises. I thank all of them for having shared these varied journeys with me and for all they have taught me along the way.

Chapter 2 appeared in the *American Journal of Sociology* 118(1): 176–230, 2012 and received the Anatol-Rapoport-Prize from the Modeling and Simulation Section of the *Deutsche Gesellschaft für Soziologie*. Chapter 3 was published in the *American Sociological Review* 75(5): 764–790, 2010. It received the best article award from the Comparative Historical Section of the American Sociological Association.

Chapter 4 was also published by the *American Sociological Review* 71(6): 867–897, 2006. It was fortunate enough to receive the best article awards from both the Comparative Historical and the Political Sociology Sections of the American Sociological Association. Chapter 5 is based on another article published by the *American Sociological Review* 74(2): 316–337, 2009.

The United States Institute of Peace offered a year-long Jennings Randolph Senior Fellowship, which enabled me to put this book together. I am grateful for this opportunity and for the congenial environment that Chantal de Jonge Outraat and her team created for the fellows of the institute. UCLA's International Institute has generously supported my research with course buy-outs over the past years, and the social science dean's research support has nourished the data projects that made this book possible.

Special thanks go to David Laitin, who has carefully and thoroughly read the entire manuscript and offered many insightful and helpful criticisms; to Stathis Kalyvas, who has encouraged my forays into the domain of conflict research in various crucial ways; to Michael Ross, with whom I regularly hike in the Santa Monica mountains to discuss life as well as the joys and disappointments of doing quantitative cross-national research; and to Rogers Brubaker for decade-long friendship, intellectual comradeship, and wise advice in matters small and large.

Introduction and summary

1 THE NARRATIVE IN A NUTSHELL AND THE MORAL OF THE TALE

Nationalism demands that rulers and ruled hail from the same ethnic background. The gradual adoption of this principle of legitimate statehood has transformed the shape of the political world over the past 200 years and has provided the ideological motivation for an increasing number of wars fought in the modern era. Before the age of nationalism set in at the end of the eighteenth century, individuals did not pay much attention to their own ethnic background or that of their rulers. They identified primarily with a local community – a village or town, a clan, or a mosque. In much of Europe and East Asia, their overlords ruled in the name of a divine dynasty, rather than "the people," and many were of different ethnic stock than their subjects. In parts of the Middle East, Africa, or Central Asia, charismatic leaders held tribal confederacies together and were respected and feared for their political skills and military bravery. Vast stretches of land in the Americas, the Middle East, and Eastern Europe were ruled by emperors whose legitimacy derived from spreading God's word across the world (as did the Ottomans and Bourbons) or bringing civilization to "backward" peoples (as France and Great Britain claimed to do in their colonies). At the beginning of the nineteenth century, such empires covered about half of the world's surface, while dynastic kingdoms, tribal confederacies, city-states, and so forth, made up most of the rest, as Figure 1.1 shows.

In this world of empires, dynastic kingdoms, city-states, and tribal confederacies, few wars concerned the ethno-national composition of government. Rather, they were fought by dynastic states over the balance of power between them or over the rightful successor to a throne. Empires conquered fertile lands

I thank Wesley Hiers, Michael Ross, Steve Ward, and Sarah Zingg Wimmer for helpful comments and suggestions on various drafts of this introduction. A previous version was presented at the New School of Social Research's Social Imagination Seminar, to which Eiko Ikegami had kindly invited me, and at the department of sociology of Columbia University.

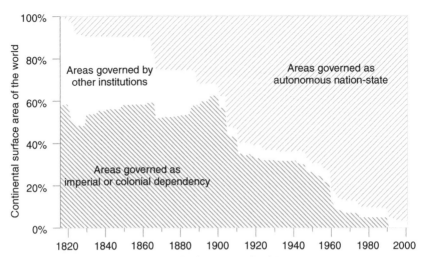

FIGURE 1.1 Empires, nation-states, and other types of polities, 1816–2001

Notes: states smaller than 25,000 km² are excluded; data are from Chapter 4.

far away from their capitals. Alliances of city-states competed over trade routes or rural hinterlands. Rebellious movements saw to bring heavenly order to the corrupt politics of the day or to repeal an unjust tax increase. At the beginning of the nineteenth century, still only one-fourth of the wars were ethno-nationalist, as can be seen from Figure 1.2, while balance-of-power wars between states, wars of conquest, and non-ethnic civil wars each comprised another quarter of all violent conflicts.

A contemporary observer looks at a different world and through different eyes. The globe is divided into a series of sovereign states, each supposed to represent a nation bound together by shared history and common culture. To us, this political map seems as obvious as the shapes of continents and the rivers that run through them. With the exception of the Middle Eastern monarchies and some small European principalities, most of today's states are ruled in the name of a nation of equal citizens, rather than dynasty or divine will. Statehood has become so much associated with nationalist principles that the terms nations and states are often used interchangeably, as in the "United Nations" or in "inter-national."

Most of today's more prominent and protracted wars are also associated with the national principle – the idea that each people should be self-ruled, that ethnic like should be governed by like. The independence struggle of Abkhazians against the Georgian state or the conflict between Protestant and Catholic parties and militias in Northern Ireland come to mind. Figure 1.2 shows that at the end of the twentieth century, over three-quarters of all full-scale wars – those armed conflicts costing more than 1,000 battle deaths – were fought either by

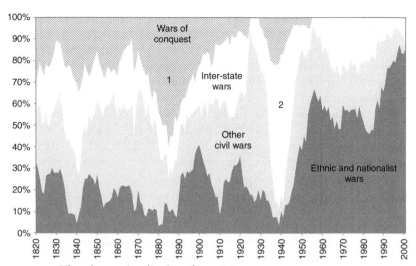

FIGURE I.2 The ethno-nationalization of war, 1816–2001

Notes: ten-year moving averages; for data sources see Chapter 4; 1 marks wars associated with the conquests of Africa and Central Asia; 2 marks wars associated with World War II.

nationalists who seek to establish a separate nation-state or over the ethnic balance of power within an existing state. Contrary to what Karl Marx had predicted, the twentieth century has turned into the age of ethno-nationalist conflict, rather than revolutionary class struggle.

This book seeks to explain this momentous transformation of the political world – from a world of multiethnic empires, dynastic kingdoms, tribal confederacies, and city-states to a world of states each ruled in the name of a nation properly seated in the general assembly of the UN; from localized political identities to large-scale ethnic or national communities with often millions, sometimes tens of millions, of members; from wars of conquest, succession, and tax rebellions to wars in the name of national sovereignty and grandeur, ethnic autonomy, and the like.

How has this transformation come about? Existing scholarship has mostly focused on how strong, territorially centralized states have emerged in Western Europe and beyond. Charles Tilly's famed dictum that "wars made states and states made war" referred to the rise of these absolutist states from the sixteenth to the eighteenth centuries. This book takes this story from the early modern period into our present day and from Western Europe to the world. It is not concerned with the development of the sovereign territorial state, as were Tilly and his successors, but why these states became nation-states and how this particular model of legitimizing political power proliferated across the world. It shows that the shift from dynasticism and empire to the nation-state was both the cause and consequence of a new wave of wars long after early modern states had been formed in previous centuries of warfare. This new wave, carried forward by the power of nationalist ideologies, reached different parts of the world at different points in time, rolling over Latin America during the early nineteenth century and finally arriving in the Soviet Union by the end of the twentieth.

In a nutshell, the argument offered in this book proceeds along the following lines. Nationalism as a new principle of legitimacy emerged from Tilly's war-making Western states. Increasing state centralization and military mobilization led to a new contract between rulers and ruled: the exchange of political participation and public goods against taxation and the military support by the population at large. The idea of the nation as an extended family of political loyalty and shared identity provided the ideological framework that reflected and justified this new compact. It meant that elites and masses should identify with each other and that rulers and ruled should hail from the same people.

This new compact made the first nation-states of Great Britain, the United States, and France militarily and politically more powerful than dynastic kingdoms or land-based empires because they offered the population a more favorable exchange relationship with their rulers and were thus considered more legitimate. Ambitious political leaders around the world adopted this new model of statehood, hoping that they too would one day preside over similarly powerful states. These nationalists subsequently were able to establish new nation-states wherever the power configuration favored their ascent and allowed them to overthrow or gradually transform the old regime, leading to cascades of nation-state creations that altered the political face of the world over the past 200 years.

This shift from empire, dynasticism, or theocracy to national principles of legitimizing political power is a major source of war in the modern era. First, nationalists who now portrayed the ethnic hierarchies of empire as violations of the like-over-like principle resorted to arms to fight for independent nation-states. Second, newly founded nation-states competed with each other over ethnically mixed territories or over the political fate of co-nationals across the border who were ruled by ethnic others. Third, civil wars broke out when the new nation-states were captured by ethnic elites who excluded others from the political and symbolic benefits of self-rule. Such ethno-political exclusion and conflict is especially marked in states that lacked the institutional capacity and organizational bases to realize the project of nation building and to offer political participation and public goods to the population at large, rather than only to the ethnic constituencies of the dominant elites.

Nationalism thus motivated a bloody, generation-long struggle over who should rule over whom. It lasted until the like-over-like principle was realized through border changes, expulsions and ethnic cleansings, assimilation and nation building or political accommodation and power sharing between various ethnic elites. Based on the global datasets introduced further below, we can calculate that the likelihood of war more than doubles after nationalism has gained a foothold in a political arena; and it remains high over generations after a nation-state has been founded.[1]

2 MAIN CONTRIBUTIONS

While the book tells this story of the rise and global spread of the nation-state and the waves of war it generated, it is not a history book, and it does not have a narrative structure. Rather, it explores the forces underlying these historical developments with the help of social science techniques of analysis and with large datasets that cover the entire modern world – the kind of datasets that make it possible to draw the preceding two figures. Besides introducing such new datasets, the analysis offers important substantial insights for our under-standing of world history over the past two centuries. Both contributions are briefly summarized here.

2.1 Bringing power and legitimacy center stage

The book aims to show that political power and legitimacy need to move center stage in all three areas of scholarship that it addresses: on nation building and ethnic politics, on nation-state formation, and on war. It will demonstrate how particular power relations between the state and other political actors combine with their varying visions of a legitimate political order to produce different political identities, forms of statehood, and dynamics of violent conflict.

More specifically, the book derives the political salience and legitimacy of political identities from a specific distribution of power and resources between the state and the population at large. Both ethnic group formation and nation building result from a renegotiation of the relationship between rulers and ruled during the process of political modernization (in line with Bates 1974; Wimmer 2002). Depending on how the distribution of resources and power between rulers and ruled change, political alliances form along ethnic lines, or the population at large shifts its loyalty to the state elite and identifies with the overarching national category. Ethnic groups and nations thus both represent equilibrium outcomes of the modernization process. This analysis contributes to the "constructivist" literature on ethnicity and nationalism by offering a precise, mechanism-based

---

[1] More precisely, the predicted probability of war is 1.1 percent in territories without nationalism – controlling for degrees of democratization, neighboring wars, the presence of oil resources, and political instability. This probability increases to 2.5 percent in the period after a first national(ist) organization has been founded. These figures were calculated on the basis of Model 1 in Table 4.2. Results are almost identical if we also control for levels of economic development and population size, which reduce the number of observations considerably.

analysis of the power configurations that provide either nations or specific ethnic cleavages with popular legitimacy and political meaning.

The book also introduces a power-cum-legitimacy approach to our understanding of the global spread of the nation-state. Shifts in the power relations between adherents of different ideas of legitimate statehood – dynasticism, imperial universalism, or national sovereignty – are crucial in understanding this momentous transformation of the political world over the past 200 years (in line with the general thrust of the work of Roeder 2007). The nation-state form was not universally adopted because one society after the other gradually ripened enough – as theories of modernization would have it – to finally fall as fully blossomed nations onto the garden of the inter-"national" community. Nor did the nation-state proliferate across the globe because the international system forced national sovereignty upon people after people. Similar to contagion processes, the global rise of the nation-state resulted from the concatenation of local and regional power shifts in favor of nationalists without much help from the global system. This power-configurational analysis sheds new light on a process that remains poorly understood, despite its obvious historical importance, in comparative sociology and international relations scholarship.

Finally, the book offers an analysis of war that again brings questions of political power and legitimacy to the foreground. It demonstrates that the shift of these principles of legitimacy – from empire to nation-state – is a major cause of both inter-state and civil wars over the past 200 years. This is often neglected in existing scholarship in international relations, which has paid only scarce attention to how transforming the nature of the units composing the inter-"national" system has affected war processes. The book also brings power and legitimacy to the study of civil wars that is at the core of a vast and fast-growing comparative politics literature. It demonstrates that civil wars and armed conflicts are most likely in ethnocracies that violate the principles of ethnic self-rule. Dominant political economy approaches to civil war, which focus on the conditions that make rebellion economically attractive or militarily feasible, need to be complemented with an analysis of the struggle over the power and legitimacy of the state.

2.2 New data to answer old questions

Studying nation-state formation and war has long been the exclusive domain of qualitative styles of historical research. The classic oeuvres on nationalism and the nation-state, for example, were written by historically minded social scientists such as Ernest Gellner, John Breuilly, or Michael Mann. They traced the origins of the nation-state in England, France, and the United States and then described, using examples from across the world, how it diffused over the globe. Besides these world historical narratives, entire libraries have been written on each individual trajectory of nation-state formation in the West. Others have teased out the differences, similarities, and interlinkages between a handful of cases, often deriving big conclusions from small numbers.[2]

Most of the chapters that follow use the tools of statistical analysis to identify recurring patterns in the tapestry woven by hundreds of such specific historical threads. They will analyze newly created datasets that cover the entire world over very long periods of time and will thus allow identifying those causal mechanisms that structure more than one context and period. Such a quantitative approach based on global datasets can counterweigh against the "European provincialism" that plagues the literature on nationalism and nation-state formation, as one of its most prominent authors has trenchantly observed (Anderson 1991: xiii).[3] Emphasizing old-world developments would be less problematic if the nation-state had remained confined to the area of its origin instead of proliferating across the world, or if the earliest nation-states had indeed all been located in Europe such that those of "the rest" could be seen as belated completions of a universal sequence. However, as Anderson reminds us, the first continent to become thoroughly nationalized was the Americas, not Europe. And many non-Western nation-states came into existence before those of Europe. There is thus no reason why Holland should be given more analytical weight than Haiti, Germany more than Japan, or Belgium more than Bolivia. A quantitative approach based on global datasets gives equal weight to all cases, while allowing analysis of how they relate to each other through diffusion and imitation.

An inverse bias exists in work on ethnic politics and conflict. Here, Western scholars see themselves standing above the abyss of violence into which the leaders of many new nation-states in the East and South have thrown their populations. Studying ethnic conflicts in Africa, for example, has developed into a small research industry among comparative political scientists. But the history of Western states is punctuated by frequent episodes of ethnic cleansing and nationalist wars as well, not least during the two world wars. To see whether the West and "the rest" indeed show similar patterns of violence and war associated with the spread of nationalism and the rise of the nation-state, we thus need a perspective looking over the long run and the entire globe, rather than restricting the horizon to the world's new nation-states or the postwar period, as is the case in most comparative politics scholarship on civil war.

In order to develop such a long-term and global perspective, one needs to turn the usual relationship between data and research questions on its head. Instead of searching for new questions that have not yet been answered with

---

[2] See the well-known critique by Lieberson (1991).

[3] The articles submitted to the leading journal in the field of nationalism studies, *Nations and Nationalisms*, illustrate the disproportionate attention given to Europe: 21.5% of all manuscripts submitted since the first issue was published in 1985 were concerned with Western Europe, followed by Eastern Europe with 13.3% of the articles, then Asia, excluding the Middle East, with 12.6%, followed by Oceania with 8.7%. Only 5.4% of the articles concerned Africa, and even fewer North America (4%) or South America (2.5%).

existing datasets, new data need to be collected to answer old questions. Creating and analyzing such new datasets with global coverage represents a second major contribution that this book seeks to make to the scholarly literature. I review these data-collection efforts briefly here.

Quantitative research on civil wars often uses the readily available ethnic fractionalization index – measuring the likelihood that two randomly chosen individuals speak the same language – to see whether more diverse societies are more war-prone. Obviously, this measurement is only indirectly related to the dynamics of ethnic competition and exclusion that a long line of qualitative researchers – from John S. Furnivall (1939) to Clifford Geertz (1963), Donald Horowitz (1985), and Roger Petersen (2002) – has identified as the source of ethnic conflict. To bring quantitative research on armed conflict closer to this rich qualitative tradition of scholarship, Lars-Erik Cederman, Brian Min, and I assembled a new dataset that measures such competition and exclusion in all countries of the world and for decades of yearly observations. As Chapter 5 demonstrates, this allows us to ask more relevant questions about the nexus between ethnicity and war and to show that it is not demographic diversity that breeds violent conflict, but rather exclusionary ethno-political configurations of power.

Similarly, the relation between nation-state formation and violence cannot be properly understood with off-the-shelf datasets. These mostly take independent states as units of observation and analysis. On the one hand, this is a matter of convenience since only modern, independent states produce statistics. On the other hand, the setup of standard datasets resonates well with how both researchers and lay observers have learned to see the world – as a "family of nations" each represented by a differently colored area on a world map.

To overcome this "methodological nationalism" (Wimmer and Glick Schiller 2002), we need a universe of observations that includes colonial dependencies or pre-colonial states. Chapters 3 and 4 explore two new datasets that contain information on all territories of the world since 1816, independently of whether or not they were governed by sovereign states. This allows tracing the destiny of the world's entire population over the past two centuries and generates new insights into the dynamics of nation-state creation and its consequences for war and peace.

Another chapter reaches even deeper back into history, at the prize of focusing on two societies only. In order to see whether nation building and ethnic group formation are indeed determined by the resource and power distribution between state elites and the population at large, I have assembled data for France from the Renaissance period to the Third Republic and for the Ottoman empire from the classical age to the Young Turk revolution. These data are then fed into the formal model developed in Chapter 2. It thus takes a step beyond most other rational choice or game-theoretic models of historical processes that often rest on plausibility assumptions alone and thus are only weakly rooted in empirical data.

All five chapters, along with the long appendices that document these various data-gathering efforts, illustrate the price to pay when going beyond existing datasets. It often means struggling for each data-point, toiling through substantial amounts of sources to find that single piece of information to be filled into the cell of a spreadsheet that seems to extend its borders overnight. Are the results worth the efforts? That is for the reader to decide.

3 FOUR METHODOLOGICAL PRINCIPLES

But who would want to promote the illusion that context-free and timeless "laws of history" could ever be discovered through quantitative analysis? By adhering to the following four methodological principles, we can avoid such an overly ambitious scientism all the while identifying repeating causal dynamics in historical processes. First, we should acknowledge that causal regularity and contingency do not rule each other out, but combine to produce particular historical outcomes (King *et al.* 1994: chapter 2). It is certainly true, for example, that the assassination of the Archduke Ferdinand was a contingent event. His driver took a wrong turn into a side street of Sarajevo, where Gavrilo Princip, a pan-Serbian nationalist conspirator, happened to be on his way to lunch. He spotted and shot the archduke. This series of coincidences kindled the powder keg of World War I. But there was a powder keg waiting for a spark: a system of dyadic, uncoordinated alliances between rival states combined with the pressure of nationalist movements that sought to escape the "prisons of nations" as which they saw Eastern Europe's empires. Contemporary Europe lacks both of these conditions and it is quite unlikely that any contingent events happening on the continent will trigger a third world war at any point in the foreseeable future.

If this book seeks to explore general causal patterns, rather than historically specific chains of events, it is a matter of emphasis and choice, and not a principled stance against the role of contingency to which historical sociology has recently paid so much attention (Wagner-Pacifici 2010). While currently rather out of favor in much of sociology (*ibid.*) and comparative politics (Pierson 2003), I hope that the search for recurring long-term historical patterns can be revitalized by demonstrating that it produces robust empirical results.[4]

Second, a quantitative approach to historical processes should carefully specify the scope conditions of causal regularities in order to avoid overdrawn claims to universal validity. Some patterns may be local – they only recur throughout the history of Thailand, for example – while others are of a regional

---

[4] Development economists (Nunn 2009), neo-Malthusians working on political history (Turchin 2003) or demography (e.g. Bengtsson *et al.* 2004), and comparative political scientists studying democratization (Boix 2011) have started to explore long-term historical patterns using quantitative techniques. Some of this research has found an intellectual home in the new journal *Cliodynamics*.

scope – they exclusively shape the trajectories of former Ottoman dependencies – and still others might affect the entire world. Some causal regularities might be period specific and only effective, perhaps, after the American president Wilson had declared national sovereignty to be the right of every people on the planet. Others are valid for the entire modern age.

When searching for globally recurring causal regularities, we therefore have to pay careful attention to possible regional and period effects (Young 2009). They are best analyzed by "converting context to cause" (Collier and Mazzuca 2006) using dummy variables – investigating, for example, whether having been an Ottoman dependency is associated with a different dynamic of nation-state creation (see Chapter 3). Regional or period-specific regularities can be also discovered by sub-sample analysis, e.g. by analyzing the post-Wilsonian period in one equation and the pre-Wilsonian period in another (also in Chapter 3). To see whether the strength or even the direction of a causal relationship changes over time, key variables can be interacted with time, or we can analyze temporal sub-samples more systematically (as done by Isaac and Griffin 1989).

This book seeks to identify the causes of nation-state formation and war in the modern age, rather than those shaping particular periods and regional contexts. This is again not a matter of principle – nobody would deny that there are elements of nation-state formation and war in nineteenth-century Latin America (Centeno 2003) that are different from those of the late twentieth century Soviet Union (Beissinger 2002). Searching for regularities that hold across as many contexts as possible does come at a price, however: the story will necessarily have to be relatively abstract and general, forming a skeleton of arguments rather than a richly fleshed out and nuanced historical narrative. Whether one prefers the bones over the flesh, or whether one needs both, as lovers of mixed-method stews would argue, is largely a matter of intellectual taste, rather than of choosing between more or less "rigor," let alone empirical accuracy.

Third, this search for global patterns does not rule out that the same outcome might have multiple causes. The forces leading to ethnic conflict in Northern Ireland, to give an example, might be different from those that produced the Lebanese civil war. Such causal heterogeneity (Ragin 1989) can be discovered in a quantitative research design, for instance, with interaction effects (as in Chapter 3) or through multinomial regression analysis (see Chapter 5).

Fourth, qualitative inspection of cases and quantitative analysis of large numbers has to be combined in order to make sure that the statistical associations capture relevant mechanisms. For example, statistical analysis might discover that oil is associated with armed conflict. When investigating which cases underlie this finding, we encounter, among other "positive hits," that Mexico has oil and it has seen the Zapatista uprising in Chiapas from 1994 onwards. But the violence was not the result of a greedy hunt for oil rents. Rather, it emerged because Chiapas' entrenched *Ladino* elite had blocked land reform for generations (Collier and Lowery Quaratiello 1994). If many more such cases underlie a correlation, it might be entirely spurious. Ideally, one would therefore check case by case whether a statistical association makes historical sense and is based on a causal mechanism that conforms to the theoretical expectations (Lieberman 2005; see also Fearon and Laitin n.d.). In other words, quantitative analysis of historical processes should be undertaken with a qualitative, historically trained, and case-oriented mind-set. It encourages us to take off the faceplate of the statistical machine and examine in detail how the products that it spits out were actually shaped and if they do relate to empirically traceable processes in meaningful ways.

4 ON THEORY: NETWORKS, INSTITUTIONS, POWER

Now that the general methodological strategy has been outlined, it is appropriate to face the theoretical challenges that understanding nation-state formation, ethnic politics, and violent conflict entail. Since the chapters address different, more specialized audiences within the broader social science community – from the comparative historical sociology of nationalism to the war literatures in comparative politics and international relations – this section sketches out the general theoretical perspective that holds the book together. Its aims are rather modest: it does not offer a new theory, but rather an analytical framework that underlies the empirical research of the coming chapters. This framework is squarely centered on how power, legitimacy, and conflict relate to each other and how they are intertwined with the politicization of social categories such as nations, ethnic groups, and the like. It brings three traditions in political sociology and comparative political science together: relational structuralism, an institutionalism focused on questions of legitimacy, and a power-configurational approach.

4.1 Political alliances and identities

The relational argument assumes that networks of political alliances determine which categorical cleavages – nations, various ethnic groups, social classes, regions, cities, or tribes – will become politically salient and the focus of popular identification. This assumption is shared by a recent strain of comparative historical work. It has shown that such cross-class networks of alliances, rather than social classes and their factions, represent the building blocks of political life and the basis on which politically relevant collective identities are often formed.[5] Such political alliances can take the form of clientelist and patronage networks (as, for example, in Thailand);[6] or of linkages between corporatist

---

[5] See Gould (1995, 1996); Wimmer (2002); Ikegami (2005); Tilly (2006); Barkey (2008); Levi Martin (2009).

[6] This is the case in many Mediterranean, Latin American and South and Southeast Asian societies or in American urban "political machines." On clientelism, see Lemarchand and Legg (1972); Scott (1972); Clapham (1982); Fox (1994); Gould (1996); Kitschelt and Wilkinson (2007).

organizations such as state-organized peasant unions and the state (see Mexico under the PRI);[7] or of networks of competing voluntary organizations allied with party machines (as in the United States); or of a system of favoritism and corruption that relate "neopatrimonial" bureaucrats to the population (as in many African states).[8]

Going beyond most relational approaches, I suggest to closely analyze the nature of the exchanges that underlie these political alliances and identities.[9] Regardless of the different dynamics that the various types of alliance networks entail, the transactions linking state elites and the rest of the population can be described by a common matrix.[10] State elites offer different degrees of political participation, sometimes through full-scale democracy, sometimes via informal influence channels. And they provide varying amounts and types of public goods, sometimes in the form of a welfare state, sometimes through patronage. The population, in turn, offers military support to a varying extent, sometimes in the form of an army based on universal conscription. And they trade public goods for different amounts of economic support, which they sometimes provide in the form of taxes, sometimes through bribes and gifts.

The nature of these exchanges is determined by the distribution of resources between state and other actors as well as the degree to which elites can obtain resources through coercion, rather than exchange. The micro-foundations of this relational part of the overall argument will be elaborated in Chapter 2. It will show how actors with various resource endowments strategize to end up in an alliance system that offers them the most beneficial exchange of goods.

Such exchange relationships are based on consent and mutual commitment and thus have long-term implications. They are not one-shot transactions, such as buying a piece of pork at a farmer's market, nor are they based on coercion, such as when a soldier takes away a farmer's pig at gunpoint. If repeated interactions generate relationships of mutual trust and commitment, exchange relationships can lead the partners to identify, over time, with each other,[11] thus producing political identities such as estates, nations, ethnic groups, tribes, cities,

---

[7] See Schmitter (1974).

[8] See Bratton and van de Walle (1994).

[9] This focus on transactions, rather than network structures, follows up on Blau (1986).

[10] For pioneering rational choice research along these lines, see Levi (1988) and Kiser and Linton (2001). See also the "state in society" approach by Midgal (2001), or the post-Tillean emphasis on coalitions and alliances between state builders and other social groups during early modern state formation in the work of Spruyt, Adams, Gorski, and others (summarized in Vu 2009).

[11] See also Tilly's (2005) analysis of the emergence and transformation of trust networks. That exchange and cooperation will be accompanied by a corresponding social classification is shown by a long line of research in social psychology, which provides the micro-foundations for this part of my argument. It stretches from Tajfel (1981) to Kurzban *et al.* (2001), who have shown how coalitional alliances determine identity patterns and that they can even trump established modes of categorization such as race in the United States.

regions, and so forth, that roughly map onto the system of exchange networks and mirror its cleavages.

Social categories that reflect a particular structure of alliances and networks will appear natural and meaningful to participants and thus become taken-for-granted, routinized, and institutionalized. Cultural assimilation – such as through the coordination around shared behavioral norms (Deutsch 1953; Coleman 1990: chapter 11) – is more likely to proceed within such taken-for-granted and salient categories, which in turn leads individuals to choose alliance partners within these categories of culturally similar others (McElreath *et al.* 2003), thus further deepening the process of social closure and leading to a self-sustained equilibrium.[12]

At the end of this "endogenous" process, the corresponding social categories become institutionalized, more resistant to change, and more "sticky."[13] Institutionalized cleavage structures provide further incentives to emphasize these cleavages over others, above and beyond the exchange gains that they entail, and to build political alliances on the basis of those categories that are "built into" everyday routines. This basic insight is shared by a variety of historical institutionalist approaches[14] and by a growing group of authors working in the fields of nationalism, ethnic politics, and conflict, many of whom followed the lead of David Laitin's (1986) pioneering study.[15]

4.2 Principles of legitimacy

The resulting institutional structure – a set of routinized exchange alliances between actors and the corresponding social cleavage structure – can be more or less legitimate in the eyes of different segments of the population. Such varying degrees of legitimacy derive from a comparison between this institutional structure and an ideal image of which categories *should* be salient (the "who should be what" question) and what the exchange relationship between members of such categories *should* be ("who should get what"). A legitimate political order is therefore based on a widespread consensus that existing rules of exchange are fair (Levi 1997) and that the sorting of individuals into social categories and power positions is plausible and morally justifiable.[16]

---

[12] A self-reinforcing equilibrium persists as long as non-intended and intended consequences of actions that are influenced by institutional incentive structures tend not to undermine these arrangements. For a brilliant formal approach along these lines, see Greif and Laitin (2004).

[13] For a more sophisticated approach to the problem of institutional stability, see Streeck and Thelen (2005a).

[14] See diMaggio and Powell (1991); Steinmo *et al.* (1992); Brinton and Nee (2001); Pierson and Skocpol (2002).

[15] See, among others, Brubaker (1996); Koopmans *et al.* (2005); Lieberman and Singh (forthcoming). Posner's (2005) institutionalism focuses on incentive structures provided by electoral systems, rather than routinized social categories.

[16] On the concept of legitimacy, see most recently Gilley (2009); Hechter (2009b). My own approach is heavily influenced by Blau (1986).

In the context of this book's topic, we are mostly interested in the cognitive and moral templates of what a "just state" should look like, or more precisely, who has the right to rule.[17] In dynastic monarchies, for example, the right to rule is restricted to the king's clan and no one in their right mind would think that an illiterate serf born in the deep provinces should ever hold the steering wheel of the state ship in her hands. In theocracies, those who have descended from the Prophet should rule, or those who have shown through lifelong religious devotion and study that they are able to act as God's representatives on earth. In some empires, the right to rule is restricted to members of the conquering tribe or ethnic group. In democracies, one needs to have gained the support of the majority of the entire citizenry in order to rule in legitimate ways.

Such principles of political legitimacy – templates of who should rule over whom and what obligations and benefits should accrue to both – can emerge through an endogenous process. When the distribution of power between actors changes, the system of alliances that these resource distributions allow, and the corresponding politically salient cleavages, will be transformed as well. Thus, new exchange relations and social categories emerge. If these offer the population at large a better deal – if fewer individuals are excluded from exchange relationships with the political center and if individuals receive more from state elites than they did under the previous arrangement – the new system of alliance and identification is likely to become transformed into the new moral standard against which reality is assessed. In other words, it will become loaded with normative expectations and thus consolidated as the new template of legitimacy.[18]

But categories and principles of legitimacy also travel between societies with differently structured alliance networks and categorical cleavage structures. This works through both a power and a legitimacy mechanism. First, certain modes of alliance and identification prove to be economically and militarily more efficient and are thus likely to draw the attention of state builders elsewhere in the world (a power competition mechanism). Second, intellectuals and other groups with a wide cognitive horizon compare their own political system with that of others and tend to adopt those with higher rewards for the population at large as templates of legitimacy against which their own socio-political order is judged (a legitimacy comparison mechanism). The spread of nationalist ideologies to societies that had not yet seen much endogenous nation building is an example of such a process of "exogenous" diffusion, to be discussed in Chapter 3.

---

[17] The idea of institutional templates stands at the center of the "new" institutionalism in sociology (for an overview, see Brinton and Nee 2001). The nation-state as an instance of such a template (or "paradigm," "modular form") is discussed by Young (1976), Anderson (1991), and Brubaker (1996). For differences in the conceptualization of institutions in political science and sociology, see Haller *et al.* (2011).

[18] A similar, exchange-theoretic approach to the emergence of legitimacy was developed by Blau (1986: chapter 8), who also provides some micro-foundations for its major propositions.

At most points in time in most societies, therefore, there are more templates of legitimacy and more modes of social categorization available than those endogenously generated and sustained by a particular alliance structure. This opens up the possibility of conflict between different visions of the legitimate political order and thus of institutional change.

4.3 Power configurations and conflict

To understand such conflicts and change – the core preoccupation of this book – we need to add elements of a theory of power configurations. In line with the "contentious politics" tradition in sociology,[19] I assume that political actors struggle for control over the central state as well as over its institutional shape – empire, theocracy, nation-state, dynastic kingdom, democracy or one-party rule, and so on.[20] Institutional stability and change is then a matter of the power relations between actors who emphasize different principles of legitimacy and different social categories they claim to represent (class, the nation, estates, ethnic groups, and so forth) (see Wimmer 1995c; Boix 2003; Mahoney and Thelen 2010).

If the power configuration is favorable enough, those who aim at changing institutional principles of legitimacy might capture the state either through a revolutionary overthrow of the old regime or in a more gradual way by winning over more and more of its exponents.[21] They can then reorganize the institutional incentive structures for the next round of political contestation and contention – either by altogether displacing existing institutions or by more gradually layering new institutional rules upon existing ones (Streeck and Thelen 2005b) – and therefore influence the future alliance structures that shape them. Accordingly, the institutional shape of a state depends upon the constellation of actor networks and the power relations between them, rather than on different stages of an evolutionary sequence, as foreseen by Marxists or scholars working in the tradition of modernization theory.[22]

According to the analytical framework outlined so far, political conflict and war spring from three different sources. They form the nucleus of the understanding of violent conflict that this book seeks to promote. First, from both the relational and power-configurational points of view, violent conflicts are more likely if certain segments of the population are not part of the exchange

---

[19] See most recently Tarrow and Tilly (2006).

[20] For a review of "state-centric" research on political revolutions, see Goodwin (2001: chapter 2).

[21] The empowering of agents of change might well be the unintended consequence of existing institutional arrangements, as argued by Goodwin (2001) and formally modeled by Greif and Laitin (2004).

[22] For a similar approach, see the elite conflict theory of Lachmann (2011) or more generally the power-distributional approach to institutional change succinctly summarized by Mahoney and Thelen (2010).

networks that bind a state and its society together because the flow of control from the top and of legitimacy from below is then interrupted. Political exclusion, in other words, fosters the mobilization of individual and collective actors, who are driven by their desire to get a more favorable balance of exchange with the state and gain access to the public and private goods at its disposal.

My argument does not specify the organizational and interactional micro-mechanisms through which exclusion produces mobilization and through which such mobilization can then escalate into violent confrontations. These micro-foundations have been elaborated by students of contentious politics (Tarrow and Tilly 2006) and need not be discussed here. The book merely specifies the conditions under which these mechanisms, such as mobilization–repression spirals, will be more likely to be triggered: the larger the population excluded from the exchange networks centered on the state and the more unfavorable the balance of exchanges with the state for those who are integrated into these networks.

Second and according to the institutionalist part of the analytical framework, conflict escalation is more likely if such political exclusion violates the principles of political legitimacy that actors have adopted because this will enhance the mobilization and determination of excluded groups. This "grievance" part of the argument rests on the assumption that frames of legitimacy are important motivational factors and organizational resources for political movements (Snow *et al.* 1986). Rather than assuming a constant level of "grievances" across history and across the world, as in some rationalist accounts of violent conflict (Fearon and Laitin 2003), or a constant demand for ethnic self-rule (Hechter 2000), I focus on variation in levels of discontent and its emotional corollaries. Such variation results not only from different power configurations, but also from different principles of political legitimacy adopted by actors. The micro-foundations for such a view have been elaborated by others (Petersen 2002; Pinard 2011) and can be bracketed for the purpose of the present study.

Third and relatedly, political conflict and war are more likely to erupt when the contending forces seek to change the very institutional setup of a state because more is at stake in such "revolutionary" struggles over who has the right to rule. Actors will therefore be more willing to escalate conflict and use violent means to defend their interests. In a nutshell, political exclusion that violates established principles of legitimacy or that involves actors who seek to change these principles represents the most violence-prone contexts.

The theoretical approach outlined so far, centered on the analysis of political alliance networks, principles of legitimacy, and power configurations, thus provides the basis on which the empirical analysis in the following chapters stands. The various feedback loops between networks, institutions, and power configurations have been discussed elsewhere in detail (Wimmer 2008b), so that I can leave it here with this rather short sketch of the theoretical framework. The five empirical chapters narrate a complex causal story, weaving together the relational, institutional, and power-configurational arguments, and giving them different weights depending on which phase in the transition from empire to nation-state we are focusing upon. The following three sections sketch out the major lines of this analysis and preview the most important findings of the book.

5 THE RISE AND SPREAD OF THE NATION-STATE

5.1 Negotiating nationhood

The analysis starts with the emergence of the first states built on nationalist principles. Existing approaches interpret nationhood either as ideological impositions by manipulative elites (Brass 1979; Mearsheimer 1990; Tilly 1994; Gagnon 2006) or, to the contrary, as popular sentiments nourished by deeply rooted ethnic memories and myths (Smith 1986) or by an eternal desire for ethnic self-rule (Hechter 2000). Both approaches tend to overlook the crucial role played by varying power distributions between elites and masses, and the types of resource exchanges that these allow. Neither ideological imposition "from above" nor popular sentiment rising from "the bottom up," Chapter 2 will argue, ethnic group formation and nation building are best seen as negotiated accomplishments involving both elites and masses.

In other words, nation building and ethnic group formation result from a new compact between state elites and the population that is built on consent and the mutually favorable exchange of resources. Following the relational argument outlined above, elites and masses will then start trusting and identifying with each other and shift the focus of loyalty to the nation or an ethnic community. The chapter introduces a formal analysis of this process. It combines an exchange-theoretic and a game-theoretic model that together allow understanding the emergence of different political alliances and identities as an interactive process, rather than as a lonely choice that individuals make between different possible identities, as in much of the rational choice literature.

The model lets elites and masses exchange political participation against military support, and taxation against public goods. The exchange-theoretic part of the model assumes that actors exchange these resources and identify with each other on an exclusive basis and close their ranks against outsiders – thus modeling a process of social closure in line with Max Weber's (1968) short treatment of the subject. The choice of who to enter into an exchange alliance with, and which competitors to best keep at arm's length, is important because it affects how much of what actors want they can actually get. The exchange model also considers how far actors take cultural similarity into account when deciding with whom they would prefer to form an alliance. In societies where voluntary organizations, such as professional associations or trade unions, have flourished, I will argue, they will be less concerned with such cultural similarity.

The game-theoretic part of the model then determines which alliance system will result, given that different actors will have different preferences regarding whom to enter into an exchange relationship with. In a nutshell, we model the unequal symbolic power of elites and masses by letting state elites propose a system of alliance and identity first – for example nationhood. Other elite segments then react with their own proposal, perhaps ethnic closure. The masses move last and choose between either of these two proposals or the existing alliance system, depending on the resources these different systems would offer them.

This model is calibrated with historical data on how three of the four resources – taxation, military support, and public goods provision – were distributed over various segments of elites and masses in France (from 1300 to 1900) and the Ottoman empire (from 1500 to 1900). Such empirical calibration represents a considerable advantage over most formal models that tend to offer mathematically elegant thought experiments often only weakly grounded in empirical data. What results does this empirically calibrated model produce?

We focus on how political modernization changes the resource distribution between actors and thus the alliance system they negotiate. Increasing centralization shifts control over political decision-making and taxation away from provincial to central elites. Mass mobilization decreases the military role of provincial elites (such as a feudal nobility with armor and horses) and increases that of the masses armed with pikes and halberds. Mass mobilization also increases the population's interest in political participation. A third aspect of political modernization is the development of voluntary organizations that allow rulers to connect with subjects in new ways.

When modernization leads to highly centralized states and mobilized masses, state elites hold political decision-making power over the entire territory and provide most public goods such as hospitals for the poor and sick, roads and waterways, or policing. According to the model results, this allows them to break out of the elite coalition to which they had confined their alliances in the pre-modern period. They now link up to the masses, across existing ethnic and status divides, because they have come to depend on the masses' taxes and military support. The masses, in turn, shift their alliances and "trade" increasing taxation and military support in exchange for political participation and the public goods that the centralized state is able to provide. Corresponding to this inclusionary and encompassing alliance system, the nation as a mode of categorization and identification replaces the older estate order in which peasants identified with peasants and nobles with nobles. Paralleling Margaret Levi's (1997) work on patriotism and consent, we thus show how a state built on coercive resource extraction – as in the pre-modern imperial order – was replaced with a state held together by an exchange system built on voluntary consent and by a shared national identity.

Where state elites were weaker vis-à-vis other elites and the population at large, they were not able to offer sufficient public goods and political participation to make the nation an attractive enough category to identify with. Furthermore, elite competition over the military support of the masses made an alliance between different elite factions – as it had existed in the imperial order – seem rather unattractive. The result is that individuals ally with their respective ethnic elites, rather than all members of the polity. Political closure then proceeded along ethnic, rather than national, lines. This tendency is even more pronounced, as will be shown, if actors do care about cultural similarity when considering with whom to exchange resources – as they do when there are few voluntary associations that could provide the organizational basis for linking rulers and ruled. Interestingly enough, this is true even if cultural similarity and difference are structured along class divisions, rather than ethnic divides. Ethnic closure can thus result as an equilibrium outcome even if ethnic groups don't share a common cultural heritage.

How well is this formal model able to make sense of actual historical developments in the two societies under consideration? According to our historical research on Renaissance France and the Ottoman empire of the classical age, low levels of state centralization and mass mobilization characterized both polities before the modern age. When calibrated with these two specific resource distributions, the model's actors negotiate an alliance between various elite factions with each other, at the exclusion of all segments of the masses. And indeed, the structure of alliances and identities had set off the nobility (in France) or the military caste (of the Ottoman empire) from the rest of the population, to which it related mainly through coercion, rather than mutually beneficial exchange. When increasing state centralization and mass mobilization until they reach the level that we empirically observe in late eighteenth-century France, the model generates nation building as the equilibrium outcome, again in line with historical reality: the French revolution first introduced the concept of the nation as a community of equals. A century later and after a further leap in state centralization, ethnic and regional identities had faded into the background and the population as a whole identified with the French nation and its state, as the famed book title *Peasants into Frenchmen* by Eugen Weber (1979) suggests.

For the distribution of resources that characterized the Ottoman empire of the early nineteenth century, the model foresees ethnic closure, rather than nation building, given comparatively lower levels of state centralization. This again makes historical sense: from the nineteenth century onward, ethno-religious communities (the *millets*) became institutionally reinforced, politically empowered, and the focus of identity for the minority population. The idea that all subjects of the Sublime Port would "fuse," in the words of Ottoman reformers, into one people loyal to the Sultan and the state was never embraced by the population of the empire. Instead, the ethno-religious *millets* – and later also Kurds and Arabs – were soon politicized and turned into aspiring nations of their own, to paraphrase Kemal Karpat's (1973) title "From Millet to Nation."

While the aim of this chapter is certainly not "retrodictions" – an impossible task given the complexity of history and the role of contingent events – it is nevertheless assuring that the equilibriums produced by the formal model do relate to actual historical developments in such meaningful ways. The main point of the chapter, however, is to show that nation building and the politicization of ethnic divisions are both the result of political modernization, but represent different equilibrium outcomes depending on the specific resource distribution that emerged.[23] Weakly centralized states will not see durable alliances with all segments of the population and nationalism will not spread and become adopted as a main framework of identity.

This is why ethnic closure – the organization of political loyalties and identities around sub-national communities – is a widespread feature of weakly centralized states with weak civil societies, with important consequences for the dynamics of ethnic politics and the potential for violent conflict, as many students of post-colonial nation building in the developing world have noticed. These consequences will be fully explored in Chapter 5. The next step in the analysis, however, is to understand why the rest of the world adopted the nation-state form, once it had emerged endogenously in France (and elsewhere) from the late eighteenth century onward, although the internal conditions were often not ripe for nation building. This is the task of Chapter 3.

5.2 The global rise of the nation-state

The early nation-states became attractive models to copy because their leaders could rely on the military loyalty and political support of the masses of the population. This had obvious advantages, as the success of Napoleon's armies demonstrated. The nation-state model was therefore "pirated," in Benedict Anderson's terms, by ambitious political leaders across the world and across times. They hoped to one day govern states that matched the military glory, political power, and economic might of the early nation-states that soon came to dominate the entire world. Nationalist intellectuals around the world were also drawn to this new model of organizing politics because it seemed to offer the population at large a better exchange relationship with the central elites – more rights, better public goods provision, and more dignity – and thus became the template of a legitimate political order they were striving for. Power competition and legitimacy comparison thus fueled a global imitation process. The spread of nationalism around the world, however, is not the focus

---

[23] Is there a problem of reversed causation? France had already reached the high levels of centralization and mobilization at which our model predicts nation building shortly *before* the French revolution produced a nation-state, thus excluding the possibility that nationalism and nation building had created such high levels of centralization and mobilization. To be sure, there is a positive feedback effect: the spread of nationalist ideologies allows further centralization and leads to additional mass mobilization, thus further pushing the exchange relationship toward the new equilibrium.

of Chapter 3.[24] Rather, it treats the proliferation of nationalisms as an antecedent and seeks to explore the conditions under which nationalists were able to establish a nation-state.

In contrast to the emergence of the first nation-states analyzed in Chapter 2, I will argue, its further spread across the world depended on a power configuration in favor of nationalists, rather than an endogenous transformation of the exchange relationships and alliance networks binding state elites and the masses together. Many nation-states thus were formed without a previous process of nation building. This analysis parallels Theda Skocpol's (1979) well-known study of the French, Russian, and Chinese revolutions, in which she showed that the political power configuration centered on the state was more crucial than class relations or the revolutionary consciousness of the masses in bringing about a revolutionary cataclysm.

Similarly I will show how a shift in the balance of power in favor of nationalists – brought about by political mobilization, wars, and diffusion effects – explains when and where the nation-state is adopted. Similar to evolutionary biology, then, the emergence of the nation-state as a new institutional form (the analogue to genetic mutation) and the mechanisms of its subsequent proliferation across the world (similar to the effects of natural selection) represent processes of a different nature that need to be analyzed with different tools and in separate steps.

This approach contrasts with much of the existing literature on the rise and global spread of the nation-state, which highlights domestic modernization processes that are supposed to bring about the nation-state whenever they reach a critical level. Political modernization, Tilly (1994) and Hechter (2000) argued, led to a shift from indirect to direct rule, often by ethnic others, which in turn mobilized the population under the banners of nationalism. Anderson's (1991) brilliant book emphasizes cultural modernization. The spread of mass literacy in vernacular languages, so the argument goes, made the imagining of national communities possible and eventually forced state institutions into this new identitarian mold. According to Gellner (1983), industrialization "needs" a culturally homogenous labor force, which is eventually provided by the educational apparatus of a nation-state. Other prominent authors such as John Meyer (Meyer *et al.* 1997) put the finger on diffusion mechanisms at the global level, rather than domestic modernization. A hegemonic world culture holds a monopoly on the definition of legitimate statehood and forces more and more state-builders all over the world to adopt the nation-state form, independent of local political conditions.[25]

---

[24] See Badie (2000).

[25] This style of reasoning can also be found in "international society-centric constructivism" in international relations scholarship (Hobson 2000).

To test these various arguments, Chapter 3 uses a new dataset containing information on 140 territories across the world before they became modern nation-states, covering all years since 1816. Analysis of this dataset shows that nation-states are created when a power shift allows nationalists to overthrow or absorb the established regime. The power balance shifts in favor of nationalists if the established regime is weakened by wars or if nationalists have had ample time to decry ethno-political hierarchies as instances of "alien rule" and to mobilize followers. Diffusion of nation-states among neighbors or within the same empire also empowers nationalists by providing them with a model to imitate and new alliance partners to rely upon. On the other hand, nationalists are at a disadvantage when they struggle against an empire that disposes of much global military and economic power. Figure 1.3 shows how these different aspects of the configuration of power between nationalists and the old regime influence the likelihood of nation-state creation.

There is no evidence, on the other hand, that industrialization, the spread of mass literacy, or increasing administrative penetration and direct rule bring about the nation-state, as maintained by the theories of economic, cultural, and political modernization mentioned above. While endogenous nation building is indeed the consequence of political centralization and the establishment of direct rule, as shown in Chapter 2, the global rise of the nation-state seems to be quite detached from a state's capacity to directly rule over a territory. Nation-states are also not more likely to emerge the more the world is already populated by nation-states or the more ties a territory has established with the centers of world culture, as predicted by those who believe in the coercive power of the world polity. It thus seems that the global legitimacy of the nation-state model *results* from its proliferation across the world, rather than the other way round.[26] As one territory after another became governed as a nation-state, a global consensus emerged that it represents the sole legitimate form of government.

Local and regional processes not coordinated or causally produced by global social forces can thus generate a global outcome: the almost universal adoption of the nation-state form over the past 200 years. As in epidemiology, processes of contagion follow established networks of political relationships and communication that span the entire world. The logic of contagion is purely local, however, and produces a decentralized pattern of diffusion, all the while generating the illusion of a systemic process when seen from a global point of view.

---

[26] This argument is in line with "second image" theories of international politics and more specifically with the revised "liberal" theory of Moravcsik (1997: 540). Note that it does not exclude a possible feedback mechanism – the more states converge on the nation-state model, the more a global cultural consensus emerges that encourages further convergence (see Risse-Kappen 1996) – but it most certainly rules out reverse causation: that world political culture *produces* nationally constituted statehood in the first place.

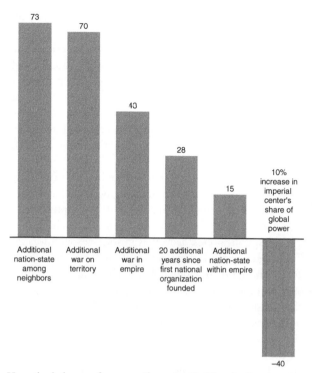

FIGURE I.3 How the balance of power affects the likelihood of nation-state formation (in %)

Notes: calculated as percentage change in the likelihood of NSC when the value of a variable is increased over its mean[27] as compared to the likelihood when all variables are set to their means; all effects are significant at the $p<0.01$ level; calculations similar to Model 7 in Table 3.1; N=16,488 observations in 145 territories.

6 NATION-STATES AND VIOLENCE

6.1 Nation-state formation and war

Chapter 4 will show that this universal shift to the nation-state model is a major cause of war in the modern world, thus challenging mainstream approaches in international relations and comparative politics according to which principles of political legitimacy and their transformation play no important role in explaining war and peace. How does the shift from imperial or dynastic to nationalist principles of legitimacy produce wars? First, nationalism with its core ideology of political self-rule – the right to be governed by "one's own" – delegitimizes

[27] For years since first national organization and the imperial share of global power I chose an increase close to a standard deviation. All other variables are increased by one unit.

the rule of imperial, aristocratic, or theocratic elites and decries ethnic exclusion hitherto accepted as part of the legitimate order. Nationalism thus motivates and enables political entrepreneurs to fight secessionist wars against "alien rule." The prolonged and bloody struggles for national independence in Algeria, Angola, Bolivia, Indonesia, Mexico, the United States, or Vietnam are well-known examples. When nationalists face a domestic old regime, rather than an empire, civil wars pitting nationalist reformers against *ancien régime* elites might bring about a national revolution – as through the short "war of the special league" in Switzerland of 1847 or the civil war after Japan's Meiji "restoration" two decades later.

Once the nation-state has been established, nationalist principles of legitimacy are reinforced and institutionalized, making both civil and inter-state wars more likely wherever these principles are violated. In Chapter 2, we will see that in modernizing states with lower degrees of political centralization and reduced capacity to provide public goods, as well as in societies with weakly developed networks of voluntary organizations, political alliances and identities tend to form along ethnic, rather than national, lines. The ruling elites thus favor their co-ethnics over all others when it comes to providing public good or shaping public policies. This may trigger the second conflict-generating mechanism identified above: leaders of excluded groups can now decry the breach of the principle of ethnic self-rule and demand a nation-state of their own, or at least a fair share of the governmental cake. They can now evoke the very principles of nationalism – that ethnic likes should be ruled by ethnic likes – to legitimize their claims and mobilize followers. The ensuing competition for control over the nation-state might escalate into full-scale rebellions.

The shift to the nation-state model and the political exclusion along ethnic lines that it fosters in weakly centralized states also increases the likelihood of inter-state war. The rulers of new states might interfere in the affairs of neighboring states to protect their co-ethnics across the border from the fate of second-class citizenship they might have to endure as ethnic minorities in a state "owned" by a different people. Apart from pure balance-of-power considerations and strategic motivations (highlighted by Mylonas forthcoming), leaders care for co-nationals across the border because they have to show to their own constituencies that they are indeed concerned by the fate of the nation and that they will not tolerate that their "brothers and sisters" across the border suffer from political discrimination. Such interference and competition over "mixed" territories increases the likelihood of armed conflict between nationalizing states. Examples are the two Balkan wars, the competing movements for independent states that emerged during the world wars, or more recently the tensions between Sudan and the newly independent Southern Sudan.

How can one show that nation-state formation leads to war? Standard datasets take independent states as units of observation and thus cannot analyze the wars associated with their emergence. To overcome this problem, we have

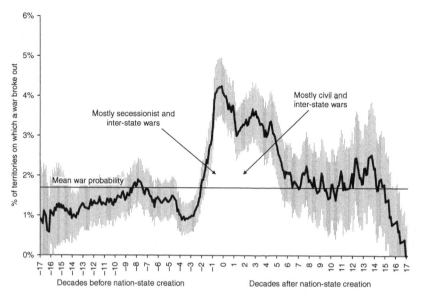

FIGURE I.4 The big picture: nation-state formation and war since 1816
Notes: moving 20-year average; 95 percent confidence interval in gray; data are from Chapter 4; N=27,700 observations on 150 territories.

assembled a new dataset that records the outbreak of war on fixed geographical territories from 1816 to 2001. The shift to constant territorial units also forced us to create a new dataset on all wars that have ever been fought on these 156 territories since 1816, using a wide range of existing war lists, compendia, and historical sources.

Are civil and international wars indeed more likely during nation-state formation? Figure I.4 offers an unequivocal answer to this question. It plots the percentage of territories on which a war broke out for each year before and after a nation-state was formed. The x-axis therefore does not record chronological time, but shows the transformation clock for all individual territories. The year of nation-state creation is set at zero, which corresponds to the year 1998 in the case of Bhutan, for example, but 1820 in the case of Spain. The vertical bars centered on the line indicate "confidence intervals at the 95 percent level." In everyday language, this means that where these bars do not cross the line representing the mean probability of war in all territories and years, we can be almost certain that the likelihood of war is different from that mean and not the product of chance alone.

Figure I.4 shows that the transformation of the international system from a world of empires, kingdoms, city-states, and tribal confederacies into a world of nation-states has indeed been associated with war. This pattern recurs in every wave of nation-state creation since Napoleon and on every continent. The shift to territorial units of observation and a long-term perspective thus reveals what has so far been hidden from view: that nation-state formation represents a crucial source of war in the modern world. To be sure, nationalism and nation-state formation do not explain all wars ever fought on the globe. My argument is not tailored to understand, for example, the American invasion of Iraq in 2003 or the communist insurgencies in Latin America of the 1970s. These are, by the way, responsible for the smaller hump in war probability 120 to 150 years after nation-state formation shown in Figure 1.4.

Still, highlighting the nationalist foundations of many modern wars represents an important insight. Traditional "realist" international relations approaches (see the overview in Levy and Thompson 2010) look at the distribution of military capabilities in an anarchic world of competing states each exclusively concerned with their own security. Rationalist accounts seek to demonstrate that states go to war if their evaluations of who would win diverge from each other. Other scholars identify those pairs of states that are most war-prone: those with territorial disputes and a long history of rivalry, or those in which one of the states is a democracy and the other an autocracy, or those not bound together by dense networks of trade.

In this vast and sophisticated literature, nationalism has not been treated as a serious candidate for explaining wars. "Nationalism," writes a prominent "realist," represents a mere "second order force in international politics" (Mearsheimer 1990: 21) because it is "caused in large part by security competition among … states, which compelled … elites to mobilize publics to support national defense efforts" (*ibid.*: 12). Obviously, as Miller (2007: 32) notes, this fails to account for why most nationalist movements are directed *against* existing states – as in the anti-imperial, secessionist nationalisms that have transformed the shape of the world in the past two centuries. With the single exception of an article by Maoz (1989), even the very creation of new states has not been treated as a potential source of war in modern history.

Mainstream international relations theory thus overlooks that "unit-level transformation"[28] – the shift from an international system composed of empires and dynastic kingdoms to a system composed of nation-states – is *itself* an important cause of war. The small literature on the role of nationalism in international relations is squarely focused either on how states militarily intervene in favor of co-nationals in neighboring states (Miller 2007;[29] Woodwell 2007; Saideman

---

[28] On the interesting lack of interest by international relations scholars in the inter-*national* nature of the world polity, see Lapid and Kratochwil (1996; also Spruyt 1996: chapter 1). Some more recent work seeks to overcome this neglect and to address the issue of "unit variation"; see the review by Kahler (2002: 66–71).

[29] Miller's (2007) argument is perhaps the most encompassing and goes beyond co-nationality as a determinant of inter-state conflict behavior. He maintains that whether or not regions (his units of analysis) are peaceful depends on the "nation-to-state balance," i.e. the degree to which there are irredentist or cross-border nationalisms seeking to redraw the existing borders between states. In regions with strong states, such revisionist nationalism leads to inter-state wars, while regions with weak states will be the arena of civil wars.

and Ayres 2008), or how political elites might stir up nationalist sentiment by attacking a neighboring country to stabilize their own insecure political position (Snyder 2000). Going beyond the important insights offered by these authors, this book shows that nationalism played a much more important role in the history of modern war than commonly assumed. It transformed the number and nature of the global system's constituent units, and this transformation is itself a major cause of war over the past 200 years, as suggested by Figure 1.4.

Moreover, the rise of the nation-state also had a profound impact on the aims and motivations for going to war.[30] As Figure 1.2 shows, wars of conquest have almost ceased to be fought since Hitler's failed attempt to build an empire stretching from the Rhine to the Urals. Why? The legitimacy of empires was based on the idea of bringing "true faith," "civilization," or "revolutionary progress" to distant places, if necessary through conquest and the "pacification" of recalcitrant locals who fail to see the light of religious truth or civilizational progress. Imperial elites thus had incentives to conquer other states and to permanently incorporate their territories into their domain. Nation-states, however, cannot legitimately rule over vast numbers of ethnic others, given that they are built on national self-rule as their legitimizing principle. Compare how the Ottoman sultan and then the British crown ruled over Iraqi lands to the policy of the United States after it had invaded the country, and it becomes clear that in a world of nation-states, conquest is no longer a legitimate war aim.[31] The transformation of the nature of states thus helps to understand why wars between states have become so rare in the contemporary period.

Ethno-nationalism, however, motivates an increasing number of wars in the world. As Figure 1.2 showed, the share of nationalist wars of secession and ethnic

---

This argument faces serious endogeneity problems, however, since the existence of revisionist nationalist movements is obviously associated with conflict, while it remains to be explained why such irredentist, secessionist, or unification nationalisms emerge in the first place. To avoid endogeneity, one could count, as Miller suggests (*ibid.*: 56), the number of national groups per state ("internal incongruence") as well as the number of ethnic groups with kin in neighboring states ("external incongruence"). However, according to an analysis of the dataset introduced in Chapter 5, neither the number of politicized ethnic groups nor the existence of cross-border ethnic kin have any effect on the probability of armed conflict or civil war (results not shown).

[30] This is in line with emphasis on domestic formation of foreign policy preference in "second image" theories of international relations (see Moravcsik 1997). For a historical overview of how the nature of states influences their motivations for going to war, see Luard (1986).

[31] An alternative explanation in international relations theory attributes the scarcity of wars of conquest in the contemporary world to the fact that multinational corporations have spread over the territories of all the major great powers, which together with the shift to knowledge-based economies decreases the economic attractiveness of conquest (Brooks 2005). This obviously fails to explain why we do not see more conquest between nation-states that host few multinationals and whose economies depend on agriculture and resource extraction, e.g. most of contemporary Africa.

civil wars rose from 25 to 75 percent over the course of a century. The spread of nationalism as foundation of political legitimacy changed the motivations and aims for which humanity goes to war: wars of conquest gave way to wars of nationalist secession, conflicts over dynastic succession or tax levels were replaced by ethno-political struggles over access to central government.[32]

6.2 Ethnic politics and armed conflict

Not all transitions to the nation-state are accompanied by war, however. Figure 1.4 shows that at the height of the transformation process, a new war broke out on only about 4 percent of all territories in that year. We thus need to more precisely specify the conditions under which nation-state formation leads to armed conflict and show that ethno-political inequality indeed plays as crucial a role as claimed throughout this book. Given data limitations, a more precise analysis cannot be offered for all phases of the process and all types of war. Chapter 5 zooms in on the period after a nation-state has been founded, and focuses on civil wars only. The analysis will now include low-intensity domestic conflicts that cost as few as 25 battle deaths as well, while previous chapters related to full-scale wars with more than 1,000 deaths. Such detailed data on armed conflicts is only available for the years after World War II.

This restricted view will allow for much more precision in the analysis. The chapter is based on a new, global dataset already briefly mentioned above. It records ethnic power relations in all countries of the world and how they changed since World War II, which will allow us to test the political exclusion hypothesis directly. Equally important and additional mechanisms that trigger ethnic conflict can be identified. I will thus pay more attention to causal heterogeneity than in the previous chapter and show that different types of ethnic conflict are caused by different ethno-political configurations of power. All these different configurations can be portrayed as ethnic underrepresentation in government and thus as violations of the nationalist "like-over-like" principle of legitimacy.

The first configuration is marked by high levels of ethno-political inequality and was already part of the analysis of preceding chapters. Ethnicity is more likely to be politicized and ethnic minority rule is more likely to emerge in weakly centralized states with a limited capacity to provide public goods, tax the population, and control the political process, as well as in societies with weakly developed civil societies. States that exclude large segments of the population on the basis of ethnicity face severe legitimacy problems since they directly violate the principle of ethnic self-rule established by the nation-state model. Saddam Hussein's ethnocracy provides a good illustration of such regimes. His Baath Party became more and more the party of Sunni Arab nationalists, and

---

[32] For a full empirical analysis of these conjectures, see Wimmer and Min (2009).

Kurdish and Shiite army officers and bureaucrats were increasingly excluded from the circles of power. A long series of insurrections by Kurdish *peshmerga* and Shiite notables followed (Wimmer 2002: chapter 6). The Alawite minority of the Assad clan has dominated neighboring Syria since the 1970s. Bloody rebellions against their ethnocratic rule were organized by the Sunni Muslim brotherhood in 1982 and by various, more dispersed forces in 2011.

Second, where state power is shared by a large number of ethnic elites, their coalition is beset with commitment problems, and competition over the spoils of government often leads to violent infighting. The higher the number of ethnic elites tied into a government coalition, the less stable their alliances and the more likely such infighting becomes. The Lebanese civil war provides an apt illustration of how this mechanism operates. The power sharing formula inherited from the French mandate period could not be adjusted to new political and demographic realities, given the rivalries and lack of predictable political alliances between the leaders of the numerous ethno-religious communities. Their elites feared losing out in the struggle over the state and being dominated by ethnic others in the future, and political tensions escalated into a full-blown civil war.

Third, the alliance networks that bind a population to the political center will be only weakly institutionalized in nation-states that have been ruled indirectly by empires in the past. Following the relational part of the theory of conflict outlined above, national identity and loyalty toward the central state are therefore expected to be weak as well, and the state and its territorial boundaries enjoy only little legitimacy – independent of the power configuration at the center. Rebels and infighters will then adopt a full-blown nationalist agenda and armed conflicts will take on secessionist forms. Examples are the separatist movements of South Ossetians and Abkhazians, whom Moscow had ruled indirectly as an autonomous republic or oblast during Soviet times. Correspondingly, they maintained only weak political ties and disidentified with the Georgian republic of which they became a part but which they perceived as largely illegitimate. When Georgian nationalists were about to declare independence, both regions hastily claimed the mantle of independent statehood for themselves, and wars of secession ensued immediately.

In summary, three different configurations of alliance and power lead to various types of ethnic conflict instigated by different actors (excluded groups or ethnic elites that share power) pursuing different aims (secession or controlling government). All remain related, however, to the principles of legitimacy – ethnic self-rule – that the nation-state established, and circle around the issue of ethnic underrepresentation and the fear of political domination by ethnic others.

Chapter 5 tests these hypotheses with the Ethnic Power Relations dataset. Since it is a fully dynamic dataset, it goes well beyond static measures of ethnic diversity – such as fractionalization indices – so often used in quantitative

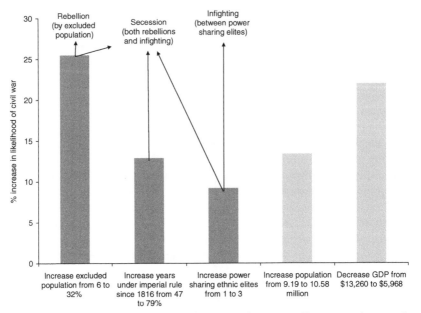

FIGURE 1.5 Ethnic civil wars in independent states since 1945: a disaggregated approach
Notes: first difference effects, calculated on the basis of Model 4 in Table 5.2. All effects are significant at the p<0.01 level, except for the years spent under imperial rule (which has a p<0.05). N=6,885 observations in 156 independent countries.

research. The dataset directly codes the ethno-political constellation of power at the state's center – rather than only focusing on politically marginalized minorities, as does the widely used and pioneering Minorities at Risk dataset. Figure 1.5 summarizes the results of Chapter 5 for readers who are not familiar with the conventions of statistical analysis. The bars tell us how much more likely armed conflict will be when the value of a particular variable (and of this variable only) is increased from its mean by one standard deviation. A standard deviation refers to the maximum difference between observed values and the mean for two-thirds of observations. This is one of the best ways to compare the effects of variables that are measured in different units and that show different degrees of dispersion from their mean.

The bars in the figure are linked with arrows to the type of conflict that the corresponding variable is affecting. Political exclusion is conducive to rebellion, both secessionist and non-secessionist. Infighting (again both in its secessionist and non-secessionist variants) is more likely the higher the number of power sharing elites. A long history of imperial rule increases the likelihood of secessionist conflict, both by excluded and by power sharing groups. These ethno-political factors are as effective and robust in predicting civil war as the two most important explanatory variables in quantitative studies of civil war: a country's level of economic development and the size of its population. Ethnic politics is clearly not only affecting armed conflict in statistically significant, but also in substantially important ways.

The chapter thus introduces a power-cum-legitimacy argument into a debate that is largely dominated by political economy approaches for which questions of state legitimacy and political inequality play no role in understanding today's civil wars. According to the most often cited article in this literature (Fearon and Laitin 2003), civil wars break out when a government is too weak to suppress the ubiquitous discontent of its population. The fact that Sweden is peaceful while the Syrian population rose up against the Assad regime in 2011 (and before) thus has nothing to do with different levels of state legitimacy, but needs to be attributed to the higher repressive capacity of the Swedish government ... Collier and Hoeffler (2004) see greedy warlords take up arms to gain control over natural resources such as oil or diamonds – leaving students of conflicts in oil- and diamond-free places such as Northern Ireland or Tibet wondering how to make sense of what they observe. Posen (1993a) argues that state collapse leaves ethnic groups no other choice than to attack each other to prevent being attacked first, thus overlooking that state collapse is often the consequence of ethnic violence, not its cause.

Chapters 5 shows that political inequality and legitimacy need to be taken into account if we want to gain a proper understanding of the drama of civil war. Rather than resource competition outside the domains of the state, or the military weakness of the state, or even the disappearance of state authority altogether, it is the ethno-political struggle *over* the state that drives many violent conflicts in the contemporary world of nation-states. This is not to deny that the repressive capacity of the state matters – an armed rebellion is obviously more difficult to organize in contemporary China than it is in a weak and fragmented state with little surveillance capacity such as Congo. Feasibility *must* matter, even if it has hitherto been impossible to establish this relationship in direct ways, perhaps due to the lack of adequate data on the repressive capacity of states. And it might also be that oil and diamonds fuel the flames of competition over the state (see Ross 2012). But perhaps military feasibility and economic resources represent mitigating and intervening factors, rather than the primary cause of armed conflict (for empirical support of this interpretation, see Thies 2010).

6.3 Can peace be engineered?

The final chapter draws some tentative conclusions for the policy debate on how to best prevent ethnic conflict. The analyses of the preceding chapters quite unequivocally suggest that the most effective way to guarantee peace is fostering inclusionary power structures. Such ethno-political inclusion can be achieved in various ways depending on historical antecedents and contemporary context: through encompassing clientelist networks tying state elites to all other segments of a society; through a governing coalition of ethnic parties such as in Malaysia; through one-party rule within which various ethnic elites find their place (as in Ivory Coast before democratization); or through a non-ethnic party system and informal power sharing arrangements such as in Switzerland. The nature of political institutions – electoral rules, degrees of federalism, levels of democratization, etc. – matters less, the chapter shows, than the power configuration that underlies them.

Most policy-makers and comparative political scientists, however, are convinced that political institutions should be the prime focus of prevention policies. In other words, they believe that peace can be engineered by adjusting the incentive structures for political leaders and followers. Policy-makers often emphasize that democratic institutions will mitigate conflict propensity in the long run. Not only can votes replace bullets as means to voice one's discontent, they argue, but democracies will also politically integrate ethnic minorities and thus produce less exclusionary power structures.

Comparative political scientists have also been engaged in a long-standing debate whether proportionalism, federalism, and parliamentarianism are fostering peaceful accommodation, as maintained by consociationalists. So-called centripetalists, on the other hand, argue that to the contrary majoritarianism, unitarianism, and presidentialism are more apt to tame the flames of ethno-political competition and avoid an escalation into armed conflict. All agree, however, that formal political institutions indeed matter in explaining why certain countries are more prone to armed violence than others.

Chapter 6 empirically evaluates these various claims. It opens by reminding readers that Chapters 4 and 5 showed no support for the idea that democracies are less prone to armed conflict and war than non-democratic regimes. Even the more circumspect finding that regimes in between autocracies and democracies – so-called anocracies – are the most war-prone has not been upheld by recent research, which showed that these earlier findings were based on a problematic coding of anocracy.

But perhaps there is evidence for an indirect effect of democracies on conflict because democracies should be more inclusionary than other political systems? Since minorities have a vote in democracies, shouldn't this allow for at least some representation at the highest levels of government? And shouldn't such more inclusionary power configurations then foster peace? Indeed, I find a strong statistical association between democracy and ethno-political inclusion – measured as the percentage of the population that is represented at the highest level of executive government. However, this is most likely due to a selection effect: more exclusionary regimes, such as the white ethnocracy of Rhodesia, are likely to resist pressure to democratization more fervently and will thus less likely transition into full-blown democracies. Democracies don't necessarily foster ethno-political inclusion, in other words, but ethno-political exclusion prevents democratization. In sum, there is no evidence that democracies are more peaceful either through a direct effect ("votes instead of bullets") or through an indirect effect via the ethno-political power structure.

But perhaps it is not so much democracy per se that prevents civil war, but either centripetal institutions (presidentialism, majoritarianism, unitarianism) or to the contrary consociational arrangements (parliamentarianism, proportionalism, and federalism)? I test these arguments using all available datasets on political institutions, which rely on different definitions and provide different data coverage. The results are quite straightforward: none of the institutional features, however defined and in whatever combination, seem to matter much for explaining ethnic conflict.

But since rules of the political game offer different incentives depending on whether an actor seeks to preserve power or to achieve it, we should perhaps again disaggregate the dependent variable and distinguish between infighting between power sharing partners and rebellions in the name of the excluded population. Such a fine-grained analysis does not yield any more encouraging results for advocates of institutional engineering, however. Using some specific codings of institutional variables indicates that presidentialism or federalism might be associated with fewer conflicts between power sharing partners. But no institutional arrangement has any effect on the much more prevalent form of ethnic conflict, i.e. on rebellions. These comprise 90 out of the 110 ethnic conflicts that occurred since 1945.

Rather than trying to engineer institutions – finding the right electoral system or the right amount of decentralization – prevention policies should aim at encouraging inclusive power configurations. But how to foster inclusion if this cannot be achieved through engineering electoral systems or decentralizing power? The rather tentative conclusions that Chapter 6 offers are not very encouraging from a policy-maker's perspective, I am afraid.

First, ethnocratic regimes can often only be overcome by violence. It is unlikely, for example, that Saddam Hussein's sultanistic regime could have been seduced to travel down a path of gradual reform that would have ended in meaningful representation of Kurdish and Shia politicians in the inner circle of power. It had to be overthrown by force. Ironically, then, violence is sometimes the only way to prevent it in the long run – perhaps the ultimately "realist" position one can take in the debate about prevention. As the peaceful South African transition away from ethnocracy illustrates, however, this position is not based on any iron "laws" or strict regularities, but on a more probabilistic argument.

Second, the ideal strategy to overcome the dynamics of ethnic competition and conflict would be effective nation building: shifting the loyalty of citizens toward the central state, increasing their identification with the nation, depoliticizing ethnicity, and thus allowing political competition and alliances to form along other lines, less linked to the basic principles of legitimacy of nation-states and thus less prone to escalation into conflict. As Chapter 2 suggests, however, nations can best be built in strongly centralized states and in the context of mushrooming civil societies. Neither state capacity nor the development of voluntary organizations can be engineered from the outside, and both are processes that evolve over generations, not years. Still, an endogenous process of nation building can be encouraged by focusing foreign aid on strengthening state capacity to deliver public goods and to tax the population effectively, thus encouraging new exchange relationships between state elites and the population at large. As the recent experience in Afghanistan shows, nation building "from the outside" is quite impossible and might delegitimize a state, rather than leading to its gradual rooting in the fabrics of society.

7 LIMITATIONS AND IMPLICATIONS

Just how exactly state capacity and networks of voluntary organizations can be fostered is a question beyond the purview of this book, however. It treats these factors as exogenously given and does not seek to explain them comparatively. Why the French state in the late eighteenth century managed to monopolize political power and the provision of public goods to a much larger extent than the Ottoman empire, to return to the empirical cases used in Chapter 2, is not the object of any systematic empirical analysis. Similarly, I do not attempt to comparatively explain why certain states in the postwar world are unable to achieve much effective nation building and exclude large segments of the population from the exchange relationships with the central government, while others have built up more integrative alliance structures and thus have managed to depoliticize ethnic relations.

This is the object of further research. Following up on the analysis presented in Chapter 2, I show in a forthcoming article (Wimmer in preparation) that the development of networks of voluntary organizations and state capacity to deliver public goods are indeed crucial factors in explaining how inclusive ethno-political power structures will be. Contemporary state capacity and organizational development are in turn related to levels of state centralization achieved during the nineteenth century before colonialism.[33] I also

---

[33] Most scholars attribute the weakness of many contemporary states to the fact that postwar international norms prevented the consolidation of weak states through conquest and absorption into stronger states

show that such long-term factors of endogenous political development are more important for explaining contemporary ethnic power structures – the success or failure of nation building – than democratization or various legacies of colonial rule.

Despite this extension of the argument presented in this book, a full empirical account of how state formation, organizational development, nation building, and war interact with each other remains beyond our current intellectual reach and capacity, at least of this author's intellectual capacity and reach. It is a major task for future research to develop a fully integrated empirical model that endogenizes all these factors, all the while taking international diffusion processes into account (for a recent conceptual move in that direction, see Levy and Thompson 2011).

Rather than offering such a full account, this book explores two major aspects of the overall history of political development in the modern era. It explains why the world has become a world of nation-states and shows that the creation of these nation-states triggered a global wave of wars and ethnic conflict. Its narrative therefore resembles a tragedy, rather than the heroic drama as which the history of modernity is often told. Indeed, the breakup of empires into a series of states, each supposed to be self-governed by a nation, made many modern achievements possible, especially when the nation-state was accompanied by effective nation building. It provided the institutional and ideological framework within which equality before the law, democratic participation, and a welfare state based on national solidarity could eventually emerge, usually generations after nation-states had been founded.

On the other hand, however, there was a price to be paid for shifting to the national principle: violent nationalist struggles against emperors and kings ended the age of imperial peace; episodes of mass violence erupted here and there, directed against civilians that ended up on the wrong side of new state boundaries and were seen as fifth columns of the nation's enemies; ethnopolitical competition over control of new nation-states often escalated into armed conflict. Tragedy is not inevitable, however, nor is it universal. After all, many histories of nation-state formation were peaceful, as the experience of the Baltic states after the end of the Soviet empire illustrates. And the book shows empirically that armed conflict is not a consequence of ethnic diversity as such and is thus not inevitable where the population speaks many different tongues or believes in many different gods. Rather, it is most likely where minorities rule, thus violating the nationalist principle of self-rule. Ethnically inclusive government is certainly difficult to achieve in institutionally weak states with a limited capacity of taxation and public goods delivery. But political inclusion

along the lines of European developments from the late medieval period onward (Jackson 1990; Badie 2000; Hironaka 2005). This argument overlooks, however, the fundamental weakness of the nation-states founded in the Americas during the eighteenth and early nineteenth centuries.

can durably mitigate the conflict-prone nature of the nation-state, as I will argue in the final chapter – whether through democratic or other institutional channels, through power sharing or power dividing, by integrating ethnically defined political networks or by depoliticizing ethnicity in a process of genuine nation building.

2

The birth of the nation

How and why did the first national communities emerge in France, the United States, and Britain? Or in more precise terms: why were political alliances and collective identities reorganized along national lines, replacing estates, tribes, village communities, and other local corporations? Obviously, the first states built on such a national compact were not able to copy this new institutional template from elsewhere. We thus will have to show how networks of alliances and identification were reorganized from *within* a society. This chapter demonstrates how high levels of state centralization and well-developed networks of voluntary associations lead to encompassing alliance structures and thus to nation building. The case of France will illustrate this trajectory. Alliances and identities will form along ethnic, rather than national, lines if states have less to offer in terms of public goods and political participation and if the relationships between rulers and ruled cannot be organized on the basis of voluntary associations. This is the path of political development that the Ottoman empire traveled down. The resulting political closure and exclusion along ethnic lines can lead to wars both between and within newly formed nation-states, as will be argued in Chapters 4 and 5.

To understand nation building and ethnic closure, this chapter introduces a formal model of domestic political alliance formation. According to this model,

This chapter is adapted from a journal article coauthored with Clemens Kroneberg.

It was presented at the Centre for International Studies, University of Zurich and Federal Polytechnical University of Zurich, in February 2007, at the FernUniversität in Hagen, in March 2007, at the workshop "Theoretical Frontiers in Modeling Identity and Conflict" at the University of Hawaii, November 2008, and the congress of the "European Network of Analytical Sociology" in Paris in spring 2011. We thank the various conveners and audiences. We are also grateful to Wesley Heirs and Nurullah Ardic for superb research assistance in collecting the historical data, as well as Christian Brumm and Luca Salvatore for help in implementing the model in C++, Python, and Gambit. Special thanks go to Theodore L. Turocy, who provided us with important advice concerning Gambit. We are indebted to Lars-Erik Cederman and Michael Hechter, who provided detailed critical comments on a first version of this chapter.

actors are endowed with different types and amounts of political and economic resources: political decision-making power, control over taxation, military support, and public goods. They seek to exchange some of their resources with some other actors while excluding yet others from the emerging alliance system. Following the relational argument introduced in the previous chapter, we assume that actor alliances will over time develop a shared identity and sense of mutual loyalty. This model allows identifying the power configurations under which nations, ethnic groups, and other types of alliance systems result from the struggles over the boundaries of belonging.

In line with the existing literature on nation building, we focus on three different ways in which political modernization affects the power distribution, and thus which actors ally and identify with each other. First, central state elites were more or less able to establish direct rule and to monopolize the political decision-making process, control over taxation, and the provision of public goods (the state centralization aspect). Second, the population at large was more or less mobilized in military and political terms: it played a more or less important role in the rulers' armies and it was more or less aware of, interested in, and indeed involved in political matters of the state, rather than just its local communities (the mass mobilization aspect). Third, political modernization also had an organizational aspect and changed the nature of ties between members of the population at large and between these and political elites. The emergence of voluntary associations – of trade unions, reading circles, professional associations, and the like – represents a crucial development here since it allowed for a different type of relationship between state elites and the population compared to the previously widespread informal patronage networks.

When did an encompassing system of alliances and identities emerge that comprised all segments of a population and thus put a society on the path of nation building? The model will show that this was most likely in highly centralized states as well as when dense networks of voluntary organizations had emerged to provide a basis for establishing alliances independent of the cultural similarity between actors. Under these conditions, a new relationship between state elites and the non-elite segments of the population evolved, a new social contract that institutionalized the exchange of political participation against taxation and of public goods against military support. Elites and masses then identified with each other over time. They started to define and perceive themselves as members of an encompassing national family worth defending and committing to, thus completing the process of nation building.

In less centralized states, no such encompassing exchange system could emerge. The central elites only disposed of enough decision-making power and public goods to ally themselves with their own ethnic constituencies. The counter-elite thus had the opportunity to do the same with their ethnic followers, who preferred an exclusive alliance with these still powerful ethnic elites over the promise of national solidarity that state elites could not keep. This tendency toward ethnic segmentation of alliances and identities was reinforced when voluntary organizations were only weakly developed. Actors thus relied on cultural commonality to stabilize their alliance networks and choose between otherwise equally attractive exchange partners. Our analysis also demonstrates, however, that such ethnic closure emerged even when actors either did not care about cultural commonality at all, or when they did care but found themselves culturally closer to their class peers, rather than their ethnic brethren. Ethnic politics and solidarity therefore represent an organizational channel to bundle the interests of various actors and do not necessarily need to be based on a deep-seated preference for those with whom one shares a set of cultural values or memories of past history.

Finally, populist nationalism – an alliance between state elites and the population at large against the "oligarchic" enemies of the nation – resulted from a situation in between these two trajectories of political modernization. The state elite was strong and resourceful enough to offer an alliance attractive for the entire population, irrespective of ethnic divisions. But they preferred to exclude the counter-elite, which remained an effective competitor for the population's support and loyalty. In the nation-building scenario, by contrast, the counter-elite no longer controlled enough decision-making power or public goods to compete with state elites. Populist nationalism becomes all the more likely the more the political and military mobilization of the masses had proceeded because this increased elite competition over the political loyalty and military support of the masses and thus provided further incentives for state elites to exclude other elite factions from the alliance system. Perhaps this helps to understand why so many populist military leaders *à la* Bonaparte populate the European nineteenth century of mass armies?

The chapter proceeds as follows: we first discuss the modeling strategy and compare our approach to that of other formal models of ethnicity and nationalism. The next section introduces the model architecture, outlines how its actors form preferences for alliance partners, and describes how they arrive at an agreement about who is to exchange which resources with whom. We then discuss how we calibrated this model with historical data on the distribution of resources between actors in France and the Ottoman empire. Three following sections discuss the equilibrium outcomes that the model produces and through which exact micro-mechanisms. Finally, we show that this model relates to the actually observed historical developments in France and the Ottoman empire in reasonably adequate ways.

I MODELING STRATEGY

Many formal models of nationalism and ethnicity are inhabited by isolated actors who choose among a set of fixed, given identities (e.g. Chai

2005).[1] By contrast, we model the formation of political alliances and collective identities as an interactive,[2] emergent process of group formation and political closure.[3] To achieve this, we combine two modeling approaches: in the first step, we use an exchange-theoretic model that explains which actor seeks to exchange resources with which other actor and to exclude which competitors from the exchange system.[4] Going beyond a purely instrumentalist approach that characterizes most rational choice approaches in historical sociology and political science (Kiser and Hechter 1998: 799), we build an additional component into the exchange model: when choosing alliance partners, actors also consider, especially if voluntary organizations are weakly developed, with whom they can identify on the basis of cultural similarity. In the second step, we use the tools of game theory to see which of the various preferences for exchange partners can in the end be realized and which overall alliance system therefore emerges.

As mentioned in the previous chapter, this modeling strategy allows overcoming one of the most conspicuous divides in the literature on nation building and ethnic politics: between explanations that focus on the actions of political elites and those that emphasize the importance of mass sentiment. Elite models argue that inventing nationalist ideologies helps to extract more resources from a population (Tilly 1994) or that ethnic elites manipulate their constituencies to gain political advantage (Brass 1979; Gagnon 2006). Such approaches have difficulty explaining why even well-crafted ethno-historical narratives or impressive nationalist rituals (Hobsbawm and Ranger 1983) sometimes fail to convince the population at large to shift their focus of loyalty and identity to the nation or ethnic group (for examples, see Anonymous 1989; C.A. Smith 1990; Kirschbaum 1993).

"Bottom-up" theories of the power of popular sentiment, on the other hand, underline the role of folk myths, established ethnic symbols, and legends in the

---

[1] See with regard to ethnic/national groups Congleton (1995); Laitin (1995); Kuran (1998); Penn (2008); as well as Dickson and Scheve (2006), who rely on the general identity model of Akerlof and Kranton (2000).

[2] Other formal models built on an interactionist logic are Fearon and Laitin (1996); Cederman (1996); or McElreath *et al.* (2003). How identity processes are embedded in social interaction has been prominently discussed by Stryker, Burke, and colleagues. They have been concerned with identity formation at the personal, cognitive level and with the impact of social networks and roles (see the overview by Stryker and Burke 2000). While compatible with these perspectives, our model is concerned with group-level boundary making, i.e. how these networks and roles emerge and change over time.

[3] On ethnic groups and nations as the result of social closure, see Weber (1968); Brubaker (1992); Wacquant (1997); Wimmer (2002).

[4] Standard game theory, by contrast, treats the preferences of its players as exogenous – a major point of critique by scholars both sympathetic (Elster 2000) and unsympathetic to rational choice theory (Somers 1998). For our analytical purposes, it is crucial to endogenize how actors come to prefer certain political alliances and identities over others.

creation of modern nationalism (Smith 1986); or they show how mass resentment against alien rule in modernizing states fuels nationalist movements (Hechter 2000); or they argue that the spread of literacy in vernacular languages makes the imagining of nations possible (Anderson 1991). But they struggle to explain why many myths, symbols, and legends are forgotten by groups who assimilate into a more powerful or culturally glorious national community; why not all ethnicities find the political elites necessary to transform into nations even when ruled by ethnic others;[5] and why many nationalisms were supported by populations who spoke different tongues.

We reconcile these two strands of the literature by conceiving of nation building and ethnic group formation as the result of a contentious and conflictual negotiation that involves both elites and masses. More specifically, we argue that the population at large only embraces national, ethnic, or populist identities if this offers them a favorable exchange relationship with elites. Nation building, ethnic closure, and populist nationalism require more than popular sentiment, on the other hand, because they need to provide elites with an alliance that serves their varying political ends as well.[6]

Another aspect of our modeling strategy needs to be highlighted at the outset. We seek to find a middle ground between micro-narratives of historical events and macro-structural approaches to political modernization. In contrast to the analytic narratives approach that uses rational choice theory to illuminate decisions taken by concrete historical figures (Bates *et al.* 1998), we do not account for specific chains of events in particular societies. Instead, we attempt to model the shift from one macro-political equilibrium to another that takes place over the *longue durée* (Carpenter 2000). We ask how political modernization shifted the balance of interests and power in favor of new modes of political alliance and identity, without trying to explain the different event chains, the conjectures of processes, and the historical reversal and contingencies through which these transformations were eventually achieved.

On the other hand, our formal approach is better able than most macro-structural theories to specify and test the key mechanisms through which modernization brings about a transformation of political alliance networks and identities. Macro-structural accounts argue that industrialization is functionally related to nation building (Gellner 1983), ethnic politics to unequal modernization (Horowitz 1985), or populist nationalism to a certain type of industrialization (Cardoso and Helwege 1991), without systematically showing that the mechanisms postulated can indeed logically and empirically bring about the

---

[5] For examples of non-politicized ethnicities, see Young (1976: 105–110); Winnifrith (1993); Wimmer (1995b: 219–229).

[6] Treating collective identities as a negotiated accomplishment extends the line of nationalism studies pioneered by Hroch (2000 (1969)) and pursued by Mann (1993b: chapter 4) and Wimmer (2002).

observed outcomes. A formal model of how actors coalesce into various alliance systems allows us to fully specify key mechanisms and assumptions and to show how macro-level outcomes are produced by micro-level interactions (thus following the program of an "analytic" sociology, see Hedström and Bearman 2009).

The chapter also aims to advance the formal modeling of historical processes by grounding it more firmly on empirical data. In much of the rational choice literature, the distribution of resources and preferences over actors is based on plausibility arguments alone and rarely fully justified. Indeed, one of the most frequently raised criticisms is that model builders often play around with input parameters until the actually observed historical outcome is produced (the problem of "post-hocery," see Skocpol 1994: 325; see also Elster 2000: 686–687; Parikh 2000). By contrast, the model introduced here relies on carefully researched historical data on the distribution of taxing capabilities, public goods provision, and military support in France (1300 to 1900) and the Ottoman empire (1500 to 1900).[7] Appendix 2.1 documents this extensive historical research.

Such calibration is not possible for the preferences of actors (for this problem in general, see Kiser and Hechter 1998). We do believe, however, that one should not simply deduce preferences from general theoretical propositions, but show their plausibility for concrete, historically situated actors (in line with Somers 1998; Parikh 2000; Skocpol 2000; and the "critical realism" of Bhaskar 1979). Absent of interview or survey data, paying attention to revealed preferences is perhaps the best strategy. Following a weak version of standard rationality assumptions, we can assume that actors did X because they wanted to achieve Y, which is widely known to result from doing X (Bates *et al.* 2000: 698). For example, if peasants stop rebelling when taxes rise, it may well be that they no longer care that much about taxes as they did before.

Our assumptions about preferences are based on such plausibility arguments that we derive from the historical literature on France and the Ottoman empire. These assumptions obviously involve a considerable degree of uncertainty. We go beyond standard practices in the formal modeling literature and perform a cutting-edge sensitivity analysis (Saltelli *et al.* 2004; Campolongo *et al.* 2007; Saltelli *et al.* 2008), which is reported in Appendix 2.3. The results show that the main findings remain largely identical even if we vary the parameter values for actors' preferences within reasonable limits.

---

[7] We chose these two societies since the comparative literature often treats them as contrasting cases of modern state building (Barkey 1991). France is one of the first states in which nationalist ideologies emerged endogenously and is considered as a prime example of successful nation building. The Ottoman empire, by contrast, is one of the earliest examples of a multiethnic empire from which ethnic minority nationalists seceded (Greeks, Serbs, Armenians, etc.). These two societies thus represent ideal cases for the analysis of the endogenous political forces behind the politicization of ethnicity and the formation of national communities.

Overall, the model that we introduce here contributes to a growing literature that attempts to translate certain insights from the constructivist literature on nationalism and ethnicity into a formal modeling architecture (Lustick 2000; Chandra and Boulet 2005; Chandra forthcoming).[8] The next section describes this architecture.

2 A GAME-THEORETIC EXCHANGE MODEL

2.1 The basics: actors and alliance systems

The model architecture foresees a simple two-dimensional social structure. On a horizontal dimension, we distinguish between actors according to the amount of power they hold, i.e. between political elites and masses, similar to the well-known polity model of Tilly (1978).[9] On a vertical dimension, we introduce a center–periphery dimension by distinguishing between a dominant and a subordinate segment of the population. This division between core and peripheral regions and populations is a universal feature of states, especially of pre-modern states that relied on indirect rule through subordinate elites to control the peripheral regions of the kingdom or empire.[10] The division between core and periphery often goes together with a marked differentiation of cultural traits and often with a corresponding ethnic cleavage or at least with strong regional identities. This vertical, ethnic, or regional division runs orthogonally to the horizontal division between elites and masses.

---

[8] Much of this emerging literature pursues a different modeling strategy, however. Evolutionary and agent-based models show how identity and group formation processes unfold on multiple social levels and within a geographic space populated by multiple societies that influence each other through diffusion processes (Young 1998; Cederman 2002; see also Lustick 2000). Our model complements these approaches since it abstracts from the diffusion mechanism (the topic of the next chapter) and instead focuses on the configurations that give rise to the very first historical examples of nation building. To adequately capture these original configurations, it is crucial to move the strategic interactions and resource exchanges between collective actors center stage – which has escaped evolutionary and agent-based modeling strategies so far. The prize is a reduction in actor complexity – and thus realism – compared to agent-based modeling strategies. As will be seen below, only four collective actors inhabit our model universe, rather than the hundreds or more that interact in the artificial societies of agent-based modelers. To see how the number of actors influences outcomes, we also constructed a model with eight actors and arrived at substantially similar results.

[9] We thus do not differentiate, as in some Weberian and Marxian traditions in sociology, between economic, political, and cultural elites, but focus exclusively on the political domain – in line with the thematic focus of this book.

[10] For empires, see Howe (2002: 14–16) and Lieven (2000: Chapter 2), who also discusses the Chinese exception; for elite divisions in pre-modern centralized bureaucratic polities, including post-feudal Europe, see Eisenstadt (1963); on indirect rule within center–periphery relations in pre-modern polities, see Hechter (2000); on the ubiquity of center–periphery distinction in modern states, see Gerring and Thacker (2008).

Four types of actors therefore inhabit the model: the *dominant elite* (dE), the *subordinate elite* (sE), the *dominant masses* (dM), and the *subordinate masses* (sM).[11] Before we move on, let us briefly envisage the real-world equivalents of these actors in the context of the two historical cases used for empirical calibration. The dominant elites (dE) represent those groups in control of the central state. In France, this refers to the king and his extended family and entourage, the royal house, until the revolution, and to the Parisian political elite thereafter. The dominant elite in the Ottoman empire consisted of the sultan and his government, including the slave administrators and elite soldiers that formed the inner palace.

The subordinate elite is made up of all those who exert political authority but who are not a member of the central state elite, thus the French nobility outside of Versailles under the *ancien régime* and the provincial political elites after 1789. In the Ottoman empire, it included the provincial *timar* holders and governors as well as the leadership of Christian *millets* that held official state functions. The masses consist of the inhabitants of towns and villages, including their notables and local leaders, who are not directly involved in the governance of the state – commoners and non-functionaries in France, and in the Ottoman empire all those who are not members of the military-administrative caste. The differentiation between dominant and subordinate masses might correspond in the case of France to the division between Paris and the provinces (or more broadly but relatedly between speakers of *langues d'oïl* vs. *langue d'oc*), and in the Ottoman empire to the provinces with Muslim majorities vs. largely Christian Rumelia, or after the loss of many of the European provinces in the nineteenth century, the Arabic-speaking provinces vs. those with Turkish-speaking majorities.

These four actors ally themselves with each other, and exchange resources. Each alliance system assigns the four actors to one of a series of mutually exclusive groups within which resources can be exchanged – thus modeling a system of political closure. Logically, four actors can combine into 15 possible alliance groups. Figure 2.1 lists those alliance patterns that are the most interesting from our point of view because they come close to what we observe in historical reality. In line with the theoretical approach outlined in the previous chapter, we assume that these actor groups also represent collective identities since actors who enter into an alliance with each other will also start to trust and identify

---

[11] Note that the two masses do not constitute groups with the ability to act collectively, but merely represent placeholders for different sets of individuals who face the same objective social conditions (i.e. who share the same position in the distributions of resources, interests, and cultural traits). As in similar game-theoretic models (e.g. Kiser and Linton 2002; Gehlbach 2006), we do not have to presuppose a shared identity or capacity to act. Our model can in principle include any number of actors, although a sufficiently realistic model of nation building can be constructed with these four types of actors. As mentioned in a previous footnote, we also built a model with eight actors (four masses and three subordinate elites), which generated very similar results.

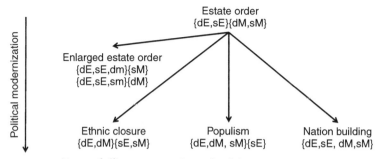

FIGURE 2.1 Types of alliance systems in modernizing states
Note: dE = dominant elites, sE = subordinate elites, dM = dominant masses, sM = subordinate masses.

with each other over time.[12] An *estate order* separates elites and masses – corresponding to Gellner's (1983) classic description of the political order of agrarian empires. We represent this classification as [dE, sE][dM, sM]. Although dominant and subordinate actors can be distinguished from an observer's point of view, the politically salient boundary here runs along the horizontal divide, creating a single elite and a single mass.[13] In a more inclusive variation of such elite rule, one of the masses is admitted into the alliance system. An example for such an *enlarged estate order* is post-Napoleonic France under the Orléanists, when the younger Bourbon king ruled a constitutional monarchy that granted full voting and citizenship rights to small segments of the population in and around Paris.

In contrast to these two essentially pre-modern alliance patterns, the three remaining groupings in Figure 2.1 represent varieties of modern systems of alliance and identity: they are all structured around at least one alliance between elites and masses, thus replacing a relationship between elites and masses characterized by force and resource extraction (as in the estate order) with one of consent, mutually beneficial exchange, and thus of reciprocal identification (for a similar analysis, see Levi 1997).

Ethnic closure describes a system of exchange and identification that is segmented along ethnic lines. The dominant elites ally and identify with the dominant masses and the subordinate groups with the subordinate masses. Such closure along ethnic, rather than along national, lines can be observed in a variety of

---

[12] Similarly, Posner (2005: 12) conceives "ethnic politics … in terms of the politics of coalition building and ethnic identity choice … in terms of the quest to gain membership in the coalition that will be most politically and economically useful."

[13] In our notation, the brackets that separate different categories (e.g. between estates in [dE, sE][dM, sM]) refer to politically salient boundaries. They thus show in which alliance group the four actors end up, without implying that the dominant–subordinate distinction was salient all the time and without assuming that there was no political conflict between dominant elites (the king's house, for example) and subordinate elites (the aristocracy) (see Eisenstadt 1963).

contexts such as in the pre-Civil War era United States and many post-colonial states in the South in which political arenas and identities are thoroughly compartmentalized along ethnic lines (Horowitz 1985; Wimmer 2002).

In *populist nationalism*, the subordinate elite is excluded from the domain of exchange and shared identity that embraces all other actors. Best known are the Latin American cases (Roberts 1996; Weyland 1996), in which the state elite portrays itself as the defender of the entire population's interest against an exploitative oligarchy allied with the evil forces of imperialism. As we will see below, however, populist nationalism is not restricted to Latin America. The Bonapartism of the Second Empire and the ideology of Tanzimat reformers in the Ottoman empire are other examples of this form of political organization and identity. Note that in our understanding, populist nationalism represents not a particular rhetorical style or mode of popular mobilization (see Jansen 2011), but a specific structure of political alliances and identities.

Finally, *nation building* corresponds to an exchange involving all four actors, thus the idea and institutionalized practice of solidarity among all elite and non-elite sections of the population. This represents the most inclusive alliance system, drawing the boundaries of belonging against non-national others rather than against a particular segment of the domestic population (Brubaker 1992; Wimmer 2002). France during the Third Republic represents a classic example, as we will see further below.

In the following, we formally model key mechanisms through which modernization leads a society onto these three different tracks of political development. Starting from the estate order as the established mode of political organization in both pre-modern France and the Ottoman empire, we analyze the conditions under which ethnic closure, populist nationalism, or nation building will become institutionalized in the modern age. The model has two parts: the first seeks to understand which actors prefer which alliance system. The second part then determines how actors with different preferences strategically negotiate with each other and arrive at an agreement – however contested and partial – over who is included in which exchange group.

2.2 The model in a nutshell

For readers not interested in the particulars of the model who would like to directly move on to the hypotheses (Section 3), I offer a brief summary of the main model features here. The exchange-theoretic part determines which actor prefers which of the possible exchange systems discussed above (nation building, ethnic closure, etc.). As a first step, we need to know who wants what and who has what: the distribution of resources over all actors as well as which actor shows how much interest in which resources. If many actors want the same resource and few actors have them, prizes for these resources will be high (a simple market mechanism). If an actor has already a lot of what she wants, she will be less interested in additional amounts of that resource (a marginal utility assumption). Actors can choose not only what to exchange, but also with whom: they want to keep those who offer the same resources at arm's length (because competition depresses prizes) and, on the other hand, get what they want from as many sources as possible (because a supply monopoly would increase prizes). All these various elements together then allow to calculate if an actor would be better off than at present under the different possible exchange systems, such as ethnic closure, the national community, an estate order, etc. Actors prefer those exchange systems from which they gain the most, leading to a ranked order of preferences for all exchange systems for each of the four actors.

We go one step beyond this purely utilitarian logic by introducing cultural similarity as another element of how actors evaluate different exchange systems. Cultural similarity and difference is expressed for each actor pair as a number between 0 and 1. 1 means that two actors have the same cultural repertoire, 0 means they don't share a single cultural trait in common. Each possible exchange system is expressed in similar ways (0 if two actors exchange with each other, 1 if they don't). Comparing these two sets of figures allows calculating how well each possible exchange system fits onto the map of "objective" cultural difference. Whether or not actors really care about such cultural similarity can change, and the model allows varying the relative weights given to the resource component and the cultural similarity component when actors rank different exchange systems.

The first part of the model thus determines which actors prefer which alliance system. Since actors are very unequal in the kind and amount of resources they control and those they want, they very likely will have different preferences (one actor prefers ethnic closure, others a national community, etc.). How then do they arrive at agreement of who will finally exchange what and with whom? To answer this question, we turn to game theory. The setup is quite simple: state elites first make a proposal (for example: "lets all exchange with each other," or nation building); the subordinate elites then can make a counter-proposal ("lets exchange between those who share the same ethnic background," or ethnic closure); the masses evaluate these proposals and determine which one comes closest to their top preference – and this is the exchange system that will finally prevail in a society. The sequentiality of the game implies that elites have more power to make proposals than the masses – but the masses can still reject any proposal that is not more advantageous for them than the status quo. And elite actors perfectly know – in the modeling environment – what the masses want and what they have, and thus take the preferences of the masses into account when making a proposal. In what follows, I outline the different parts of the model in more detail.

2.3 The exchange model in detail

The exchange of resources is modeled using Coleman's "linear system of action" (Coleman 1990). The two basic elements are, on the one hand, actors' interest in the four resources, and on the other hand their control over these resources. C_{ij} describes the control which actor i (i = 1,...,n) exercises over resource j

$(j = 1,...,m)$ and x_{ji} describes her interest in these resources. These parameters are scaled such that all actors' control over each resource sum to one and the interests of each actor also sum to one. Hence, an actor's control over a resource equals her share of control, relative to shares held by the other actors. Likewise, her interest in a resource is measured relative to her interest in the other resources. The initial distributions of interests in and control over resources can thus be summarized in a control matrix C and an interest matrix X.

The preferences of actor i are expressed by the Cobb–Douglas utility function $U_i^{control} = c_{i1}^{x_{1i}} \cdot c_{i2}^{x_{2i}} \cdot \cdots \cdot c_{im}^{x_{mi}}$. It is based on the usual assumption that the utility of control over additional resources diminishes the more the actor already possesses of that resource. Furthermore, actors demand control over resources proportional to their interests in them, while taking into consideration their prices and their own budget (see Coleman 1990: 682–684). Those who are more interested in the resources controlled by others than in their own will engage in exchanges until no further mutually beneficial exchange is possible.[14]

Coleman's exchange model thus describes a simple logic of trading. However, we do not want to model a free market world untainted by power and exclusion. Rather, we take into account that actors may also want to exclude others from the exchange system because the prizes they can fetch for their resources depend on who else offers these very same goods to the same actor who demands them.[15] We assume that when they have decided and agreed upon with whom to ally

[14] The control after exchange or equilibrium control can be calculated as $c_{ik}^{*} = \dfrac{x_{ki} \sum_{j=1}^{m} c_{ij} v_j}{V_k}$, where v_j

denotes the value of resource j. Intuitively, this formula states that an actor i's control over resource k after the exchange will be higher the more he is interested in it (x_{ki}), the lower the value (or price) v_k of this resource and the more actor i has to offer in return (the sum of products in the numerator describes his initial budget). The budget of each actor can be interpreted as an actor's exchange power. It is equal to the sum of her initial shares of control, each weighted with the price of the respective resource:

$$b_i = \sum_{j=1}^{m} v_j c_{ji} \quad \text{for all } i=(1,...,n).$$

The prices of the resources derive from the distributions of interests and control. In equilibrium, they can be computed by solving the matrix equation v = XCv, i.e. they equal the elements of the eigenvector v of the matrix XC (for the derivation, see Coleman 1990: 682–684).

[15] We thus apply Kalter's (2000) extension of the Coleman model. It involves a simple method to analyze situations in which actors split up into two or more subgroups. Exchanges only occur within these separated subgroups. Technically, one simply has to normalize the shares of control within each subgroup (Kalter 2000: 447). This is done by dividing the shares of control over a resource k by the sum of control that remains in the respective system of exchange. One then derives the equilibrium in the same way as before. To compare the equilibrium values of demand and supply as well as the utilities across exchange systems, one has to reverse the normalization by multiplying the equilibrium control values by the respective weighting factor (i.e. with the total share of control over the respective resource available in the subgroup).

themselves, they will exclude all others from this network of relationships. Actors therefore not only consider what they want and at which prices they are willing to exchange resources; they are also concerned with whom to enter into an exchange relationship in the first place. In general, they attempt to monopolize the supply of resources they offer by excluding competitors; and they try to de-monopolize the demand for these resources by including as many potential buyers as possible.[16]

In other words, we model a process of monopolistic closure with important consequences for the structures of political exchanges and identities in a society (Tilly 2006; Wimmer 2008b).[17] The model architecture also allows us to consider how inequality in the distribution of resources affects the group formation process and thus helps to avoid the assumption that actors operate on a level playing field, a problem of many game-theoretic models (Parikh 2000: 682).

2.4 Considerations of cultural commonality

So far, the actors that populate our model prefer an alliance system that allows them to maximize their control over political and economic resources. However, it is not enough to focus exclusively on such instrumental interests, as the majority of rational choice models do (Elster 2000). Rather, a sufficiently realistic model should incorporate the insight that some social categories and collective identities are more plausible or more desirable than others for other than purely instrumental reasons. Since nationhood and ethnicity are related to matters of cultural difference and similarity, the correspondence between an alliance system and the distribution of cultural traits might matter for actors. Examples of such traits are religion, language, skin color, cultural dispositions, and the like (see the "diacritical markers" in Barth 1969).[18] Why should actors care about the correspondence between alliance groups and trait distribution. The literature offers various suggestions and mechanisms, from emotional to cognitive and evolutionary (see Cornell 1996; McElreath *et al.* 2003; Hale 2004). Here, we shall pursue

---

[16] Note that expanding a group to incorporate an additional exchange partner can yield costs, but also benefits to group members. Thus, we do not model social closure as a zero-sum game and therefore do not predict coalitions of minimum winning size as does Riker's (1962) classical work on coalitions in political science.

[17] Assuming total closure between groups of exchange partners is not to deny that individuals from different sides of a boundary engage in transactions in their everyday lives (such as in paternalistic and clientelist social systems). However, we focus on exchanges that are institutionalized and involve major political and economic resources.

[18] Agent-based models offer the most sophisticated formal approach to this aspect of group formation processes (Axelrod 1997; Lustick 2000). They start from two-dimensional grids inhabited by a high number of agents who are characterized by strings of cultural traits. In Cederman's artificial social world, for example, actors in each grid choose the most similar neighboring actors as co-nationals as soon as the ideology of "nationalism" enters this world from the outside. Cultural difference and similarity henceforth start to matter for alliance formation and processes of cultural drift

an interpretation in line with the general approach underlying this book: actors will care about the empirical correspondence between an alliance group and the landscape of cultural similarity and difference when voluntary organizations are only weakly developed. This argument will be more fully developed below.

To model the correspondence between possible alliance systems and the trait distribution, we assume a stable distribution of traits over actors. For simplicity, we express the cultural difference between each pair of actors as a number between 0 (no difference at all) and 1 (maximum possible difference).[19] This allows us to represent the empirical distribution of traits over actors as a vector in which each cultural element corresponds to the dissimilarity between a pair of actors (for a similar approach, see Shayo 2009). In the analysis that follows, we distinguish between two ideal-typical trait distributions. In one of them, dissimilarity runs along ethnic divides – as when Armenian, Greek, and other Christians are culturally distinct from Sunni Muslims in the Ottoman empire. In the other, class boundaries are marked by differences in cultural traits, as for example in France during the *ancien régime*, where nobles pursued a cultural lifestyle meant to distinguish them from the ordinary commoner.[20]

We can now compare this structure of similarity with that of each possible alliance system. In an alliance system, two actors are either members of the same exchange group (0) or find themselves on opposite sides of the boundary (1). An alliance system S_j can therefore also be represented in the form of a vector, but with only zeros and ones as values. To measure the overall empirical correspondence between an alliance system and the landscape of cultural similarity, we simply sum the differences between the two vectors.[21]

We can now finally calculate which actors prefer which alliance system. They evaluate each system with respect to the exchange gains it would allow and with respect to how well it corresponds to an observed trait distribution. The exchange gains that an actor i can expect from adoption of an alliance system S_j are equal to the difference $\Delta U_i^{control}(S_j)$ between her utility after exchange under this alliance system and her utility after exchange under the established system. The second part of the utility function consists of the empirical correspondence $m(S_j)$, i.e. the perceived match between the alliance system S_j and the empirical distribution

and assimilation come to an end (Cederman 2002). Since we operate in a simpler game-theoretic environment with many fewer actors, we adopt a more parsimonious, but comparable specification of how cultural similarity influences social boundary making.

	dE|sE	dE|dM	dE|sM	sE|dM	sE|sM	dM|sM
TD =	(0.2	0.8	0.8	0.8	0.8	0.2)

[19] Conceptually, this number should be thought of as expressing differences in *averages* between groups with respect to the relevant traits, so that empirical plausibility is judged based on those group averages. Hence, we do not have to assume trait homogeneity within groups.

[20] Here is an example of a class differentiation.

[21] The empirical correspondence $m(S_j)$ of an alliance system S_j is defined as 1 minus the (unweighted) average of the absolute differences between all elements of S_j and the elements of the empirical

of traits across actors, weighted by $U_i^{meaning}$. The exogenous parameter $U_i^{meaning}$ describes the relative importance of such empirical correspondence in the utility function, which later on will be interpreted as a consequence of how well developed networks of voluntary organizations are. This produces the following simple, additive[22] utility function: $U_i(S_j) = \Delta\, U_i^{control}\,(S_j) + m(S_j) \cdot U_i^{meaning}$.

2.5 The negotiation process in detail

Now that we have described actors and their preferences, we turn to the strategic interaction between actors with different preferences and differential power to enforce them. The outcome of this contentious negotiation determines which exchange system will eventually prevail – and thus who will come to identify with whom, and who will remain excluded from the system of alliance and identification. An alliance system should be stable as long as no actor has an incentive to unilaterally deviate from it. From a game-theoretic perspective, the struggle over the boundaries of belonging therefore constitutes a non-cooperative game: if one actor stops believing in the usefulness and/or empirical accuracy of an alliance system and retreats from it, this system will subsequently break down.

We model this struggle as a sequential game, which allows us to capture the effects of symbolic power in two simple ways. First, we assume that only elites are able to formulate and propose new alliance systems in the public domain – for example by arguing against the exploitative *ancien régime* and proposing a new national compact based on equal rights and duties for all citizens. Masses can react toward these proposals or choose to stick to the existing alliance system. This assumption is realistic, since in modernizing states the power to effectively propose new political identities and alliances was restricted to political elites, even if such new ideas were originally developed by others, such as nationalist intellectuals, street-level populist firebrands, or ethnic entrepreneurs in the rural hinterland. Note, however, that the masses influence the proposals of the elites through their control over crucial economic and political resources (e.g. military support) and through their capacity to reject any proposal that does not conform to their perceived interests. As we will show below, it is the masses' exchange power that at times led elites to envision inclusive alliance systems and propose the national community as a new form of collective identity. Our model therefore stays clear of the elite manipulation arguments criticized in the first section of this chapter.

A second assumption is that the dominant elites move first. This reflects their superior symbolic power compared to that of subordinate elites. The dominant elites have more control over cultural institutions such as schools or the media

---

distribution of traits (vector TD): $m(S_j) = 1 - (\sum | S_j(1,k) - TD(1,k) |)/n$, where n denotes the number of columns of the vectors S_j and TD (this number being a function of the number of groups).

[22] Robustness analyses with a multiplicative linkage produced qualitatively identical results.

and can thus more effectively propagate their "vision of the legitimate divisions" of society, to paraphrase Bourdieu. In any case, we modified the order in which actors move to check the results for robustness, and report results in footnotes.

The strategic interaction process thus comprises three stages: first, the dominant elites propose one out of eight possible alliance groups of which they are a part (or an "in-group," for short). In the next stage, the subordinate elites likewise propose an in-group. In the third and last stage, the dominant and subordinate masses choose simultaneously between the dominant elites' proposal, the subordinate elites' proposal, and the established alliance group.[23] Since elites propose in-groups, the masses accept membership either in one of these two in-groups (if it includes them) or in the corresponding out-group (if they are excluded). Thus, the sets of alternatives among which actors choose are not entire exchange systems but in-group proposals – reflecting the greater psychological and instrumental importance that individuals attach to their own identity and interests vis-à-vis those of others.

The outcome of the game is derived according to the following aggregation rule: two actors i and j belong to the same alliance groups, if and only if both prefer identical in-groups (Hart and Kurz 1983; Yi and Shin 2000). This so-called principle of consensus means that actors who enter into an exchange relationship with each other have to agree on belonging to the same group – trading resources, in other words, is modeled as an act of voluntary exchange, rather than forced extraction. This is a crucial model feature if the goal is to understand the formation of alliances and identities without embracing an elite manipulation argument. Still, this principle of consensus does not imply that everybody gets what they want: the struggle over the boundaries of belonging involves conflicting interest, and stronger actors can often altogether exclude weaker ones from the exchange system – whether the latter like it or not.

As a solution concept for this sequential game, we employ "sub-game perfect equilibrium in pure strategies."[24] Basically, this means that actors anticipate the alliance system that might result from their proposal and evaluate their empirical correspondence as well as the exchange gains that would result. The elites take into account the interests and equilibrium behavior of the actors who move after them. On the side of the masses, however, no such sequential rationality needs to be assumed, since they move last and simultaneously.[25]

[23] These are not necessarily distinct alternatives, since the elites' proposals and the established classification could imply identical in-groups for the masses. Thus, the number of distinct alternatives faced by the masses varies between one and three.

[24] In equilibrium, actors' strategies are mutually best responses that involve no incredible threats (see, e.g., Osborne and Rubinstein 1994).

[25] The masses only need to have consistent preferences regarding three alternatives and to choose mutually best responses in equilibrium, i.e. arrive at an outcome from which they have no incentive to deviate. Thus, our sequential game makes rather modest rationality assumptions with respect to the masses (Elster 2000).

We now have outlined all the different parts of the model: the resource exchange system as well as the system of cultural similarity and difference, which both influence which alliances the various actors prefer. The game-theoretic part captures the strategic struggle between these actors and elucidates how a system of exchange finally emerges from these struggles. Taken together, the high number of exogenous parameters makes a mathematical solution to the game infeasible. We therefore derive the equilibrium outcomes computationally.[26]

3 HYPOTHESES AND EMPIRICAL CALIBRATION

3.1 Hypotheses

This model architecture allows analysis of the key mechanisms through which the estate order of pre-modern polities is transformed either into an encompassing national community, into an ethnically segmented political arena, or into a populist mode of alliance and identity. Under which conditions do we expect these three different political trajectories to emerge? Building on the qualitative literature, we suggest the following four hypotheses. First, a highly centralized state will lead actors to negotiate an encompassing nationalist compromise. We define the strength of the state by the degree to which the dominant elites have been able to establish direct rule and thus to monopolize control over political decision-making, taxation, and the provision of public goods (Tilly 1994; Hechter 2000). Second, other authors have emphasized the role of the political and military mobilization of the masses, i.e. the degree to which they have become engaged in the politics of the center and to which they provide manpower for the ruler's armies (Mann 1995; Lachmann 2011).

Combining hypotheses 1 and 2, we arrive at two different scenarios. In a centralized state with a highly mobilized mass of citizens, which we term the "strong scenario," we expect an exchange of political and military loyalty of the masses against political participation and public goods provision by the state elite – and thus the most encompassing system of alliances and identity (nation building). Conversely, ethnic segmentation will emerge in states that are weakly centralized and whose population is less mobilized, in other words

---

[26] The model is programmed in the following way: the user specifies the distributions of control and interests, the trait distribution, the status quo, and the relative weight of empirical correspondence in the overall utility function ($U^{meaning}$). Based on the control and interest matrices, a $C++$ program calculates exchange equilibriums and actors' gains from exchange for all 15 classifications, using Kalter's (2000) normalization method for segregated exchange systems. Based on the trait distribution, the program computes the empirical correspondence of the 15 classifications. Combining these results gives the overall utility of each social classification for each actor. This yields complete preference rankings over classifications, which provide the basis for the strategic interaction model. To calculate the sub-game perfect equilibriums of the sequential game, the program uses the *Python* interface of the game theory software *Gambit* (McKelvey *et al.* 2007).

in a "weak scenario." Under these conditions, the elites do not have the political and economic resources to distribute public goods and grant political participation evenly over the population. The masses, on the other hand, can expect less from the state elites and are thus less likely to identify with an encompassing nationalist project and more likely to find the ideology and practice of ethnic solidarity attractive. The result should be political closure along ethnic lines (Wimmer 2002).

As mentioned in the previous chapter, we treat state centralization and mass mobilization as two exogenous variables and do not model how they are affected by the structure of the international system, especially the nature and frequency of war between competing states. This is the object of Tilly's (1975) classic work on early modern state formation, which thus provides the backdrop for our analysis. The model focuses on how increasing centralization and moblization transformed domestic exchange relationships without further exploring these processes.

Our third hypothesis states that ethnic closure is all the more likely in states with weakly developed networks of voluntary organizations. This hypothesis is derived from Wimmer's (2002) comparative work on nation building in Iraq, Switzerland, and Mexico, as well as from Varshney's (2003) study of the conditions under which communal violence is more likely in Indian cities. When only few voluntary clubs, associations, trade unions, and the like have been established, political elites and followers alike will be more likely to rely on ethno-cultural similarity as a means to organize trans-class alliances. In other words, they prefer to ally themselves with actors who share certain ethno-cultural traits because this allows them to choose between otherwise similarly attractive alliance partners. Conversely, where dense networks of voluntary organizations have emerged, elites will rely on these in order to mobilize followers and to gain military support. Elite competition is then more likely to follow the dividing lines of ideology and interest.

Fourth, populist nationalism should result from medium state centralization. Drawing on analysis of the reemergence of populist nationalism in Latin America (Roberts 1996; Weyland 1996), we suggest that medium state centralization leaves the central state elite with too few resources and too little political power to integrate and co-opt all elite segments of society. But they are resourceful enough to ally themselves with the masses who will follow populist and anti-elite appeals in the hope of gaining access to public goods and political participation. Thus, by being able to attract both masses with an attractive exchange offer, the central elites win the struggle for support against competing elite factions. We therefore expect populist forms of political alliances to lie between the nation building and the ethnic closure variants, both in terms of the conditions that produce them as well as the degree of inclusiveness that they imply.

Fifth, populist nationalism will be more likely in societies with weak civil societies because appeals to the undifferentiated "people" are especially attractive, as the literature on waves of populist mobilizations in Latin America suggests, where large segments of the population are not integrated into stable, institutionalized networks of political organizations, and thus constitute a reservoir of political support that can be used in the struggle against competing elite segments. A weak network of voluntary associations thus makes nation building less likely by providing incentives to negotiate either ethnic closure or a populist compromise.

We use the game-theoretic exchange model to test whether these hypotheses hold against an explicit specification of the underlying micro-mechanisms. In order to proceed in as transparent a way as possible, we first model scenarios in which voluntary associations have developed and actors therefore do not care about cultural similarity when choosing alliance partners (setting the parameter $U^{meaning}$ to o). In a second step (in Section 6), we will modify this assumption and calculate scenarios with weak organizational networks and different distributions of cultural traits over actors, following class division in one scenario and ethnic division in the second. Before we can present results, however, we need to familiarize the reader with the empirical data used to calibrate the model.

3.2 Empirical calibration I: empire and strong scenario

As can be seen from Appendix 2.1, the empirical data used for model calibration refer to various stages of political modernization. The French Renaissance kingdom (thirteenth and fourteenth centuries) and the Ottoman empire of the classical age (sixteenth and seventeenth centuries) provide the data for modeling the pre-modern imperial scenario. The absolutist French state of the eighteenth century, the Ottoman empire under the modernist Sultan Abdul Hamid, who reigned until the Young Turk revolution in 1908, as well as the fully centralized state under the French Third Republic before World War I represent further points along the continuum of state centralization and mass mobilization. The model calibration for the strong state scenario – defined as a combination of high state centralization and high mass mobilization – lies in between those of absolutist France and late nineteenth-century Ottoman empire – thus reflecting the points in the developmental trajectory just before nationalism emerged in the French and Young Turk revolutions.

Before we discuss the calibrations for the strong scenario in more detail, a word about the pre-modern situation is in order. According to the model calculations that are detailed in Appendix 2.2, the specific distribution of resources and interests in the French Renaissance kingdom and the Ottoman empire of the classical age lead the four actors to negotiate an estate order – pitting masses against elites. The model thus generates an alliance system that was indeed characteristic of these two societies and can thus capture the historical starting point of subsequent historical developments in adequate ways. In the following tables, we include the empirical estimations of resource controls in the French Renaissance kingdom and the Ottoman empire of the classical age in order to provide the benchmark information against which the different paths of modernization can be specified.

Let us now turn to the calibration of the strong scenario that combines high state centralization with high mass mobilization. According to the historical research described in Appendix 2.1, the dominant elite almost exclusively control public goods provision in such highly centralized states (their share increases from an average of 5% in the two pre-modern situations to 91% under the strong scenario)[27] and hold the greatest share of control over taxation as well (from an average of 42% in the two pre-modern situations to 88%).[28] This reflects the change from indirect rule through subordinate elites to direct rule, a key aspect of political modernization. Conformingly, the subordinate elites gradually lost control over their two main sources of power: public goods provision and taxation, and thus no longer served as intermediaries between the central elites and the masses of the population. As part of the same transition, we assume that the dominant elite came to almost exclusively control political decision-making (from an average 60% in the pre-modern age to 9% in strongly centralized states). Given the scarcity of historical data, we could not empirically calibrate control over political decisions and instead relied on plausibility assumptions here. Extensive sensitivity tests (in Appendix 2.2) establish that our results do not change if we vary these assumptions within reasonable limits.

We further assume that the development of such strong, centralized states also changed the interests of actors. The masses and the subordinate elite show

---

[27] As described in Appendix 2.1, we use data on expenditures to estimate which actor provides how much of public goods. We assume that the highest institutional level through which money used for public service provision circulates "controls" these resources. Compared to earlier periods, the Ottoman state of the classical age had vastly wider concerns in the area of public goods provision and was involved in public works, education, the administration of justice in both Muslim and non-Muslim areas, policing, pensions for former government workers, postal and telegraph services, funding of the holy cities and pilgrimages, and so on. In eighteenth-century France, the king financed the police, postal services, major infrastructure construction and repair projects, education, and also spent considerable sums for the support of hospitals. Under the Third Republic, the state provided all of this and declared major public services (including caring for the needy, policing, and mandatory schooling) a municipal task mandated by law and financed through centrally collected taxes (see Appendix 2.1 for details).

[28] As described in Appendix 2.1, these figures are estimated based on tax revenue data. The development of a centralized French bureaucracy under absolutism, such as the system of royal intendants (Harding 1978), is well documented, as are the corresponding efforts under the Tanzimat reformers in the Ottoman empire (Lewis 1962: chapter 4). The capacity to directly tax the population increased accordingly. By the late eighteenth century, the French state was collecting a wide variety of taxes, both direct (property taxes, income taxes, and a general head tax) and indirect (mostly sales taxes levied on a wide variety of goods). Some of these indirect taxes were collected by the state, others by tax farmers. The French state still lacked the bureaucratic capacity for gathering all taxes through its own administration – contrary to the tax systems under Abdul Hamid (Shaw 1975) and the Third Republic (Kiser and Kane 2001), which formed part of a more efficient, bureaucratically integrated state apparatus.

a heightened relative interest in public goods, given that the absolute volume and quality of state-provided goods and services increases so dramatically. Conversely, their *relative* interest in control over taxation decreases compared to the pre-modern situation.

The other aspect of the strong scenario relates to the mobilization of the masses. This process had a military, as well as a political, dimension. First, the evolution of military technology implied a shift in control over military support in favor of the masses (from an average of 5% in the empires to 45% each, as the historical data documented in Appendix 2.1 show).[29] The second, political aspect of mass mobilization is best modeled as a change in the interests of the masses. We assume that they became strongly interested in political decision-making (relative interest of 50%), because the shift from indirect to direct rule, the centralization of power, and the administrative penetration of society dramatically increased the relevance of the decisions of the central state for the everyday life of its citizens (see Mann 1995; Hechter 2000). Together with their increased interest in public goods provision discussed above, this implied that the masses' *relative* interest in taxation sank considerably (from 85% in empires to 10%; note though that this does not imply a decrease in absolute interest in maintaining a low taxation level).

And indeed, after the Fronde rebellion of the mid-seventeenth-century tax increases no longer produced rebellions in France (Kiser and Linton 2002), arguably because the king was becoming more efficient at preventing them, but also, as Kiser and Linton suggest (2002: 905), because the population may have started to identify with the state, and envision, as I would argue, a different exchange relationship with the central elites. Also note again that we test whether a certain degree of variation in the specific values of relative interests and control change our main findings – which is not the case (see Appendix 2.3). The various model assumptions and the empirical data that support them are represented in Table 2.1.

3.3 Empirical calibration II: the weak scenario

The weak scenario of political modernization ends in a state with a lower capacity to tax directly, less control over decision-making processes and the provision of public goods, as well as in lower levels of popular mobilization.

---

[29] In the case of France, the evolution of military technology rendered the feudal *arrière-ban* increasingly irrelevant, thus undermining the military power of the subordinate elite, while navy sailors and infantrymen became even more important and effective. This development culminated in the introduction of universal conscription by the French revolution and the Ottoman army reforms of 1843 and 1869 (see Appendix 2.1 for details). In the Ottoman empire, the tribal militias that Abdul Hamid institutionalized in 1892 and that wrought havoc on the Armenian population of Anatolia were the only remaining bulwarks of military power left for the subordinate elites, while the role played by the nobility in the army of the Third Republic was comparatively even much smaller.

TABLE 2.1 *Control and interest distributions in empires and in the strong scenario*

	Model assumptions strong scenario									
Control over:					**Interest in:**					
	Pol. decision making	Publ. goods Military	Military Support	Taxation			dE	sE	dM	sM
dE	0.9	0.91	0.05	0.876	Pol. dec. making		0.2	0.3	0.5[a]	0.5[a]
sE	0.1	0.03	0.05	0.05	Public goods		0.01	0.2	0.4	0.4
dM	0	0.03	0.45[a]	0.037	Military support		0.2	0.25	0	0
sM	0	0.03	0.45[a]	0.037	Taxation		0.59	0.25	0.1	0.1
Empirical data on control in "strong scenario"										
France 1690–1789										
dE	NA	0.865	0.12	0.873						
sE	NA	0.018	0.08	0.083						
dM	NA	0.0585	0.4	0.022						
sM	NA	0.0585	0.4	0.022						
Ottoman empire 1876–1908										
dE	NA	0.934	0.005	0.9						
sE	NA	0.915	0.12	0						
dM	NA	0.03	0.44	0.05						
sM	NA	0.03	0.435	0.05						
France 1870–1914										
dE	NA	0.934	0.004	0.9						
sE	NA	0.06	0.042	0.04						
dM	NA	0.003	0.477	0.03						
sM	NA	0.003	0.477	0.03						
Empirical data on contol in "empire"										
France 1280–1350										
dE	NA	0.005	0.185	0.42						
sE	NA	0.915	0.68	0.46						
dM	NA	0.04	0.065	0.06						
sM	NA	0.04	0.065	0.06						
Ottoman empire 1470–1670										
dE	NA	0.152	0.325	0.36						
sE	NA	0.588	0.61	0.49						
dM	NA	0.13	0.05	0.07						
sM	NA	0.13	0.015	0.07						

Notes: [a] Indicators of a strong mass mobilization. The control matrix gives the pre-exchange distribution of control for each resource (i.e. the relative shares of control exercised by the actors). The interest matrix gives the distributions of interest for each actor (i.e. her relative interest in the resources). Values for control over taxation, however, represent post-exchange values because pre-exchange controls cannot be measured empirically.

We specified the control and interest matrices for this scenario by using the midpoints between the pre-modern situations and those of a highly central-ized state. We preferred this strategy over collecting additional historical data because we realized that the various "snapshots" of the French and Ottoman resource distributions aligned almost perfectly along a linear continuum, lead-ing from Renaissance France to the sixteenth/seventeenth-century Ottoman empire of the classical period to eighteenth-century absolutist France, Abdul Hamid's empire, and finally the Third Republic (see again Appendix 2.1). It thus made sense to define the weak scenario as the midpoint on this continuum – thus a situation resembling the Ottoman empire in the Tanzimat era or France in the sixteenth century.

However, we deviated from this interpolation principle on one point, because weak states also differ from the Tanzimat Ottoman empire or sixteenth-century France. While in these societies the midpoints represent transitory phases in a steady political development, in weak states they conform to a longer-term equilibrium. This has two consequences. First, the masses regain some control over taxation because neither indirect rule nor direct rule is fully institutional-ized in a permanently weak state (10% of control over taxation by each mass, vs. 5% under the empire or strong scenarios). Second, when the weak state is permanent, the subordinate elites become predominately interested in military support because they seek to secure their position in the situation of uncertainty created by the weakness of the political center (38% vs. 15% under the empire scenario and 25% under the strong scenario). The interpolation procedure plus these two modifications produces the following control and interest matrices for the weak scenario (Table 2.2).

4 RESULTS: STRONG AND WEAK SCENARIOS WITH WELL-DEVELOPED CIVIL SOCIETIES

We are now ready to present the results for strong and weak scenarios, still assuming that civil societies are well developed and actors thus do not take the distribution of cultural traits into account when deciding with whom they prefer to exchange resources. This assumption will be modified in Section 6 below. The first panel of Figure 2.2 depicts the social classifications that result in equilibrium for different levels of state centralization (y-axis) and mass mobilization (x-axis).

We describe the results as a series of scenarios that lie in between the strong and the weak scenario. Each point in the graph corresponds to a specific dis-tribution of control and interest. The point in the lower-left corner represents the weak scenario. The point in the upper-right corner conforms to the strong scenario; the diagonal connecting them thus is the continuum between weak and strong scenarios. All other points were calculated by varying the indicators of state centralization and of mass mobilization in equal-sized steps from the values of the weak to those of the strong scenario.

TABLE 2.2 *Control and interest distributions under the weak scenario*

Control				Interest				
Pol. dec. making	Publ. goods	Mil. supp.	Tax		dE	sE	dM	sM
dE	0.75	0.56	0.13	0.20	Pol. dec. making	0.20	0.10	0.20^a	0.20^a
sE	0.25	0.38	0.38	0.20	Publ. goods	0.01	0.15	0.20	0.20
dM	0	0.03	0.25^a	0.30	Mil. supp.	0.20	0.50	0	0
sM	0	0.03	0.25^a	0.30	Tax	0.59	0.25	0.60	0.60

Notes: [a] Indicators of a weak mass mobilization. The control matrix gives the pre-exchange distribution of control for each resource (i.e. the relative shares of control exercised by the actors). The interest matrix gives the distributions of interest for each actor (i.e. her relative interest in the resources). Values for control over taxation, however, represent post-exchange values because pre-exchange controls cannot be measured empirically.

The negotiation process results in three types of equilibriums: nation building (black squares), populist nationalism (white squares), and a multiple equilibrium in which each elite group aligns with only one of the masses (black triangles). For simplicity, we identify this as ethnic closure, although it also includes the reverse assignment of elite groups and masses. If we allowed for only an infinitesimal significance of an ethno-cultural trait distribution in actors' preferences, ethnic closure would obviously be the sole equilibrium in these cases.

Overall, the results depicted in the left-most panel of Figure 2.2 lend strong support to the first hypothesis according to which state centralization is positively related to more inclusive forms of alliance and identity: nation building results only if the state is strong, while ethnic closure is the equilibrium outcome only if the state is weakly centralized. Populist nationalism emerges when state centralization reaches medium levels. We also see that the mobilization of the masses has hardly any effect on the resulting exchange system, contrary to our second hypothesis. It is only under conditions of medium-to-high degrees of state centralization that mass mobilization matters, by leading to populist nationalism and away from nation building. Thus, contrary to our expectations, mass mobilization does not emerge as a factor promoting nation building and acting against ethnic closure. We will see why this is the case as soon as we discuss the preferences and the strategic interactions between actors in detail.

Remarkably, our model also shows that given our assumptions, ethnic closure can be the equilibrium outcome *even* if actors do not care at all about cultural similarity. In other words, ethnic closure may result from a purely instrumental negotiation process that is exclusively geared toward maximizing exchange gains and is not influenced by considerations of culture or identity. This supports the conjecture that ethnic groups are not necessarily characterized by stronger symbolic or emotional attachments than other modes of social categorization and identification – they may emerge even in the absence of any deep primordial or

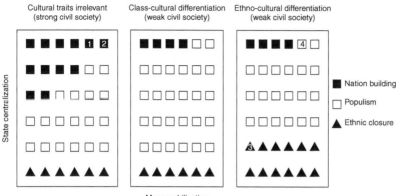

FIGURE 2.2 State centralization, mass mobilization, and alliance systems in three different model universes
Notes: 1 corresponds to France 1690–1780; 2 to France 1870–1900; 3 to the Ottoman empire in the early nineteenth century; 4 to the Ottoman empire 1870–1908.

psychological bond. The mechanisms underlying this finding will become clear in the next section where we have a closer look at the negotiation process itself.

5 THE NEGOTIATION PROCESS UNDER THE MAGNIFYING GLASS

How did elites and masses, according to our model, arrive at these different, more or less encompassing agreements over where the boundaries of belonging should lie? We begin with the weak scenario, under which actors end up aligning themselves along the ethnic divide.

5.1 Ethnic closure

A first step shows that actors prefer certain alliance systems over others depending on the exchange gains that these would imply for them. Note that these preference orders are not based on plausibility assumptions, but calculated with the help of the exchange-theoretic part of the model introduced above. For the sake of simplicity, we will not show prices, equilibrium offer, and demand for the various resources, or the resulting exchange gains for each actor under each exchange system. Rather, the main points will be introduced narratively. The upper part of Table 2.3 displays the resulting preference orderings for the weak scenario. The two elite groups compete for the military support of the masses and therefore have an incentive to draw a social boundary that excludes the other elite group. This competition for the military support of the masses explains why the first preference of both elite groups is to form a coalition with both masses and without the other elite group, as can be seen from Table 2.3.

TABLE 2.3 *Actors' preferences over alliance systems under the weak and strong scenarios*

		Rank-ordered preferences for alliance systems				
Scenario	Actor	1.	2.	3.	4.	5.
Weak	dE	dEdMsM/sE	dEsEdMsM	**dE*M/sE–M**	dEsE*M/–M	dEsE/dMsM
	sE	sEdMsM/dE	**dE*M/sE*M**	dEsEdMsM	dEsE*M/–M	dEsE/dMsM
	*M	dEsE*M/–M	**dE*M/sE–M**	dEsEdMsM	sE*M/dE–M	dEdMsM/sE
Strong	dE	**dEsEdMsM**	dEdMsM/sE	dEsE*M/*M	dE*M/sE–M	dEsE/dMsM
	sE	sEdMsM/dE	dEsE/dMsM	dE*M/sE*M	dEsE*M/–M	**dEsEdMsM**
	*M	dE*M/sE–M	dEsE*M/–M	dEdMsM/sE	**dEsEdMsM**	sE*M/dE–M

Notes: Equilibrium outcomes in bold. dE = dominant elites, sE = subordinate elites, dM = dominant masses, sM = subordinate masses. *M = either dM or sM, –M = the other masses (–M = sM if *M = dM, –M = dM if *M = sM).

However, the competition is not symmetric. Because the dominant elites hold twice as much decision-making power, their gains from an exchange between all actors would be somewhat greater than those of the subordinate elites. This is why nation building and ethnic closure rank differently in the preference orders of the two elite factions.

For both elites, these two alliance systems involve a trade-off, since ethnic closure would allow them to avoid the competition with the other elite group at the cost of losing the support of one of the masses. The subordinate elite prefers ethnic closure to nation building, because they do less well in the competition with the dominant elites. For the dominant elite, the trade-off plays out in favor of nation building.

The masses likewise compete with one another. Each of the masses is willing to give away its military support. However, the amount of resources that the masses receive in return is lowered when the elites can simultaneously also exchange with the other masses (since increased supply lowers the price). Their most-preferred classification is therefore to be included in an extended estate order, i.e. to exchange with both elites while excluding the other masses from the exchange system. For the masses, ethnic closure carries a similar trade-off as for the elites. It prevents competition with the other masses, but entails losing one supplier of elite-controlled resources. Both masses end up preferring an extended estate order to aligning with the dominant elite only. Nation building follows on the third rank, and aligning with the subordinate elite only is the least attractive alliance system.

Given these preferences, ethnic group formation is the equilibrium outcome. To understand this, one has to turn from preferences to the strategic interaction between actors (the game-theoretic part of the model). Because the dominant elite cannot convince the other actors to embrace their first or second preference, they cannot do better than ethnic closure. The subordinate elite will counter a populist alliance system by proposing ethnic closure, which the masses prefer over populist nationalism. Alternatively, the dominant elite could propose nation building, their second preference. This classification would be preferred by both masses relative to aligning with the subordinate elite only. However, the latter can make nation building infeasible: they can decline to join the national community by proposing to align only with one or both of the masses. This will again lead to ethnic group formation: one of the masses will follow the proposal of the dominant elite, while the other will agree to exchange with the subordinate elite.

The subordinate elite likewise cannot do better than ethnic closure, which is their second preference. Their first preference, a populist alliance with both masses under exclusion of the dominant elite, is not at all attractive for the masses. Compared to this outcome, both prefer to align themselves with only one of the elites.

A critical assumption of this analysis is that the masses know the value of the public goods and decision-making power controlled by the elites. The masses do not align with the dominant elites, but follow the subordinate elites' counter-proposal of ethnic closure, because they know that the dominant elite has only a limited amount of goods at its disposal. This assumption of perfect information can be relaxed in the following way: while both elites know that the state is only weakly centralized, the masses attach a certain probability to the possibility that the state is highly centralized. Populist nationalism becomes more prevalent the more the masses tend to believe that they are facing a strongly centralized political center, as additional analysis shows. Thus, by misleading the masses about their resourcefulness, the dominant elites can more easily attain their most preferred outcome. Maybe this helps to understand why populists often overemphasize their capacity to deliver public goods and their effective political power?

5.2 Negotiating nationhood

We now turn to the strong scenario that leads to nation building. As Figure 2.2 reveals, a high level of state centralization is crucial to bring about this outcome. Contrary to what the second hypothesis postulates, however, high levels of mass mobilization are irrelevant. More specifically, where the state is strongly centralized, the preference orderings of the dominant elite and the masses, as shown in the lower part of Table 2.3, stay the same *regardless* of the degree of mass mobilization. We can therefore abstract from this dimension for the moment and focus on the mechanisms by which high levels of state centralization lead to nation building. The issue of why mass mobilization does not support nation building, but rather populist nationalism, will be taken up in the next section.

In a strongly centralized state dominant elites control even more of decision-making and public goods than in the weak scenario, while subordinate elites as well as the masses show more interest in these resources. As a consequence, the subordinate elites switch from being a supplier of public goods to demanding them along with the masses, and they no longer are serious competitors when it comes to offering political participation to the masses. Both attenuate elite competition, and nation building becomes the first preference of the dominant elite. Populist nationalism drops to the second rank of their preference order compared to the weak scenario, while extended elite coalition replaces ethnic closure as their third preference.

The preferences of the masses are also markedly different compared to the weak scenario, mostly because they now value public goods more highly, which are now predominantly controlled by the dominant elite. The masses therefore prefer *any* classification in which they end up together with the dominant elite to an exchange exclusively with the subordinate elites (see the lower part of Table 2.3). The preferences of the subordinate elites therefore do not matter much because the masses are no longer interested in an alliance with them. The nation thus becomes the system of alliance and identification that all actors will agree upon.[30]

5.3 The populist compromise

We now briefly turn to populist nationalism as the most prevalent outcome in between strong and weak scenarios – and to the question of why increasing mass mobilization in moderately centralized states produces a shift from nationhood to populist nationalism. Separate analyses (not shown here) demonstrate that the military mobilization of the masses is responsible for this outcome. For the dominant elites, an increase in the supply of military support by the masses makes the subordinate elites less attractive as an exchange partner. There is even an incentive to exclude the latter: the central elite's exchange power vis-à-vis the masses is weakened if they have to compete for their military support with subordinate elites. Through these two mechanisms, mass mobilization works against nation building and leads to populist nationalism.

Our model thus suggests that the increasing military role of the masses may not have contributed much to nation building, contrary to the crucial role

---

[30] Additional robustness analyses show that letting the subordinate elite make its proposal first produces identical equilibriums. If both elites move simultaneously, however, some additional equilibriums emerge: due to a coordination problem between the elites, nation building ceases to be a unique equilibrium and is always accompanied by populist nationalism as a second (pareto-inferior) equilibrium outcome. However, strict simultaneity (or non-observability) is rather unrealistic given that we model how elites propose alliance systems in the public sphere and react to the proposals by others. When one of the masses moves first, the general pattern is similar, but there are more multiple equilibriums than in the other variants of the game. Especially in the middle ranges of state centralization, these multiple equilibriums include ethnic closure. This finding adds another aspect to the picture: the symbolic power of elites (represented by the fact that they move first) enhances nation building.

accorded to universal conscription by Lachmann (2011). Rather, it leads to populism as long as the central elites cannot swim free of the competition with subordinate elites and thus cannot afford to integrate them into an encompassing exchange system. Overall, state centralization seems to be the more important ingredient of successful nation building, in line with Tilly's (1994) and Hechter's (2000) analyses.

6 WHEN CULTURAL TRAITS MATTER

So far our analyses assumed that actors only care about the resources they obtain from different exchange systems. We now take into account that they might also consider how well the various alliance systems fit the empirical landscape of cultural difference and similarity. In the context of our theoretical framework, we interpret a *lack* of such concerns as evidence of a well-established, densely woven network of voluntary organizations that may serve as a basis for establishing and stabilizing alliances between actors (Wimmer 2002). When such voluntary organizations are absent, however, actors will take cultural similarity into account when forming alliances, since no other institutional channels to support and stabilize a coalition are available.

Obviously, how considerations of cultural similarity affect the prospect of nation building also depends on how cultural traits are distributed over actors. We analyze two cultural landscapes: a horizontal, class-cultural differentiation in which both elites resemble each other and both masses; and a vertical, ethno-cultural differentiation in which subordinate elites and subordinate masses show similar traits, and dominant masses and elites are also culturally similar. Recall that we represent cultural differentiation as a vector in which each element corresponds to the dissimilarity between a pair of actors and varies between 0 (no difference at all) and 1 (maximum possible difference).

The ethno-cultural differentiation involves a dissimilarity of 0.4 between dominant elites and masses, as well as between subordinate elites and masses, whereas all other pairs of actors are assumed to be dissimilar by 0.6. In this situation, ethnic closure obviously has the best empirical fit, followed by populist nationalism. Nation building and the estate order have the lowest correspondence to this distribution of cultural traits. The class-cultural differentiation assumes a dissimilarity of 0.4 between the elite groups and between the masses, and a dissimilarity of 0.6 for all other pairs. The alliance system corresponding best to this trait distribution is the estate order, with ethnic closure, populist nationalism, and nation building following.

To calculate actors' preferences, we set the parameter $U_i^{meaning}$ to 0.4. It expresses how much actors weigh the correspondence between alliance system and cultural traits relative to the exchange gains that come with an alliance system. Other parameter values either lead to qualitatively similar results or are less interesting:[31] trivially, assuming a very high $U_i^{meaning}$ ultimately leads to the alliance system with the highest correspondence – irrespective of the gains from exchange. In turn, a weight close to 0 makes correspondence irrelevant and brings back the equilibriums of the "strong civil society" scenarios discussed above.

The middle graph in Figure 2.2 reports the results when cultural differentiation has proceeded along class lines. The right-hand graph depicts the equilibriums for an ethnic trait distribution. Overall, there are only six instances of nation building in the two scenarios with weak civil societies (middle and right-hand graphs) compared to the 12 instances in the strong civil society scenario (left-hand graph), and 12 instead of only six instances of ethnic closure when cultural differentiation follows ethnic lines. Clearly more encompassing alliance and identity systems emerge when voluntary organizations are strong and actors do not take cultural similarities into account when building alliances. This supports our hypothesis that the density of networks of voluntary organizations promotes inclusive forms of political alliance and identity – independent of whether cultural traits align with ethnic or class divisions.

More specifically, populist nationalism becomes more prevalent under both scenarios with weak civil societies (middle and right-hand graphs),[32] replacing some instances of nation building when state centralization reaches medium to high levels. The reason is that populist nationalism instead of nation building is now the first preference of the dominant elites because of its better correspondence with either of the two trait distributions. As shown in the previous section, the dominant elites can push through their vision of the legitimate division of society in a strongly centralized state.

When cultural differentiation follows ethnic lines (right-hand graph), we observe an additional row of ethnic closure compared to the strong civil society scenario (left-hand graph). Remarkably, this is true even though the dominant elites' first preference continues to be populist nationalism (as in the strong civil society scenario). But the masses prefer ethnic closure when networks of voluntary organizations are weakly developed and cultural difference is aligned with ethnic divisions, although in terms of exchange gains both masses would do better under populist nationalism. Thus, if the dominant elite proposes populist nationalism, the subordinate elite can successfully counter by suggesting a political alliance and identity based on ethnic commonality.

---

[31] The same holds true for different specifications of the trait distributions. As robustness analyses show, more extreme trait distributions lead actors to develop stronger preferences for alliance systems that are in line with the respective distribution.

[32] The apparent prevalence of populist nationalism in all three matrices of Figure 2.2 does not mean that this is historically or globally the most frequent outcome. It is so prominent in the figure because we truncate both axes by looking at the data range between c.1600 and 1900. All post-1900 resource and interest distributions would lead to nation building, while the pre-1600 distributions would result in ethnic closure or the estate order.

Under the class-cultural differentiation, the exchange gains continue to dominate preferences as long as the state is only weakly centralized. Thus, we observe the same equilibriums as in the strong civil society scenario. This is mostly because the estate order does not offer the masses an attractive resource exchange – thus offsetting that it provides the best fit in terms of cultural similarity. We thus arrive at the counterintuitive finding that even when cultural markers are horizontally aligned with class cleavages and actors *do* care about cultural similarity, modernization will lead to the politicization of vertical, ethnic, or national dividing lines, and to corresponding forms of political alliances. This supports the "modernist" school in ethnicity and nationalism studies, according to which political closure either along ethnic or national lines forms an integral part of the modern political order (Geertz 1963; Young 1976; Rothschild 1981; Wimmer 2002). Our model explores the micro-mechanisms that produce this global pattern even when the cultural landscape is not structured along ethnic divisions. The complementarity of resource exchanges in modernized states binds elites and masses into networks of alliances, and replaces the coercive resource extraction that had characterized feudal and other pre-modern polities. Such elite–mass alliances make class-based identities and forms of closure comparatively unlikely. Nationalism and ethnic politics therefore take center stage in the age of modern, centralized territorial states.

7 HISTORICAL ANALOGIES: FRENCH NATION BUILDING, OTTOMAN DISINTEGRATION

Retrodictions are not the aim of this chapter nor are they possible given the host of important factors that our model is not considering, not least the role of contingent events. Still, it is encouraging to see that the model produces results in line with the political identities and alliances that effectively emerged in the two societies to which our data refer. Figure 2.2 contains numbers that display where in these three matrices the historical data on resource distribution would locate France and the Ottoman empire at various points in time. We also had to assign the two societies to one of the three scenarios related to the development of organizational networks and the type of cultural trait distribution. While we can find both ethno-cultural and class-cultural types of differentiations in early modern France and the Ottoman empire, it is probably safe to say that there was *less* ethno-cultural differentiation in France and *more* cultural differences along class lines than in the Ottoman empire.[33]

---

[33] Intergenerational status mobility was institutionalized in the Ottoman empire, which had no *de jure* hereditary caste of nobles comparable to that of France but had long relied on the subordinate Christian provinces for recruiting its top slave administrators and generals (Shaw 1976: 113–150). At the same time, the Sublime Port made fewer conscious efforts to homogenize the country in religious or linguistic terms (Grillo 1998) but rather sought to preserve its heterogeneous communities (Barkey

In any case, cultural difference mattered much less in France than in the Ottoman empire because the Enlightenment movement had created strong networks of voluntary organizations that transcended class and regional boundaries (as argued in the classic oeuvre of Habermas 1989; see also Horn Melton 2001) – in contrast to the Ottoman empire, where such organizations were confined to a much smaller elite of *literati* in the major cities and where horizontal links between various communities were sparse (Barkey 2008).[34] Thus, the ethno-culturally differentiated scenario (the right-hand graph in Figure 2.2) corresponds best to the empirical reality of the Ottoman empire, while the French case resembles the strong civil society scenario in which cultural differences hardly mattered for the formation of political alliances (left-hand graph).

We can now see what outcomes the model produces for the specific resource distributions that our historical research has identified for the various points in time. The French case is more straightforward. The model "retrodicts" nation building for the period immediately preceding the French Revolution (see number 1 in Figure 2.2). In historical reality, the democratic, republican nationalism first developed by Girondists and Jacobins (Sewell 1996) competed over almost a century with other forms of political alliances and identities, until nation building was completed under the Third Republic. Until this new "equilibrium" state was reached permanently, various developments on and off the equilibrium path can be noted and their potential meaning explored with the help of the model.

The revolutionary process and the domestic and international wars that it entailed led to the unprecedented military mobilization of the population under Napoleon's leadership. Conforming to our analysis of the conditions under which populist nationalism emerges, the strong militarized leadership of Napoleon depended on mass military support and loyalty, and he therefore excluded competing political elites – both the old nobility and the new republican forces – from his political coalition. The result has been described in Karl Marx's *18th Brumaire* as "Bonapartism," which roughly corresponds to populist nationalism in our terminology.

Subsequent political developments then led further away from what our model would identify as the equilibrium path: the collapse of Napoleon's empire and the Congress of Vienna in 1815 brought the Bourbon and later Orléanist kings back to

---

2008). The Ottoman empire had institutionalized religious, and to a certain degree therefore also linguistic, differences through the millet system that granted legal autonomy in matters of family law and a certain degree of self-rule to religious minorities. The French kings, by contrast, had eradicated religious diversity by revoking the Edict of Nantes and elevated their own dialect to a national language (Lodge 1993).

[34] In France, a government study of historical rates of literacy published in 1880 showed that for the 1686–1690 period, 25% of the overall population (and 36% of men) could sign their name, and 90% of the urban bourgeoisie was literate (Cipolla 1969). By contrast, only 2–3% of Ottoman subjects were literate in the early nineteenth century, and about 7% in the middle of the century. In the Turkish heartland of the empire, literacy rates had only reached 10.5% in 1924, when the Republic was founded (for sources of these estimates, see Appendix 3.3).

power. They did not undo the principle of legal equality, but offered only limited political inclusion to the bourgeoisies of the country's center, a configuration that resembles what we have called an enlarged estate order – indeed a partial return to pre-revolutionary forms of political alliance and identity. Our model does not foresee these developments toward a British-style constitutional monarchy. But the failure of this system to become permanently institutionalized might be explained by the fact that state centralization had already proceeded far enough to make the demands for popular political participation and effective public goods delivery both legitimate and politically appealing – as the 1830 and 1848 revolutions illustrate.

The subsequent Bonapartist regime of the Second Empire (1852–1870) under Louis Napoleon II brings back a populist mode of alliance and identification. With the Third Republic comes a massive further strengthening of the central state, especially in the domain of public goods provision, as the torrent of reforms regarding schools, hospitals, welfare for the poor, and public infrastructure indicate (see Appendix 2.1 for details). As a consequence, provincial elites no longer provided such services, but became dependent on them, and no longer effectively competed with the Parisian political elite, as they still had at the time of the 1789 revolution – aptly illustrated by the Vendée revolt in its aftermath, which was led by the provincial clergy and nobility. The dominant elites thus no longer had to fear political competition with the provincial elites and integrated them into a more tightly organized administrative apparatus.

As our model foresees (see number 2 in Figure 2.2), this provides the background for the development of a truly encompassing nationalist ideology by the central elites of the Third Republic – greatly helped by the defeat at the hands of Prussia in the 1870 war, the effects of which again escape our model. Nationalism was now embraced by the subordinate provincial elites as well and gradually diffused into the peripheral regions (Weber 1979), where the public service provided by schools, hospitals, and the gendarmerie made it more and more attractive for the common men and women to embrace the nationalist ideology – rather than to enter into an alliance and identify with provincial elites, which no longer had much to offer them.

As this brief discussion shows, the model is not able to predict or to make sense of the back-and-forth between various forms of alliance and identification, but it explains why those forms that conformed to what it describes as equilibrium outcomes became permanently institutionalized and stabilized. Rather than offering a stylized version of history, then, the model helps to understand the overall direction of historical developments, leading from the estate model of society under the *ancien régime*, through populist nationalism, to effective nation building. It cannot and is not meant to grasp other aspects – the international dimension, the balance of power between various contending political factions – or the appearance and disappearance of Robespierres and Napoleons, and thus is not a model *of* history, but a theoretical specification of the equilibrium states that once reached – through whatever historical circumstance and concatenation of events – will be stabilized and institutionally "locked in."

The Ottoman case is less straightforward and understandably so, given that the French revolution had already created a new template of political legitimacy to emulate and adopt. Diffusion and imitation effects thus might come into play – the focus of the next chapter. Furthermore, non-domestic actors played an important role by instigating and promoting various minority nationalisms. Neither diffusion effects nor the power struggle between competing empires and states are accounted for in our model, however.

Still, the model outcomes for the early nineteenth-century Ottoman empire are roughly in line with historical developments. The model produces ethnic closure as the equilibrium for the late eighteenth and early nineteenth centuries.[35] Graphically, this corresponds to number 3 in Figure 2.2. And indeed, from the nineteenth century onward, ethno-religious communities (the *millets*) became institutionally reinforced, politically empowered, and the focus of identity for the minority population. With the help of Western imperialists and missionaries, the Christian *millets* – and later also Kurds and Arabs – were soon politicized and turned into aspiring nations of their own, to paraphrase Kemal Karpat's (1973) subtitle "From Millets to Nation." The Greek, Serbian, and Romanian ethno-nationalisms of the early nineteenth century and their eventual success in achieving independence are the result of that process.

For the late nineteenth century, the model generates populist nationalism as the equilibrium outcome (see number 4 in Figure 2.2) – now in an empire that had lost almost all of its European domains. Indeed, with the 1876 constitution, the estate order was definitively abandoned and the principle of equality irrespective of citizens' religion was supposed to foster a shared identity and the "fusion" of all Ottoman subjects into a single peoplehood, a goal that Tanzimat reformers and Young Ottomans had long advocated (Davison 1954, 1963: chapter 10). Conforming to the populist model, the Christian, Arab, and Kurdish elites of the provinces were to be disempowered by continued centralization and the democratization of the *millets*. This stance against Christian elites that "misgoverned" their population and were manipulated by Western imperialists increased further under Abdul Hamid (i.e. in the period to which the last data point refers), who gave this populist conception of society a distinctively Islamist touch, without, however, abandoning the principle of equality and inclusion for Christian citizens (Karpat 2002).

But was the populist mode of alliance and identification also embraced by the masses? While it is clear that the Muslim population were generally supportive of this reconfigured empire and its populist-Islamist ideology (*ibid.,* but see Davison 1954 for Muslim resentment against equality), most historians argue that the non-Muslim population did not embrace this vision of society but increasingly identified with a trans-class minority nationalism (or ethnic closure in our terminology, see Karpat 2002). However, it remains unclear how much popular support minority nationalisms had after 1878 and before the Young

---

[35] This model was run using data interpolated between the sixteenth and late nineteenth centuries.

Turk revolution. There are some signs that the Christian Orthodox and Jewish rank and file welcomed and supported the new order, as shown by the enthusiastic reception of the 1878 constitution among some Christian communities (Davison 1963: 383ff.). The counterfactual thus holds that *without* further outside encouragement for and instigation of Christian nationalisms, lost wars, and the immigration of millions of Muslim refugees from Rumelia, Ottoman patriotism might have become the dominant and widely accepted ("equilibrium") mode of political organization and identity.

8 SUMMARY AND CONCLUSIONS

This chapter showed how state centralization and the development of networks of voluntary organizations gave birth to the first national community. It introduced a formal model of political closure that offers precise, actor-based mechanisms to elucidate how the boundaries of belonging are realigned during modernization processes. We found that ethnic closure emerges in the context of weakly centralized states with weak civil societies. In such states, the system of indirect rule has eroded without being replaced by a strong center with full control over political decision-making, public goods provision, and taxation. The resulting uncertainty leads to competition among the elites for military support by the masses. Since the latter likewise compete in their demand for state resources, actors end up negotiating separate alliance blocks based on ethnic commonality.

Populist nationalism becomes more likely when state centralization is stronger but still of medium strength. More centralization implies an increased attractiveness of the dominant elites as an exchange partner, which gives them the power to exclude subordinate elites. Contrary to our expectations, however, we also find that populist nationalism is more prevalent and nation building less likely when the entire male population has become militarily active. This is also at odds with the reasoning of historical sociologists who have emphasized the role of the military mobilization of the population for understanding the rise of nationalism. Going beyond the insights that can be drawn from our model architecture and data, we have speculated whether this could help to explain the recurrence of Napoleonic figures – populist military leaders – in the long nineteenth century of European mass armies.

The situation is different when state centralization proceeds further and the dominant elite gains enough exchange power to make an inclusion of all three other actors profitable. The subordinate elite is now integrated into this encompassing alliance system since it no longer can effectively compete for the military support of the masses and has itself started to demand public goods from the state elite. Strong state centralization therefore leads to nation building, a system of alliance and identity that is all the more likely when voluntary organizations are well developed.

Absent such organizational networks, actors prefer alliance partners that are culturally similar, since cultural commonality offers a way to choose between otherwise equally attractive exchange partners and avoid the instability of shifting alliance structures. This works against nation building since a nation comprises relatively dissimilar groups, irrespective of whether cultural traits are aligned with class or ethnic divisions. Populist nationalism and ethnic closure therefore become more likely where voluntary organizations are only weakly developed, even when cultural traits are aligned with class rather than with ethnic divisions. This might help to understand one of the most striking features of the modern world: in contrast to Karl Marx's prediction that the twentieth century would be the age of revolutionary class struggles eventually leading to the dissipation of the bourgeois state and of nations as its ideological corollary, it has turned out to be the age of nationalist, ethnic, and populist politics.

Chapter 5 on ethnic conflicts in the postwar world will come back to the analysis offered on the preceding pages. Many recently founded nation-states became thoroughly compartmentalized along ethnic lines because low state capacity and weak civil societies made the establishment of encompassing networks of political alliances difficult. Nation building remained a political ideal impossible to achieve, and ethnicity was politicized in similar ways as happened with the ethno-religious communities of the Ottoman empire during the Tanzimat period. Chapter 5 identifies additional conditions, related to the specific configuration of power between such ethnic alliance clusters, that will make violent conflict between them more likely.

This chapter thus explored the macro-historical processes that led to the emergence of the first nation-states. As the notes on Ottoman and French political developments indicated, the model cannot and is not intended to account for the exact course that history charts out over time. Many other factors come into play that will determine whether or not a particular society will realize the nationalist compact between elites and the masses: an unfavorable constellation of political power between nationalist forces and representatives of the *ancien régime* may delay nation building, as in France, even though a strong state and a well-developed network of voluntary organizations had made French society ripe for the transition. Furthermore, once the nation-state model was propelled onto the world stage by the French and American revolutions, it could be adopted by political movements such as the Christian intellectuals and bureaucrats of the Ottoman empire, quite independently of whether or not domestic exchange relations between rulers and ruled allowed for endogenous nation building.

This suggests that in later episodes of nation-state formation – from the establishment of the Latin American republics in the early nineteenth century to the recent foundation of Southern Sudan as an independent state – such diffusion and balance-of-power effects might be more important than endogenous nation building upon which this chapter has focused. This hypothesis forms the core of the next chapter.

3

The global rise of the nation-state

How did the nation-state model, once it had emerged in France and else-where in the West, proliferate across the globe? Why did the world order of dynastic states, tribal confederacies, and multiethnic empires change into a world made up of states each ruled in the name of its nation? This chapter shows that in contrast to the first nation-states, their subsequent rise across the world was rarely the result of previous nation building. Rather, whether or not a nation-state emerged depended on the configuration of power between adherents of different political projects. Nation-states were established wher-ever nationalists – who had adopted the model of the first nation-states as their template of political legitimacy – gained the upper hand over representatives of the pre-national regime. More specifically, the balance of power tilts in favor of nationalists the longer they had been mobilizing the population and decrying the ethnic hierarchy of the ancient regime as an instance of "alien rule"; when the imperial center commanded little global economic and mili-tary power or was weakened by wars; and when nation-states had been created

This chapter is adapted from an article coauthored with Yuval Feinstein.

We wish to thank Nurullah Ardic, Phillippe Duhart, Wesley Hiers, Hazem Kandil, Yana Kucheva, Joy Morgen, Anoop Sarbahi, Frank Yen, Jeremy Yobe, and Sarah Zingg Wimmer for superb research assistance. Mauro Guillén, Robert Mare, Brian Min, Gabriel Rossman, Art Stinchcombe, and Don Treiman provided help and advice regarding research methods and data management. We are especially grateful for discussions with Robert Mare. Angus Maddison helped with the standardization of economic data. We received advice regarding the early literacy rates of individual territories from Harvey Graff, Aaron Althouse, Nola Jean Cook, Keith Weller Taylor, Olöf Gardarsdóttir, Loftur Guttormsson, Luca Godenzi, Alois Gehart, Jörg Baten, Brian Min, and Gustav Brown. Previous versions of the paper have been presented at the sociology departments of Northwestern University, UCLA, and the University of Washington, the political science departments of the University of Chicago and George Washington University, at the conference "Comparing Past and Present" organized by the Comparative Historical Section of ASA in 2009, the Social Science History Association Annual Meeting of 2009, and the Association for the Study of Nationalism meeting in 2010. We thank conveners and audiences for stimulating comments and challenging criticisms. Rogers Brubaker offered extensive comments and suggestions on a first draft.

in the neighborhood or within the same imperial domain, thus offering models of successful nation-state creation and new alliance partners that further tilted the balance of power in favor of nationalists. This chapter thus highlights the exogenous diffusion of the nation-state form, which is adopted wherever the power configuration allowed overthrowing or absorbing exponents of the pre-national order.

We test this power-configurational theory with a global dataset covering most of the world over the past 200 years. It thus aims at overcoming two of the limitations in the rich literature on nation-state formation that has emerged in the past decades – stretching from the early treatises of Kohn (1944) and Deutsch (1953) to the classical oeuvres of Gellner, Anderson, Smith, and others. First, most of these general theoretical statements are meant to explore universal processes that account for the rise of the nation-state in the modern world as a whole. But empirical support for these generalizations is often based on examples picked selectively from here and there, sometimes in a merely illustrative manner (deplored by Breuilly 2005; Wimmer 2008a). Second, more detailed empirical research on particular trajectories of nation-state creation tends to be segmented along regional and disciplinary lines. For example, the political science literature on decolonization (Strang 1990; Spruyt 2005) and nation building in the post-colonial world (Bendix 1964) developed quite independently from the debates among historical sociologists about the origins of the nation-state in the West. Yet another strand of historical scholarship investigates the historical developments that led to the collapse of the land-based Ottoman, Habsburg, or Soviet empires and subsequent waves of nation-state creation (e.g. Barkey and von Hagen 1997; Roshwald 2001; Esherick *et al.* 2006; Saideman and Ayres 2008). Given that nation-states cover almost the entire world by now, one wonders whether an integrated view on all these various routes to the nation-state might be within reach.

To develop such an integrated and systematic analysis, we assembled a new, global dataset that allows identifying those patterns of nation-state formation that recur across continents, empires, and time periods. This required considerable efforts because only independent nation-states systematically collect information on their economies and societies. Available datasets thus don't allow us to understand why such states emerged in the first place, perhaps the main reason why quantitatively minded scholars have so far shied away from a more systematic evaluation of existing theories of nation-state formation (but see the work of Strang and Roeder, to be discussed below). The new dataset introduced below includes independent states, colonies, and imperial dependencies over two centuries, and contains almost the entire universe of nation-state creations. It provides information on 145 of today's states from 1816 until the years they achieved nation-statehood (or 2001 if they did not). Many of the variables in this dataset – for example, the length of railways, government expenditures, and literacy rates – had to be assembled by extracting information from secondary sources, such as country histories. This global dataset allows assessing the plausibility of major theories of the nation-state from a global, comparative perspective.

Alas, a quantitative approach to historical processes comes at a price, as noted in the introduction. Not only must we content ourselves with proxy variables that measure the hypothesized processes imperfectly, we also cannot test the rich arguments offered by past scholarship in a very nuanced way. We need to focus on crucial elements of theories – the association between core conditions and outcomes – and cannot evaluate whether the postulated mechanisms linking conditions to outcomes are actually at work. The empirical analyses that follow therefore do not pretend to submit whole theories to a sort of Popperian falsification test. Rather, they simply evaluate the plausibility of key theoretical arguments that lend themselves to a test using data that can be gathered for a wide range of territories over long periods.

What are these theories theories *of?* They do not mainly concern the emergence of the nation-state model in the United States, France, or perhaps earlier in Britain, but rather its subsequent proliferation across the world. While sharing this common focus, many classical works are somewhat ambiguous as to whether their primary aim is to explain nationalism as a political movement, the spread of national consciousness among a population (i.e. nation building), or the shift in the institutional setup of the state (i.e. the creation of a nation-state). They all concur, however, that these three phenomena are closely related to each other, even if they disagree on the precise nature of these relationships. In Anderson's account, nationalism leads to nation building and eventually a nation-state, while according to Gellner, nationalists form nation-states that then build their nations. World polity theorists such as Meyer, by contrast, consider neither nationalism nor nations to be a necessary condition for nation-states to emerge. My own power-configurational approach assumes that nationalists create nation-states, whether or not nations have already been built. All of these arguments therefore contain the nation-state as a central element in the analytic tableau; the emergence of nation-state institutions therefore represents an appropriate dependent variable for this study. It is now time to introduce these various approaches to nation-state formation in more detail.

1.1 Economic modernization

According to Ernest Gellner (1983), the epochal shift from agricultural to industrial society brings about nationalism and eventually the nation-state. In the agricultural empires of the past – such as in late medieval France or the

Ottoman empire of the classical age that formed the focus of the previous chapter – the economic system contained many highly specialized niches reproduced through on-the-job training in the specific skills demanded. Culture and
language marked and reinforced the boundaries between rulers and ruled (producing what we have termed the "estate order" in the previous chapter). The
industrial mode of production, by contrast, needs a mobile and flexible labor
force. A rationalized, standardized education in a common language provides
workers with the generic skills to shift from job to job and communicate effectively with each other. The educational apparatus of the nation-state inculcates
this new, standardized, rational, homogenized culture into the population and
thus enables industrial societies to function properly(*ibid.*: 37f.).

This functionalist analysis is complemented with a subtle study of four historical
pathways through which industrial society's needs were met. I will discuss only the
two most important here. First, uneven industrialization drew rural peasants into
industrialized centers, where their ascent and prospects remained limited if their
language and culture did not correspond to the center's high culture. Resentment
fed into nationalism and eventually led to the creation of nation-states, as in the
Balkans and the peripheries of the Habsburg empire. Second, a similar process
unfolded in the colonial world, where visible traits (e.g. skin color) were associated
with unequal power, unleashing anticolonial nationalisms as soon as industrialization set in and delegitimized the colonial hierarchy.

Both trajectories specify how industrialization, arriving at different times in
different parts of the world (*ibid.*: 52), reorganized political boundaries along
cultural lines and led to the formation of nation-states. Focusing on this general
association, rather than the different mechanisms that bring it about, we can
state the simple hypothesis that the likelihood of nation-state creation should
increase with industrialization (Hypothesis 1).

1.2 Political modernization

Tilly's (1994), Mann's (1995), and Hechter's (2000) political modernization theories shift our attention to the system of governance. Starting in the sixteenth
century, permanent war between competing European states made techniques
of governmental control and resource extraction ever more effective and efficient. Indirect rule via regional elites and notables was replaced by direct rule
through a unified and hierarchically integrated bureaucracy, as elaborated in
the previous chapter. From there, two major pathways led to the nation-state.
In autonomous states (e.g. France), state elites gradually nationalized and
homogenized the population over the course of the nineteenth century and
developed an assimilatory nationalism to legitimize their rule (Tilly 1994;
Hechter 2000). In Mann's (1995) related, yet differently accented account of
this process, nationalism emerged from below to justify the public's demands
for democratic representation vis-à-vis the increasingly interventionist state.

As we have seen in the previous chapter, a combination of these two perspectives is useful for understanding the emergence of the first nation-states in the West.

Far more frequent than the transition to the nation-state within existing boundaries, however, is the second trajectory foreseen by political modernization scholars: peripheral, state-seeking nationalism. In the multiethnic empires of the Habsburgs and the Ottomans (and according to Hechter also in Yugoslavia and beyond), the shift to direct rule led to nationalist mobilization by regional elites who resented being governed by ethnic others and sought to reestablish self-rule. Whether such state-seeking nationalists were successful depends on additional (including international) factors and forces. Simplifying these accounts by subsuming these additional factors and forces under a *ceteris paribus* clause, we can derive Hypothesis 2: the more directly a territory is ruled, the more likely nation-state formation should be.

This is compatible with the argument introduced in the previous chapter. It showed how increasing centralization of decision-making power and public goods provision in the hands of state elites led to endogenous nation building, especially if it was accompanied by the growth of voluntary organizational networks. However, Hypothesis 2 is not concerned with the origins of the nation-state; rather, it assumes that state centralization is also responsible for its subsequent adoption by the rest of the world.

1.3 Cultural modernization

Benedict Anderson's theory of nationalism distinguishes between three mechanisms that combine in different ways in four different waves of nation-state creation. The first mechanism is related to the alphabetization of the population. The Reformation, state bureaucratization, and, most importantly, the rise of print capitalism enabled and propelled literacy in vernacular languages, replacing complex elite languages such as Latin. The emerging reading public thus shared a narrative cosmos and soon imagined itself as a national community of common origin and future political destiny (Anderson 1991: chapter 3).

Mass literacy was less important for the first wave of nation-state creation than for subsequent waves. Overall literacy levels were still low when the first wave rolled over Latin America, but Anderson nevertheless sees the emergence of provincially oriented newspapers and reading publics as crucial (*ibid.*: 61–64). Mass literacy then became the central force behind the second-wave linguistic nationalisms in nineteenth-century Europe (*ibid.*: 80), as well as the third wave's official nationalisms (*ibid.*: 109f.), developed by dynastic rulers such as the Romanovs who sought to contain nationalism by adopting it as a state doctrine. Mass literacy remained a central causal force during the fourth wave as well, leading to decolonization after World War II (*ibid.*: 119ff.). Hypothesis 3 captures the effects of this first mechanism: an increase in the literacy rate in vernacular language should make nationalism, nation building, and ultimately the transition to the nation-state more likely.[1]

Anderson's second mechanism comes into play during the first and fourth waves of nation-state creation. Why did Bolivia, the Ivory Coast, and Vietnam become independent, rather than Spanish Latin America, French West Africa, and French Indochina as one would expect in view of the popular literacy argument? Low-level colonial administrators recruited from the local population could not aspire to positions above the provincial levels, Anderson argues, which led to resentment and growing nationalist dissent. Being confined to the provincial bureaucratic space laid the groundwork for imagining the nation along these provincial lines, rather than those of common language. During the fourth wave, colonial governments vastly expanded the educational systems. This not only helped fuel nationalism by spreading literacy, but at the same time also cast these nationalisms into a provincial mold because colonial provinces often had separately administered school systems, thus again confining the horizon of future nationalist imaginations (as in Indonesia; Anderson 1991: chapter 7). This suggests Hypothesis 4: a territory that corresponds to a province or an independent state should be more likely to see nationalism arise and more likely to eventually become a nation-state.

The third, and perhaps least crucial mechanism in Anderson's account relates to global diffusion processes (*ibid.*: 80–82, 113f., 116f.), which are especially important for the last wave of nation-state formation in the former colonies, as well as in Japan (*ibid.*: 94–99), Thailand (*ibid.*: 99–101), and Switzerland (*ibid.*: 135–139). Such global influence is at the heart of Meyer's world polity approach.

1.4 World polity theory

Meyer's diffusion theory emphasizes external influences rather than domestic modernization processes. He and his coauthors show that the nation-state template is part of a world culture that emerged over the past 200 years and eventually became institutionalized in the League of Nations and later the United Nations. This world culture gradually forced state elites and political challengers alike to adopt nationalism as the universally accepted template of political legitimacy and the nation-state as the most legitimate form of statehood (Meyer *et al.* 1997).

World polity theory offers a cross-sectional and a longitudinal argument. First, the more linkages a territory maintains to the centers of global culture and

---

[1] Keith Darden's (2011) recent work lends considerable support to an Andersonian line of reasoning. Based on data on Eurasia, he shows that a population inoculated by a nationalist doctrine through alphabetization in the corresponding language remains loyal to that national identity even in the face of subsequent attempts at assimilation into other languages and nationalist projects.

power, the more its elites are exposed to this culture and the more likely they will adopt world-cultural templates and create a nation-state (Hypothesis 5). Second, the likelihood of transition to a nation-state should increase the more territories of the world have already adopted the nation-state (Hypothesis 6), because this further reinforces the pressure on the remaining states to finally adopt the hegemonic model of statehood.

1.5 A power-configurational approach

My own approach emphasizes the configurations of power that are largely absent from the picture drawn by both modernization and global diffusion theories. Transitioning from one form of legitimate statehood to another is seen as the outcome of a struggle between various politically organized segments of society. The balance of power between these actors determines which vision of a legitimate political order and which institutional principles will prevail. These templates may emerge endogenously through a change in the power relations between actors, as analyzed in the previous chapter. The introduction already pointed out, however, that templates of legitimacy can also travel across societies – a process that the analysis of the previous chapter has bracketed. Once we have understood how the nation-state model first emerged and focus on its subsequent proliferation across the entire world, however, such diffusion processes need to be taken into consideration.

This raises the question why nationalists appeared in political arenas across the world – an obvious antecedent condition for the power-configurational argument to touch empirical ground if we no longer assume that all nationalisms emerged endogenously, as in the modernization theories discussed above. The first nation-states (France, Great Britain, the United States, the Netherlands) became the most powerful states in the world because the new national compact, explored in the previous chapter, produced a hitherto unseen military loyalty of and political support by the masses (see also Levi 1988, 1997). These political and military advantages were clearly demonstrated by the success of Napoleon's armies across the European continent.[2] And indeed, a systematic examination of what happens when nation-state armies encounter those of dynastic or other pre-national regimes confirms this historical impression: between 70 and 90 percent of such wars were unambiguously won by nation-states, depending on whether or not we exclude wars of conquest in which the technological superiority of Western colonial powers played a crucial role as well.[3] Political elites

---

[2] On how the nationalist mobilization of the masses allowed Napoleon to defeat his dynastic rivals, see Posen (1993b); more generally on the diffusion effects entailed by the military superiority of nation-states, see Taliaferro (2009).

[3] I am grateful to Wesley Hiers for his research assistance. The numbers are based on the Wimmer/Min dataset of wars between 1816 and 2001, which will be introduced in the next chapter. Out of the 164 inter-polity wars in this dataset, 79 pitted a nation-state against a

across the world therefore sought to adopt the nation-state model in order to effectively compete with the first nation-states that soon dominated or conquered the entire world.[4]

The global spread of nationalism was fueled not only by such power competition, but by legitimacy comparison as well: nationalist intellectuals – priests, secondary school teachers, journalists, low-ranking officers, etc. (Hroch 2000 [1969]) – considered the new model of statehood more legitimate because it seemed to offer the population at large a more favorable exchange relationship than with dynastic kings, colonial administrators, or tribal chiefs: it offered equality before the law, the possibility to ascend to the highest political office, the provision of public goods, and the symbolic capital of representing a sovereign nation rather than the "plebs" owing obedience to the king, Sultan, or sheikh.

The subsequent adoption of nationalist ideologies by a variety of political movements across the world thus represents an imitation process quite unrelated to domestic processes of nation building analyzed in the preceding chapter. Ambitious political elites from around the world embraced the ideology of nationalism, hoping that they would one day preside over states as militarily powerful, politically potent, and culturally glorious as the early nation-states. This imitation process proceeds along established networks of political and cultural relations: African nationalists were inspired by the might of France or Great Britain (Fieldhouse 1966); Turkish and Japanese nationalists resented these two imperial powers and thus looked at France's and Britain's German nemesis for inspiration; Kurdish and Arab nationalists oriented themselves on Turkish models, and so on. According to the power-configurational perspective developed here, this diffusion process is neither driven by the hegemonic power of a uniform world culture, nor by domestic modernization processes, but rather follows the logic of a decentralized contagion mechanism.[5]

---

non-nation-state. Sixty-four of these 79 wars resulted in an unambiguous victory, 59 times by the nation-state(s). When we exclude wars of conquest, there are 22 wars pitting national against non-national states, 13 of which led to a clear victory, nine times in favor of the nation-state.

[4] How resentment of French and British superiority fueled nationalism further East in Europe is explored by Greenfeld (1992). Mufti (1996) shows how the entrenched interests of post-colonial elites at controlling a state of their own prevented Pan-Arabism in Iraq and Syria from reshaping colonial boundaries. A similar argument for Africa is made by Herbst (2000). This contrasts with the argument that postwar nation-states were created because the international system insisted on sovereignty within colonial boundaries (Jackson 1990).

[5] We conducted a rather preliminary quantitative analysis of this hypothesis, taking the year when the first national organization was founded on a territory as a dependent variable (for coding rules see below). The data include only successful nationalisms, since a large number of nationalist movements that never managed to reach their goal are excluded from consideration. We find that modernization variables (proxying for industrialization, the rise of mass literacy, and direct political rule, all discussed below) are not robustly associated with nationalism. But there is evidence that nationalism owes its global rise to a diffusion process: the establishment of a

If this accounts for nationalism's global appeal and its subsequent spread around the world, under what conditions are nationalists able to establish nation-states? We propose the following set of hypotheses that refer to various domestic and international aspects of the power configuration. A power shift in favor of nationalism is more likely when nationalists are able to convert existing elites to their cause or reach out to larger segments of the population, beyond the intellectual circles, army factions, monasteries, or colonial bureaucrats who are often the first supporters of nationalist movements.

This process of empowerment has political and symbolic aspects. Nationalists need to build networks of political organizations and alliances, and effectively portray the existing regime as an instance of "alien rule" or as a sclerotic and fragmented *ancien régime* unable to withstand domination by powerful nation-states in the neighborhood. This effectively undermines the legitimacy of the ethno-political hierarchy that characterizes many empires and dynastic states. Disregarding short-term cycles of popular mobilization and demobilization (Beissinger 2002), we assume that nationalists' political and symbolic power increase monotonically: the more time nationalists have to propagate their worldview and establish networks of followers, the more powerful they will be vis-à-vis non-nationalist forces and the more likely they will succeed in eventually establishing a nation-state (Hypothesis 7).

The power balance also depends on the strength of the established regime – its capacity to resist nationalist forces and to avoid conversion to the nationalist cause, institutional reform in the direction nationalists propose, abdication, or the loss of territory to nationalist secession. Following Theda Skocpol's (1979) lead, we assume that wars fought either on the territory in question or elsewhere in an empire reduce the established elites' staying power and make a nationalist revolution possible. The likelihood of nation-state creation thus increases with an increase in the number of wars fought on a territory or within an empire (Hypotheses 8 and 9). Similarly, the global military and economic standing of a pre-nationalist regime should influence its capability to co-opt or suppress nationalist movements and thus maintain the status quo, making nation-state creation on its territories unlikely (Hypothesis 10, as proposed by Strang 1990).

Finally, diffusion of the nation-state within empires and between neighboring territories can also shift the power balance in favor of nationalists.[6] Recently established nation-states within the same imperial domain demonstrate that the center is no longer willing or able to prevent independence. The new

---

national organization in a neighboring territory during the past five years as well as a nationalist war of independence elsewhere in the empire seem to inspire the foundation of nationalist organizations.

[6] Gleditsch and Ward (2006) find a similar relation between regional diffusion and local empowerment in their analysis of democratization.

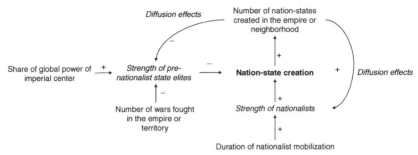

FIGURE 3.1 A power-configurational model of nation-state formation

nation-states not only provide a model to follow, but also new alliance partners in the imperial political arena, and thus empower nationalist movements
and further delegitimize the pre-national regime. This leads to Hypothesis 11:
the more territories within an empire that have become nation-states, the more
likely other territories will follow. Note that this imperial diffusion effect is theoretically distinct from global diffusion because the source of the external influence is different (i.e. the empire versus the world), as is the mechanism through
which it operates (i.e. contagion versus imposition).

Within neighborhoods, a nation-state creation may propel its own replication
in adjacent territories through similar demonstration and alliance mechanisms.
It might also take the more bellicose form of a domino effect through competition over ethnically mixed or ill-defined territories (Weiner 1971; Wimmer 2002:
chapter 3). If one territory is organized as a nation-state and demands inclusion of its ethnic kin population across the border, this increases pressure in the
adjacent territory to adopt the nation-state model as well. Hypothesis 12 thus
states that the likelihood of nation-state formation increases with the number of
nation-state creations in a neighborhood. This power-configurational argument
can now be summarized in Figure 3.1.[7]

1.6 Existing datasets and quantitative findings

To date, only two quantitative studies have explored the dynamics of nation-state
formation, both with a different focus and a much universe of cases than the present chapter. Strang's work attempts to understand the conditions under which

---

[7] Our argument incorporates several of the diffusion mechanisms identified by Dobbin *et al.* (2007).
The diffusion of nationalism corresponds to the effects of "following the leader" emphasized
by constructivist sociologists. Imperial diffusion of the nation-state is similar to mechanisms
of "copying between similar countries" identified by sociologists or the "channeled learning"
between networked actors studied by political scientists. Finally, neighborhood diffusion contains
aspects of the copying mechanism, but also of the competition effects studied by economists.

colonial dependencies became independent states from 1879 to 1987.[8] We build on this endeavor by enlarging the empirical horizon to include autonomous states, dependencies of land-based empires (e.g. of the Ottomans, Romanovs, and Habsburgs), and the former Soviet Union and Yugoslavia. Our dataset also improves on data quality and adds variables that are relevant to the classic literature on nationalism and the nation-state summarized above.

Roeder conducted the second quantitative study. He developed a global dataset to test an institutional capacity argument: a large degree of institutional autonomy, he maintains, allows provincial elites to establish cultural and ethnic hegemony within their territories and provides them with the political resources necessary to successfully challenge the metropolis and establish an independent state. This argument parallels Anderson's provincial confinement hypothesis and can thus be tested, in an approximate way to be sure, with Hypothesis 4: territories that correspond to a province or an autonomous state should be more likely to become nation-states than territories that do not correspond to political boundaries.

His institutional capacity model advances the theoretical understanding of nation-state formation by revealing the importance of the balance of power between nationalist contenders and representatives of the *ancien régime*. Many of his arguments thus parallel my own understanding of the rise of the nation-state. However, his quantitative analysis displays certain weaknesses that raise doubts about the validity of his findings. Most important are sample selection problems. Roeder's (2007: 323–331) dataset uses autonomous provinces, including colonial dependencies, as units of observation and provides information on 336 such units from 1901 to 2000.[9] But his list misses many provinces that never became nation-states, such as German *Bundesländer*, American states, and Swiss cantons, although these enjoyed as much autonomy as the states of India that do appear in his list. The Ottoman empire has only Bulgaria, Crete, and Samos listed as sub-state units, and none of the *vilayets*, none of which developed into nation-states.

---

[8] He finds support for Wallerstein's hegemonic cycles theories (decolonization is more likely when a global hegemon rules), world polity theory (decolonization accelerated after the UN adopted an anticolonial statement in 1960), balance-of-power arguments (colonies governed by a metropolis with strong naval capability are less likely to become independent), and imperial diffusion effects. Strang (1991b) obtained similar findings in a related study with fewer variables but a longer time span, thus including the Iberian colonies as well. This second study also reports a global diffusion effect, measured by the number of colonies that have already achieved independence.

[9] Roeder shows that the likelihood of nation-state formation increases if a sub-state unit is self-governing, if central elites are weakened by internal strife and political turmoil, if the provincial population is excluded from political participation or is linguistically and religiously different from the core population, and if the province experienced independent statehood prior to incorporation into the current state.

2 DATASET AND MODELING APPROACH

The two existing quantitative studies thus leave ample room for improvement. Each exclude parts of the world that were candidates for making the transition to the nation-state: the land-based Eurasian empires stretching from Vienna to Vladivostok, or the nineteenth-century waves of nation-state creations in the Americas, the Balkans, and Western Europe. Furthermore, both studies include a list of variables that are mostly unrelated to classical theories of nation-state formation discussed above, perhaps because corresponding data is not readily available.

2.1 Units of observation

Our dataset contains information on 145 territories from 1816 until a nation-state was created. By 2001, 139 of these territories had made the transition to nation-statehood, while the others were still governed as absolutist monarchies. All territories refer to the geographic boundaries of countries that existed in 2001, extending these fixed geographic units back to the beginning of our dataset in 1816. For example, this means that we observe the territory of "Bosnia," as defined by the geographic shape of the Bosnian state today, from 1816 onward, independently of whether Ottomans, Habsburgs, Yugoslavia, or the independent state of Bosnia ruled over the territory.

The dataset covers almost the entire world. It only misses mini-states with less than 20,000 km² surface and eight larger states for which no literacy data are available.[10] We also exclude the early nation-state creations of Great Britain, France, Paraguay, and Haiti because they occurred before our data series starts in 1816. Conforming to the focus of this chapter, the following analysis is thus not about the origins of the nation-state – analyzed in the previous chapter – but about the general mechanisms that might help explain its subsequent proliferation across the world.

Some notes on the units of observation may be in order. To clarify, we combine data from various polities in the case of territories that did not correspond to a political unit at a given point in time. Data for Poland in the 1870s, to give an extreme example, are proportionally combined from the Russian, German, and Austrian empires that controlled pieces of what is today Poland. The disadvantage of creating units that do not conform to political entities is outweighed by the advantage that these units actually experienced the event: it is Poland that became a nation-state, not any of the Russian, German, or Austrian provinces on their own. Medical studies of mortality take a similar approach: they use individuals, rather than families or couples, as units of observation because it is

---

[10] We had to exclude Albania, Belize, Djibouti, Equatorial Guinea, Greenland, Iceland, Lesotho, and Namibia. We did include, however, Gambia, Kuwait, Cyprus, Bahrain, Qatar, and Mauritius, all of which control less than 20,000 km² of territory.

individuals, not families, who die. Constant territorial units also have the advantage of defining a stable risk set. They allow us to pursue "Poland" and other territories throughout history, rather than having to deal with a different set of units every time a state ceases to exist or comes into being, or every time provincial boundaries are redrawn, as would be the case in a dataset composed of provinces or states.

Does choosing today's countries as units mean that we select on the dependent variable because we include only successful instances of nation-state creation and not failed ones? Note that the grid of states defines our units in 2001, independent of whether these are nation-states. Most are nation-states simply because the nation-state has proliferated so widely, not because our research design excludes non-national states. Second and as discussed below, we include the creation of nation-states that existed in the past but then were subsequently swallowed again by an expanding empire or fell apart into smaller nation-states. Examples for the first set of cases include the Baltic and Caucasian states that became nation-states after World War I but were then reintegrated into the Soviet empire. The second group includes Gran Colombia, the Central American Republic, Yugoslavia, Czechoslovakia, Vietnam, and Germany, which were subsequently divided (at least during certain periods of their history) into smaller nation-states. All these instances of the creation of nation-states are included in the analysis, as long as the state survived for at least three years and was recognized by at least three other states.

To be sure, using 2001 states as units means that we define the risk set retrospectively; there is no Kurdistan, Tibet, West-Sahara, or Southern Sudan in our dataset, although they could eventually (and Southern Sudan in the meantime did) become nation-states. This potential selection problem is less severe than it might first appear. We know from the next chapter on nation-state formation and war that few secessionist states break away from nation-states and most emerge from imperial polities. No such empires are left today. We thus do not expect a large number of nation-states to be created in the foreseeable future. We believe our risk set, while certainly not complete, nevertheless captures the overwhelming majority of possible events.[11] Furthermore, there is no reason to

---

[11] A brief discussion of the advantages and disadvantages of five other possible definitions of the risk set might be in order. First, one could choose the states of 1816 as fixed units of observation, which avoids the problem of "coding history backwards." With the exception of Germany, Italy, and Yemen, however, these units are much larger than those that actually made the transition to the nation-state, which makes it difficult to identify a single event. Second, one could code on the state units that exist in any given year, rather than on fixed territorial units. This would have the advantage that all independent variables would relate to meaningful political entities, while again producing the problem that the outcome (nation-state creation) could often not be attributed to units that actually experienced it, as in the case of empires that dissolved into a series of nation-states.. A third alternative research design would be to choose fixed spatial units of observation, such as 100 x 100 km² grid cells. This would

believe that the dynamic of future nation-state creations will differ from that of the past (as would be the case if a sorting mechanism biased our results).

2.2 Variables

Dependent variable

In order to use event history methods, we need to identify the particular year in which a territory became a nation-state. Finding data for a continuous dependent variable, such as a coding for "degrees of nation-statehood," is practically unfeasible. Furthermore, most transitions to the nation-state – with exceptions such as those in Sweden or the United Kingdom – occurred through a clearly identifiable rupture. We code as year of nation-state creation when kings, emperors, or theocrats were no longer the source of political legitimacy of the state, but the nation. The sovereign right to rule, in other words, is from now on vested in "the people." Sovereignty has a domestic and an external component. Domestically, a written constitution claims a nationally defined community of equal citizens as the sovereign and foresees some institutional representation of this community (not necessarily a freely elected parliament, see below). Internal sovereignty thus stands in opposition to dynasticism, theocracy, feudal privilege, or mass slavery. Externally, sovereignty means control over foreign policy decisions that affect the nation, and it stands in opposition to foreign rule of all sorts. Both conditions must be cumulatively fulfilled. This definition and most data were adopted from Wimmer and Min (2006; for more details on coding rules, see Appendix 4.2).

How does this definition of nation-statehood relate to democratization and the granting of citizenship rights? Our definition of the nation-state focuses on principles of political legitimacy, rather than their effective realization. We

generate a risk set that is completely independent of the outcome. One would then have to deal with the problem that the multiple events coded for all units that eventually formed a nation-state together are obviously not independent from each other.

Fourth, one could argue that today's federal states (such as Nigeria or India) contain units that have been at risk of becoming nation-states of their own, especially if the federal provinces are populated by ethnic minorities. We redefined our risk set accordingly (using data from Christin and Hug 2009) and found no major differences in the results. This research design obviously increases measurement error because we assign the same values for all independent variables to all those sub-state units; and it is based on an *ex-post* definition of which states contain federal sub-units.

Finally, one could take ethnic groups as units of analysis, which would help to overcome the potential selection bias implied by our approach. Unfortunately, the ethnic makeup of the world in 1816 is unknown and we therefore could not operate a varying risk set. A fixed risk set based on contemporary ethnic groups creates the same potential selection bias as our research design. Whether using a varying or fixed risk set, it would be quite challenging to find yearly data on thousands of groups from 1816 onward. To illustrate the magnitude of the challenge: *Ethnologue* lists close to 7,000 living languages, of which roughly 900 languages are spoken by at least 100,000 individuals today, perhaps enough to form a microstate.

therefore code autocracies as nation-states as long as the dictator claims to rule "in the name of the people." Only one-fifth of nation-states also became democracies during the first two decades of their existence (see the figure in Appendix 3.1).[12] The proportion of democracies then continuously rose until it reached 60 percent, sometimes 150 years after the foundation of nation-states. In other words, nation-state formation is a precondition for democratization, since nationalism defined the boundaries of the people to which democratic and citizenship rights were eventually to be granted (see Nodia 1992; Wimmer 2002: chapter 3). But otherwise the two processes are independent from each other. Government *for* the people (nation-statehood) and *by* the people (democracy), to use Lincoln's famous formula, are ideologically and empirically intertwined, but separate aspects of political modernity. Conformingly, less than 50 percent of independent states were democracies by 2000 (Gleditsch and Ward 2006: 913), while over 95 percent were nation-states.

The extent to which citizenship rights are effectively granted to the entire population is also not of concern for our definition of nation-statehood. The transition into the nation-state again provided the necessary precondition for the expansion of citizenship rights to ever-larger segments of the population (Marshall 1950). We therefore disregard the fact that property restrictions on voting rights and denial of full citizenship rights to women usually lasted many decades into nation-statehood.[13] Similarly, we do not consider whether a government is able to exercise sovereignty over the entire territory and to uphold the monopoly of violence. Independent nation-states that suffered from a continued series of civil wars since their foundation – such as Burma or the Democratic Republic of the Congo – are still based on nationalist principles of political legitimacy.

Following these coding principles, 24 territories experienced more than one episode of nation-state formation, which we treat as independent from each other. As mentioned above, the Baltic territories for example were independent national states from 1918 to World War II, when they were swallowed again by the Soviet Union, and they regained the status of nation-states in 1991. In other cases, a territory transitioned into nation-statehood as part of a larger state, which subsequently broke apart into smaller nation-states. Such was the case for

---

[12] Nation-state creation went hand in hand with a democratic revolution in Switzerland, Austria, Czechoslovakia, some of the Yugoslav successor states, the Baltic states, Ukraine, Armenia, and Moldova in the 1990s, as well as in Finland, Belize, Suriname, Cyprus, Gambia, Sierra Leone, and Nigeria. Only a handful of states, most of them British settler states in the New World, were already democratic when becoming fully independent nation-states.

[13] However, we do not define states whose constitutions exclude segments of the population from the citizenry as modern nation-states (such as the United States before abolition of slavery or Liberia before granting voting rights to the indigenous majority of the population). When governments revoke the citizenship status of minorities, such as Jews in Nazi Germany, we do not code this as a "reversal" to a pre-nation-state situation. Changing this handful of coding decisions does not affect the results.

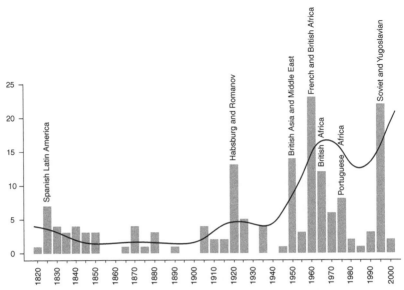

FIGURE 3.2 The global spread of the nation-state, 1816–2001
Notes: Left scale refers to number of nation-state creations per five-year period; the line represents a smoothed hazard rate (based on 20-year moving averages).

Gran Colombia (which later gave birth to Colombia, Venezuela, Ecuador, and eventually Panama), the Central American Republic (which fragmented into Guatemala, Honduras, Costa Rica, Nicaragua, and El Salvador), Yugoslavia, and Czechoslovakia. To check for selection bias in this definition of the risk set,[14] we ran all our models with a restricted definition of the outcome that excludes these repeated events (see Table 3.2). Our results remain almost identical. A list of nation-state creations per territory can be found in Appendix 3.2.

The above figure gives a descriptive overview of how many nation-states were formed in five-year periods since 1816. Figure 3.2 also shows that many nation-states were created as part of waves following the collapse of empires. The first wave led to the dissolution of the Spanish empire in the New World; the second wave occurred after World War I with the breakup of the Habsburg empire; a third wave brought the nation-state to the Middle East – which France and Britain had recolonized after the fall of the Ottoman empire – as well as South and Southeast Asia; the next wave followed around 1960, as the British and French colonial empires receded from Africa; the fifth and final wave rolled over the Soviet empire during the early 1990s. Not all transitions to the

---

[14] One could fear bias since only weaker nation-states are later reconquered by empires or fall apart into a series of smaller nation-states.

nation-state start from empire, however, since there are 18 states (Switzerland, Thailand, Ethiopia, Nepal, Japan, and so forth) that were never part of an empire and where the transformation was therefore brought about without a mobilization against "alien rule." An additional group of former imperial dependencies transitioned into nation-statehood after independence had already been achieved.[15]

Independent variables

To test Gellner's economic modernization argument, we code the length of railway tracks (in km) per 1,000 square kilometers. We adopt some data from the monumental compendium of historical statistics assembled by Mitchell (various years) and code other data from primary sources, which are remarkably rich thanks to the enthusiasm that the history of railways has sparked among lay and professional scholars.[16] Is this an adequate proxy to measure Gellner's notion of industrialization? A flexible labor market is the crucial element in Gellner's argument, while the manufacturing of industrial goods is not given much consideration. It therefore makes sense to include fully commercialized agricultural and extractive economies into his definition, both of which are historically associated with railway construction. This proxy is also justified by Gellner's treatment of African colonies as representing early stages in industrial society's development – despite the almost complete absence of manufacturing.

Certainly, a more direct measurement of the flexibility of labor markets would be preferable. The railroad variable, however, offers the possibility of full data coverage for the entire dataset, while it would be unthinkable to collect global data on the sectorial distribution of the labor force, for example. The railroad variable is also very precise; it is possible, for instance, to find out how many kilometers long the railways of colonial Burma were in 1880, but it is quite impossible to learn how many people were employed in which professions.[17]

---

[15] This includes a number of Latin American countries as well as Morocco and Ireland, which became independent before a constitution was passed; and a group of independent states that continued to constitutionally exclude large segments of the population from its citizenry during the first decades of independence (Liberia, the United States, Rhodesia, South Africa, and Australia).

[16] For the Habsburg empire, we relied on Strach (1906), Heinersdoff (1975), and Oberegger (2008); for the successor states of Yugoslavia on Oberegger (2008); for the Romanov empire on Perl (1872), Roll (1915), and Rautavuiori (2008); for Germany on Roll (1915); for the former Soviet Union republics, on Central Statistical Administration (1957) as well as Sakari and Likka (2003); for the Ottoman empire, on Karkar (1972) and Bonine (1998).

[17] Still, railway track length is correlated ($r = 0.45$ or 0.65 for years before 1970) with the percentage employed outside agriculture, based on 196 data points from Vanhanen (2000).

We did experiment with existing historical data on energy consumption, urbanization, iron and steel production, as well as the percentage of labor force employed outside agriculture as alternative measurements, although these are available for only 1,000 to 2,000 pre-nation-state observations. These models (not shown) are substantially identical to those with the railway variable.

To test Anderson's main argument about the role of literacy in generating nationalist imaginaries, we assembled data on adult literacy rates for all territories in the database, relying on published country studies, government censuses, historical research on particular regions, existing quantitative datasets, and so on. The sources are listed in Appendix 3.3. In all cases, we found estimations within a ten-year range from the year of nation-state creation; to interpolate, we combined these data with the best estimates available for the beginning of the time series in 1816,[18] as well as several later data points. The reliability and comparability problems characteristic of literacy estimates (Reis 2005: fn. 9–12), especially before census taking became widespread in the 1870s (Kaestle 1985), also haunt our efforts. In view of the substantial variation of estimated literacy rates over time and across territories, however, we believe that the quality of the data is sufficient to justify including this variable in the analysis.

To test Anderson's "provincial horizon of identity" argument and Roeder's theory of institutional capacity, we code for each year whether a territory *corresponds to an autonomous state or a sub-state unit* (1) or not (0). Such variables are called "dummy" variables and one tests their effect by comparing whether observations with a 1 affect the outcome differently from those with a 0. Given that our territorial grid is fixed, while political boundaries might change over time, we effectively evaluate whether nation-state creation is more likely if a territory previously enjoyed some degree of institutional autonomy as a province or a state. We count provinces, colonies, mandate territories, *vilayets* and *sanjaks*, and Russian governorates, for example, as relevant sub-state units, and we took into account dozens of reorganizations of colonial and imperial provinces. We code pre-colonial territories that were divided between various indigenous states or were stateless as 0 on this variable.

But doesn't the advent of the automobile make the length of railway tracks an increasingly poor proxy variable for industrialization over the course of the 20th century? Those industrialized countries that ceased to build railways after World War I or World War II mostly achieved nation-statehood *before* they started to rely on automobiles, thus minimizing the potential problem. And while some communist dependencies or colonies let their railway systems decline, many more continued to build railways after World War II and well into the 1970s and beyond. This is the case, for example, in Zimbabwe, Mozambique, South Africa, Angola, Bangladesh, Malaysia, Armenia, Slovakia, Croatia, Uzbekistan, and Tajikistan. We also ran models for the pre-World War I period alone and found that results do not change significantly.

[18] In a handful of cases where no data are available for these early years, we chose the data for the most similar society: Vietnam and Korea were given the same literacy rates as early nineteenth-century China; Laos and Cambodia got Thailand's early figures; the figures calculated for mid-century Tunisia were also used for Morocco, Libya, Algeria, and Malaysia; the Cisleithanian provinces of Austria borrow data from Prussian Westphalia. For a couple of British colonies in Africa, we assumed the same growth rate over the twentieth century as in Ghana, the best researched case. All pre-colonial territories in societies that had no indigenous writing culture were assigned the value of 0.

The degree of directness of rule plays a crucial role in Tilly's and Hechter's theories of nationalism and the nation-state. It can be approximated by calculating *government expenditure* for a particular territory, assuming that the more a government spends on a territory, the denser and deeper administrative penetration will be, increasing the government's interference in local affairs and its ability to circumvent local power brokers. We again use data from Mitchell (various years) and complement this with additional sources for the Ottoman and Spanish empires and the Soviet Union.[19] We give imperial dependencies (but not colonies) the same values throughout an empire, assuming that land-based empires were more uniform than seaborne colonial empires in modes of territorial control. Pre-colonial territories that had not developed indigenous states are assigned a value of 0 because, by definition, they cannot be ruled directly. All other polities, including pre-colonial states such as Dahomey, Burma, and Morocco, are given their proper values if data is available or coded as missing values and thus excluded from the analysis.[20] These coding rules generate many such missing values; we therefore test this variable in separate models. All figures were standardized as per capita figures, converted into US constant dollars using time-varying conversion rates, and then additionally adjusted for purchasing power differences using Maddison's (2003) GDP estimations.[21]

Is this variable a good proxy for directness of rule? Lange (2005) has developed a more specific measurement for British colonies, using the percentage of court cases handled by traditional or "native" courts as a proxy. This variable shows a high correlation with our measurement of direct rule via government expenditure ($r = 0.82$ for 19 data points, using non-standardized values).

---

[19] Our prime sources for calculating figures for the Spanish empire were Klein (1998); for the Ottoman empire, Shaw (1978) and Akar (1999) provided figures for government expenditure, while Cem Behar (1996) and Karpat (1985) are our sources for population data; for the Soviet Union government expenditure data come from Plotnikov (1948/1954) and Svodnii otdel gosudarstvennogo byudzheta (various years), and population data from New World Demographics (1992) and Kozlov (1988). The Soviet budgets included basically the entire economy, given the nature of the Soviet economy (on Soviet budgets, see Hutchings 1983). To make these figures comparable to others, we excluded all expenses related to the production and distribution of goods from the provincial budgets, including those related to pensions, health care, and the like.

[20] Nominally dependent, but de facto self-ruled territories under the Ottomans were also assigned their proper values or coded as missing data if not available. We also used different codings of the direct rule variable to accommodate different possible interpretations. In one variant, we assigned all pre-colonial, pre-modern states 0 in order to exclude non-bureaucratic regimes from our definition of direct rule, thus effectively interpreting it as "modern, bureaucratic forms of direct rule." Another variant defined de facto autonomous territories nominally controlled by the Ottoman empire (mostly Algeria, Bahrain, Egypt, Kuwait, Libya, Tunisia, and the UAE) as 0, while assigning pre-modern or pre-colonial states their values or coding them as missing. This represents a coding of direct rule that does not distinguish between modern and pre-modern forms. The results presented below do not depend on which of these various coding variants are used.

[21] We ran all models with unadjusted data as well and found no differences.

In addition, our measurement seems to capture historical shifts in directness of rule quite adequately. For example, the decentralization of the Habsburg monarchy after the *Ausgleich* in 1867 – which effectively created two federal states, one under Hungarian control and one under Austrian control – is faithfully reflected in a dramatic decrease in Vienna's government expenditure for the Hungarian lands.

We generated the diffusion variables by counting the *number of territories governed as nation-states in the neighborhood, within the same imperial domain, or in the world*. We then created a variable that reflects the number of nation-states established during the previous five years because imitation and domino effects are best captured by a dynamic coding. All results reported below also hold when using a total count or the percentage of nation-states in the world, empire, or neighborhood.[22] To test the cross-sectional version of the global diffusion argument, we code the *number of memberships in international governmental organizations* by the polity to which a territory belonged. We assign imperial and colonial dependencies the same value as their centers, assuming that world cultural values spread from a metropolis to the peripheries.[23] All data were adopted from the Correlates of War (COW) project.

To evaluate whether *wars in the territory or the empire* affect the creation of nation-states, we use a dataset of wars in all territories of the world from 1816 to 2001, which will be discussed in more detail in the next chapter. This dataset allows us to distinguish between inter-state wars, civil wars, and nationalist wars of independence. We code a large number of different war variables to test whether specific types of wars are more effective in weakening the political center and thus shifting the balance of power in favor of nationalists.

The *strength of nationalist challengers* is proxied by counting the years elapsed since the foundation of the first national organization. To be considered a *national organization*, its membership must be defined formally (thus excluding clientelist networks and informal factions) and leadership roles must be institutionalized independent of individuals (thus not considering the personal followings of a nationalist leader). In addition, an organization had to claim to represent the national community in the name of which the territory eventually became governed – without being necessarily nationalist in the strict sense

---

[22] Obviously, we coded all territories in the neighborhood, empire, or world, including those on which we lack data on other independent variables and which are thus not included in the rest of the analysis. For the imperial diffusion variables, we extended membership in the empire five years after independence. To calculate the neighborhood variables, we used the matrix of contiguity provided by the Correlates of War project, using a maximum distance of 150 miles to define neighbors separated by water (COW 2008), and excluded same-empire neighbors in order not to confuse imperial and neighborhood effects.

[23] If all dependent territories are assigned 0 on this variable, the results reported below do not change.

of the term.[24] To statistically distinguish the monotonically increasing strength of nationalist challengers from the mere presence or absence of nationalism as such, we include a dummy variable that codes 1 for *all years since the first national organization* was founded. The existence of nationalism should make nation-state creation much more likely, given that the power-configurational argument is premised on this antecedent.

To take the political center's *capacity to resist* nationalist movements into account, we rely on COW's "composite index of national capabilities," which combines energy consumption, military expenditure, number of soldiers, steel production, urbanization, and population size (Singer 1987). This index reflects a country's share of total economic and military power available in the world (ranging from 0 to 100 percent). All dependent territories are assigned the value of the imperial or colonial center; pre-colonial, stateless territories are coded as having no global power at all. Unfortunately, we have to code autonomous states not listed in the COW dataset as missing values and exclude them from the analysis.

2.3 Modeling approach and time specification

We use "discrete-time event history models," estimated via a logistic regression analysis of territory-years, to estimate the effect of covariates on the likelihood of nation-state creation. In everyday language, this statistical model estimates how the different variables – railroad length, literacy rates, etc. – affect the probability that a territory becomes a nation-state from one year to the next.[25] We take into account that next year's values on the independent variables depend to a certain degree on this year's values (you cannot possibly build tens of thousands of kilometers of railways in one year, to give an example), by clustering standard errors on territories.

Given the chronic instability of cross-national regression results (see Young 2009), we ran all models with different ways of defining dependent and independent variables and with different combinations of variables. We only rely on results that are robust to all different model specifications – meaning that the results have to remain stable whether you standardize government expenditure by today's American dollars or not, to give an example, and whether you test the government expenditure variable together with the railways variable or just on its own, and so forth.

One of the major challenges for this kind of analysis is how to conceptualize the effects of time. Obviously, much has changed between 1816 and 2001 that is not captured by our independent variables but that might affect the likelihood of

---

[24] Most of the information is based on Woronoff (various years).
[25] The dataset was set up as an unbalanced panel. All independent variables were lagged one year to reduce reverse causation problems.

nation-state creation systematically. There are various ways to take such unmeasured differences across historical periods into account. The simplest way is to include a time trend into the statistical model (as in most diffusion models, see Strang 1991b). This tests whether the passing of time itself affects the outcome, each year being more (or less) likely to see nation-states created than the one preceding it. One can also use discrete time periods, such as decades, to explore whether some decades are particularly likely to produce nation-states. We also used a more complex technique, called "natural cubic splines" (the standard in comparative political research, following Beck *et al.* 1998). This allows considering non-linear trends such as an increase of the probability of nation-state creation until World War I and a decrease thereafter. We ran all models with all three time specifications and we only rely on results that remain similar. In the tables below, we show the results generated with cubic splines.

Substantively, the splines describe a more or less constant risk of nation-state creation until World War II and a sharply increasing risk thereafter, similar to the smoothed hazard rates in Figure 3.2. This trend could be interpreted in line with Strang's world polity argument by attributing it to an increase in the nation-state's legitimacy after the United Nations' founding in 1945 – though Strang himself points to an anticolonial UN declaration of 1960 as a critical turning point.

We are uncomfortable with the post-hoc-ergo-propter-hoc nature of this interpretation. The post-1945 surge in the baseline probability might be due to the increased global power of the United States, champion of decolonization and self-determination. Or it may relate to the unprecedented growth of the global economy that made many more nation-state projects economically feasible. Or it may capture the decreasing popularity of the colonial project in France and Britain – which may or may not be related to the decreasing legitimacy of colonialism in the world as a whole.[26] In conclusion, period dummies and general time trends rarely provide conclusive evidence in support of a particular substantive argument.

3 RESULTS

Many of the variables associated with modernist theories of nation-state formation are strongly correlated with each other (see the correlation matrix in Appendix 3.4) since they all increase over time: literacy rates tend to go up, railway tracks tend to become longer, government spending tends to increase, and so forth. This makes it more difficult to disentangle their separate effects. To test their explanatory power independent from each other, we therefore introduce them in separate models. We include continental dummies in all main models to account for unobserved heterogeneity across world regions – in other words,

---

[26] In contrast to world polity arguments, Britain had already started to prepare for decolonization from the late 1930s onward (Flint 1983), while Nazi Germany's imperial project was in full swing.

to test whether being located in sub-Saharan Africa, in Western Europe, and so forth makes a territory more likely to become a nation-state, for reasons that we have not adequately captured by our variables and data.

3.1 Main findings

Model 1 in Table 3.1 includes the length of railway tracks to test a core hypothesis derived from Gellner's work. The variable fails to achieve standard levels of statistical significance (significant variables are marked with * in the table). In everyday language, this means that we are less than 95 percent certain that railways are associated with the likelihood of nation-state creation. This holds true even if we restrict the sample to pre-1914 years, during which the length of railways is a better proxy for industrialization than afterward. The main reason why we find no general association between industrialization and nation-state formation (according to additional analyses not reported here) is that early nation-states in Latin America were created in a pre-industrial environment and many weakly industrialized African territories achieved nation-statehood in the 1960s, while the highly industrialized Soviet and Yugoslav provinces had to wait another generation to accomplish the same.[27] This combination of historical developments might explain why there is no statistically significant association between industrialization and nation-state creation.

This hints at the importance of political and power-configurational factors largely missing from Gellner's account and to be explored further below: the Soviet Union had the power to keep nationalist movements in its highly industrialized provinces in check for generations, not least by co-opting and controlling minority elites into the governments of the republics. Spain, preoccupied

---

[27] This explains why territory-fixed effect models (not shown here), which control for time-invarying differences across territories and give greater weight to within-territory comparisons over time, create a negative significant coefficient for railways – which turns positive significant if Eastern Europe is excluded and insignificant without Africa.

The railway variable achieves significance in two combinations of variables: first, in models that do not include a general time trend *and* at the same time control for the specificities of the Latin American, African, and Soviet territories either through continental controls or a fixed effect model (*with* such a time trend, the variable is also significant in fixed effect models but the coefficient is negative, as noted above). Second, the effects of Latin American and Soviet territories is weakened by eliminating the second episodes of nation-state creation (on the territories of Gran Colombia, the Central American Republic as well as in the Caucasian and Baltic regions). However, these results are significant only when specifying time effects with cubic splines. If the *first* episodes in South America and Yugoslavia are not considered, i.e. when only the establishment of Colombia, Venezuela, etc. are taken into account, the variable again loses significance.

Sub-sample analysis shows that railways are significantly and positively associated with nation-state creation only in the Middle East and Eastern Europe and only if we control for previous episodes of nation-state creation with a dummy variable. The coefficient is negative significant for Africa alone. Change in the length of railway tracks over time also has no significant effect on the likelihood of nation-state creation.

TABLE 3.1 *Explaining nation-state creation (logit analysis)*

	Model 1	Model 2	Model 3	Model 4	Model 5
Length of railway tracks per km^2	0.005 (0.004)				
Territory corresponds to state or province		−0.300 (0.222)			
Percent literacy among adults		−0.016** (0.005)			
Central government expenditure for territory			−0.213* (0.084)		
Center's membership in international governmental organizations				0.008 (0.005)	
Total number of nation-states in world				−0.025** (0.008)	
No. of nation-states created in the empire past five years				0.165** (0.038)	0.124** (0.034)
No. of nation-states created in neighborhood past five years				0.780** (0.121)	0.512** (0.124)
Existence of national organization					1.087** (0.292)
Years since first national organization founded					0.007* (0.003)
Number of wars fought in the empire					0.297** (0.051)
Number of wars fought in the territory					0.481** (0.182)
Center's share of global power					0.061* (0.029)
Center's share of global power x dependency					−0.108** (0.03)
Dependent territory					0.406 (0.287)
Observations	17,500	17,522	9,821	17,522	16,488

Notes: Continental dummies, cubic splines, and constant not shown; robust standard errors in parentheses; * significant at 5 percent; ** significant at 1 percent.

with the Napoleonic invasion and a subsequent civil war, failed to achieve the same in its faraway colonial empire, long before it had been touched by industrialization.

Model 2 contains variables associated with Anderson's (and Roeder's) approach. Territories that correspond to the boundaries of provinces or states are not more likely to become nation-states.[28] The literacy variable is negative and significant (indicating that more literate societies are *less* likely to become nation-states). This result is not robust to other time specifications, however, which all produce insignificant results. We therefore do not consider this a reliable finding. What happens if we look more precisely at only the types of territories for which Anderson thought mass literacy or being a province would be most effective in bringing about a nation-state? The political entity variable is also insignificant for the colonial dependencies of Europe, where it should matter most (results not shown). The literacy variable also fails to reach standard levels of significance if we analyze only European territories, that is, the domains of second- and third-wave nationalisms for which high literacy levels should be a catalyst, according to Anderson (results not shown).[29]

Why does the literacy variable not behave as Anderson expected?[30] Additional analysis (not shown here) suggests the following: after World War I, literacy was promoted heavily by communist regimes all over Eastern Europe and by the colonial bureaucracies especially of Africa, long before the creation of nation-states in these areas of the world. Perhaps these regimes were able to keep nationalists at arm's length by inducing the population to imagine – at least temporarily – other, non-national communities, such as a global family of subjects loyal to Her Majesty, or the revolutionary working classes of the world. The relationship between mass literacy and nationalism might therefore be less straightforward than Anderson's account suggests.

Model 3 integrates our measurement of directness of rule, which reduces the number of observations by almost half because we could not find data for most pre-colonial territories. The variable is robustly significant but with a negative coefficient, indicating that the more directly a territory is ruled by the political

---

[28] This result is not dependent on the number of years that we lag this variable. A 20-year moving average produces comparable results.

[29] The literacy variable is positive significant only in models without continents as controls (thus attributing the fact that African territories achieved nation-statehood so late to their low literacy rates) and with a linear time trend as a specification of the baseline hazard rate. It is insignificant for all continental sub-samples except Asia.

[30] Perhaps the emergence of nationalist imaginaries would be a better dependent variable to test Anderson's mass literacy argument? We find no significant association between levels of literacy and the foundation of a national organization as soon as continental dummies are included in the model (results not shown); the same holds true for the railroad length and government expenditure variables. However, diffusion mechanisms within empires and among neighbors seem to be at work again, as noted in a previous footnote.

center, the less likely it is to eventually become a nation-state. This is contrary to expectations derived from Hechter's and Tilly's arguments.[31] It seems that more directly ruled states are more capable of resisting the pressure to shift to the nation-state model and can keep nationalists in check by "buying" the consent of the population and building a network of alliances and dependencies that incorporates segments of the population that might otherwise succumb to the siren song of nationalism. This result, however, is mostly driven by the Middle Eastern kingdoms that have not yet experienced a transition to the nation-state as per 2001 despite very high government expenditures per capita. This is the only such dependence on few observations in all the results that we report in this chapter.

To analyze the full dataset again, we exclude the government expenditure variable from subsequent models. Model 4 introduces diffusion variables. The term for global diffusion is negative and significant, meaning that the more the world is populated by nation-states, the less likely additional nation-states will be founded. This result is substantially meaningless, however. It is entirely due to the fact that the time trend and the number of nation-states in the world are very highly correlated with each other.[32] In contrast to Strang's (1991b) analysis of decolonization,[33] we thus do not find any support for the longitudinal version of the world polity argument.[34] A political center's number of IGO memberships – the

[31] Model 3 remains substantially identical for different codings of direct rule: as modern, bureaucratic rule (assigning o to all pre-modern states such as Dahomey or Ethiopia); as pre-modern as well as modern direct rule (coding missing values for pre-modern states where no data are available and o for de facto self-ruled, but nominally dependent territories, such as Tunisia under the Ottomans). Restricting observations to the developing world also does not change results. In sub-sample analysis, the variable is insignificant for all continents except for Eastern Europe (where it is negative) and Asia (where it is positive).

 The direct rule hypothesis can only be confirmed in a coding that could be described as "direct alien rule": all pre-colonial territories, nominally dependent but de facto autonomous territories, and all autonomous states are coded as self-ruled. These coding rules thus create a contrast between self-ruled pre-colonial lands (which never experience a nation-state creation) and foreign-ruled imperial/colonial dependencies, which all eventually transform into nation-states. Since it is more than doubtful that pre-colonial states were mostly ethnically self-ruled (as the examples of the Zulu, Durrani, and Bemba empires illustrate), we think that this coding of the independent variable is not the most plausible one.

 All these different versions of the government expenditure variable were also coded without standardizing its values according to the level of development of a territory. All results remain fairly similar, except that the "direct alien rule" variable discussed above is completely insignificant in its unstandardized version.

[32] The global diffusion variable is only positive significant in models that include a linear time specification that does not capture the post-1945 upward trend in the baseline hazard rate.

[33] In contrast to Strang, we also found no robust effect of his other global-level variable, i.e. Wallerstein's period of hegemony (results not shown). Also contrary to his analysis, nation-states are not more likely to emerge among dependencies of democratic centers, nor in settler societies. Our results do confirm, however, that nation-states diffuse within empires (see below) and that militarily powerful imperial centers can prevent nationalist secession from their domains.

[34] One might argue that the deepening and broadening reach of world culture itself describes the change in the baseline event risk appropriately and that one therefore does not need to include a

variable to test the cross-sectional aspect of the world polity argument – also fails to achieve significance. A territory that is more integrated into the world polity is not more likely than an isolated territory to become a nation-state.

Let us now explore how the power-configurational argument fares in a statistical test. In Model 4, we find strong and meaningful evidence for diffusion at the imperial and neighborhood levels. The number of nation-states founded during the past five years within an empire and within a territory's neighborhood increases the likelihood of nation-state creation substantially, pointing toward imitation and domino mechanisms.[35]

Here are some of the cases that underlie these results. For diffusion within empires, they include how the political and military pressure on Bolivia's remaining royalists increased after the Bolivarian spirit of nationalist revolution had gained a foothold in most other former Spanish dependencies; how the Committee for Union and Progress abandoned the Hamidian project of imperial restoration and instead embraced the nation-state model after so many Ottoman provinces in Rumelia had already become independent nation-states; and how Indian independence inspired and encouraged many nationalist movements elsewhere in the British empire.

The competing nation-state building projects on the Spanish peninsula, born out of nationalist resistance against Napoleon's occupation, provide an example of the neighborhood diffusion effect. The Portuguese liberal revolutions, and thus the creation of a modern Portuguese nation-state, were directed as much against the absent emperor (who fled to Brazil) as against the state's traditional rival, Spain, whose newly formed mass army – modeled after the French *peuple en arme* it had just defeated in the world's first guerilla war – threatened Portugal's independence.

Model 5 explores how the other variables associated with the power-configurational argument fare in the statistical tests. The proxy variable for the

---

time trend in the event history models, thus avoiding the collinearity problem. However, the diffusion variables never fitted the data as well as simple chronological time (results not shown). Furthermore, we regressed the predicted hazard rates from a discrete-time model (using decades) first on the predicted hazard rates produced by a global diffusion variable and then on the predicted hazard rates produced by linear time. The secular time trend has a stronger association with the discrete-time hazard rates. Global diffusion thus cannot substitute for chronological time.

[35] But are these really imitation and domino effects operating at the imperial and neighborhood level, or rather the regional or local manifestations of the pressure to adopt the nation-state emanating from the *global* level? First, these variables are significant for the pre-1915 sub-sample as well, when global pressures to adopt the nation-state were much weaker (see Model 1, Table 3.2). Second, additional analysis shows that the absolute number of territories in the empire or neighborhood that already made the transition to the nation-state also increases the likelihood of nation-state creation in the remaining territories. Such a *cumulative* effect would not be expected if we were dealing simply with local manifestations of a global adoption pressure. Our findings thus parallel research on the transition to democracy, which has been shown to diffuse within networks of related states (Torfason and Ingram 2010: 20) or between geographical neighbors (Gleditsch and Ward 2006: 925f.), rather than within a uniform global space.

strength of nationalist movements – the years that have passed since the foundation of the first national organization – has a significant effect on the likelihood
of nation-state creation in Model 5. Because we also include a dummy variable
for the period after the foundation of the first national organization, this effect is
net of the existence of nationalism per se. However, the results suggest that the
existence of nationalism is itself a very strong predictor of nation-state creation.
This is in line with the basic theoretical framework of the power-configurational
model, which trivially implies that nationalist forces first need to emerge before
they can eventually take over an existing state or found a new one.[36]

Another core hypothesis associated with the power-configurational argument
is that nationalists will be more successful if the center is weakened by wars –
similar to Skocpol's analysis of revolutions. Indeed, both the number of wars
fought within a territory during the past year and the number of wars fought
within an empire (excluding those fought on a territory) significantly affect the
likelihood of nation-state creation. Examples of the latter include the civil war
in Bolivia between royalists and Bolivarists, the nationalist wars of liberation
that helped bring about the Baltic republics' independence after World War I,
and the Russian-Turkish war that allowed Bulgaria to become an independent
nation-state in 1879 after Ottoman forces had crushed a Bulgarian rebellion four
years earlier.

Note that this short list contains examples of nationalist wars of liberation
such as in Bolivia or the Baltics, which are thus a direct cause of the creation of
these nation-states – a mechanism that will form a crucial element of the next
chapter. The Russian-Turkish war, on the other hand, was causally unrelated to
the struggles of Bulgarian nationalists, but weakened the Ottoman empire enough
to allow for the establishment of a Bulgarian nation-state. This is a good example
of what could be called a Skocpolian "midwife" effect. If we excluded nationalist
wars of liberation from the coding of the war variables, which would then capture
this midwife effect alone, it would still significantly affect nation-state creation in
Model 5 (results not shown). The war on the territory variable thus captures two
different mechanisms: first, a specific avenue through which nationalists achieve
nation-statehood thanks to successful nationalist wars of independence. Second,
the tilting of the balance of power in favor of nationalists through wars that are
unrelated to the nationalist struggle in a particular territory, but still weaken the
established state elites and thus facilitate a nationalist revolution.

World War I, which debilitated the Habsburg and Soviet empires and enabled
a wave of nation-state creations in their domains, provides a prime example for
how wars in one part of an empire can facilitate nation-state creation in other
parts. Other cases include the Mau Mau rebellion in Kenya and the Malaysian

---

[36] The years since the foundation of a national organization variable is sensitive to the inclusion of a
small group of territories. If we exclude the dummy variable from the model, however, this sensitivity
disappears entirely.

anticolonial communist insurgency, which decreased the British empire's willingness to hold on to its imperial possessions and helped accelerate Ghana's independence – the first on the continent. Similarly, the bloody struggles in Algeria and French Cameroon weakened France's capacity and willingness to erect further obstacles against decolonization in its West African domains.[37]

According to our configurational theory, a center's power to resist nationalist challengers also depends on its international standing. We found out, however, that the effect of the "center's global power" is different for self-ruled territories compared to imperial or colonial dependencies. The interaction term in Model 5 is significant and negative, while the sign of the coefficient of the non-interacted term is positive and significant. What does such an interaction effect mean? It explores if the effect of one variable is dependent on the values on another variable. In the case at hand, the "center's global power" *decreases* the likelihood of nation-state creation *if* the value of the "dependency" variable is set at 1 – in other words, if we look at colonial and imperial dependencies. The non-interacted "center's power" variable then refers exclusively to those territories in which the "dependency" variable is set at 0 – meaning territories that are independent countries. Since this "center's power" variable is positive and significant, it would indicate that independent states are less likely to become nation-states, the more powerful they are in the global arena. But this latter result disappears if we would use decades or a linear time trend instead of cubic splines to specify the effects of time (not shown); thus, we do not rely on this finding for independent states.

The results for imperial and colonial dependencies are robust, however. Imperial states that are powerful players in the international arena can more easily co-opt, control, or suppress nationalist movements and prevent the establishment of nation-states in their dependent territories. As an example for the opposite case, we can again point to Spain, which could not contain or co-opt Creole nationalists in its New World possessions or fight independence movements effectively after its fleet was dramatically decimated in the famous battle of Trafalgar and its attention was further diverted by Napoleon's occupation of her lands.

3.2 Context and contingency

Model 5 therefore lends strong and consistent support to the various hypotheses associated with a power-configurational model of nation-state creation.[38] Do these findings hold across time and across the different waves of

---

[37] All results relating to the war variables are similar if we code the average number of wars fought over the past five years. Note that the coding of the imperial war variable excludes wars that are also fought on the territory in question. Thus, the imperial war variable is *not* directly connected to the independence struggles on the territory itself.

[38] We also ran Model 5 with "territory-fixed effects," which takes into account that many time-invariant characteristics of individual territories, not adequately captured by our set of variables, might

nation-state creation that rolled over the modern world? Isn't the story of the dissolution of the Habsburg empire quite different from that of the breakup of the Soviet Union? And should we expect variables to affect outcomes in different ways in the early-nineteenth century than in the late twentieth century? Table 3.2 shows the results of some additional tests that answer these questions.

Model 4 in Table 3.2 demonstrates that none of the various imperial domains – such as Ottoman, Romanov, or British – is significantly different from the others or from the 18 territories that remained autonomous throughout history, such as Japan or Switzerland.[39] No decade stands out as particularly prone to nation-state creation (see Model 3), with the exception of the decades starting in 1956, when Africa was decolonized, and the 1990s, when the Soviet Union dissolved and Yugoslavia disintegrated (more on this below). If we look only at observations either before 1914 (Model 1) or after 1914 (Model 2), roughly the midpoint in our data series, we discover that the results remain fairly similar. After World War I, however, wars fought in a territory no longer significantly affect the likelihood of nation-state creation, and the center's share of global power variable is only borderline significant.[40]

We took a closer look at how the effects of the share of global power variable change over time. It is negative (making nation-state creation less likely) until the 1970s, but it has a positive effect thereafter (making nation-state creation

influence the likelihood of nation-state creation. To put it simply, fixed effect models give much more weight to *within* territory changes *over time* than standard models. With the exception of the center's share of global power variable, to which we will turn in a moment, all variables remain statistically significant in the expected direction (results not shown). We also ran Model 5 without instances of repeated nation-state creation on the same territory, thus only counting the foundation of Czechoslovakia, but not the subsequent independence of the Czech Republic and of Slovakia. The results (not shown) are substantially identical. The same holds true if we consider only the last events in cases of repeated nation-state creations (i.e. if we exclude the foundation of Czechoslovakia, but count the independence of the Czech Republic and Slovakia) or if we drop all observations of one continent from the sample (results also not shown).

[39] Maybe transitions to nation-statehood in independent states (such as Switzerland) are different from those of imperial dependencies (such as Ghana)? Sub-sample analysis of both groups of territories reveals that this is generally not the case. The share of global power of the center, however, is insignificant in the sub-sample of nation-states created after independence had already been achieved (in line with the findings discussed above); wars in the territory are only borderline significant in the sub-sample of nation-states that were created out of empires. If we analyze the 18 territories that were never part of an empire separately, however, the only variable that still influences the chances of nation-state creation in significant ways is the time since the foundation of a national organization.

[40] We lose significance on the share of global power and the wars in the territory variables from 1880 onward. The model is much more robust to right-hand truncation (which in contrast to left-hand truncation does not create an incomplete, and thus problematic, risk set): all covariates remain significant in sub-samples that exclude years after 1880 or beyond, and only the neighborhood diffusion variable is borderline or insignificant when years after 1850 are dropped.

TABLE 3.2 *Does context matter? Logit analysis with sub-samples and additional covariates*

	Model 1 Before 1914	Model 2 After 1914	Model 3 Decades[a]	Model 4 Empires[b]	
No. of nation-states created in the empire past five years	0.297** (0.104)	0.134** (0.037)	0.110** (0.04)	0.135** (0.049)	
No. of nation-states created in neighborhood past five years	0.496* (0.232)	0.634** (0.158)	0.486** (0.123)	0.630** (0.124)	
Years since first national organization	0.025** (0.005)	0.010** (0.003)	0.018** (0.003)	0.019** (0.003)	
Center's share of global power x dependency	−0.15* (0.059)	−0.028 (0.017)	−0.056** (0.014)	−0.047 (0.026)	
Number of wars fought in the empire	0.521** (0.097)	0.239** (0.051)	0.289** (0.047)	0.318** (0.043)	
No. of wars fought in the territory	0.818** (0.230)	0.394 (0.224)	0.661** (0.173)	0.555** (0.183)	
1821–1840			1.58 (1.013)	0.65 (0.53)	Spanish
1841–1855			0.636 (1.068)	0.08 (0.403)	Habsburg
1856–1870			0.414 (1.073)	0.461 (0.4)	Romanov
1871–1885			0.303 (1.102)	−0.391 (0.513)	Ottoman
1886–1900			−1.084 (1.408)	−0.588 (0.37)	Yugoslav
1901–1915			0.868 (1.062)	−0.777 (0.505)	Soviet
1916–1930			0.82 (1.041)	0.444 (0.347)	French
1931–1945			−0.153 (1.119)	0.455 (0.458)	British
1946–1955			1.379 (1.025)	0.168 (0.373)	Dutch

TABLE 3.2 (*cont.*)

	Model 1 Before 1914	Model 2 After 1914	Model 3 Decades[a]	Model 4 Empires[b]	
1956–1965			2.456* (1.008)	-0.732 (0.569)	Portuguese
1966–1975			1.906 (1.032)	0.748 (0.607)	Other empires
1976–1985			-0.411 (1.409)	0.168 (0.299)	Independent states
1986–1995			3.129** (1.026)		
1996–2001			2.761* (1.28)		
Observations	11,116	5,372	16,488	16,421	

Notes: Cubic splines and constant not shown; robust standard errors in parentheses; * significant at 5 percent; ** significant at 1 percent.
[a] Years 1816–1820 are the reference category; [b] pre-colonial territories are the reference category.

more likely).[41] This is because many nation-states were created within the domains of the Soviet Union in the 1990s, while Moscow still commanded an extraordinary share of global military and economic power, especially compared with some small Gulf monarchies that continued to resist nationalism and are thus still in the risk set during the 1990s. We thus need to account for what seems to be the specificity of African decolonization and the dissolution of the Soviet empire.

According to our model and data, Moscow would have had the capacity to fight or co-opt independence movements – yet nation-states popped up all over its domains. Similarly, the dissolutions of the French and British empires in sub-Saharan Africa were engineered in advance (for British Africa, see Flint 1983) and in the very end supported, rather than fought, by the imperial center (on French West Africa, see Chafer 2002). Does the lack of willingness to uphold and defend an imperial domain explain why so many territories achieved nation-statehood in 1960 and 1991, making the two corresponding decades stand

[41] We interacted all independent variables with linear time in order to determine whether there is causal heterogeneity across history. For none of the independent variables this is the case, except for the center's share of global power, for the reasons discussed below.

out compared to all others in Model 3? Does contingency play a role in these two waves of nation-state creation – contingent, that is, from the point of view of a power-configurational argument that does not foresee a lack of willingness to use one's power?

I suggest that we might deal with a problem of data resolution here, rather than a flaw in the theoretical argument or a lack of empirical support. The following discussion focuses on the Soviet case, but similar arguments could be made with regard to African decolonization (see Hiers and Wimmer, in press). First, it might be that the Kremlin was already too weak domestically to use its global military and economic power against nationalist independence movements, even if it had wanted to. Our data are not fine-grained enough to capture power relations between the Russian president Boris Yeltsin – who famously stood on a tank in the center of Moscow amid thousands of supporters – and the putschist generals who wanted to roll back the nationalist movements and reestablish the USSR's control over the empire, including over Russia. It is well possible that the generals were no longer in a position to use the empire's global military and economic might against the nationalist movements. If we had finer-grained and better data, the Soviet Union's lack of effective control over its power resources would have been captured and no reverse effect for the center's share of global power variable would have resulted for the decades following 1970.

Second, the yearly resolution of our data does not capture faster-moving diffusion effects. The Baltic declarations of "sovereignty" (in 1988) and later of full independence (in September 1991) inspired leaders of the Caucasian republics to declare independence in early December of 1991. In mid-December Yeltsin's Russian nationalism and declaration of independence provoked the collapse of the remaining Soviet Union and left Central Asian republics no choice but to embrace independence themselves, which they did later that very same month. If our data resolution was weekly, rather than yearly, such fast-paced diffusion processes could be captured, as shown by Hale (2000). It may well be, then, that the 1990s would no longer stand out from other decades if we had such more fine-grained diffusion data.

With better data and a more detailed analysis, we could thus gain a deeper understanding of the complex dynamics of political mobilization, contestation, repression, diffusion, and imitation that change the balance of power between nationalists and existing elites within days or weeks (see the superb analysis of the Soviet case by Beissinger 2002). Our global dataset, stretching from the fall of Napoleon's empire to the beginning of the twenty-first century, is not well equipped to handle this task. It can, however, highlight those waves of nation-state formation, such as those leading to the dissolution of the Soviet and African colonial empires, that were propelled by such fast-moving dynamics.

4 CONCLUSIONS

Past comparative historical scholarship has explored various routes of nation-state formation: reform from above as in Japan; gradual transition into nation-statehood as in Sweden and Thailand; the overthrow of an *ancien régime* through revolution as in Russia or through civil war as in the United States and Switzerland; nationalist secession as in Yugoslavia and Mexico; and unification movements such as in Germany and Yemen. Independent of which of these routes a territory travels down, our analysis suggests, nation-states are created whenever the configuration of power favors nationalist movements and factions over imperial centers or *ancien régimes*, quite independent of whether domestic modernization processes have readied a society for nation building. Such a power shift is more likely when nationalists have had ample time to mobilize followers and propagate their ideology or when the established regime is weakened by wars. Diffusion of nation-states among neighbors or within the same empire also empowers nationalists by providing a model to follow and new alliance partners on which to rely. On the other hand, nationalists are at a disadvantage when facing an empire with considerable global military and economic power.

We thus integrate balance-of-power and diffusion mechanisms into a simple power-configurational model that includes domestic and international dimensions as well as military, political, and symbolic aspects of power. In contrast to political modernization arguments, this model emphasizes more proximate political factors, such as war or the political standing of imperial elites. Political modernization and, more specifically, state centralization are thus crucial to understand endogenous nation building in the early cases such as France, discussed in the previous chapter. But they are less relevant for the subsequent adoption of the nation-state in the rest of the world.

With regard to Gellner's and Anderson's classic theories of economic and cultural modernization, the analysis suggests that the rise of the nation-state across the world is decoupled – or at least only indirectly related – to these slow-moving historical forces.[42] In contrast to world polity theory, we find diffusion effects operating within neighborhoods and imperial domains, while the

---

[42] We should mention two other interesting non-results here. First, we tested whether the size of the largest ethnic group (data for the 1990s are from Fearon 2003) has an effect on the likelihood of nation-state creation, which is not the case. This variable can be seen as a proxy to test Anthony Smith's argument that nationalist mobilization is easier to achieve among groups with a rich ethno-history and within territories with a demographically dominant ethnic group that can form the "ethnic core" of a future nation (A. D. Smith 1990: 14, 11). The result is of course unreliable because of endogeneity problems: early nation-state creation could result in ethnic homogeneity through subsequent assimilation or ethnic cleansings, not the other way round. Other authors have argued that Protestantism provided the best breeding ground for the nation-state, mostly because of its ideological affinities to nationalism (Gellner 1983: 40f.; Smith 2003). However, we were somewhat surprised to find that Catholicism is robustly associated with the likelihood of nation-state creation (data on religious composition of the population is available for 1900 and from the 1970s onward in Barrett 2001).

growing global hegemony of the nation-state template – certainly a historical fact worth underlining – is not a good predictor of individual instances of nation-state creation. This hints at the possibility – already alluded to in the introduction – that this global hegemony results from the worldwide rise of the nation-state, rather than the other way around.

The last two chapters have explored how the first nation-states emerged in the eighteenth century, and why nationalism and the nation-state then proliferated across the world during the nineteenth and twentieth centuries. We have seen how wars facilitated these developments in multiple ways: the increasing involvement of the population in the wars of the early modern period was crucial in bringing about a new exchange relationship with state elites and the nationalist ideology expressing and cementing it. This new, national compact made these states more legitimate and militarily even more powerful – allowing them to soon dominate the rest of the world. This triggered a wave of political movements across the world that attempted to appropriate the secrets of this success and replicate the institutional structures that made it possible. Nationalist movements often came to power, this chapter demonstrated, when the old regime was weakened by wars that often were unrelated to the nationalist cause itself (what I have termed a Skocpolian midwife effect). The next chapter will analyze the relationship between nation-state formation and war more systematically.

4

Nation-state formation and war

"Events of the recent past have once again clearly demonstrated that the world is not yet ready for perpetual peace" (Hintze 1975: 215). This sarcastic statement is as true today as it was when penned 100 years ago by Otto Hintze in what is perhaps the first systematic treatise on warfare in the social sciences. In the meantime, a vast literature on why and when wars are more likely to break out has emerged. As briefly discussed in the introduction, this literature largely overlooks that nationalism and the global spread of the nation-state might represent major causes of war. This chapter seeks to correct this omission by showing that both wars between and within states are most likely to be fought during and because of the process of nation-state formation.

1 BLIND SPOTS IN CONVENTIONAL STUDIES OF WAR

The existing literature in international relations started from a different angle, however: from the basic insight that the world is not governed by a global state, but divided into competing sovereign entities. This anarchic structure makes wars between states a recurrent feature of global history. Decades of debate ensued to determine which exact distribution of military power between states and which features of their internal decision-making processes will make war more likely. Is

This chapter is adapted from a journal article coauthored with Brian Min.

    We thank Nicole Busse, Wesley Hiers, Veronika Lenarz, Ani Sarkissian, and Nusrat Sheikh for excellent research assistance. The following colleagues have given generous advice regarding research design and data coding (in chronological order): Indra de Soysa, John O'Neal, Rob Mare, Lillian Min, Xiao Chen, Lars-Erik Cederman, Christopher Blattman, Michael Ross, Havard Hegre, and Felix Elwert. The methodological framework and first results were discussed in the methodology course of UCLA's sociology department, organized by Jack Katz and Rob Mare. Sections of the article were presented at the conference on "Alien Rule and Its Discontent" convened by Michael Hechter at the University of Washington. Stathis Kalyvas invited us to present a first full version of the paper at the Yale Center for Conflict, Order, and Violence. We received stimulating comments and critiques on all occasions. Lars-Erik Cederman, Michael Ross, Nicholas Sambanis, and Christopher Winship gave generous comments and helpful advice on a later version.

a bipolar system such as during the Cold War more war-prone than a multipolar system (Waltz 1979)? Are global wars breaking out every time a new state rises to global dominance (Organski and Kugler 1980)? Will security-maximizing states always attack each other when they have the military upper hand (Mearsheimer 2001) or only when offensive military doctrines and technologies dominate over defensive ones (Van Evera 1999)? Are states with a long and persistent history of saber rattling and competition, such as between India and Pakistan, more likely to fight each other on the battlefield (Diehl and Goertz 2000)? What issues over which states compete are more likely to lead them into war (Senese and Vasquez 2008) and which types of informational asymmetries or commitment problems make the costly pursuit of war more attractive than a bargained solution (Fearon 1995)? Can international norms and institutions (Keohane 1984) or intense trade between countries (Polachek 1980) countervail the consequences of anarchy and prevent war? What kind of domestic coalitions of actors can succeed in pushing for expansionist wars and how do they manage to rally the population behind them (Snyder 1991)? And relatedly: why are democratic states not fighting other democracies (Russet 1993)?

1.1 Nationalism and nation-state formation

These are the key questions that have been asked over the past decades of research (see the excellent overview in Levy and Thompson 2010). As this list makes clear, there is very little concern of whether different types of states have different motives and frequencies of going to war – with the exception of the discussion of why democracies don't fight each other.[1] There is even less concern whether a change in the nature of the units composing the international system might itself be associated with war, apart from the rather obvious observation that the global likelihood of war increases with the number of states (for references see Vasquez 2009: 406). The main focus in international relations scholarship since its inception remained on the distribution of military and political power between states or the logic of decision-making within them. Conformingly, the transformation of the nature of these constituent units over the past 200 years – from a world of dynastic states or empires to a world of nation-states – is not considered a major cause of war, nor is the process through which states emerge or disappear. Only one article in this vast and sophisticated literature is specifically dedicated to understanding the conditions under which the creation of new states is associated with war (Diehl and Goertz 1991); and one other piece of scholarship investigates how such violent creation of new states leads these to fight wars with other states in the neighborhood (Maoz 1989).

---

[1] Luard (1986) offers a broader sociological approach that squarely focuses on how the nature of states affects the issues, motives, and decision-making processes leading to wars between states over the past 500 years. This chapter builds on this general theoretical outlook.

Conformingly, nationalism plays only a marginal role in international relations theories of war. It is sometimes thought that state leaders conveniently use nationalism to justify wars with neighbors and to thus divert attention from domestic problems or shore up domestic political support when needed (Snyder 2000). Other authors, to be discussed further below, have shown that concern for co-nationals living across an international border can lead to war between neighboring states. This chapter goes a step beyond theories of "diversion" and beyond acknowledging the role of co-nationality in inter-state war. It will show that the global spread of nationalism and the subsequent formation of nation-states are major causes of war during the past 200 years. Nationalism led to the often-violent creation of new states; these new nation-states often went to war with each other over ethnically mixed territory; and ethno-nationalist civil wars over who controlled these newly founded states haunted many of them decades after independence was achieved.

Extending our purview beyond the process of nation-state formation and thus allowing a slight digression from the main topic of this book, we also discuss a second major transformation in the nature and number of states in the past 200 years: the expansion of empires during the nineteenth century, which swallowed most of the non-Western world except Nepal, Bhutan, Ethiopia, Thailand, and China. This chapter thus pays attention to the two most important processes of institutional transformation in the modern world and the wars associated with them: the shift from hereditary kingdom, tribal confederacy, or village societies to empire, and the shift from empire to nation-state that followed subsequently. The large majority of states and populations – with the exception of Western Europe – was first incorporated into empires before transitioning into nation-statehood, and we focus on this by far most frequent historical trajectory here – in line with the global purview of this book.

This chapter therefore focuses on the institutionalist part of the overall argument. It shows that periods of institutional transformation are much more war-prone than periods of institutional stability because the stakes in the political struggles are particularly high and escalation into armed conflict therefore more likely. Its main goal is to empirically show that there is indeed a systematic association between imperial incorporation and nation-state formation on the one hand, and war on the other hand. The next chapter will then zoom in on one part of this broader picture and investigate more closely the power configurations that trigger civil wars once nation-states have been established.

1.2 Long-term processes

That empire building and nation-state formation are major sources of war can only come to the foreground if we look at long-term processes that unfold over extended stretches of time. Research on both inter-state war and civil war, however, has moved away from the preoccupation with such slow-moving, macro-level transformations and toward a detailed analysis of faster-moving decision-making processes involving key political actors, often at the sub-state level. In the international relations literature, the once prominent long-wave theories of war sought to explain the periodic recurrence of world wars as a consequence of global economic cycles stretched over six decades (Goldstein 1991) or of the century spanning rise and fall of global hegemons (Modelski and Morgan 1985; Thompson 1988). Although there is no doubt that the past two centuries have seen several such global wars involving the major power centers of the world, most researchers now recognize that they do not follow a clear pattern of periodicity. In other words, there are no cycles of a uniform length between global wars, and the search for such regularities has now been largely given up (including by its most prominent early proponents, see Levy and Thompson 2011). The related issue of whether multipolar or bipolar global distributions of power are more war-prone, once hotly debated between various strands of "realism," has similarly been abandoned, perhaps because the N in such global-system-level analysis is so small that no firm conclusions can be reached (see most recently Bennett and Stam 2004).

The current focus in international relations research has thus shifted to the decision-making processes within states or the nature of pairs of states that make them more war-prone. While many approaches continue to use data that cover vast stretches of time, they are mostly concerned with processes that unfold over a handful of years, not decades. In the debate over whether recently democratized states are more war-prone (Mansfield and Snyder 1995), for example, democratization is conceived as a short-term process – operationalized as a democratic transition in the past five years. Perhaps the only systematic exception to this trend toward the short-term are certain strands of rivalry theory, where pairs of countries are pursued over decades and the history of past engagements and confrontations is shaping contemporary inter-state relations in path-dependent ways (Senese and Vasquez 2008).

In the civil war literature, a similar move toward faster-moving processes at ever more disaggregated levels of analysis can be observed. In the most prominent quantitative study in the field, the effects of independence are studied over a mere two years (Fearon and Laitin 2003). Other scholars have begun to assemble ever more fine-grained datasets, including detailed civil war event histories that decompose a civil war into various battle episodes, each with the exact dates when they occurred (Raleigh and Hegre 2005), or studies of war theaters at the regional level, allowing the location of battle events in grid cells of 100 km^2 (Buhaug and Rød 2005; Aas Rustad *et al.* 2010). Long-term processes of political development or of the transformation of principles of statehood play only a marginal role in the contemporary study of civil war.

This chapter revitalizes the macro-political perspective by examining processes that unfold over the span of decades rather than across a handful of years or months. In contrast to long-cycles theory and classical realism, however, I do not conceive of the globe as an integrated system, nor as a single unit of observation, but rather as an arena for the discontinuous diffusion of institutional forms. To be sure, revitalizing the macro-historical tradition in the study of war represents a complement, rather than an alternative, to mainstream lines of research. Many of the war-generating factors identified in the recent literature are indeed important to understanding the conditions under which political conflict may develop into full-scale war, remain virulent over time, or give way to the possibility of peace. These factors include political instability at the centers of power (Fearon and Laitin 2003), the availability of natural resources to support warring parties (Ross 2004), a specific dynamic of rivalry that may lead states to fight each other on the battlefield (Vasquez and Leskiw 2001), various mechanisms which make autocracies more prone to inter-state war than democracies (Levy 1998), and so forth. Our approach helps to understand at what point along the long-term history of institutional transformations political tensions are likely to build, allowing these other war-promoting factors to come into play.

1.3 Beyond methodological nationalism

In order to be able to observe the conflictual consequences of empire building and nation-state formation, we need to go beyond existing datasets. The standard units of analysis in international relations and comparative political research are existing independent states, which are treated as continuous and comparatively stable entities once they enter the global system. According to this view, what varies is the power distribution between or within states, not their institutional nature. And the process of their emergence or disappearance is given only scarce attention (Maoz 1989). Conformingly, standard country–year datasets exclude those parts of the world that are not governed by independent states – still more than half of the globe by 1900, as we have seen in Figure 1.1. From such a restricted perspective, we therefore cannot observe the *consequences* of macro-institutional transformations such as the colonization of the world in the nineteenth century or the shift to the nation-state during the twentieth.

To overcome these difficulties, we again created a dataset with fixed geographic territories as units of analysis, independently of whether a territory is part of an internationally recognized independent state. By relating each territory's conflict history to its history of institutional change over a 200-year period, we are able to identify a recurring pattern: the likelihood of war is highest during the two institutional transformations that have so dramatically reconfigured the political landscape of the modern world. We thus bring the world of empires and the entire period of colonial domination into the analytical horizon of quantitative research. And we can show that nation-state formation is itself a major cause of war over the past 200 years.

1.4 Civil and inter-state wars

A final contribution of this chapter is to further attenuate the entrenched segregation between students of civil and international war. The literature has until recently overlooked possible linkages between domestic and international conflict (as noted by Gleditsch 2007; Levy and Thompson 2010: 3, 103) apart from the realist assertion that states weakened by civil wars might become easy prey for rivaling states or that domestic political war might be diverted to international conflict to profit from the rally-round-the-flag effect (Davies 2002). More recently, Gleditsch *et al.* (2008) have shown that domestic civil war is a good predictor of conflict between neighboring states. States meddle into each other's civil wars in retaliation for rebel support by the neighboring government or to influence the outcome of the civil war. Their engagement is thus not merely opportunistic in nature or the result of a diversion effect.

While we build on this new strand of research, we also go one step beyond merely establishing the fact that states are (self-)interested in the outcome of their neighbors' domestic conflicts. The following analysis will suggest that both inter-state and civil wars have the same causes: both are associated with the transformation of principles of political legitimacy and the corresponding changes in the number, institutional makeup, and territorial extension of states.

2 FROM EMPIRES TO NATION-STATES: AN INSTITUTIONALIST ARGUMENT

This institutionalist argument will now be outlined in greater detail by discussing the various mechanisms that link empire building and nation-state formation to war. Before I do so, however, a short definition of empires, nation-states, and other polities is in order, as well as a brief account of the history of their mutual displacement over the past 200 years. This will add some more nuance and detail to the historical sketch offered on the first pages of this book.

2.1 Imperial expansion and nation-state formation, 1816–2001

Following Eisenstadt (1963: 10–24), Howe (2002: 13–20), as well as Burbank and Cooper (2010: 8–17), empires are characterized by centralized bureaucratic forms of government, the domination of a core region over peripheries, an ethnically or culturally defined hierarchy between rulers and ruled, and claims to universal legitimacy – whether referring to a revolutionary ideology as in the Soviet Union, to a *mission civilisatrice* as in colonial empires, or to religious conversion as in Spanish Latin America.[2] Nation-states are also based on centralized

---

[2] Note that we exclude "informal empires" (Mann 2006) such as the contemporary United States or the dispersed hegemonic "empire" of Hardt and Negri (2000) from our definition, since these are not politically coherent entities. Note also that following the territorial logic of the analysis,

bureaucratic forms of government, but are ruled uniformly without an institutionalized differentiation between core and periphery, embrace the principle of equality of citizens (replacing hierarchy), and govern in the name of a bounded national community rather than some universal principle.

Dynastic kingdoms also govern through centralized bureaucracies, but lack the center–periphery structures and the universalist forms of legitimacy of empires.[3] In contrast to nation-states, such absolutist states are not based on the equality of all citizens, and ruled in the name of dynasty, rather than a nation.[4] Feudal states, tribal confederacies (e.g. the Sanusi of Libya), city-states (e.g. Switzerland before 1848), and patrimonial empires (e.g. the Tukulor or Mongol empires) all lack centralized bureaucracies.

At the time of the Congress of Vienna in 1814/1815, empires ruled over roughly half of the world's surface, while "other" political systems such as tribal confederacies, city-states, or dynastic kingdoms controlled the rest of the globe, as we have seen in Figure 1.1. In 2001, modern nation-states governed almost the entire globe. The two centuries in between tell the story of a struggle between empire building and nation-state formation. Empires replaced "other" forms of governments during the nineteenth century, mostly due to the expansion of Western colonial empires in Africa and Asia, but also because the Romanov empire swallowed the khanates of Central Asia. At the same time, empire was replaced by nation-states in the Western hemisphere, most importantly all over Latin America. The expansion of empires during the nineteenth century does not match, however, the dramatic proportions of their decline during the twentieth century, when the nation-state form spread across the globe, as discussed in the previous chapter.

2.2 A long-term, institutionalist model of modern war

Why should these two institutional transformations – empire building and nation-state formation – cause war? In the previous chapter, we considered

we code the political institutions governing a particular territory, not those of entire states. The territory of Great Britain is classified as a nation-state, even though it was the core of a colonial empire. The territory of the contemporary United States is a nation-state, although Guam is governed according to imperial principles.

[3] In contrast to Eisenstadt (1963: chapter 1) and in line with Howe (2002) as well as Burbank and Cooper (2010), we exclude the absolutist kingdoms and principalities of Western Europe from our definition of empire. It makes little sense to assign Württemberg before Bismarck or the Papal State before Garibaldi to the same category as imperial China or the Spanish empire.

[4] As already discussed in the previous chapter, we assume that the difference between nation-states and dynastic kingdoms asserts itself even if both are ruled autocratically. The dictators of nation-states such as Idi Amin cannot rule in the same way as Louis XIV. They cannot evoke dynastic legitimacy, but instead have to show that their government benefits "the people," for instance, by expelling Indian traders as "parasites" from the national home. Louis XIV, by contrast, revoked the edicts of Nantes not so much to protect the national majority, but because he saw the presence of heretics among his subjects challenged his God-given might.

wars as an independent variable. They weakened pre-national regimes such that nationalist forces were be able to capture government and create a nation-state. We have seen that both nationalist and non-nationalist wars can facilitate nation-state formation in this way. In this chapter, wars represent the dependent variable, and we show that the diffusion of nationalism and the nation-state themselves cause wars. Before we get into the details of this argument, let us first describe its general contours.

Following the theory outlined in the introduction, we assume that wars are particularly likely if the most basic institutional principles of political legitimacy are at stake: the informal and formal rules that determine who legitimately can lay claim to governmental power and what the legitimate borders of a polity should be. It is thus a genuinely political understanding of war in which economic interests or military-technical feasibility play a secondary role. From this perspective, war does not result from the anarchic nature of the international system (as in realist theory), from the rise and fall of global hegemons, or from revolutionary class conflict, but from the struggle between competing projects of state-building based on different principles of political legitimacy.

But isn't it self-evident, a realist might object, that creating new states or absorbing existing ones into an expanding empire will be accompanied by war – independent of the institutional transformation process? This potential misunderstanding needs to be addressed early on. First, where wars do coincide with the creation or destruction of states, these territorial changes are the consequence of the institutional transformation process, rather than a separate causal mechanism. A new principle of political legitimacy implies a new definition of those that should legitimately be included in the territory of a state and those that should not, as we will see in a moment. Attempts to create new states or destroy existing ones are therefore part and parcel of the fight over the institutional form of the state. Second, most of the wars fought over the past 200 years were not associated with the creation or absorption of states, as we show in greater detail later. This is true for most civil wars as well as for many inter-state wars. Third, and conversely, not all territorial expansions and contractions of states are automatically associated with war. A study by Diehl and Goertz (1988: 115) shows that only one-fourth of all territorial changes in the world state system from 1816 to 1980 have involved some violence. Without offering any systematic evidence here, we suggest that those border changes associated with empire building or nation-state formation are more war-prone than other territorial changes.

2.3 Imperial incorporation and war

What are the causal mechanisms that link imperial expansion and nation-state formation to war? We briefly discuss imperial incorporation first. Empires are defined, as discussed above, by center–periphery relations, hierarchical inclusion, and claims to universal legitimacy. They therefore know no natural borders and may potentially cover the entire globe to bring civilization, Christianity, Islam, or revolutionary progress to all of humanity. As mentioned in the introduction, empires therefore show an institutionalized drive to expand their domain through conquest, even if at high military, political, and economic costs, and irrespective of the ethnic composition of the population of the new territories. Claims to universal legitimacy make the extension of the imperial domain a benchmark for judging the success of the military-political elite. Moreover, the center–periphery structure allows for easy incorporation of newly conquered populations. They are simply added as new pieces to the ethno-national mosaic and henceforth ruled indirectly.

Local political units – tribal confederacies, alliances of city-states, feudal kingdoms – may resist imperial expansion and refuse to be "pacified" and "civilized" by the encroaching army and the imperial administration. A shift toward imperial principles of rule not only implies a loss of power, but also a delegitimation of the very institutional rules that allowed elites to struggle for and perhaps gain power. Tribal sheikhs, for example, risk losing not only military control over a territory once an imperial army starts to establish garrisons. The very possibility of gaining power by holding a centripetal alliance of clans together is undermined by the new bureaucratic system of administration. Similarly, bourgeois elites that were organized in city councils lose their political standing and capacity for forging alliances with other city-states once their government is incorporated as the lowest tier of the administrative and political apparatus of an empire far removed from the reach of elite councils.

Under conditions not specified by our model (such as military opportunities, a given distribution of resources between actors, etc.), tribes or city-states may choose to fight against expansionist empires. Once the crucial turning point is reached and a territory is governed according to imperial principles, the hinterland may continue to resist imperial expansion. When the entire territory is militarily subdued or "pacified," the process of expansion is complete and imperial peace should prevail, interrupted by occasional rebellions against higher taxes, violations of traditional rights, undue interference in local political affairs, or attempts by ambitious provincial governors to establish their own mini-empires by ceasing to pay tribute to the center.

2.4 Nation-state formation and war

The second institutional transformation starts with the spread of the major competing project of state building in the modern world: nationalism. The previous chapter has briefly analyzed the diffusion of nationalism, and we can thus treat it as an exogenous process here. Once nationalism has been adopted by significant actors in a political arena, the process of nation-state formation enters its first phase. During this first phase, we expect a higher likelihood of secessionist wars than during any other period of modern history. In the political order for which nationalist leaders aspire, each ethno-national group should govern itself, and the government in turn should be representative of the ethno-national makeup of the population. Imperial hierarchy is now reframed as an instance of "alien rule" under which human progress and individual liberty cannot ever be achieved. Many nationalist movements will thus encounter the resistance of imperial elites who stand no chance of being admitted to the new game for power, given that they are often of a different ethnic background than the local population.

Wars of secession against an imperial center are thus one road toward nation-statehood. We note again, however, that other roads are traveled as well. Absolutist dynastic states such as France, Japan, or Thailand, or alliances of city-states such as Switzerland, may transform into modern nation-states without significant changes in their territorial extension. In these cases, the struggle over the institutional shape of the state may lead to non-secessionist civil wars between representatives of the old order and nationalist contenders. Examples are the French revolution, the wars leading to the Meiji restoration, or the "war of the special league" in Switzerland.

Once the turning point is reached, the institutional logic of the nation-state creates further incentives for going to war, both between and within newly established states. Because the new state is now governed in the name of a nationally defined people (a "Staatsnation" in Meinecke's well-known terms), the new political elite tends to treat members of this "Staatsnation" preferentially. In other words, access to public goods and political participation are confined to members of the dominant ethnic group. This tendency is ubiquitous among modern nation-states because it results from the very incentive structures embedded in its principles of legitimacy: rulers now have to show that they represent and care for "the people." Ethnic favoritism is especially pronounced, however, in weak states with weakly developed civil societies. Such states lack the resources for universal provision of public goods as well as the non-ethnic political alliances on the basis of which more encompassing alliance networks could be built. This has been the topic of Chapter 2 and will be discussed in more detail in the following chapter. For the present purposes, it suffices to note that the differential treatment of individuals on the basis of their ethnic or national background now contradicts, from the point of view of those excluded from access to the state and its public goods, the fundamental institutional principle of ethnic self-rule.

This in turn increases the likelihood of both inter-state wars and civil wars. To protect co-nationals living across a state border from ethnic discrimination, state elites may be tempted to annex the corresponding territory in the name of "national unification" (as argued by Weiner 1971; Saideman and Ayres 2008). They do this to show their own constituency that they care "about our ethnic brothers" across the border and can act as legitimate representatives of the entire nation. In line with this reasoning, previous quantitative research has shown that the likelihood of inter-state wars increases significantly if such territorial and ethno-political conflicts emerge in a pair of countries (Huth 1996; Vasquez and Leskiw 2001), if irredentism (Carment and James 1995) or decolonization

(Mishali-Ram 2006) is the issue over which a foreign policy crisis emerges, or more generally if ethno-political actors are involved in the dyadic conflict between two states (Ben-Yehuda and Mishali-Ram 2006).

A basic factor affecting the probability of inter-state war during the process of nation-state formation is therefore the ethno-demographic makeup of a region. War is more likely if the new states contain substantial minorities that are majorities in neighboring states and thus have a "home-state" that is supposed to represent their interests and aspirations (Brubaker 1996; Miller 2007; for statistical evidence, see Woodwell 2004).[5] More precisely, and in line with our theory, Davis and Moore (1997) show on the basis of a cross-sectional analysis that pairs of states will see higher levels of conflict (including war) if an ethnic group is dominant in one state and dominated or mobilized in antigovernment protest in the neighboring state.[6]

The second factor is that inter-state war will be more likely if a neighboring territory is already involved in such a war.[7] Ethnic kinship relationships can motivate governments to protect their cross-border co-ethnics from the consequences of power shift that a war in the neighboring state might bring about. The neighboring government, in turn, may not tolerate such "outside interference" and tensions may escalate into another inter-state war. Unfortunately, we have no data on ethnic kin relationships across states,[8] but we can at least see if the postulated, spillover effect occurs.

We now turn to mechanisms that link nation-state formation to civil wars. The shift to the nation-state may lead to civil war when elites of excluded groups mobilize and attempt to overthrow and replace the ethnocratic regime by force,

---

[5] Woodwell also finds that two neighboring states in which the same ethnic group represents the majority are also more prone to develop conflictual or even violent relationships. However, this finding might well be an artifact of his coding scheme. Most Latin American states are described as having the same, Spanish-speaking ethnic group as a majority – though Argentineans and Chileans would be surprised to learn that their nations are considered ethnically identical even after 200 years of nation building. It is only slightly less problematic to code Arabs in the Middle East as one single ethnic group dominating most adjacent states in the region. Some other pairs of states with the same majority group (Germany, Korea, Vietnam) resulted from Cold War competition.

[6] Note that such irredentist wars over borders and territory are of a different nature than wars of conquest. The very logic of nationalist doctrine impedes modern nation-states from expanding much beyond the domains of their core ethno-national group, as noted in the introduction. This does not exclude the possibility that nation-states conquer territory for their own ethno-national core group. A (rare) case in point is the history of American westward expansion to fulfill its "manifest destiny."

[7] A review of the older literature on the spread of inter-state war is offered by Maoz (1989: 201–203). None of these existing international relations approaches consider nationalism as a major factor in the spread of inter-state conflict.

[8] Coding the ethnic makeup of all states and their neighbors for every year since 1816 would represent a challenging (and rewarding) data project that I hope someone will take on in the future.

or to secede and create a new state in which they would represent the national majority, or to join their co-ethnics in a neighboring state. The next chapter offers a much more detailed account of the different mechanisms leading to ethnic rebellions or nationalist secessions. Here, we limit the analysis to the political exclusion mechanism that underlines both secessionist and non-secessionist forms of rebellion. In contrast to empire, where ethno-political hierarchies were often seen as legitimate and God-given, they now appear as a violation of the "like-over-like" principles of legitimacy on which nation-states are supposed to rest. The spread of nationalism, in other words, is a precondition for rebellions against political domination by ethnic others (a point overlooked by Hechter 2003). Such rebellion was indeed quite rare before the advent of nationalism, even in directly ruled territories such as some of the French colonies.

Obviously, political mobilization against ethno-political inequality does not always lead to civil war. The analysis of this chapter specifies three major intervening variables, while the next chapter will offer more nuance. First, rich countries are characterized by less political exclusion since state elites can offer public goods to the entire population, thus depoliticizing ethnicity and leading to a process of endogenous nation building, as discussed in Chapter 2. Even if ethnicity is politicized and some groups excluded from state power, however, rich states find it easier to react to ethno-national protest through a policy of power sharing, affirmative action, or redistribution. In poor countries, state resources are scarcer and alternative sources of income are lacking, transforming competition over state revenue into a zero-sum game. Indeed, much empirical research finds that gross domestic product (GDP) per capita is one of the most robust factors in predicting civil war onsets (Sambanis 2004).

Second, different sources of state revenue have different effects on the structure of political alliances, which in turn affect war propensity. Oil resources in particular have been linked to an increased likelihood of civil war (Ross 2004; but see Sambanis 2004). Our model incorporates one of the explanations that have been brought forward in the literature (Humphreys 2005): state elites who do not depend on taxes but on oil rents may indulge more in clientelism than the governing elites of tax-dependent and resource-poor states. Ethnic clientelism in turn reinforces the dynamics of ethnic exclusion and competition leading to ethno-political mobilization and eventually civil war.

Third, civil war in one country are likely to affect relations between politically relevant ethnic groups in neighboring countries,[9] resulting in an escalation of political tensions into full-blown civil war there. Since we again lack data on

---

[9] Gleditsch (2003) shows that the likelihood of civil wars increases if an ethnic group stretches across the territories of two neighboring states (however, the results are not supported by Ellingsen 2000).

relations of ethnic kinship across states, we confine ourselves again to determine whether such spillover effects indeed occur.[10]

In summary, the transition from empire to nation-state increases the likelihood of both inter-state and civil wars because the institutional principles of legitimate government are at stake. Claims to universal legitimacy struggle against the demand of national self-determination, ethno-political hierarchy is delegitimized and portrayed as a violation of the principle of self-rule, and the realm of the state is reduced to the territory occupied by members of the nation. Nationalism, in other words, changes the rules of the political game and provides new incentives and motivations for the pursuit of power, including by violent means.

This model obviously does not attempt to explain all wars in the modern world, as indicated in the introduction. Revolutionary wars are not driven by the politics of nation building and ethnic exclusion. We thus expect that the likelihood of war recedes back to a baseline rate after the process of nation-state formation is completed, i.e. once the struggles over the ethno-national character of the state and its borders are settled, and ethno-political exclusion and hierarchy have been overcome. This may be reached through a stable, institutionalized arrangement of power sharing (as in the Swiss case), through a series of ethnic cleansings in civil and inter-state wars (as in Eastern Europe), or through successful nation building that achieves the nationalist dream of homogeneity through assimilation and the depoliticization of ethnic dividing lines (as in France). During this last stage of the process of nation-state formation, a post-hegemonic state embracing and affirming the "diversity" of its population may finally emerge.

2.5 Summary: institutional transformations and war

In summary, we expect the *ceteris paribus* likelihood of violent conflict to be highest near periods of institutional transformation, when the struggle over the institutional principles of government is most intense. Figure 4.1 summarizes this expectation. The likelihood of war is predicted to crest at the two turning points of the process of empire building and nation-state formation and to drop to lower levels of risk during periods of institutional stability. The result is a double inverted U-shape that resembles the back of a camel.

The model also predicts which type of violent conflict should be most likely during a territory's institutional transformations. Wars of conquest will be the most frequent type of war in territories undergoing the first transition, as empires replace other forms of governance. During the first half of the nation-state

---

[10] Sambanis (2001) finds that war in a neighboring state increase the likelihood of ethnic civil war much more significantly than the probability of non-ethnic civil war. For further statistical evidence of the "contagion effect" of ethnic conflicts, see Gurr (1993b: 181) as well as Lake and Rothchild (1998).

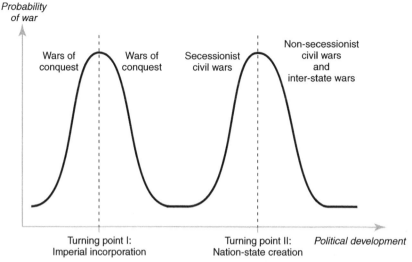

FIGURE 4.1 A stylized model of institutional change and war

formation process, secessionist civil wars against "alien rule" should be the dominant war type. After the turning point, non-secessionist struggles against ethno-political exclusion and wars between competing nationalizing states will be more frequent.

This model stylizes and simplifies complex historical event chains and thus describes a certain developmental pattern rather than a relationship between independent variables that affect stable units in a history-free space (Abbott 1998). This does not mean, however, that the model is not causal. During the first phase of the transformation process, wars *cause* institutional shifts (and are thus independent variables, as in the previous chapter), whereas in subsequent phases, wars are the *consequence* of this shift (and thus dependent variables). The model can be tested with standard methods by measuring institutional shifts independently from warfare and thus determining whether their temporal relationship follows the predicted patterns.

3 A NEW DATASET

To do this, we had to create a new dataset that records the outbreak of wars on all territories of the world over the past 200 years. We again used fixed geographic territories as units of analysis because only this would allow us to determine whether changes in the institutional form of governance are indeed related to the onset of war. If we took independent states as our units of observation, for example, such institutional shifts would be impossible to trace. You could not observe the wars associated with the expansion of the British empire in Africa and the creation of African nation-states a century later if you had only Great Britain as a state in your dataset during the nineteenth and first half of the twentieth century and if Uganda, Kenya, etc. only entered the data universe from the moment of independence onward. We thus departed from the standard country–year datasets and collected data for fixed geographic units both for the dependent variable (onset of war) and independent variables. This section describes the most important coding principles. More details can be found in Appendix 4.

3.1 Units of observation

As in Chapter 3, we used the world's states in 2001 as a territorial grid. Wars were coded as occurring on the territory of its major battlefields, defined, according to conventions in war research, as an armed conflict with more than 1,000 battle deaths. If colonial subjects rebelled against Her Majesty's government in what today is Kenya, the war is attributed to the territory of "Kenya," and not to the United Kingdom, of which Kenya was a part at the time of the rebellion. Episodes of nation-state creation or imperial incorporation also were attributed to individual territories.

Before we proceed to a description of the dataset, we note two possible objections to this choice of observational units. These are more specific than those discussed in the previous chapter because they relate to this territorial coding of wars. First, the war fought *on* a territory is sometimes not related to the political dynamics *of* that territory. The Russo-Japanese war, to give the most striking example from our dataset, was entirely fought on the territory of current China, and is thus attributed to "China" rather than to the territory of Russia or Japan, where the decisions of going to war were made. However, this is an exceptional case. Overall, our dataset contains less than a handful of wars for which the territorial coding logic leads to such problems of misattribution.

A second possible objection is that our units of observation are not independent of the causal processes we observe. The 2001 grid of states indeed has resulted partly from the past 200 years of war associated with empire building and nation-state formation. However, our explanandum is not the territorial shape of states, but rather the occurrence of war. That we observe this occurrence through a grid that is the result of future wars would be problematic only if wars fought in the future influenced the state of variables at present, which at least according to traditional Humean notions of causality is quite unlikely.

3.2 The war dataset

We invested considerable effort to create a reasonably complete war dataset (for more details, see Appendix 4.1). The starting point was the widely used war list assembled by the Correlates of War (COW) project. We first had to find and code wars that occurred in territories that were excluded from COW because they were not part of the international system centered on the West – in line with the traditional international relations view of the world. This limitation has been mostly overlooked by researchers who use the COW data (other problems are discussed by Sambanis 2004). Among territories not covered by COW are nineteenth-century Latin America, Central Asia before the Russian conquest, and the like. Our major sources were Richardson (1960), whose list of wars also provided the basis for COW's dataset; a detailed historiography of wars across the modern world (Clodfelter 2002); and a number of online sources such as onwar.com. We are confident that our new war dataset is reasonably complete, with the exception of some areas in pre-colonial Africa and Central Asia.[11] We also updated the list to 2001 relying on Gleditsch *et al.* (2002), and followed some of the revision of the COW dataset proposed by Gleditsch (2004).

We then added locational codes for all wars in our database so that wars could be assigned to one of the fixed territories. In the COW dataset, wars are attributed to states, independently of their actual territorial extension. Thus, COW codes a war in early twentieth-century Morocco as a French war because Morocco was part of the French empire.[12] Most of the information regarding the location of battlefields was collected from Clodfelter (2002).

Finally, COW's classification of wars depends on the status of actors within the Western state system – again in line with the traditional international relations perspective on the world. "Imperial wars" occur between a recognized state actor and an actor that is not part of that system (a tribe, an independent kingdom). A "colonial war" is fought between a recognized state actor and a non-state actor that is part of the system. "Inter-state wars" take place between independent system actors, and "intra-state wars" are waged between a state actor and a domestic non-state actor.

Because our units of observation are fixed geographical territories rather than actors, we had to come up with a new typology of wars that would be independent of the character of the actors involved. Our institutionalist model suggests that the aims of warring parties may change according to the institutional

---

[11] We guess that some of the following wars may have reached the 1,000-battle-death threshold: the wars among Yoruba states in pre-colonial Nigeria, the civil wars in Ethiopia and Afghanistan during the middle of the nineteenth century, the wars connected to Buganda's expansion in Uganda in the pre-colonial era, and the wars between the khanates of Central Asia before Russian conquest. Unfortunately, we were not able to gather reliable data on battle deaths and thus did not include them into the current version of the dataset.

[12] Sambanis (2004) discusses this problem and suggests another possible solution: to take the entire territory of an empire as the unit of observation. However, this would create difficult data problems, as GDP and other figures would have to be averaged over the entire empire. Furthermore, important differences in the living conditions – including human rights and democratic participation – of the "motherland" and the colonies would disappear from the picture.

incentive structures provided by different principles of legitimacy. We thus reclassified all wars according to a simple typology of war aims (for a similar typology see Holsti 1991: chapters 1 and 12).

According to this typology, war participants can fight for domestic power (civil wars) or to enlarge the power of the state vis-à-vis other states (inter-polity wars). Civil wars are subdivided depending on whether the participants try to establish a new independent state (secessionist war) or gain/retain control over an existing one (non-secessionist civil war). Inter-polity wars are subdivided into wars of conquest, which aim at the permanent incorporation of the territory and population of the enemy state, and inter-state wars, in which the balance of power between states is at stake and participants are not trying to absorb the enemy state completely. Coding depends on intentions rather than outcome: when secessionists fail to establish their own state, the war is still classified as secessionist. When conquest is successfully resisted, the war is nevertheless coded as one of conquest. The classification of wars into types is therefore independent from who won them. We dealt with the difficult coding problem of changing or conflicting war goals by focusing on the original intentions of the most important actor. Table 4.1 gives an overview of this new classification scheme. More details can be found in Appendix 4.1.

It should be noted that the definition of these war types is independent from our definitions of political systems. Indeed, all types of wars can occur in pre-modern states, in empires, and in nation-states, which is not to say that we expect them to be equally frequent.[13] Quite to the contrary, I have already argued in the introduction that institutional frames influence the political aims that actors pursue, including the aims of warfare, and that certain types of war are therefore more likely to occur in certain types of political systems.

To test the model, we had to determine when the turning points in the two processes of institutional transformation occurred in calendar time. For nation-state creation, we relied on the same definitions and data as the preceding chapter. With regard to imperial incorporation, we established the following coding rules (for more details see Appendix 4.2): as soon as a territory was effectively administered by an empire, or militarily controlled by a garrison, or legally made a protectorate or colony (whichever came first), we coded this as the year

---

[13] It may be useful to briefly illustrate this for inter-polity wars, for which the assumption could be more problematic. Inter-state or balance-of-power wars may occur between competing empires trying to snatch territory from each other, such as when the Romanov and the British empires fought over control of Afghanistan. But neither Britain nor Russia aimed at absorbing the entire territory of the other empire, as in a war of conquest. Inter-state wars also occur between city-states vying for control of trade routes (think of Venice and Genoa), between nation-states over disputed territory, between absolutist states, and between tribal confederacies. Wars of conquest have historically occurred between empires (e.g. the dismembering of the Ottoman empire by an assorted group of Western imperial powers during World War I), nation-states (e.g. the American conquest of the Dominican Republic), between city-states, and tribes.

TABLE 4.1 *A new war typology*

Wars between independent polities		Civil wars	
Wars of conquest	Inter-state wars	Secessionist civil wars	Non-secessionist civil wars
Expansion of state territory, permanent incorporation of new territories and populations; resistance against such expansion	Fight between states over borders and territory, regional hegemony (but without aim of permanent incorporation as in wars of conquest)	Fight against the political center with the aim of establishing an independent state; resistance against such independence by the political center	Fight between groups, at least one of which represents the central government, over domestic power relations, degree of autonomy of provinces or ethnic groups, tax burden, dynastic succession, etc.

of imperial incorporation. Note that a territory can experience various episodes of imperial incorporation or nation-state creation (as discussed in the last chapter). Examples include the current territory of Poland, which has gone through various partitions and imperial annexations, and the multiple nation-state creations that today's Croatia has experienced over the past 100 years.

We arrived at a dataset with 484 distinct wars, including 77 wars of conquest, 111 inter-state wars, and 296 civil wars, 109 of which were secessionist and 187 non-secessionist. The dataset includes 156 territorial units, 140 of which were incorporated into an empire at some point (92 during the temporal range of this chapter, 1816–2001), and 150 of which experienced nation-state creation. We use this slightly reduced set of 150 territories for all subsequent analysis, thus effectively excluding the dynastic kingdoms of the Middle East from our purview.

4 DISCOVERING THE PATTERN: TEMPORAL VARIATION IN WAR RATES

4.1 Rates of war around the two transformations

Figure 4.2 shows strong support for the main claim of this chapter: wars are indeed more frequent during the two periods of major institutional transformation that have characterized the modern world. We calculated rates of war onset

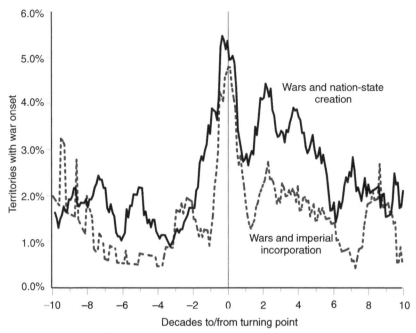

FIGURE 4.2 Rates of war relative to imperial incorporation and nation-state creation (ten-year moving averages)

for each year before, during, and after the two turning points by tabulating the number of territories at war versus those at peace. As in Figure 1.4 shown in the introductory chapter, the x-axis is made up of the years before and after a territory experienced either imperial incorporation or nation-state creation. It thus represents the institutional transformation clock for each individual territory, the year of the turning point being set at zero. The y-axis shows the percentage of territories in which a war broke out in a particular year before, during, or after these two transformations. We depict the war rates associated with the two transformations separately.

The dashed curve shows the rate of war as a ten-year moving average in relation to the year of imperial incorporation – excluding territories that were never part of an empire.[14] The wave pattern that we expect is clearly visible: the rate of war rises dramatically during imperial incorporation and is roughly twice as high at its turning point as in the decades that follow.[15]

[14] We also experimented with moving averages of 20-, five-, and one-year periods. The main pattern does not change.

[15] Almost half of the wars that constitute a second peak between 70 to 100 years after imperial incorporation consist of nationalist wars of secession, which already relate to the second

The solid curve shows how the war probability changes before, during, and after a nation-state was created, this time including all territories of the world except the six territories that were still not governed as a nation-state in 2001. Again, the pattern conforms to our stylized model. The rate of war increases sharply as territories move closer to the date of nation-state creation. Roughly speaking, wars break out twice as frequently during the immediate years around nation-state creation compared with several decades before or afterward. Even at this high level of aggregation, these graphs show that violent conflict does not occur at a uniform rate across time, and that there is a systematic pattern of temporal dependence that must be caused by some underlying mechanism beyond chance or randomness.

4.2 Rates of onset for different types of war

Our stylized historical model also made specific assumptions about the types of war that should be associated with different phases in the transformation process. We limit our focus to the transition to nation-statehood, which is at the center of this book.[16] Figure 4.3 confirms our expectations regarding inter-polity wars. Wars of conquest are less frequent once a territory is governed as a nation-state and thus conforms to the principles of legitimacy that diffuse and gradually acquire an uncontested hegemony in the modern world. These results confirm the findings of Strang (1991a): few states, once recognized as nation-states, have rarely been the victims of wars of conquest. The most prominent exception is the attempt by Nazi Germany to establish an imperial polity in Eastern Europe.

The frequency of inter-state wars rises dramatically around the time of nation-state creation – according to our argument of the "Macedonian syndrome" (Weiner 1971) of irredentist claims on the territory of neighboring states – and drops steadily throughout the century after the nation-state has been created. The war rates for secessionist wars show a dramatic peak immediately before nation-states are formed, conforming exactly to our model. Secessionist wars are much less likely once a nation-state is established and the nationalist principle of legitimacy has been established.[17]

---

transformation, to nation-statehood. It may be useful to note here that the picture is not distorted by the fact that our war data start in 1816 only, whereas many territories have been incorporated into an empire centuries ago. A graph that includes only territories that became part of an empire for the first time after 1816 displays the same pattern (not shown here).

[16] For the imperial incorporation process, the number of observations is too small to produce a significant pattern for most war sub-types and years. Still, the peak in the probability of war is mostly related to wars of conquest – just as our model assumes. These become gradually less likely after incorporation and are no longer significant 40 years thereafter. After incorporation, civil wars and inter-state wars occur from time to time, in the random pattern our model predicts.

[17] In contrast to the analysis of the preceding chapter, this finding relates only to conflicts that directly brought about the foundation of the nation-state in question. In the previous chapter, I showed that

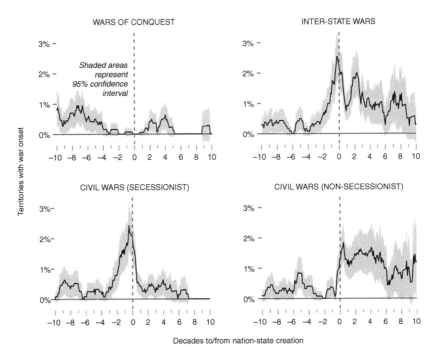

Territories with war onset

FIGURE 4.3 Nation-state creation and types of war (ten-year moving averages with 95 percent confidence intervals)

The pattern for non-secessionist civil wars is more complex. As we expect, the rate rises from an average of 0.4 percent in the years between −150 to −10 to nearly 2 percent immediately after the creation of a nation-state. According to our model, this results from the struggles over the ethno-national distribution of power that the shift to the modern nation-state often brings about. We were surprised, however, that war rates did not decline more steeply once nation-states had been created. After two generations, the conflict potential of nation-state formation should have been absorbed through secession, ethnic cleansings, or institutional accommodation such as power sharing, federalization, or minority rights (McGarry and O'Leary 1993). At closer examination, the civil wars beyond 100 years after nation-state creation are almost all revolutionary wars in Latin America (e.g. the *cristero* rebellion in Mexico, the "dirty" wars in Argentina and Chile, the *sendero luminoso* rebellion in Peru), as mentioned briefly in the introduction.

---

wars fought *outside* of a territory, but *within* the same empire, weakened its capacity to resist nationalist forces and thus helped the latter's rise to power. I also mentioned that non-nationalist wars on a territory facilitated the creation of nation-states. These two effects are obviously different from the direct causation that we are looking at here.

In general, Latin America's civil wars are not well captured by our model. In many countries on the continent, large shares of the population were excluded from state power on the basis of ethnicity. This was (and often still is) the case for the Amerindian population in Peru, Bolivia, Ecuador, Guatemala, and Mexico, as well as the black populations in many former plantation societies. But few of the civil wars were instigated by rebels with an ethno-nationalist political program – even though many recruited heavily among the excluded population. The pathways leading to revolutionary civil wars – not covered by our theoretical model – seem to be traveled with considerably higher frequency in Latin America than elsewhere, for reasons beyond the scope of this chapter. Suffice to note here that if we were to exclude Latin American territories from Figure 4.3, the war rates would indeed decline to a baseline probability after 60 years, as our model predicts.

While the patterns of war described in this section generally conform well to the model, they might be generated by other mechanisms unrelated to the shift from imperial or dynastic principles of legitimacy to nation-statehood. For example, the high number of civil wars after the creation of a nation-state might simply be due to the military weakness of newly established governments that are left without the fighting power of the imperial army – in line with Fearon and Laitin's (2003) "insurgency model" briefly introduced below. Alternatively, independence might bring about an economic crisis, which then triggers civil wars without any relation to new principles of legitimacy, incentives to fight ethno-political wars, and the like. The following two sections evaluate this possibility by controlling for other factors previously shown to be robust predictors of war onset. We again limit the focus to nation-state formation, and look at onsets of civil war and of inter-state war separately. We first introduce the variables to be included in the statistical models along with hypotheses of their expected effects.

5 VARIABLES AND HYPOTHESES

5.1 Testing the institutionalist model

To test whether war onsets are indeed related to nation-state creation, we use natural cubic splines (Beck *et al.* 1998). In the previous chapter, this technique[18] allowed the capture of possible effects of chronological time. We now use it for a different purpose: to determine whether the likelihood of

---

[18] Natural cubic splines are constructed of piecewise cubic polynomials such that the function, its derivative, and its second derivative are continuous at each of the specified knots. In addition, the spline function is constrained to be linear beyond the end points, simplifying their calculation. Splines are an efficient way to estimate non-linear time dependence, which can be traced easily using the estimated spline coefficients, as we will show later. We placed the three knots at the 10th, 50th, and 90th percentiles of the time-to-nation-state-creation variable. We tried alternate numbers of knots and locations but there were no major changes in the results.

war systematically depends on the timing vis-à-vis the year of nation-state creation. The splines offer an ideal way of achieving this because they can trace non-linear time dependency. We can thus test whether the relationship between time to/from nation-state creation and war probability indeed takes the shape of an inverted U.

As discussed above, other factors influence the probability of war and we need to take these into account in order to make sure that the nation-state formation hypothesis is evaluated correctly. First, the governments of rich countries might be less characterized by exclusion and in any case can afford to co-opt ethno-political protest movements through redistribution. We therefore expect per capita GDP to be correlated negatively with the likelihood of war. All our GDP and population data come from Maddison (2003), who offers the best available GDP estimates for the nineteenth century and full data for all territories except the Soviet and Yugoslav successor states from 1950 onward.

Second, we have argued that not only levels of development, but also its source matter. Oil-rich territories should have a higher probability of civil war than countries that rely on taxes for revenue generation because oil encourages rent-seeking behavior that reinforces ethnic clientelism and discrimination. To measure the impact of oil, we generate an oil production per capita variable based on historical data (Mitchell, various years).[19]

Finally, we construct a variable to test the spillover effects that our model postulates. Ethnic civil wars in one territory tend to stir up tensions and civil wars in neighboring territories that harbor similar ethnic groups, and inter-state wars of an irredentist nature have a tendency to draw in other states that seek to influence the ethnic balance of power in their neighborhood. We counted the number of wars that were ongoing in any contiguous territory during the same or any of the preceding three years, and thus constructed a neighboring war variable.

There are other variables – not related to our model – that have been identified by various authors as crucial for understanding the dynamics of war. We have included the most robust (see Hegre and Sambanis 2006) or theoretically interesting ones and present them briefly below.

5.2 Other independent variables

According to the hegemonic cycles theory of Modelski and Morgan (1985) briefly mentioned above, inter-state wars occur during the transition from one world

---

[19] Most published studies (e.g. Fearon and Laitin 2003) use either a dummy variable for oil exporters or calculate the share of oil exports to GDP. However, a per capita figure represents an improved operationalization since it is not dependent on the strength of other economic sectors, as are the percentage of GDP figures, and the risk of collinearity is reduced considerably, as compared to dummies (cf. Humphreys 2005).

hegemon to the next.[20] We introduced dummy variables for phase of the hegemonic cycles that Modelski and Morgan identified and that should be associated with a different likelihood of war.

Democratic peace theory refers to the risk of war between dyads of countries (Russet 1993). It assumes that two democratic countries will not go to war with each other, whereas the likelihood of warfare between an autocratic and a democratic country is highest. Various specific mechanisms have been proposed to make sense of this relationship (see for example Bueno de Mesquita *et al.* 1999), all of which are outside of the purview of this chapter. To make the democratic peace hypothesis testable with our monadic territory–year dataset, we constructed an interaction variable between a territory's democracy indicator and the percentage of its directly contiguous neighbors that were also democratic. This means that we check whether the percentage of democratic neighbors affects the likelihood of inter-state war on a territory, *given* that it is itself a democracy.

Whereas democratic peace theory refers to dyads of established democracies, other models have related war to the *process* of democratization. As mentioned above, Mansfield and Snyder (2005a) maintain that societies experience a higher likelihood of inter-state war in the early stages of democratization because the nationalist spirit conjured up when power shifts to the people is channeled by politically threatened old elites toward the outside. Our regime type data are unfortunately not fine-grained enough to test this theory in a way that does full justice to their argument.[21] Still, all democratizing regimes will be situated somewhere between autocracy and democracy. Such "anocracies" should thus be more prone to go to war with their neighbors than either full democracies or autocracies.

Yet another group of authors have related democracy to civil wars. The "democratic civil peace" theory states that democracies should be able to solve internal disputes through the ballot. Autocracies on the other hand can prevent rebellions through ruthless repression. Civil wars should therefore be less likely in democratic and autocratic societies and thus – again – most likely in "anocracies" (Müller and Weede 1990).[22] All regime variables are based upon Polity IV data, and use the widely adopted cutoffs of +6 and −6 (on a scale that goes from −10 to

---

[20] Originally, the hegemonic cycles theory was supposed to explain only the major "system wars," such as the two world wars. However, as Pollins (1996) has shown, there is no reason to treat system wars and small-scale wars involving only two countries as principally different. Since hegemonic power is by definition global in its reach, its effects on conflict behavior should be the same for all states.

[21] For an empirical critique of the "dangerous democratization" hypothesis, see Narang and Nelson (2009).

[22] A number of quantitative studies have confirmed this so-called democratic civil peace argument (Ellingsen 2000; Hegre *et al.* 2001). Reynal-Querol (2002) and Sambanis (2001) arrived at similar results, but for ethnic wars only. All these studies, however, might be biased because their definition of "anocracy" includes periods of state-breakdown and conflict, as shown by Vreeland (2008).

+10 to identify democracies, autocracies, and anocracies). In addition, we created an anarchy category for territories with no central government (including years of interregnum).[23] Since Polity IV only includes independent states, we had to add new coding for dependent territories. Colonies were coded as autocracies since several test codings of individual colonies, using the Polity codebook, revealed that one would never arrive at an anocracy score. Dependent territories of land-based empires received the same score as the imperial center. Independent territories were coded as "anarchy" if they had no central government at all, "autocracy" if they could be classified as traditional states such as emirates, or "anocracy" in the case of elite democracies such as the Swiss confederation.

Fearon and Laitin's (2003) much-discussed "insurgency model" maintains that wars are not driven by questions of political legitimacy, but by military opportunity. If government forces are weak and disorganized, and if mountainous terrain allows rebels to hide and retreat, ambitious leaders will be able to organize a rebellion in whatever name: national liberation, fewer taxes, religious renewal, elimination of class oppression, or straightforward self-enrichment. We included a measure of mountainous terrain, previous regime change (which weakens the government vis-à-vis rebels), and change in the repressive capacity of government as control variables. The mountainous terrain data are adopted from Fearon and Laitin's dataset. Regime change in the previous two years is defined as any shift between regime types (e.g. from anocracy to autocracy or from anarchy to democracy), and the repressive capacity is proxied by the percentage change in the number of government soldiers (taken from COW data) relative to the average over the previous decade. Following Fearon and Laitin, we should expect rebels to descend from their mountain retreats and fight as soon as the military strength of the government decreases – especially when a departing imperial government leaves a military vacuum.

Finally, we included population size as an important control variable. A larger population simply offers more opportunities for fighting with each other, as the following thought experiment illustrates. Imagine a one-person country where the likelihood of warfare is necessarily 0 and contrast this with a world-state in which all wars would be counted as civil wars. Similar thought experiments could be made regarding inter-state wars. In this chapter, population size is thus included as a simple control variable, while the next chapter on ethnic conflict in independent nation-states will introduce a more substantial interpretation of the effects of population size.

6 TWO REGRESSION MODELS

Finding data on all of these independent variables becomes more difficult the further back in time beyond 1950 one moves, and it is especially difficult for

---

[23] This should take care of the coding problem mentioned in the previous footnote.

former colonies or the pre-colonial areas of the developing world. Still, we were able to create a dataset with a reduced set of independent variables (including time to nation-state creation, regime type, neighboring wars, and oil production) for all of the world's territories and years. Once we include GDP and population into the equation, the two most robust variables in the quantitative civil war literature, we have to drop almost half of the observations, excluding most of Africa and Central Asia before 1950, most of nineteenth-century Latin America, and pre-1870 Eastern Europe. However, the main results remain remarkably stable even if we reduce the empirical universe in such drastic ways, as shown in the following.

6.1 Civil war onsets

Table 4.2 presents a series of logit regressions on civil war onset.[24] The dependent variable is whether a new civil war breaks out in a specific territory and year (which is then given the value of 1) or if peace prevails (coded as 0). All models include natural cubic splines to test whether wars are more likely the closer a territory is to the year of nation-state creation.[25] We discuss three models. Model 1 has full data for all territories of the world from 1816 to 2001, while Model 2 includes only half of the observations because we now include the GDP and population size variables. Model 3 cuts the number of observations further, because we now only include territories that have data for the five years preceding the creation of a nation-state – thus avoiding the potential "truncation" problem to be discussed below.

The results demonstrate that even after controlling for a range of important independent variables and despite variations in the size of the samples analyzed, our main finding remains the same: the likelihood of war depends significantly on the time to/from nation-state creation. Simply looking at the coefficients of the spline variables, however, tells us little about the shape that this time dependency assumes. When is the likelihood of war onset highest and when is it lowest? To facilitate interpretation, we graphed predicted probabilities for each year relative to the turning point while other variables were held at their mean or modal values. Figure 4.4A presents the predicted probability curve calculated on the basis of Model 2, along with confidence intervals.

---

[24] Because standard errors are likely to be correlated for observations within territories, we specify the robust and cluster options to correct the standard errors.

[25] When we include splines defined as a function of calendar year in the civil war models, as we did in the analysis of nation-state creation in the previous chapter, they are insignificant. We thus proceed by focusing only on potential time dependence to nation-state creation. However, there is evidence of dependence on calendar time for inter-state war onsets. In addition to the splines for dependence on time to/from nation-state creation, we include a set of four hegemonic cycle phase dummies to account for calendar time period effects.

TABLE 4.2 *Explaining the outbreak of civil war (logit analysis)*

		Model 1[1]	Model 2[2]	Model 3[3]
Time to/from nation-state creation	Spline 1	0.0215[***]	0.0145[***]	0.0202[***]
		(0.0061)	(0.0042)	(0.0058)
	Spline 2	−0.0194[***]	−0.0205[***]	−0.0374[***]
		(0.0055)	(0.0057)	(0.0124)
Civil wars in neighboring territories		0.0902[***]	0.0529[**]	0.0541[**]
		(0.0172)	(0.0265)	(0.0261)
Regime type (compared to autocracy)[a,b]	Democracy	−0.3448	−0.0349	−0.0474
		(0.2860)	(0.2385)	(0.3170)
	Anocracy	0.1442	0.2657	0.0666
		(0.1801)	(0.2112)	(0.2900)
	Anarchy	1.1079[***]	1.2117[***]	1.2749[***]
		(0.4166)	(0.3778)	(0.4399)
Previous regime change[a]		0.6935[***]	0.6077[***]	0.6194[**]
		(0.1965)	(0.2082)	(0.2568)
Mountainous terrain (log)		0.26[***]	0.3326[***]	0.3081[***]
		(0.0633)	(0.0767)	(0.1157)
Oil per capita[a,c]		0.0317	0.146[**]	0.2098[***]
		(0.0498)	(0.0652)	(0.0672)
Population size (log)[a,b]			0.3029[***]	0.3335[***]
			(0.0566)	(0.0871)
GDP per capita[a,b]			−0.0003[***]	−0.0003[**]
			(0.0001)	(0.0001)
Previous change in army size[a]			−0.4475	−0.2234
			(0.2732)	(0.3264)
Number of observations		24,779	13,707	6,554

Notes: [1] All observations; [2] without most of pre-independent Africa, some nineteenth-century Latin America, pre-1870 Central Europe, some small territories; [3] excludes territories with no data for years before NSC. Continental dummies and constant not shown; Huber–White robust standard errors in brackets; * significant at 10%; ** significant at 5%; *** significant at 1%; [a] lagged one year; [b] in 1000s; [c] in metric tons.

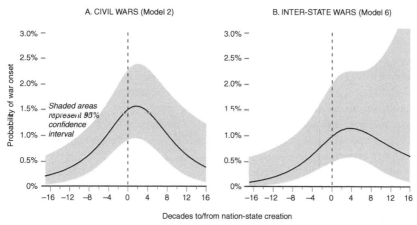

The graph confirms our theoretical expectations and the descriptive results presented in previous sections. There is a marked increase in the likelihood of civil war onset in the years around nation-state creation. The risk of civil war peaks in the second decade after nation-state creation, with new civil wars starting in 1.5 percent of territories. The risk of war is 25 percent higher than average in the 50-year window beginning in the decade before a nation-state has been created. Outside this high-risk window, the predicted rate of war drops off rapidly.[26]

How does this basic finding relate to the existing literature on civil war? It is certainly consistent with Fearon and Laitin's (2003) study, which finds that the odds of civil war onset is over five times higher in the first two years after independence than in the other post-independence years. They suggest that this supports their insurgency model of civil war because they suppose that the departure of the imperial army and the power vacuum of the immediate post-imperial period provide insurgents with an opportunity to rise up in arms. However, our results show that the likelihood of civil wars increases already well *before* independence, when the imperial army is still firmly in place. Their "new state" argument thus captures only a very small part of the temporal relationship between the formation of nation-states and the odds of civil war. Furthermore, a change in the size of the government's army does also not significantly affect

---

[26] This pattern of time dependency is basically the same for the other regression models (figures not shown). We also ran Model 1, for which we do not have significant missing data, for different cohorts of territories that became modern nation-states during the same time period, usually because they emerged from the same empire. The results (not shown here) demonstrate that with the exception of the Latin American cases of the first half of the nineteenth century (for reasons discussed above), all cohorts display a strong and stable pattern of time dependency.

the likelihood of civil wars (Models 2 and 3). Civil wars don't seem to be mostly a matter of the repressive capacity of the state.

To further explore the insurgency model, I conducted some additional analysis on secessionist wars before independence. It turns out that they are not more likely if the military capacity of the empire decreases or if its overall share of global economic and military power declines (results not shown). They thus cannot be interpreted as merely opportunistic reactions to a weakening imperial grip on power, but are driven by the power of nationalist ideologies. To be sure, whether the imperial elites indeed put up a fight and whether nationalists are willing to take up arms also depends on the power configuration between them, as additional analysis shows: nationalist wars of independence are less likely the larger the absolute share of global power of the center (to be distinguished from change over time) and if a territory had already gained independence before and was subsequently reintegrated into empire. Both discourage nationalists to take up arms. On the other hand, they are more likely to do so the longer they have already decried "alien rule" and mobilized the population.[27]

Let us now explore how the other variables in the model affect the outbreak of civil wars. In all the three models, the civil-war-in-a-neighboring-territory variable significantly increases the chances of civil war in the territory under consideration, consistent with our argument that ethno-national struggles in one territory often spill over into neighboring territories. Closer investigation shows that nationalist wars of independence are responsible for much of this spillover effect (results not presented). This confirms the analysis of the preceding chapter, according to which nationalist movements spread from territory to territory, leading to a concatenation of armed struggles against the imperial center. Also consistent with our expectations, we find that oil resources increase the risk of civil war. The results become more significant the more observations of the pre-oil era are dropped. The regime variables show no support for the democratic civil peace hypothesis: anocratic territories are not more likely to see civil wars than autocracies – the omitted category with which all three others are compared.[28] Conditions

---

[27] These findings contrast with those of Diehl and Goertz (1991): a military confrontation is more likely if the imperial center has recently lost some of its global power; the more of its dependencies have already become independent; the more independent states exist in the world as a whole (legitimizing decolonization); and the more economically important the dependent territory is for the center. This latter argument cannot be evaluated with the dataset used in this chapter. None of the other variables identified by Diehl and Goertz affect the likelihood of nationalist wars of independence in my models. Maybe this is because they do not seem to include controls for chronological time, which would quite likely make the total number of independent states in the world insignificant. They also operate within a different universe of cases, referring to successful secessionist wars only and without considering the breakup of Yugoslavia and the Soviet Union.

[28] These findings stand in contrast to much of the quantitative literature. As mentioned in a previous footnote, this is because most other research clumps together all mid-range Polity scores into an anocracy category, including years of interregnum (Vreeland 2008). To avoid this problem, we assigned interregnum years to the "anarchy" category.

of anarchy and instability following a regime change are closely related and are both positive and significant, as Fearon and Laitin's insurgency model predicts.

In Models 2 and 3, we also control for population size and per capita GDP. As mentioned previously, we have to drop observations for much of pre-1950 Africa and Central Asia as well as much of nineteenth-century Latin America and Eastern Europe because very little time-series data exist for these regions of the world. Population is positive and significant across all models, confirming that territories with larger populations have a higher risk of civil war. Consistent with the entire empirical literature on civil war, we find poverty to be a significant predictor of civil war onset. According to our interpretation, this is because the governments of richer territories are characterized by less exclusionary power structures and can react to ethno-political protest with redistribution and co-optation.

In Model 3, we test the robustness of our findings by dropping all territories for which we lack data, on any of the independent variables included in Model 2, for the five years preceding the creation of a nation-state. In this way, we make sure that there is no problem of "left truncation": it could be that our results are distorted because for many territories, we only have observations for decades *after* they became modern nation-states, but no data on the period *before* that. Even after dropping 73 territories for which we lack pre-nation-state data, there is no major change in the results.[29]

6.2 Inter-state war onsets

Table 4.3 presents results from a similar analysis, but with the outbreak of inter-state wars as the dependent variable. The territory–year structure of the data-set is not ideally suited for analysis of inter-state wars because studies that use dyadic datasets routinely show that country-level attributes do not explain war as well as the characteristics that describe country pairs. We conduct our analysis with the modest aim of suggesting plausibility for our model and to encourage future tests using dyadic research designs.

To see whether the likelihood of wars between states depends on the stage in the process of nation-state formation, we again use natural cubic splines created as functions of the years to the creation of a nation-state. Model 4 includes independent variables for which we have data covering the entire globe from 1816 to 2001. Model 5 adds control variables, which again results in the loss of many observations including those for pre-independent Africa, much of nineteenth-century Latin America, and pre-1870 Central Europe. In both

---

[29] Some right-hand truncation remains, it should be noted, because we do not observe patterns of war and peace that have not yet occurred in the recently founded states of the former communist bloc.

TABLE 4.3 *Explaining the outbreak of wars between states (logit analysis)*

		Model 4[1]	Model 5[2]	Model 6[3]
Time to/from nation-state creation	Spline 1	0.0162***	0.015***	0.0121
		(0.0047)	(0.0056)	(0.0076)
	Spline 2	−0.0115**	−0.0157*	−0.0083
		(0.0046)	(0.0087)	(0.0108)
Inter-state wars in neighboring territories		0.2013***	0.155***	0.1026*
		(0.0288)	(0.0379)	(0.0600)
Regime type (compared to autocracy)[a]	Democracy	0.145	0.6493	0.4428
		(0.4020)	(0.3566)*	(0.4150)
	Anocracy	0.5704***	0.425*	0.1353
		(0.1868)	(0.2518)	(0.3523)
	Anarchy	0.8547**	1.0649**	1.393***
		(0.4196)	(0.5419)	(0.4974)
Democracy x % democratic neighbors[a]		−3.0307*	−6.8142***	−8.7757***
		(1.5851)	(1.9310)	(2.8671)
Previous regime change[a]		0.1201	0.1225	0.5017
		(0.2487)	(0.2617)	(0.3128)
Population size[a,b]			0.2878***	0.3212***
			(0.0710)	(0.0682)
GDP per capita[a,b]			−0.0002*	−0.0002*
			(0.0001)	(0.0001)
Previous change in army size[a]			0.3082*	0.4606**
			(0.1726)	(0.2022)
Hegemonic cycle phases (compared to hegemony)	Delegitimation		−0.4218	0.3074
			(0.3355)	(0.4133)
	Deconcentration		−0.122	0.1105
			(0.3943)	(0.5646)
	Global war		0.27	0.7798
			(0.3472)	(0.5163)
Observations		26,307	14,511	7,169

Notes: [1] All observations; [2] without most of pre-independent Africa, some nineteenth-century Latin America, pre-1870 Central Europe, some small territories; [3] excludes territories with no data on the five years before NSC. Continental dummies and constant not shown; Huber–White robust standard errors in brackets; * significant at 10%; ** significant at 5%; *** significant at 1%; [a] lagged one year; [b] in 1000s.

models, the signs and significance of the spline coefficients are as predicted, tracing out an increase in wars during the years approaching nation-state creation, followed by a decline afterward. Model 6 includes only the 76 territories for which we have data on all independent variables in the five-year period preceding the creation of a nation-state, thus reducing possible truncation problems. The spline coefficients are no longer significant at standard levels, but the signs and relative magnitudes remain similar to those of the earlier models, suggesting that although the smaller number of observations contains too much noise for time dependency to emerge, the general pattern is consistent with our argument.

To make the spline coefficients easier to interpret, we again plot the predicted war probabilities to create Figure 4.4B, which is based on estimates from Model 5. The spline coefficients are only weakly significant, but the shape of the calculated war probability conforms exactly to our model. Together, the two graphs of Figure 4.4 suggest that similar historical processes might cause inter-state wars and civil wars, a possibility that is often overlooked in the specialized literatures. Struggles over the ethnic distribution of power in emerging nation-states can drive irredentist wars that extend across borders, just as they can drive secessionist wars and ethno-political conflicts within states. Conforming to this broad historical argument, we also find strong spillover effects for inter-state wars, as we did for civil wars: the fight over the ethno-national character of states may draw in neighboring territories populated by related ethnic groups.

What do the results reported in Table 4.3 tell us about other theories of inter-state war? The "dangerous democratization" hypothesis of Mansfield and Snyder (2005a) postulates that anocratic regimes are more likely to be engaged in inter-state wars than democracies or autocracies. Model 4 in Table 4.3 provides clear support for this argument: anocracies are more likely sites of inter-state wars than autocracies. The results are weakened but still significant when we control for per capita GDP in Model 5. As soon as we exclude territories with no data for the years immediately before a nation-state was created (Model 6), however, the association is no longer statistically significant. A more dynamic measurement of democratization – rather than using a static anocracy dummy – would represent Mansfield and Snyder's hypothesis in a more adequate way, and perhaps produce even stronger results (but see the reassessment of the hypothesis by Narang and Nelson 2009).

The democratic peace theory is tested with an interaction term between democracy in a territory and the percentage of democratic neighbors. It is significant in all three models, indicating that democratic territories are less likely to be attacked by – and to attack – other democracies. In contrast to our findings with regard to civil wars, a previous regime change does not increase the likelihood of inter-state wars. The population variable, included for simple control purposes, strongly influences the likelihood of inter-state war onsets. Also as expected, richer territories are less likely to be the arena of an inter-state war than poor territories. A prior increase in military personnel is associated with an increased risk of inter-state war, in line with the expectations of rivalry theory (Vasquez and Leskiw 2001), which hypothesizes that states with a history of saber rattling are likely sites of future inter-state war.

We find no support for Modelski's hegemonic cycle argument, which we test in Models 5 and 6 by adding period dummies, one for each of the four phases in the cycle. We omit the "hegemony" phase from the regression, during which the theory predicts peace, and thus effectively test whether the other three phases are indeed more war-prone than periods of the "hegemony." The results show that not even the "global war" phase is significantly different from "hegemony." More important than global constellations of power, it seems, are domestic institutional transformations that shape the incentive structures for political actors, including the motives and opportunities to pursue foreign policy ends with military means.

7 CONCLUSIONS

As much of other social science research, the study of war has been dominated by approaches that take the institutional form of the independent nation-state as given and exclude most other types of polities from analysis. Conformingly, existing scholarship has not paid much attention to the profound change in the nature of the units composing the international system and has only occasionally looked at the formation of new states as a source of war (Maoz 1989). In contrast, this chapter demonstrated that the emergence of the nation-state structure provides the macro-historical context within which an explanatory model of war should be situated. More generally, periods of transition from one type of political institution to another are much more war-prone than periods of institutional stability.

This perspective puts long-term political developments at the center of analysis and provides an important complement to established theories of war and peace. The "realist" international relations approach focuses on the anarchic nature of the international system (Waltz 1979) and investigates how the rise and fall of great powers (Gilpin 1981) within that system or specific distributions of military capabilities (Van Evera 1999; Mearsheimer 2001) and information (Glaser 1997) between two states entices them to go to war with each other. Alternatively, "liberals" have shown how institutionalized cooperation between states can overcome the implications of anarchy (Keohane 1984) and that democracies have fewer incentives to fight each other than autocracies (Russet 1993).

The "realist" focus on war-prone inter-state relations needs to be complemented by analysis of the transformation of the international system's constituent units. This transformation is itself a major source of war – quite independent of the distribution of capabilities between existing states. Furthermore, politics in the age of empires followed a different logic than politics in the current world of nation-states, and conformingly, the reasons for going to war also have changed considerably over the past two centuries, as shown in the introductory chapter (see also Luard 1986).

With regard to democratic peace theory, we postulate that basic principles of legitimacy beyond the varying degree of democratization affect how frequently and with which motives wars between states will be fought. To restate the point, empires behave differently toward other polities than do nation-states, and the transition from the former to the latter has redefined the political character of dyadic relationships between states, independently of whether these are governed according to democratic principles or not. This is most clearly illustrated by the finding that nation-states are rarely the objects of wars of conquest by others.

Our model also complements established findings in comparative politics. We confirm that political instability and oil resources do matter and make a territory more prone to civil war. Should we conclude that wars are primarily driven by military opportunities to rebel (Fearon and Laitin 2003) or by the greed for resource rents (Collier and Hoeffler 2000)? We have argued that larger processes of institutional transformation shape such military and economic incentives for war-making. These incentives represent circumstantial triggers that explain the timing of war – but are in themselves not a driving force comparable to the crisis of legitimacy that empires face once nationalists have successfully decried alien rule. As discussed above, nationalists have often instigated secessionist wars against an imperial center that had maintained a constant military capability to suppress rebellions. It is the lack of legitimacy, not military weakness, that makes empires vulnerable to secessionist war as soon as nationalist ideologies have gained a foothold on a territory. Once a nation-state is established, new incentives to protest and rebel and new opportunities to pursue ethno-nationalist goals in civil and irredentist wars are created. Oil resources, which can be distributed along ethnic lines and thus used to consolidate ethnic clienteles, provide further fuel for the dynamics of ethno-political competition and conflict, but they are perhaps not their primary cause.

Empire building and nation-state formation are thus two important sources of war in the modern world. While this chapter has established that this claim is empirically plausible, it has not provided much evidence for the mechanisms supposed to generate these associations. Is ethnic exclusion indeed the consequence of nation-state formation in weak states with weak civil societies – as argued in Chapter 2? And do ethnic wars break out where such ethno-political

exclusion is more marked and the like-over-like principle of nationalist legitimacy therefore more obviously and blantantly violated, as I have maintained?
The next chapter seeks an answer to these questions by investigating more
closely the dynamics of ethno-political competition, inequality, and conflict
after World War II.

5

Ethnic politics and armed conflict

This chapter shifts the focus back from the struggle over principles of political legitimacy to the power configurations that will make this struggle more
war-prone. After all, war remains a rare event even at the height of the process
of nation-state formation. Many territories transitioned into nation-statehood
peacefully (as the Baltic states in the 1990s) or remained peaceful after a violent
overthrow of the pre-national regime (as Switzerland). To empirically evaluate whether an exclusionary power configuration indeed explains the differences between violent and peaceful trajectories, we need to restrict the analysis somewhat so that the collection of high-quality data becomes feasible. This
chapter looks at the post-1945 period exclusively and examines civil wars only,
showing that they are more likely to erupt in countries with marked degrees of
ethno-political inequality. Compared to the previous two chapters, it also uses a
much more fine-grained coding of violent conflict that includes all armed confrontations that cost as few as 25 lives. Therefore, we are now interested both in
small-scale incidents of armed conflict as well as in the full-scale civil wars that
were already analyzed in the previous chapter.

This chapter is adapted from a journal article coauthored with Lars-Erik Cederman and Brian Min.
    we wish to thank the many individuals who have helped assemble the dataset on which this
chapter relies. While we cannot list all country and regional experts who have generously shared
their knowledge, we should like to at least mention Dennis Avilés, Yuval Feinstein, Luc Girardin,
Dmitry Gorenburg, Wesley Hiers, Lutz Krebs, Patrick Kuhn, Anoop Sarbahi, James Scarritt,
Manuel Vogt, Judith Vorrath, Jürg Weder, and Christoph Zürcher. Luc Girardin implemented
the software for the online expert survey. The data project relied on financial support from
UCLA's International Institute and the Swiss National Science Foundation through the project
"Democratizing Divided Societies in Bad Neighborhoods." I am grateful to Michael Ross as well
as audiences at the department of sociology of the University of Arizona, the Conference on
Disaggregating the Study of Civil War and Transnational Violence held at the University of Essex,
the Program of Order, Conflict, and Violence at Yale, the Mannheim Center for European Social
Research, the Graduate School for Public and International Affairs of the University of Ottawa,
and the Graduate Institute for International and Development Studies in Geneva for encouraging
comments and criticisms on an earlier draft of this chapter.

To test the political exclusion hypothesis, the chapter introduces a new dataset that records ethnic power relations in all countries of the world since World War II. The Ethnic Power Relations (EPR) dataset contains a yearly list of all politically relevant ethnic groups and their degree of access to executive-level state power – from total control of the government to overt political discrimination and exclusion. The EPR dataset overcomes the limitations of existing data compilations, especially the widely used Minorities at Risk (MAR) dataset, which contains information on disadvantaged minorities and is thus less suited to capture the dynamics of ethnic politics at the power center. The EPR dataset also improves upon conventional demographic indices of diversity that are only tangentially related to the ethno-political struggle over newly established nation-states, as will be discussed in more detail below.

This new dataset allows for a somewhat more complex and nuanced analysis of ethnic civil war than offered in the previous chapter. So far, I have argued that ethno-political inequality in new nation-states with weak state capacity and weakly developed voluntary organizations are more likely to experience civil wars. It is now time to broaden the analysis and consider other war-prone power configurations as well, thus adopting a multicausal mode of analysis. The chapter identifies two additional configurations that are associated with ethnic conflict. First, the larger the number of ethnic elites who share power with each other, the more likely their ongoing struggles over "fair representation" in government will escalate into a violent confrontation. The fear of being dominated in the future by competing ethnic elites who might renege on the current power-sharing arrangements makes such configurations especially conflictual. Second, a long history of imperial rule leads the populations in the peripheries to distrust and disidentify with the newly established state. The discontent of both excluded groups and power-sharing elites then takes on secessionist forms: to avoid political domination by ethnic others, founding a new state controlled by one's own ethnic elites appears as an attractive project worth fighting for. All three configurations can all be portrayed as violations of the like-over-like principle enshrined in the nationalist doctrine, leading actors into an escalating struggle over who symbolically owns and politically controls the nation-state.

This more fine-grained analysis follows in the footsteps of others in the quantitative literature who have emphasized that war has different causes (Sambanis 2001; Buhaug 2006). And indeed, one would not expect that an army coup in Brazil would have the same roots as the Maoist insurgency in Nepal, the Biafra civil war in Nigeria, or the conflict in contemporary Afghanistan. This chapter shows how such causal heterogeneity can be taken into account within the framework of a quantitative research design. Before I do so, a more detailed review of past research is in order.

I MAIN APPROACHES TO ETHNICITY AND ARMED CONFLICT

The quantitative literature on ethnicity and civil war struggles with two major problems. First, most empirical research tends to overlook such causal heterogeneity by assuming that a single set of processes is responsible for all ethnic conflicts – or even for all conflicts in general. Second and more importantly, the mechanisms linking ethnicity to armed conflict are specified in theoretically and empirically problematic ways. We first discuss this problem of specifying relevant mechanisms, focusing on three prominent schools in civil war research: greed and opportunity, diversity breeds conflict, and minority grievances.[1]

The most influential and often cited articles argue that civil war dynamics have nothing to do with ethnic exclusion, ethnic claims ("grievances"), ethnic diversity, or any other aspect of ethnicity. Conformingly, the increase in ethnic conflicts during the twentieth century – shown in Figure 1.2 – is not seen as a meaningful trend. It is simply due to the unfortunate tendency of both contemporary scholars and rebels themselves to attribute conflict to primordial ethnic identities – a collective delusion of sorts (Laitin 2007: 20–27). More important than ethnic identity or political exclusion along ethnic lines are the material and organizational incentives to stage a rebellion against government.

According to Fearon and Laitin's (2003) well-known insurgency model, briefly discussed in the previous chapter, wars erupt when governments are weak and rebels can hide from troops while recruiting unemployed young men. "Grievances" about a lack of political representation or access to public goods or more general doubts about the legitimacy of government are considered to be ubiquitous and thus cannot possibly help to understand rare events such as violent conflict. A constant, after all, is not able to explain a variable outcome. Similarly, Collier and Hoeffler (2004) maintain that civil wars occur where rebellions are most feasible, rather than where actors are facing ethno-political inequality or social marginalization. More specifically, lootable economic resources facilitate organizing and sustaining a rebel organization and thus explain where and when civil wars break out (see also Collier *et al.* 2006).

A second group of scholars insists on the opposite: that ethnicity *does* matter for conflict processes because diverse states experience more armed conflict. Different possible mechanisms have been highlighted by different authors. Some maintain that ethnic diversity contradicts the assumption of cultural homogeneity on which modern nation-states are based, thus triggering waves of separatist wars and ethnic cleansings (Gellner 1991; Nairn 1993). Vanhanen (1999), the most ardent proponent of the diversity-breeds-conflict argument, relies on a sociobiological theory of

---

[1] This review does not cover all existing approaches. The "horizontal inequality" argument, for example, posits that economic inequality increases the risk of armed conflict if aligned with ethnic cleavages (Stewart 2008). Quantitative evaluations of this claim produce a rather more complex picture (Cederman *et al.* 2011).

ethnic nepotism, according to which humans tend to favor kin and co-ethnics over others. As a result, more ethnically heterogeneous states will see more antagonism between nepotistic groups and thus more armed conflict. Finally, societies divided into a large number of ethnic groups face higher risks of ethnic war, Sambanis argues, because shared ethnicity decreases the organizational costs of building a rebel force (Sambanis 2001: 266; see also Easterly and Levine 1997).

These two positions – the greed-and-opportunity school and the diversity-breeds-conflict tradition – both rely on demographic diversity indicators to test their core propositions. Many use a linguistic fractionalization index, calculated as the likelihood that two randomly drawn individuals would speak a different language. This indicator is obviously quite unrelated to the political dynamics associated with ethnic conflict. First, not all ethnic groups matter for politics (Posner 2004; Chandra and Wilkinson 2008). Second, ethnic conflicts are not the outcome of everyday encounters between individuals; rather, they result from interactions between the state and ethno-political movements that challenge its authority (Cederman and Girardin 2007). A fractionalization index based on population demographics obviously cannot capture the nature of these political relationships.

Given these conceptual and measurement problems, it is not surprising that empirical studies produce conflicting results regarding the relationship between diversity and armed conflict. Some find that ethnic fractionalization does not explain war (which by definition costs more than 1,000 battle deaths per year) (Fearon and Laitin 2003; Collier and Hoeffler 2004). Others show that ethnic fractionalization is a significant factor when the dependent variable includes low-intensity wars as well (Hegre and Sambanis 2006) or if we focus exclusively on ethnic wars (Sambanis 2001) or secessionist armed conflicts (Buhaug 2006). Some find a parabolic relationship between ethnic fractionalization and the prevalence of civil war (Elbadawi and Sambanis 2000). Still others maintain that polarization between two equally sized ethnic groups, rather than fractionalization, best explains armed conflict (Montalvo and Reynal-Querol 2005).[2]

This chapter moves beyond these demographic indicators so far removed from how ethnicity works in political practice (Chandra and Wilkinson 2008). The EPR dataset brings us closer to the actual logics of ethnic politics by directly recording politically relevant groups and their access to executive state power. This allows us to test whether ethno-political inequality and thus "grievances" are indeed ubiquitous, as maintained by the greed-and-opportunity schools, or whether variation in the ethno-political power configuration is systematically associated with ethnic conflict. Once we account for the political dynamics of ethnic exclusion and competition, this chapter will demonstrate,

---

[2] Ellingsen (2000) finds support for both a linear association between conflict and fractionalization and a U-shaped association with polarization.

ethno-demographic diversity is no longer systematically associated with armed conflict.

The third major approach is the minority-grievance school. Its proponents analyze the relationship between ethnicity and armed conflict at the level of groups rather than countries. Gurr (1993a) explored the conditions under which ethnic minorities protest or rebel, including intense communal grievances and a political opportunity structure that facilitates political mobilization. Gurr and colleagues have also assembled a worldwide dataset on such "Minorities at Risk" (MAR). The MAR dataset has produced a quantum leap in the study of ethnic politics and has provided an invaluable service to researchers in political science (Saideman and Ayres 2000; Toft 2003; Walter 2006; Elkins and Sides 2007, among others) and sociology (Chai 2005; Olzak 2006).

Compared to the other two schools, the minority-grievance perspective undoubtedly comes much to the empirically observable mechanisms linking ethnicity to armed conflict and civil war. We thus incorporate some of its insights into the model of ethnic politics developed below. This research paradigm, however, is limited by the exclusive focus on disadvantaged minority groups. By "hard-wiring" the degree of access to central state power into the sample definition, the comparative horizon is limited to excluded groups, and ethnic groups in control of government therefore disappear from the picture. This makes it harder to capture the effects of political exclusion in unambiguous ways: one needs to compare excluded and included groups to effectively demonstrate how exclusion breeds conflict. Moreover, in many countries with dramatic shifts in power constellations over time (Chad, Afghanistan, Liberia), the political status of an ethnic group may change from discriminated minority to ruling elite from one period to the next. In other words, students of ethnic politics should treat representation within government as a variable rather than as a constant. Finally, focusing on demographic minorities overlooks the possibility that majorities – rather than minorities –suffer from political disadvantage as well, as the fate of Africans under the South African apartheid regime aptly illustrates.

Accordingly, the MAR coding scheme does not fit countries with ruling *minorities* or complex coalitions of ethnically defined elites, as in Nigeria, India, or Chad, where ethnic conflict will be pursued in the name of excluded majorities (rather than minorities) or of ethnic groups that share power (and are thus not "at risk").[3] Roughly half the observations in our dataset conform to such ethno-political constellations and thus escape the logic of the MAR

---

[3] The MAR project tries to address these limitations by including five "advantaged" minorities who *benefit* from political discrimination. MAR also codes some "communal contenders" (i.e. groups that share power with others while at the same time mobilizing in protest or rebellion), mostly in Africa (Gurr 1993b). However, ethnically defined elites that do not mobilize their constituencies in protest are omitted from the MAR dataset.

approach. By reducing its focus to the political mobilization of disadvantaged minorities – perhaps using the American civil rights movement as model – the minority-mobilization model therefore overspecifies the conditions under which ethnicity leads to armed conflict or civil war.

I conclude that neither of the three schools offer fully convincing analyses of how ethnicity relates to conflict. They either rely on a version of the ethnic diversity argument that is unrelated to the logic of ethnic politics, or they define ethnic conflicts too narrowly as a matter of minority mobilization. A second problem in the existing literature is that it conceives ethnic conflict as a unitary phenomenon caused by uniform factors.[4] Qualitative comparative work, however, shows how important it is to take different ethno-political constellations into account and that qualitatively different causal pathways lead to violence. The following four vignettes of well-known ethnic conflicts illustrate this point.

In Northern Ireland, the American civil rights movement had inspired segments of the educated Catholic middle class to mobilize against their long-standing political marginalization. The state apparatus, controlled by Protestant elites who ruled Northern Ireland as an internal colony of the British state, reacted with repression and intimidation. The ensuing escalation reinvigorated the Irish nationalist underground army, which fought to unite Northern Ireland with the rest of the country. This in turn led to the emergence of Protestant militias and terrorist groups opposed to the nationalist project (Bardon 2001).

In Bosnia shortly before independence, the leadership of the Serbian territories withdrew from the provincial government that they had shared with Croatian and Bosniak politicians. Mobilization for war proceeded quickly on both sides. Serbian militias, supported by the army of neighboring Yugoslavia, soon attacked Croatian and Bosniak villages that they intended to incorporate into the territory of a future Serbian state (Burg and Shoup 1999).

In January 1994, the now iconic *commandante* Marcos led a group of masked followers to the main square of San Cristóbal de las Casas and announced that the indigenous peoples of Chiapas and Mexico were no longer prepared to accept their fate as second-class citizens. He demanded profound constitutional, economic, and political change. Decades of political mobilization had preceded his rebellion, including by left-wing organizations fighting for land reform and by members of the lower clergy inspired by liberation theology. The central government reacted to this provocation by ordering the army to occupy indigenous villages that supposedly harbored members of the Zapatista guerilla. After a series of armed encounters, the Zapatistas eventually withdrew into the Lacandon jungle (Collier and Lowery Quaratiello 1994; Wimmer 1995a).

---

[4] The MAR dataset allows for a more disaggregated perspective by coding different types of ethnic groups. Gurr's (1993b) analysis, however, mostly focuses on the difference between peaceful protest and violent rebellion, rather than between types of groups.

In Iraq after the fall of Saddam Hussein, former Baathist officers and high-level functionaries joined tribal leaders from the Sunni triangle and foreign *jihadists* in a fragile alliance. They fought what they perceived as an illegitimate government controlled by Shiite apostates and Kurdish separatists. Opposing any federalization and power sharing on the national level, they dreamt of restoring the ethnocratic regime they once controlled. Meanwhile, factions within the Shiite bloc jockeyed for power, exploiting the unpopularity of the new government and its dependence on American military power. The Sadr Army harnessed the support of marginalized urban youth to oppose power sharing with Sunni and Kurdish political parties, advocating instead a strong, central state under Shiite command (Cole 2003; Wimmer 2003; Bengio 2004).

The factors affecting these four conflict histories and the mechanisms at play are quite different. While Irish Catholics and indigenous *Chiapanecos* represented excluded groups that mobilized against the state, representatives of Bosnian Serbs and Shiite Arabs were partners in coalitional governments. Serbian Bosniak elites and Iraqi ethno-religious factions faced a disorganized and ethnically fragmented state, while Catholics in Northern Ireland and the Zapatistas in Mexico opposed an entrenched state apparatus. The IRA and Bosnian Serb nationalists developed separatist agendas aimed at joining established neighboring states, while the Zapatistas and Iraqi groups focused on changing ethnic power relations within existing states. It seems doubtful that any single indicator can accurately grasp these different ethno-political dynamics. The power configurations are different, as are the mechanisms and logics relating ethnicity to armed conflict.

2 A CONFIGURATIONAL THEORY OF ETHNIC POLITICS AND CONFLICT

This section introduces a configurational approach that links such different ethno-political constellations via distinct causal pathways to specific types of ethnic conflict. Before we do so, we remind the reader that these various war-prone configurations would not have emerged without the previous politicization of ethnicity, which thus represents an important antecedent condition for any type of ethnic conflict.

As shown in the second chapter, central elites who command a great deal of public goods and decision-making power can make nation building an attractive option for regional elites and the population at large. The system of political alliances and exchanges therefore bridges ethnic divides and includes larger segments of the population, leading to successful nation building and the depoliticization of ethnicity.[5] By contrast, political closure will proceed along ethnic, rather than national lines in weak states where the central elites lack the

---

[5] For empirical evidence that successful nation building is associated with better public goods provision, see Miguel (2004).

resources for including all citizens into an encompassing alliance system, as well as in states with weakly developed networks of voluntary organizations where such non-ethnic channels for aggregating political interests and rewarding political loyalty are therefore scarce.

In weak states with weak civil societies, those holding political offices will favor co-ethnics over others when distributing public goods and government jobs; judges will apply the principle of equality before the law more for co-ethnics than for others; policemen provide protection for co-ethnics, but less for others; and so forth. The expectation of ethnic preference and discrimination works the other way too. Voters prefer parties led by co-ethnics, delinquents hope for co-ethnic judges, and citizens prefer to be policed by co-ethnics.[6] In such ethnically compartmentalized states, political leaders and followers alike have therefore good reasons to avoid dominance by ethnic others and to strive for self-rule or at least for getting as big a part of the state cake as possible. The aggregate consequence of these strategic orientations is a struggle over control of the state between ethnically defined actors – or ethnic politics for short (Rothschild 1981; Esman 1994).

2.1 Ethno-political configurations of conflicts

Under which configurations of power is ethnic politics more likely to escalate into violent conflict? To answer this question, we need appropriate conceptual tools to describe different configurations of actors and the power relations between them (see Figure 5.1). Relying on Tilly's (1978, 2000) polity model, we distinguish between various politicized ethnic groups that control or have access to the central government (the inner circle in grey), those who are excluded from government but are citizens of the country (the next circle in white), and finally, the political world beyond the territorial boundaries of the state. Note that this is a more complex setup than in Chapter 2, where the formal model included only two ethnic categories and where I treated state boundaries as given.

In this more complex world, each ethno-political constellation of power can be described by three types of boundaries: (1) the *territorial boundaries* of a state define which ethnic communities are considered a legitimate part of a state's citizenry; (2) the *boundary of inclusion* separates those who share government power from those who are not represented at the highest levels of government; (3) finally, the number of ethnic cleavages among the included sections of the population describes the structure of the power center.

Each boundary can become the focus of ethno-political conflict: who is included or excluded from state power, how power is shared among ethnic elites and their constituencies, and which ethnic communities should be governed

---

[6] For experimental evidence of such strategic cooperation among co-ethnics, see Habyarimana *et al.* (2007).

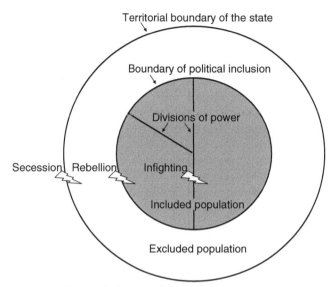

FIGURE 5.1 Types of ethnic conflict

by which state. We can thus distinguish between three types of ethnic conflict, depending on which of these boundaries is at stake. When politically marginalized segments of the population fight to shift the boundaries of inclusion, I call these conflicts *rebellions*. When ethnic elites in power are pitted against each other in a struggle over the spoils of government, we speak of *infighting*. Finally, *secession* aims at changing the territorial boundaries of a polity and can be pursued by both excluded and included groups. As mentioned above, the three types of armed conflict are related to the patterns of legitimacy established by the nation-state model. Its protagonists all evoke the "like-over-like" principle and the ideal of the ethnic representativity of government when they demand a state of their own, fair representation in government, or an end to political exclusion.

2.2 War-prone configurations: hypotheses

Following the configurational argument outlined so far, I propose separate hypotheses for rebellions, infighting, and secession. First, a high degree of ethnic exclusion will increase the likelihood of rebellion (Hypothesis 1) because it decreases the political legitimacy of a state and thus makes it easier for political leaders to mobilize a following among their ethnic constituencies and challenge the government for violating the principle of ethnic representativity.[7] The

---

[7] For additional specifications of the mechanisms leading to successful ethnic mobilization, see Hechter and Levi (1979), Gurr (1993b), and Wimmer (1997).

exact micro-mechanisms of this process have been analyzed by others and need not concern us here. Nor can we explore in detail under which conditions and through which sequences of interactions – such as mobilization–repression spirals – history is steered toward a violent cataclysm (for a first step in the direction of such an analysis, see Sambanis and Zinn 2006). We thus confine ourselves to the simple exclusion argument already underlying the analysis of nation-state formation and war in the previous chapter. We can now take advantage of the EPR dataset and test it empirically. We expect that the most war-prone configurations are ethnocracies – the rule of an elite with an only small ethnic constituency, such as the Tutsi regime in contemporary Rwanda, white settlers in Rhodesia, or Sunni rule under Saddam Hussein.

Second, we assume that infighting is more likely when many partners share government power, that is, in states characterized by a segmented center. The greater the number of political partners, the more severe commitment problems will be, increasing the fear of losing out in the ongoing struggle over the distribution of government spoils. Other authors have elaborated on the micro-foundations for this argument. Tsebelis (2002) shows that the larger the number of veto players, the more difficult it becomes to adjust policy-making, and therefore the less stable a governing coalition. The veto-player argument is compatible with a commitment theory of civil war (see overview in Walter 2009): since possible alliances between actors increases with their number, the uncertainty over one's future power position increases as well. The promise not to take advantage of other coalition partners in the future becomes accordingly less credible.[8] Elite factions are therefore more likely to mobilize their ethnic followers preventatively and challenge other power-sharing partners by demanding a "fairer" share of the government cake. Or they might use their control over parts of the security apparatus and stage a violent coup to prevent being driven from power in the future (Roessler 2011). Thus, the higher the number of power-sharing elites, the greater the likelihood of infighting (Hypothesis 2).

Third, I introduce another legitimacy argument that is independent of the two power-configurational aspects discussed above. It refers to the acceptance and taken-for-grantedness of a state and its territorial shape, rather than the question of who controls its government. In states with a long history of indirect, imperial rule before achieving nation-statehood, large segments of the population are not accustomed to being governed by the new political center and therefore see the new state as a whole as less legitimate. As argued in the introduction, exchange relationships between state elites and the population need to

---

[8] Cunningham (2011) uses veto-player theory to address the question of civil war duration and shows that the larger the number of fighting parties, the longer a civil war lasts. Lijphart (1977: 55–61) offers another argument that relates the number of power-sharing partners to conflict. For a variety of reasons, he expects that three or four power-sharing groups represent the least conflict-prone configuration.

be routinized and institutionalized in order to develop, over time, into a shared identity and a sense of mutual loyalty.

Peripheral groups with a long history of indirect rule maintain only weakly institutionalized ties to the new, post-colonial center and can therefore be mobilized more easily for a secessionist project with the argument that only independence will avoid the future danger of alien rule and guarantee self-government in line with nationalist ideals. To put this into more rationalist terms, peripheral groups in new states will find it hard to believe promises by the ruling majority not to abuse its power (Fearon 1998) – thus creating a commitment problem that might lead to preventative secession and a corresponding armed conflict independent of the exact distribution of power at the center. Georgia was the example cited into the introduction, which spent most of the nineteenth and twentieth centuries under Romanov and later Soviet rule, and which thus commanded little routinized loyalty and trust by its citizens once it became an independent state. South-Ossetians and Abkhazians, whom Moscow had previously ruled indirectly as an autonomous republic or oblast, hastily declared independence as well, and long wars of secession followed. States with a long history of indirect rule, I hypothesize, are therefore more likely to see secessionist conflicts (Hypothesis 3).

Fourth, I postulate that secession is also more likely in large states (Hypothesis 4), thus giving a substantial interpretation to a variable already explored in the previous chapter. Large states are less likely to have penetrated the outer reaches of their territory in the past, and thus the population is less accustomed to being ruled by the political center, especially in the provinces far away from the capital.[9]

Imperial past and population size are both measurements of state cohesion, that is, the degree to which the population takes a state's territorial borders for granted and identifies with a state independent of who controls its government.[10] Secessionist groups claiming to represent power-sharing partners or excluded populations are more likely to challenge states that lack coherence. Low state cohesion thus reinforces the dynamics of exclusion and segmentation and leads them onto the path of secessionist conflict.

Additional factors may halt the spiral of mobilization, counter-mobilization, contestation, and escalation, and instead lead to accommodation and de-escalation. First, the governments of rich states can better accommodate

---

[9] For empirical evidence of this geographic aspect, see Wucherpfennig *et al.* 2011.

[10] Existing typologies of ethnic power configurations mostly refer to exclusion, elite segmentation, and state cohesion as well. Hechter and Levi (1979), Lustick (1979), Horowitz (1985), and Wimmer (2002) distinguish states on the basis of levels of exclusion and segmentation. Anthropologists working in the "complex society" tradition have analyzed different degrees of institutional pluralism (Despres 1968; Smith 1969; Simpson 1995), thus referring to the cohesion dimension. Cohen (1978) cross-classifies cohesion and exclusion, while Schermerhorn (1970) does the same with segmentation and exclusion. Young (1976) and Rothschild (1981) offer the most comprehensive typologies integrating all three aspects.

protest movements by providing public goods to hitherto underserved communities and by co-opting movement leaders into the power elite – as already argued in the previous chapter.[11] An example is the Great Society and affirmative action programs in the aftermath of the civil rights movement in the United States, which helped to co-opt the increasingly radicalized young urban leadership and avoid a violent escalation. The same holds true for dissatisfied members of a power-sharing arrangement: new government institutions can be created and staffed with their followers, and new infrastructure projects can be directed toward their ethnic constituencies.

Both rebellions and infighting, therefore, should be less likely the greater a state's level of development (Hypothesis 5). Our model thus again incorporates one of the most robust findings in the civil war literature (Hegre and Sambanis 2006), that civil wars happen in poor countries, and gives it a new and more nuanced interpretation in line with theories of contentious politics.[12]

Second, the likelihood that a particular actor will instigate an armed conflict depends on the entire power configuration, not just on that specific actor's position within it. More precisely, we expect that power-sharing partners are less likely to fight each other when there is a high risk of rebellion by the excluded population. We therefore postulate that the likelihood of infighting *decreases* as the degree of exclusion increases (Hypothesis 6) and as states become larger (and thus less coherent) (Hypothesis 7). Exclusion and cohesion will therefore have opposite effects on different types of ethnic conflict. Ethnocracies will experience more rebellions (Hypothesis 1), but less infighting between power-sharing partners (Hypothesis 6); incoherent states will have more secession (Hypothesis 4), but less infighting (Hypothesis 7). Only a disaggregated research design distinguishing between different types of ethnic conflicts can do justice to such multicausality.

2.3 Existing theoretical traditions and empirical findings

How do these hypotheses relate to existing analysis of ethnic conflict and to previous findings of quantitative research? The model introduced above incorporates two arguments usually conceived as mutually exclusive. Much debate has emerged over whether exclusion and segregation (as in the "internal colonialism" model of Hechter 1975 or the "split labor market" theory of Bonacich 1974)

---

[11] Note that in contrast to the previous chapter, we now control for different ethno-political configurations of power, such that levels of development are no longer associated with conflict because of their relationship to degrees of political exclusion. We therefore now focus on the other potential effect of economic development, i.e. on the limited ability of governments of poor countries to co-opt leaders of protest movements and satisfy their clienteles through a politics of redistribution.

[12] See Tarrow and Tilly (2006: 145). For empirical support of this interpretation of the effects of GDP, see Fjelde and de Soysa (2009).

or to the contrary, competition and increased contact (Bates 1974; Horowitz 1985; Olzak and Nagel 1986), are more conflict-prone. The configurational model of conflict maintains that both hierarchical exclusion and vertical competition are relevant mechanisms that link ethnic politics to violence. But they affect different types of actors, as defined by their positions in the overall power configuration.

The model also specifies what competition and exclusion are about: not primarily about individual goods such as housing or jobs (as maintained by both competition and split labor market theory), nor more generally about the fruits of modernization (as argued in Horowitz 1985), or a vaguely defined "relative group status," as in much sociopsychological research on prejudice (Blalock 1982). Rather, actors struggle over who controls the state and the public goods and services at its disposal. This focus on the state as both an object and agent in ethno-political conflict is in line with an older tradition of thinking that derived from the modernization and pluralism schools (Geertz 1963; Young 1976; Rothschild 1981) as well as with Hechter's (2000) theory of nationalism that we have encountered several times already.

What does existing quantitative research say about the plausibility of the various hypotheses introduced above? In line with the argument that a long history of imperial rule is conducive to secession, quantitative research based on the MAR dataset shows that previous political autonomy predicts the likelihood of secessionist conflict at the group level of analysis (Gurr 1993b; Walter 2006).[13] And according to Buhaug (2006), population size affects secessionist conflicts only, while offering a different explanation for this finding than the one suggested above.

Quantitative tests of the exclusion hypothesis (Hypothesis 1) have produced more conflicting results, even when using the same data sources. Regan and Norton (2005) as well as Walter (2006) use MAR group-level data and find strong evidence that political discrimination increases rebellions or secessionist civil wars. But Fox (2000) fails to find any clear relationship for the subset of ethno-religious groups. Saideman and Ayres (2000) show that discrimination does not explain secession (but see Jenne *et al.* 2007), and Gurr's (1993b: 179) own study of ethno-nationalist rebellions in the 1980s even suggests that political discrimination is associated with *less* rather than more armed rebellion.

---

[13] According to Jenne *et al.* (2007), however, previous autonomy encourages separatist claims, but not rebellion (they analyze MAR data from 1985–2000 only). Two other factors that we do not incorporate into our theory are thought to be associated with the likelihood of secession: according to Gurr (1993b), Davis and Moore (1997), Gleditsch (2007), and Forsberg (2008), kin groups across the border increase secessionist conflict. Walter (2006), however, finds a significant effect going in the opposite direction; Jenne *et al.* (2007) did not find any association at all; Cederman *et al.* (2009) confirm the mechanism for large groups only; Saideman and Ayres (2000) only for groups whose kin are separatist as well. The second factor is geographic concentration and peripheral location, which are quite unequivocally related to conflict in a series of independent studies conducted by: Saideman and Ayres (2000); Toft (2003); Walter (2006); Jenne *et al.* (2007); Buhaug *et al.* (2008); Cederman *et al.* (2009).

Olzak (2006: 124) aggregates MAR data to the country level for a subset of 55 countries from 1965 to 1989. She arrives at the somewhat conflicting conclusion that both formal recognition of ethnic group rights and political discrimination increase the likelihood of armed rebellion. Wimmer and Min (2006) used a global dataset and also aggregated MAR data to the country level; they found that countries with more politically discriminated groups are more likely to have civil wars (similar results were obtained by Bates *et al.* 1998). Using data covering all countries from 1945 to 2001, Fearon and Laitin (2003: 85) find that a lack of minority language rights and a constitutional preference for certain religious groups do not increase the likelihood of high-intensity civil war. Cederman and Girardin (2007) made a first attempt to code ethnic groups' access to state power in the countries of Eurasia and found evidence that exclusion breeds armed conflicts. This result has been contested by Fearon *et al.* (2007), who use the head of state's ethnic background as a proxy for the ethnic power configuration.

There are good reasons to believe that this inconclusiveness is because of measurement problems and data limitations, some of which have already been discussed above in relation to the MAR dataset. Fearon and Laitin define exclusion narrowly, focusing on minority rights rather than explicitly measuring access to state power. Cederman and Girardin use a broader definition of exclusion, but their data are limited in geographic scope and are cross-sectional in nature, which makes it impossible to analyze how changes in ethnic power relations affect the likelihood of conflict. There is thus ample room to improve on existing findings.

3 THE ETHNIC POWER RELATIONS (EPR) DATASET, 1946–2005

The Ethnic Power Relations (EPR) dataset was designed for this purpose. For the sake of brevity, I introduce only the major aspects of the dataset here and refer readers to Appendix 5.1 for more details. The dataset contains two parts. The first lists politically relevant ethnic groups for each country and each year since 1946, and notes how far group representatives had access to central state power. The second is a conflict dataset, based on the widely used Armed Conflict Data-set (or ACD for short) assembled by the Peace Research Institute, Oslo, and the University of Uppsala. This dataset includes all armed conflicts with more than 25 battle deaths. We extend the ACD with new codings of whether rebels pursued ethnic or non-ethnic goals as well as whether they aimed at secession. We then link armed conflicts to politically relevant ethnic groups if rebels claimed to fight in the name of a particular ethnic community.

3.1 Politically relevant ethnic groups and access to power

According to EPR's coding rules, an ethnic category is politically relevant if at least one significant political actor claims to represent the interests of that group in the national political arena, or if members of an ethnic category are systematically and intentionally discriminated against in the domain of public politics. We do not distinguish between degrees of representativity of political actors who claim to speak for an ethnic group, nor do we code the heterogeneity of political positions voiced by leaders claiming to represent the same community (Brubaker 2004). The coding scheme allows us to identify countries or specific periods in which political objectives, alliances, or disputes were never framed in ethnic terms. This makes sure we do not force an ethnic frame on situations where ethnicity is not politicized, such as in Tanzania or Korea.

If access to political power changed over time, coders divide the 1946 to 2005 period and provide separate coding for each sub-period. This is also necessary when the list of politically relevant categories changes from one year to the next either because certain categories cease to be relevant or because they become relevant for the first time. Next, we code the degree of access to power enjoyed by political leaders who claim to represent a particular group.

We focus on executive level power only, that is, representation in the presidency, cabinet, and senior posts in the administration, including the army. The weight given to these different institutions depends on their de facto power in a given country. In all cases, coders focus on absolute access to power irrespective of the question of under- or overrepresentation relative to the demographic size of an ethnic group.

To describe different degrees of access to central state power we use three basic categories and several subcategories. Some group representatives hold full control of the executive branch with no meaningful participation by members of any other group, some share power with representatives of other groups, and some are excluded altogether from decision-making authority. Within these three basic categories, coders differentiate between further subtypes, choosing from monopoly power, dominance, senior or junior partner in a power-sharing arrangement, regional autonomy, powerless, and discriminated (see Appendix 5.1 for details). For the analyses of this chapter, we distinguish only between power-holding groups (from monopoly to junior partner) and the excluded population (comprising regionally autonomous, powerless, and discriminated-against groups).[14]

The dataset counts 733 politically relevant ethnic groups in 155 sovereign states. On average, countries have between five and six politically relevant ethnic groups (see Appendix Table 5.1). In the most frequent configuration of political power, a single majority group holds either a monopoly or dominant position, with one to three groups excluded from power, typically representing between 10 and 20 percent of the population. This configuration describes about half of the 7,155 country–year observations in the dataset. Some 340 of

[14] For a more differentiated analysis on the group level that uses the full array of categories, see Cederman *et al.* (2010b).

these country–years reflect extreme cases of ethnocratic rule, in which a single group representing less than 20 percent of the population controls the executive branch completely.

How does this universe of ethnic groups in the EPR dataset compare to that of other datasets? Do our coding rules produce a systematic selection bias in favor of the exclusion argument since we only include groups with a minimum level of political organization? Does the EPR dataset therefore systematically overlook severely discriminated groups that do not even appear on the political landscape let alone were able to mount an armed rebellion? To alleviate such concerns, I compared EPR's groups list to the well-known and often used compendium of ethnic groups assembled by Fearon, as well as to the MAR dataset.

Fearon's (2003) list contains 777 groups in countries covered by EPR. They are categories that "an average citizen" of a country would consider to be meaningful – independent of their political relevance. Of these 777 groups, 563 are listed in EPR, either directly or as a group subsumed under a higher-level category. Twenty-eight groups are excluded from our list because EPR omits non-citizen immigrant groups, such as Yugoslavs and Spanish in Switzerland or Vietnamese in Cambodia. A further 180 groups in Fearon's list are not politically relevant in the national political arena according to EPR's coding rules, such as Blacks in Canada, Mandinka in Guinea-Bissau, or Moravians in the Czech Republic. What would their power status be if these *were* politically relevant? I was able to track 130 of these groups. Roughly 6% might be coded as discriminated, 54% as powerless or with limited autonomy, and 40% as groups represented in power. In the EPR dataset, there are 15% discriminated groups, 45% are powerless or autonomous, and 40% included (see Appendix Table 5.1). There is thus no selection bias and the EPR group list is not systematically geared either toward included or excluded groups.[15]

The Phase IV Minorities at Risk data lists 340 groups of which 284 remain "at risk" and are actively tracked. EPR includes coverage of 310 of these groups. Of the 30 groups that EPR does not code, four are non-citizen groups excluded from EPR (immigrants in Switzerland, Turks in Germany, non-citizen Muslims in France, and Vietnamese in Cambodia), and five are groups we do not consider ethnic (such as the regionally identified Honamese in Korea or clans like the Issaq in Somalia). The remaining 21 groups do not appear in EPR because they are not politically salient according to our scheme, including Native Hawaiians in the United States, Chinese in Panama, and the Mossi-Dagomba in Ghana. Again, EPR does not suffer from a systematic selection bias in favor of groups that are politically disadvantaged *and* at the same time rise up in arms against the state.

---

[15] Meanwhile, the EPR dataset incorporates 138 groups in 1995 that do not appear in the Fearon list, including dozens of small groups that maintain regional autonomy in Russia and China, as well as some large politically salient groups, such as Muslims in India.

3.2 War coding

As mentioned above, the following analysis relies on the Armed Conflict Dataset to identify conflict events. These are defined as any armed and organized confrontation between government troops and rebel organizations or between army factions that reaches an annual battle death threshold of 25 people (Gleditsch *et al.* 2002). Massacres and genocides are not included because the victims are neither organized nor armed; communal riots and pogroms are excluded because the government is not directly involved.

The ACD does not contain information on whether an armed conflict should be classified as ethnic. Based on our own research, we classify each conflict as either ethnic and non-ethnic depending on rebel aims and recruitment patterns (this is in line with other ongoing coding projects, e.g. Sambanis 2009). Ethno-national self-determination, a more favorable ethnic balance of power in government, ethno-regional autonomy, the end of ethnic and racial discrimination, or language and other cultural rights are all considered "ethnic aims." In order to be coded as an ethnic conflict, the rebel organization also needs to recruit fighters predominantly among their leaders' ethnic group and forge alliances on the basis of ethnic similarity.

We look at the aims and recruitment patterns of each armed organization involved in a conflict separately. In some complex cases (e.g. Afghanistan, Burma, Chad, Uganda, Angola, and Zaire), we disaggregate the conflict into sub-conflicts because the non-governmental side made different ethnic claims and rebel organizations acted independently from each other. Our dataset thus contains a higher number of armed conflicts than the original ACD (for details see Appendix 5.1).

We then link all ethnic conflicts to the politically relevant ethnic category in the EPR dataset. To avoid endogeneity problems, we make sure that the coding of ethnic power relations reflects the power constellation *before* the outbreak of armed conflict in cases where political changes occurred in the same year as the onset of conflict. To test the configurational theory of ethnic conflict, we then divide ethnic conflicts into those fought in the name of ethnic groups that were excluded from central government power (rebellions) and those fought in the name of power holders (infighting).

We also code whether rebels or infighters aimed to establish a separate, independent state or join another existing state, using the same definition of separatism as in the previous chapter. In order to deal with the tricky issue of changing or conflicting war aims, we focus on the initial aims of the most important actors. Cross-classifying actor type and war aims produces a fourfold typology of ethnic conflicts with separatist rebellions, non-separatist rebellions, separatist infightings, and non-separatist infightings.

The dataset includes 215 armed conflicts fought between 1946 and 2005, 110 of which were ethnic conflicts. Of the 215 conflicts, 60 had secessionist aims, the vast majority of which were also ethnic in character. Among the 110 ethnic conflicts,

TABLE 5.1   *The conflict dataset*

	Ethnic conflicts		Non-ethnic conflicts	Total
	Infighting	Rebellions		
Secessionist	9	48	3	60
Non-secessionist	11	42	102	155
Total infighting/ rebellions	20	90		
Total		*110*	*105*	*215*

20 were fought by groups in power (of which nine were separatist) and 90 by excluded groups (of which 48 were secessionist; see Table 5.1). One half of the armed conflicts reached the standard threshold of civil war, i.e. claimed more than 1,000 battle deaths in a year.

4   VARIABLES AND DATA SOURCES

4.1 Exclusion, center segmentation, state cohesion

To test Hypothesis 1, we compute the share of the excluded population in the total population that is ethno-politically relevant. We assume that at lower levels of exclusion, an increase in this share will have a greater effect on the likelihood of armed conflict than at higher levels, and we therefore use a logged transformation of this variable.[16] Hypothesis 2 is tested with a variable that counts the number of power-sharing ethnic elites. It ranges from 1 to 14 in India, the state with the most segmented center. Following Hypothesis 3, the cohesion of a state is lower the longer it had been ruled indirectly by an empire before becoming independent. We calculate the percentage of years spent under imperial rule between 1816 and independence, including years as a colonial or imperial dependency (for example of the Soviet Union or Habsburgs) or as the heartland of a land-based empire (e.g. Turkey under the Ottomans), but not the "mother country" of an empire with seaborne colonies (such as Portugal).

4.2 Other variables

As in the previous chapter, we again control for other variables that may cause violent conflict or foster peace, especially those identified by Hegre and

---

[16] We hypothesize that an initial break with the "like-over-like" principle of legitimacy carries more political risk than the shift to an even more exclusionary ethnocracy.

Sambanis (2006) as the most robust variables in civil war research. Many of these control variables have already been discussed in the previous chapter and we can thus introduce them here more briefly. We include linguistic fractionalization (as found in Fearon and Laitin's dataset) to show its limited significance once ethnic politics variables are part of the equation. GDP per capita[17] and a state's population size play important roles in the configurational model of ethnic conflict introduced above (Hypotheses 4 and 5). Democratic civil peace theory – briefly introduced in the previous chapter – states that civil wars should be most frequent in states that are neither democratic nor autocratic, i.e. in anocracies (Müller and Weede 1990; Ellingsen 2000; Hegre *et al.* 2001; Mansfield and Snyder 2005a; but see Vreeland 2008). We again include a corresponding dummy variable, based on the Polity IV dataset. We also consider major variables associated with Fearon and Laitin's (2003) insurgency model according to which wars break out when government forces are weakened by political instability and when mountainous terrain allows rebels to hide and retreat.[18]

The disaggregated analysis pursued in this chapter will allow us to specify the link between oil and conflict with more precision. Ross (2003) explores how natural resources affect different types of violent conflict. When rebels can obstruct the extraction of natural resources, as with oil, he expects conflicts to take on secessionist forms (see also Collier and Hoeffler 2004). Buhaug (2006), on the other hand, argues that oil fosters non-secessionist conflict because oil fields are usually controlled by the central government. This increases the incentives to capture a state, rather than to secede from it. According to the argument introduced in the previous chapter, oil resources reinforce the dynamic of ethnic patronage and clientelism. We can now specify that increased patronage should lead to more violent conflict *over* the state, rather than attempts to secede *from* it, in line with Buhaug's argument. To measure the possible impact of oil, we use the same oil production per capita variable as in the previous chapter.

5 MODELS AND FINDINGS

The following analysis uses the same modeling approach as in the previous chapter, evaluating the effects of independent variables on a binary dependent variable coded as 1 in the first year of an armed conflict and 0 otherwise.[19]

---

[17] The GDP per capita data refer to constant 2000 American dollars. Data for 5,737 observations (79 percent) come from Penn World Table 6.2. Using growth rates from the World Bank's World Development Indicators provided 229 additional observations (3 percent). Using Fearon and Laitin's data, we calculated annual growth rates and extended values back to 1946. Total data coverage is 7,105 observations (99.6 percent).

[18] We adopt the mountainous terrain data from their dataset and again define regime change as any change in the Polity score of three points or more over the prior three years.

[19] We test all models against two versions of these dependent variables, both commonly used in the literature. The first version includes years during which another war was already ongoing, and adds

We control for possible time trends by including a simple calendar year variable, which should capture a possible global trend toward more peace or more conflict.[20]

The analysis proceeds in three steps, each leading to a more fine-grained, disaggregated analysis. First, we determine whether ethnic politics matters at all in predicting when and where armed conflicts occur. We do this by including all types of conflict – whether ethnic or not – in the dependent variable. Second, we focus on ethnic conflicts only, while maintaining our global purview and keeping all country–years in the analysis. Third, we look at the four different types of ethnic conflicts represented in Table 5.1 and determine whether secessionist rebellion, secessionist infighting, non-secessionist rebellion and non-secessionist infighting are indeed caused by different configurations of power, as maintained in the hypotheses section.

5.1 Explaining armed conflict: ethnic exclusion matters

Quantitative civil war research often produces conflicting results, not the least because war is a rare event and even small differences in the war lists used by a researcher can make a difference. We also know that different factors cause high-intensity conflicts with more than 1,000 battle deaths compared to low-intensity conflicts with as few as 25 battle deaths (Hegre and Sambanis 2006). To mitigate these two problems, we go beyond standard practice in the field and include, wherever possible, additional models based on the war lists assembled by other researchers. For the first steps in the analysis, we can use the well-known civil war dataset of Fearon and Laitin (2003), which includes a coding of whether or not wars are "ethnic" in nature, as well as the equally widely used dataset of Sambanis (2004) that so far contains no information on the ethnic nature of war.

---

a dummy control for such ongoing war. The second version drops ongoing war years by coding them as missing, thereby omitting wars that begin while a first conflict is still active. This coding of the dependent variable results in approximately 15 percent fewer observations. In contrast to the previous chapter, we here present results with a control for ongoing war (for models with dropped observations, see the tables in Appendix 5.4). The results of the two sets of models are very similar, but in general our hypotheses fare better when ongoing war years are dropped.

[20] Since conflict processes are path different, we also include the number of peace years since the outbreak of the last conflict, as well as a cubic spline function on these peace years following Beck *et al.* (1998). We thus use the same technique as in the previous chapter, but for a different purpose: we are no longer interested in the overall relationship between nation-state formation and conflict, but in the exact ethno-political configurations of power that make it more likely. For the sake of space, we do not show these time control variables in the following tables (see Appendix 5.3). As a robustness check, we ran all models with continental dummies and without time controls, and found no large differences in the main findings (see Appendix 5.4). Throughout, we again specify robust standard errors clustered by country to account for the non-independence of observations from the same state. Because armed conflict is a rare event, we also ran all models using the "rare events" logit estimator and found no substantive differences from our main findings (see Appendix 5.4).

As we will see, we arrive at basically the same results despite the fact that both Fearon and Laitin and Sambanis only include high-intensity conflicts with more than 1,000 battle deaths in their war lists, while our own ACD-based dataset also contains low-intensity armed conflicts.

The first three models in Table 5.2 explain the outbreak of all types of armed conflicts, whether ethnic or non-ethnic, separatist or non-separatist. The percentage of excluded population, the central variable in our configurational model of ethnic conflict, is significant for all model specifications: when using the ACD that includes conflicts with as few battle deaths as 25 (Model 1) and when regressing on Fearon and Laitin's or Sambanis' coding of the dependent variable that both refer to full-scale civil wars (Models 2 and 3). Ethnic exclusion is as consistently related to conflict as is GDP per capita, one of the most robust explanatory factors in the study of civil wars (Hegre and Sambanis 2006).

These results challenge greed-and-opportunity theories, according to which ethnicity and more specifically ethnic grievances should not play any role in a proper understanding of civil war. Models 1 to 3 also demonstrate that once the dynamics of ethnic politics are measured with appropriate variables, the linguistic fractionalization index loses its significance – contrary to what the diversity-breeds-conflict school assumes. Rather than ethnic diversity as such, the results suggest, it is political exclusion along ethnic lines that fosters conflict.

This is the first time that the exclusion argument has been statistically confirmed based on a global, time-varying dataset that measures degrees of exclusion directly and at the polity level, rather than the group level, as in the MAR dataset. The robustness of this finding is remarkable, given that Models 1–3 analyze all types of armed conflicts. The configurational model of ethnic conflict, however, obviously cannot explain non-ethnic wars, such as the revolutionary conflict in El Salvador, army coups in Brazil, or the Katanga conflict in Congo – all of which are part of the dependent variable in these models.

The number of power-sharing partners (Hypothesis 2), however, does not have a robust impact on the onset of armed conflict or civil war in Models 1 to 3. This is not surprising, given that actors representing ethnic groups in power initiated only 20 of the 200 conflicts in the dataset. We therefore expect to see the effects of a high number of power-sharing partners only when distinguishing between rebellions and infighting. The duration of imperial past variable is positive but only significant in Model 2 (Hypothesis 3). We will demonstrate further below, when regressing on different types of ethnic conflict, that a lack of state coherence is associated with *secessionist* conflicts only.[21]

---

[21] Among a large number of robustness checks, we controlled for endogeneity (the possibility that past conflict determines future conflict) by running models that include a variable for the number of past conflicts. This did not affect our results (see Table 5.3c in Appendix 5.3).

TABLE 5.2 *The big picture: ethnic exclusion and armed conflict (logit analysis)*

	All conflicts			Ethnic conflicts only	
	Model 1	Model 2	Model 3	Model 4	Model 5
	All conflicts in the Armed Conflict Dataset (ACD)	All conflicts in Fearon and Laitin's dataset	All conflicts in Sambanis' dataset	Ethnic conflicts in ACD	Ethnic conflicts in Fearon and Laitin's dataset
Ethnic politics variables					
% excluded population	0.1291*	0.2564**	0.2792**	0.3191**	0.3667**
	(0.0558)	(0.0779)	(0.0808)	(−0.0875)	(−0.1214)
Number of power-sharing partners	0.0587	0.0771	0.0177	0.1120**	0.0969
	(0.0389)	(0.0586)	(0.0491)	(−0.037)	(−0.0747)
Duration of imperial past (in years)	0.4579	0.7899*	0.5932	0.9301*	1.5761**
	(0.2886)	(0.3568)	(0.3307)	(−0.4426)	(−0.4244)
Other variables					
Linguistic fractionalization	0.6298	−0.0283	0.0261	1.2800**	0.599
	(0.3227)	(0.4474)	(0.3989)	(−0.3997)	(−0.6156)
GDP per capita	−0.1093**	−c.1267**	−0.1750**	−0.1256**	−0.1554**
	(0.0276)	(0.0374)	(0.0472)	(−0.0448)	(−0.0585)
Population size	0.1397**	0.2354**	0.2135**	0.2102**	0.3609**
	(0.0532)	(0.0672)	(0.0616)	(−0.0656)	(−0.0894)

	(1)	(2)	(3)	(4)	(5)
% of mountainous terrain	0.1241*	0.1581*	0.1320	0.1749	0.0701
	(0.0601)	(0.0794)	(0.0765)	(−0.0984)	(−0.109)
Political instability	0.3454	0.2693	0.2655	0.1544	−0.0441
	(0.1764)	(0.2754)	(0.2412)	(−0.2726)	(−0.3549)
Anocracy (compared to autocracy and democracy)	0.4292**	0.7218**	0.6478**	0.4469*	0.9738**
	(0.1625)	(0.2369)	(0.1863)	(−0.2263)	(−0.2614)
Oil production per capita	0.0171**	0.0056	0.0176*	0.0180*	0.0064
	(0.0063)	(0.0165)	(0.0078)	(−0.0091)	(−0.0284)
Observations	6,865	6,034	5,818	6,865	6,034
No. of conflict onsets	197	97	121	102	66

Notes: Time controls, ongoing war dummy, and constant not shown; robust standard errors in parentheses; * significant at 5%; ** significant at 1%.

How do other theories of civil war fare in these models? Regime change and mountainous terrain play a key role in the insurgency model but receive rather limited support here, although the mountainous terrain helps to explain low-intensity conflicts (Model 1) and Fearon and Laitin's civil wars (Model 2).[22] Oil production per capita is associated with conflict in two models as well (Models 1 and 3). Meanwhile, the findings for democratic civil peace theory are more robust: anocracy increases the risk of armed conflict in all models. This association, however, will disappear as soon as we start to disaggregate the dependent variable.[23]

5.2 Explaining ethnic conflict: exclusion, segmentation, incoherence

Because half of the armed conflicts in our dataset are not related to ethnic politics, a more focused investigation needs to exclude these conflicts. We do so in Models 4 and 5 in Table 5.2. Once we analyze ethnic conflicts only, the other two ethnic politics variables become statistically significant as well. The duration of imperial past, which measures a state's cohesion and should be associated specifically with secessionist conflicts, is significantly associated with conflict in both models. The number of power-sharing groups is highly significant in Model 4, but not in regressions on Fearon and Laitin's coding of ethnic civil wars (Model 5), which does not include low-intensity conflicts.

Significance levels do not tell us how much a variable affects the outcome, however. And the coefficients themselves are often hard to interpret. We thus calculated "first differences" effects, which report how the probability of ethnic conflict changes when we increase the value of one of the independent variables (and only this one) by a standard deviation. As already reported in the introductory chapter, it turns out that exclusion, segmentation, and incohesion affect the dynamics of war and peace in quite substantial ways: increasing the share of the excluded population from 6% to 32% (an increase of one standard deviation from the mean) results in a 25% increase in the probability of ethnic conflict

---

[22] Sambanis (2004) as well as Collier and Hoeffler (2004) also find no support for the mountains variable – but it appears in Hegre and Sambanis' (2006) list of the "25 most robust variables," as does political instability. We also experimented with Fearon and Laitin's "new state" variable discussed in the previous chapter. It is not robustly related to armed conflict and quite sensitive to alternative codings. It is insignificant except when regressing on Sambanis' coding of civil wars (this is for models that control for ongoing war). When recoded as relating to the first five years after independence instead of two, and regressed on ethnic conflicts, the "new state" variable is insignificant for all codings of the dependent variable.

[23] As noted in the previous chapter, the anocracy variable unfortunately includes periods of state-breakdown and other conflict-intense situations, which is largely responsible for the statistical association with armed conflict, as Vreeland (2008) has demonstrated. In the previous chapter, I assigned such periods and situations to an "anarchy" category to avoid endogeneity. Here, we don't modify the coding of this variable in order to maintain strict comparability with widely used models of civil conflict.

(calculated on the basis of Model 4). A one standard deviation increase in center segmentation leads to a 9% increased risk of armed conflict, while a similar increase in years under imperial rule augments the chance of armed conflict by 13%. A one standard deviation increase in GDP per capita and population size, the two most robust variables in the civil war literature, influence the probability of conflict by 22% and 13%, respectively. Clearly, ethnic power configurations are substantially as important as basic economic and demographic factors that are well known to influence the prospects of war and peace.

The strength and robustness[24] of the exclusion, segmentation, and cohesion variables are noteworthy because the dependent variable in Models 4 and 5 still comprises different types of ethnic conflict. Our theory assumes, however, that infighting, rebellion, and secession are caused by different ethno-political configurations and that the same variable might therefore have *opposite* effects on the likelihood of different types of conflict (see Hypotheses 1, 6, 4, and 7). In the next step, we therefore disaggregate the dependent variable and use multinomial logit regressions to predict the onset of different types of ethnic conflicts.

In non-technical terms, a multinomial logit asks how independent variables affect the likelihood that a given country–year will be peaceful, *or* marked by the outbreak of a conflict of type 1, *or* by the outbreak of a conflict of type 2, and so forth. Rather than analyzing each conflict type separately, multinomial regressions allow for the joint estimation of their determinants in a single model. It is therefore a good tool to discover causal heterogeneity: the possibility that different causes generate similar outcomes.

As discussed above, combining actor types with war aims produces four kinds of ethnic conflict in the dataset, which will be the outcomes that the multinomial logit regression seeks to explain: secessionist wars fought in the name of excluded groups (secessionist rebellions for short), non-secessionist rebellions, secessionist conflict started by power-sharing groups (secessionist infighting for short), and non-secessionist infighting.

5.3 Explaining different types of ethnic conflict: a configurational analysis

Table 5.3 reports the results of a multinomial regression on these four types of armed conflict. Let us first analyze the difference between rebellions (the dependent variable in both Columns 1 and 2) and infighting (Columns 3 and 4). In line with Hypothesis 1, exclusion affects rebellions only – whether secessionist[25] or not. Confirming Hypothesis 2, the number of power-sharing partners

---

[24] For a series of robustness checks, see Appendix Tables 5.3.

[25] The result for secessionist rebellion in Column 2 depends on using a logged version of the share of the excluded population. A non-logged version, although it does not change any results of previous tables, fails to come close to standard significance levels (results not shown here).

TABLE 5.3 *The disaggregated view: explaining different types of ethnic conflict (multinomial logit analysis)*

	Conflicts involving excluded groups (rebellion)		Conflicts involving power-sharing partners (infighting)	
		Secessionist conflicts		
	Non-secessionist rebellion (Column 1)	Secessionist rebellion (Column 2)	Secessionist infighting (Column 3)	Non-secessionist infighting (Column 4)
Ethnic politics variables				
% excluded population	0.7501**	0.2554*	−0.2032	−0.4504
	(0.1277)	(0.1109)	(0.3306)	(0.3156)
Number of power-sharing partners	0.0689	0.0008	0.4956**	0.3176**
	(0.1001)	(0.0417)	(0.1164)	(0.0960)
Duration of imperial past (in years)	−0.8041	1.9524*	14.6269**	1.1870
	(0.7777)	(0.8152)	(2.8503)	(1.6311)
Other variables				
Linguistic fractionalization	0.9796	1.9997**	1.4433	0.9991
	(0.8709)	(0.6431)	(1.2707)	(1.6116)
GDP per capita	−0.1833*	−0.0226	−0.6017	−0.1914
	(0.0814)	(0.0584)	(0.3302)	(0.1750)
Population size	0.2498	0.4835**	−0.1882	−0.7321**
	(0.1329)	(0.1256)	(0.1925)	(0.1841)

Mountainous terrain	−0.0913	0.3943	0.6948	0.5656*
	(0.1608)	(0.2211)	(0.3751)	(0.2815)
Political instability	0.0291	0.3655	−35.2497**	1.0312
	(0.4485)	(0.5128)	(0.6728)	(0.7487)
Anocracy (compared to autocracy and democracy)	0.6533	0.2931	1.4050	0.0115
	(0.3639)	(0.3892)	(0.9854)	(0.7129)
Oil production per capita	0.0296**	0.0016	−0.3692	0.0126
	(0.0085)	(0.0452)	(0.4031)	(0.0088)
No. of conflict onsets	42	41	9	10

Notes: Time controls, ongoing war dummy, and constant not shown; 6,865 observations; robust standard errors in parentheses; * significant at 5%; ** significant at 1%.

increases the chances of both secessionist (Column 3) and non-secessionist infighting (Column 4), but has no significant effect on rebellion (Columns 1 and 2). Hypothesis 6 maintained that power-sharing partners that exclude large proportions of the population would stick together and avoid infighting. While the sign of the coefficient of the exclusion variable turns from positive for rebellions (Columns 1 and 2) to negative for infighting (Columns 3 and 4), it fails to reach standard levels of statistical significance for the latter.

How do we explain whether rebellions and infighting turn secessionist (Columns 2 and 3)? Conforming to Hypothesis 3, the longer a country had been ruled by empire in the past the more likely secessionist conflicts instigated by both power sharers (Column 3) and the leaders of excluded groups (Column 2). The duration of imperial past has no effect, again confirming our expectations, on non-secessionist ethnic conflicts (Columns 1 and 4). Countries with large populations are also more likely to be haunted by secessionist conflicts (Hypothesis 4). Both a long imperial past and a large population imply that many citizens were accustomed to self-rule and do not consider the newly established nation-state as legitimate. As expected by Hypothesis 7, population size is significant and positive for rebellions only (Column 2), while the sign of the coefficient is negative for infighting (and significant for the non-secessionist type reported in Column 4).[26]

Our expectations regarding the effects of levels of economic development are not fully confirmed. Richer states' governments are indeed able to avoid non-secessionist rebellions (Column 1) because they can afford to co-opt the leadership of ethnic protest movements, but they do not experience less non-secessionist infighting (Column 4), as Hypothesis 5 had maintained. That said, the frequency of violent infighting is rare (nine secessionist and 10 non-secessionist cases) and the signs of the coefficient for GDP in Columns 3 and 4 are at least pointing in the right (negative) direction.

Table 5.3 again includes linguistic fractionalization as a control variable. The disaggregated perspective now allows us to see that linguistic diversity is significantly associated only with secessionist rebellions (Column 2). Perhaps linguistic fractionalization captures – in an indirect and rough way – another aspect of state coherence. It expresses the extent to which the central state has linguistically assimilated its population in past centuries; this provides an indicator of a state's capacity to extend its reach over a territory over a prolonged time frame. However, additional analysis shows that this finding is not robust to

---

[26] Population size is insignificant in regressions on the onset of non-ethnic wars (results not shown), supporting our interpretation that population size represents a proxy for state coherence. This is contrary to the interpretation of Fearon and Laitin, who hypothesize that governments find it more difficult to logistically and militarily control large populations. Dropping years with ongoing wars or running the models with additional continental dummies produces some minor changes to the results of Table 5.3 (for details see Appendix Tables 5.4).

other specifications of the statistical model and we should therefore not rely on it.[27] All in all, it becomes evident that ethnic diversity is not a robust predictor of armed conflict, as soon as we introduce measurements for the ethno-political power configurations and operate within a multicausal framework that allows distinguishing between various pathways to ethnic violence.

Among other control variables, anocracy and regime change are no longer associated with any of the four types of armed conflict, while mountainous ter-rain is increasing the chances of one type of infighting (Column 4) but not rebellion, contrary to what the insurgency model predicts. Oil resources increase the likelihood of non-secessionist conflicts fought in the name of excluded groups (Column 1), but none of the other types of armed conflict. This is consistent with Buhaug's hypothesis that oil resources – which according to our own inter-pretation reinforce ethnic clientelism – provide incentives to capture the state, rather than to secede from it.

Overall, the results of Table 5.3 demonstrate that a configurational approach to the study of civil wars yields important insights. Measures of ethnic politics have heterogeneous effects on different types of ethnic conflict, as do other key variables such as population size and oil. A configurational approach allows to better understand why ethnic conflicts and wars might erupt in such different ethno-political constellations as seen in Bosnia, Northern Ireland, and Mexico – even if statistical associations are generally unsuited to generate precise point predictions.

Bosnian Serbs participated in a segmented power-sharing arrangement within which elite competition for control over the newly founded state quickly escalated to incompatible positions and demands. The long history of indir-ect rule – from Ottoman to Habsburg to Yugoslavian – meant that all but the Bosniak segments of the population disidentified with the new state, which fur-ther increased the likelihood of armed conflict and gave it a secessionist form. In Northern Ireland, however, the conflict erupted when the large Catholic population no longer tolerated its exclusion from political power. Ireland had long been ruled as an internal colony of Great Britain and the northern parts of the island thus disidentified with the British state, increasing the likelihood that rebels would pursue secessionist aims. In Mexico, *commandante* Marcos led a group of former peasant activists to rebel against the political domination that the indigenous populations of Chiapas had suffered for centuries. In contrast to Northern Ireland and Bosnia, the Mexican state had enough time over the past two centuries to project its symbolic and political power over the population,

---

[27] As explained in a previous footnote, we ran all models with a different method of dealing with cases with multiple conflicts. In the above models, second (and third) conflicts are included and we add a control variable for "ongoing war." If we exclude these additional conflicts from the analysis, the linguistic fractionalization variable will no longer be significant in Column 2 of Table 5.3 (see Appendix Table 5.4A, Model 4).

which thus learned to see their membership in the Mexican state as self-evident and legitimate. The rebellion did not develop into a separatist endeavor, even though ample opportunities would have existed to unite with Guatemaltecan Mayas and their rebel organizations.

6 CONCLUSIONS

This chapter sought to identify the precise conditions under which violent ethnic conflicts erupt after a nation-state has been established. Conflicts are more likely when the center of power is divided between a large number of ethnic elites or when large proportions of a state's population are excluded from power. In incoherent states where the population is not accustomed to be governed by the new political center, violent conflict is even more likely and will take on a secessionist form.

These results stand in opposition to the greed-and-opportunity school, which discounts ethnicity and more specifically ethnic exclusion and grievances as relevant factors in explaining civil war. To be sure, our argument is not that ethnic "identity" or "grievances," as opposed to "interests" and "greed," motivate people to found and join armed organizations. Rather, in weak states with weakly developed civil societies, ethnicity will channel the pursuit of power and prestige such that political factions will align along ethnic cleavages. Ethnicity is therefore not an aim in itself, but a perceptual lens through which individuals identify reliable alliance partners as well as the organizational means through which they struggle to gain access to state power and its public good. Our approach specifies the conditions under which this political logic of ethnic solidarity comes into play, as well as the power configurations that make an escalation into armed conflict more likely.

This chapter also goes a step beyond the minority-grievance model by showing that ethnic mobilization and conflict do not exclusively involve discriminated minorities fighting for their rights. Ethnic conflict often concerns the entire configuration of power, most importantly the question of who controls the state and what share of it. Our results thus lend themselves to a broader perspective not focused on demographic minorities at risk, but on the dynamics of ethnic politics at the center of state power. After all, armed rebels are more likely to emerge from excluded majorities, not minorities, and groups in power instigate an important number of armed conflicts.

In contrast to the diversity-breeds-conflict school, this chapter demonstrates that ethnic conflicts are not any more likely in more diverse countries: ethno-demographic diversity indices are rarely associated with conflict in statistically significant ways and they do so only for a circumscribed subset of armed conflicts. Ethno-demographic indices, and many theories of war and peace that rely on them, measure the degree of linguistic and religious heterogeneity without taking relations of power between ethnically defined actors into account, and without analyzing the different relationships between such actors and the state. Violence is thought to erupt between ethnic groups –nourished by nepotistic instincts or primordial antagonisms – and only then to involve state authorities. These approaches overlook the crucial fact that the state is neither a neutral actor nor a passive arena within which ethnic groups operate, but might itself be "captured" by one of these groups. Such capture creates serious legitimacy problems in modern nation-states and is thus a major source of war in the contemporary world.

With this more fine-grained analysis of today's civil conflicts, we have reached the end of a journey that began when a new template of legitimacy – in the name of a nationally defined people – entered the stage of world history some 250 years ago. As argued throughout this chapter, ethno-nationalism remains the central ideological principle that motivates all the different types of ethnic conflicts that this chapter has disentangled from each other: rebels decry the breach of the like-over-like principle as much as do infighters who complain about "underrepresentation" in government and secessionists who struggle to free themselves from "alien rule." Given that nationalist forms of legitimizing and contesting power are ubiquitous in the modern world and that ethno-political inequality is widespread, is conflict unavoidable? This question stands at the heart of the next chapter.

6

Can peace be engineered?

During the first decade after the fall of the Berlin Wall, preventing armed violence around the world became an important preoccupation of Western policy-makers. Many hoped that the sole remaining superpower, no longer preoccupied with containing communist insurgencies across continents, could now afford to lead "the international community" into a peaceful future. The September 11 attacks shifted the attention away from preventing civil war and toward fighting and dismantling terrorist networks around the world.

Two recent developments have helped to bring the idea of civil war prevention back onto the agenda of Western policy-makers, however.[1] First, the wars in Afghanistan and Iraq have led to a military and political overstretch of the United States and its allies. Preventing additional civil wars that would demand Western intervention has very much become a matter of necessity. Second and more importantly, the discussion on how to prevent terrorism focuses increasingly on the role of failed states that provide the environment within which radical groups can flourish. Most of these states "failed" in the wake of civil war.

Parts of this chapter have been presented at the United States Institute of Peace. I thank the discussants Jack Goldstone and Philip Keefer as well as Chantal de Jonge Oudraat and Elizabeth Cole for having organized the event. Andries Odendaal, Marc Sommers, and Sarah Zingg Wimmer offered helpful comments and suggestions. A later version was presented at a session of the annual meeting of the Midwest Political Science Association, to which Ben Smith had invited me, as well as at a panel of the Annual Political Science Association Meeting in Seattle organized by Gwyneth McClendon. I am especially indebted to my friends and colleagues in comparative politics who offered this sociologist venturing into their core disciplinary domain crucial advice, made helpful suggestions regarding datasets to use, or pointed out pitfalls to avoid and holes in the argument: Emmanuel Teitelbaum, Patrick Kuhn, Nicholas Sambanis, and Kanchan Chandra.

[1] From an American foreign policy point of view, see Woocher (2009); from a strategic planning point of view, see Stares and Zenko (2009).

This book is not mainly written to provide insights on how violent conflict can be avoided. Nevertheless, the analysis presented so far contains some important lessons for current debates, and additional analysis in this chapter will offer further support for the main argument:[2] prevention should foster inclusionary power configurations, rather than democracy, decentralization, and other institutional reforms commonly considered prime tools of peace promotion. I will show empirically that formal political institutions either don't influence conflict dynamics in any systematic way, or only show a rather unstable and fragile association with infighting between power-sharing partners. As we have seen in the previous chapter, such infighting accounts for only one-fifth of all ethnic conflicts fought in the postwar world. Encouraging inclusive government or depoliticizing ethnicity altogether through a long-term process of nation building should therefore be the focal goals of prevention policies.

This general message is somewhat at odds with the current debate among policy-makers and "constitutional engineers" about which political institutions promote peace.[3] The holy trinity of prevention "tools" for ethnically divided societies consists of democracy, federalism (e.g. Lijphart 1977: 42–44; Heper *et al.* 1997; Ghai 1998), and minority rights (Kymlicka 2007). There is some disagreement, however, as to exactly which democratic institutions are best at preventing violence – a strong president or a strong parliament, proportional systems of representation, in which parliamentary seats are distributed according to vote shares, or majoritarianism, where "the winner takes all." What can quantitative research tell us with regard to the peace-promoting effects of these and other political institutions? I first evaluate whether democracy brings peace, either through a direct effect ("ballots replacing bullets") or indirectly because democracy might foster political inclusion and thus prevent ethnic rebellions.

---

[2] In the discussion that follows, I will bracket the important question of whether prevention is politically feasible given that it may conflict with other policy goals such as access to natural resources, the wish to see friendly regimes in place, or a balanced domestic budget. I also will sideline the issue of how prevention could become the focus of policy-makers and their electorates who have a notoriously short time horizon and limited capability to focus on other than fully escalated conflicts that make headlines in the Western media. The argument thus will be limited to identifying what should be done, rather than how it can be achieved politically.

[3] Note that political institutions here refers to explicit and formalized rules regulating access to power, rather than to principles of political legitimacy as I have used the term in previous chapters. For an overview of different understandings of the concept in political science and sociology, see Portes and Smith (2010).

I DEMOCRACY AND DEMOCRATIZATION

1.1 Direct effects of democracy

Chapters 4 and 5 showed no support for the idea that democracies are more peaceful than autocracies. This is in line with the entire quantitative research literature.[4] Even the more modest claim that democracies and autocracies are *both* more peaceful than the "anocratic" regimes that lie in between them is not systematically supported by the results of Chapters 4 and 5, nor by the most recent research on this specific issue. Previous studies that reported that anocracies are more war-prone (Ellingsen 2000; Hegre *et al.* 2001) were mostly based on the Polity IV dataset, whose measurement of "anocracy" includes intense political conflict or even violence (Vreeland 2008) – such that the previous findings boiled down to showing that conflict explains violence.[5]

There is, however, some evidence that the *democratization* of authoritarian regimes is often violence-prone (Cederman *et al.* 2010a). The analysis of previous chapters offers some interpretation of the possible mechanisms at work: when multiparty democracy is introduced, encompassing clientelist networks that stretched from the center of power down to individual villages break apart along ethnic lines, thus giving rise to a party system with clear ethnic connotations. Research on Africa has shown that ethnicity then becomes more salient when elections near and are expected to be close (Eifert *et al.* 2010). The losers of such elections, along with their ethnic clienteles, might subsequently be excluded from access to central state power with the known consequences for the prospects of peace (for examples, see Rothchild 2004). This is in line with the finding of Cohen (1997), who reports, on the basis of an analysis of MAR groups from 1945 to 1989, that ethnic rebellion is less likely in one-party systems than in multiparty systems. Democratization, to conclude, is not an effective tool of preventing armed conflict.[6]

---

[4] The only exception is Saideman *et al.* (2002), who found that democracies are more prone to ethnic rebellion in a subset of 110 countries analyzed from 1985 to 1998, using the MAR dataset to construct their dependent variable.

[5] Gleditsch *et al.* (2009) defend the democratic civil peace argument by using another measurement of democracy. However, the inverted U-shape relationship only holds when controlling for a host of other political variables (*ibid.*: 184, model 1), but not in a simple model with only the basic covariates (*ibid.*: model 2). According to Schneider and Wiesehomeier (2008), democracies are more peaceful than autocracies, but in ethnically homogenous societies only.

[6] The foreign policy implications of this conjecture are discussed by Mansfield and Snyder (2005b).

1.2 Indirect effects of democracy, parliamentarianism, proportionalism, and federalism

But aren't democracies more inclined to include minorities politically, given that their votes count in electoral competition? And shouldn't political inclusion then promote peace, as argued throughout this book, such that there could be an indirect effect of democracy on armed conflict? Indeed, democracies on average exclude less than half as many of their citizens than non-democratic countries on the basis of ethnicity. In multivariate regression analysis, democracy is strongly associated with the percentage of the population that is excluded from central government power, as Model 1 in Table 6.1 shows.[7] This association remains significant even in country-fixed effect models (results not shown), in other words, even if we take into account that countries differ from each other in many ways not captured by the democracy variable.

How are more specific institutional arrangements, such as proportionalism, parliamentarianism, and federalism, related to ethno-political inequality? Scholars of the "consociationalist" school have argued that proportional systems of electing parliament are more conducive to political power sharing when compared to majoritarian rules that tend to produce two-party systems with limited minority representation (Lijphart 1994, 1999). Consociationalists also argue that parliamentarianism should foster minority representation. In such systems, the executive is elected by parliament and depends on the support of its major parties. This often allows minority parties to enter a governing coalition, consociationalists argue, and to be rewarded with senior government posts. A presidency that is independent from parliament, by contrast, tends to be occupied by a member of the national majority. Finally, federal institutions are also seen as conducive to a more equal distribution of power since minorities that control a federal unit are able to use this as leverage to gain representation at the center as well.

Model 2 reveals, however, that neither proportional representation nor parliamentarianism nor federalism is associated with a more inclusive power configuration. These results are based on Gerring and Thacker's dataset (2008), which does not consider autocracies. We obtain the same results (not shown here) if we use the more precise World Bank dataset on political institutions (Thorsten Beck *et al.* 2001), which includes autocracies but has data from 1975 onward only, or the encompassing and equally granular Institutions and Elections Project

---

[7] Models 1–4 are generalized linear models with a logistic link function and the distribution specified as binomial. This is the most appropriate model specification since the dependent variable is a proportion and shows excess zeros due to countries that are ethnically homogenous (such as Korea) or where ethnicity is not politically relevant (as in Tanzania). In both groups of cases, the power structure is coded as fully inclusive (the dependent variable is therefore set at 0). Since the values of the exclusion variable can only change discontinuously and in "chunks," depending on the size and number of ethno-politically relevant groups, all models include these two control variables.

TABLE 6.1 *Democracy and exclusion: which influences what?*

	Dependent variable				
	Share of the excluded population			Future change in exclusion	Democratic transition next five years
	Model 1	Model 2	Model 3	Model 4	Model 5
Democracy, lagged	−0.5630**	−0.8109**	−0.5796*	−0.0048	
	(0.216)	(0.297)	(0.237)	(0.009)	
Fully proportional systems		0.4561			
		(0.280)			
Fully parliamentary systems		0.0753			
		(0.358)			
Fully federal systems		−0.3006			
		(0.525)			
Democratic transition during past 10 years			0.0303	−0.0147	
			(0.212)	(0.012)	
Share of the excluded population					−0.9679*
					(0.465)
Number of observations	7,024	3,404	6,819	6,092	4,439
Notes on no. of observations		Without autocracies			Non-democracies only

Notes: Controls for the size of the largest ethnic group and the number of groups (Models 1–4), GDP, cubic splines on calendar year, and constant not shown; robust standard errors in parentheses; * significant at 5%; ** significant at 1%.

dataset (Regan and Clark 2011) that covers all countries from 1972 onward,[8] or if we code federalism based on the Polity III dataset, which includes all regime types and all postwar years up to 1994.

It thus seems that democracy is associated with more inclusionary power configurations, while consociational institutions (federalism, proportionalism, parliamentarianism) don't show any such effects. Is the association between democracy and inclusion that Models 1 and 2 reveal due to a causal effect? Does democracy *make* a country more inclusionary? This question is evaluated in Model 3. It explores if having transitioned to democracy during the past 10 years led to a more inclusionary power structure today – which is not the case. But maybe this is because Model 3 compares young with old established democracies, and the younger ones haven't yet had the time to realize the inclusionary potential of democracy? To evaluate this possibility, Model 4 uses a different dependent variable: the change in levels of exclusion in the next five years. It shows that recent democratization does not push a country along the path of a more inclusionary future (note that results from Models 3 and 4 do not depend on how many years the independent or dependent variables are lagged).

These findings make us suspect that high levels of exclusion might inhibit democratization, thus producing a reverse causal relation between democracy and inclusion. This is exactly what Model 5 suggests. It refers to non-democracies only and evaluates which factors influence the chances of a democratic transition. The model is specified as a logistic regression on a dichotomous dependent variable. It shows that the higher the percentage of the population excluded from government power, the less likely the country will become a full democracy within the next five years. The same results from a country-fixed effect model based on the 72 countries that underwent a democratic transition since 1945 (results not shown).

Democracies are therefore more inclusive because of a selection mechanism: ethnocratic rulers who exclude large proportions of their population cannot possibly risk democratization since this would most likely mean that they would have to vacate the throne. Think of current Rwanda dominated by a small Tutsi elite of former exiles from Uganda; or think of Saddam Hussein's ethnocratic and sultanistic regime. These certainly tentative and preliminary findings run parallel to other studies that show how economic inequality hampers the prospects of democratization (Boix and Stokes 2003; for a more nuanced interpretation, see Houle 2009).[9]

---

[8] Autonomous provincial governments, as coded in the IAEP dataset, are significantly associated with less exclusion – but a similar coding for autonomous regions in the WB dataset shows no such association, nor does a variable that records if provincial governors are locally elected (also from the WB dataset) or IAEP's coding of constitutional federalism.

[9] A more detailed analysis of the relationships between ethno-political exclusion and democracy would have to take into account that yet other, unobserved variables could cause both.

In short, these additional analyses provide support to the argument that inclusion, rather than democratization, should be the top priority of prevention policies. More inclusionary power configurations will then also generate an environment within which democracy can flourish better. This argument is in line with the power-configurational view on institutional change that underlies this book: institutions reflect a specific distribution of power between coalitions of actors and change when these configurations shift.

2 DIRECT EFFECTS OF PROPORTIONALISM, PARLIAMENTARIANISM, AND FEDERALISM

The above analysis has shown that neither democracy nor more specific institutional arrangements such as proportionalism, parliamentarianism, or federalism have a demonstrable causal effect on the ethno-political power configuration, thus ruling out an indirect effect on conflict dynamics. Similarly, Appendix Table 6.2 shows that none of these political institutions – whatever the dataset used to capture them – shows a clear-cut association with the number of power-sharing partners, which represents the other aspect of the power configuration explored in the previous chapter.

I have also argued above that there is no evidence that democracy fosters peace directly, a mechanism often described with the seductive alliteration "from bullets to ballots." What is left to examine is whether there is a direct effect of proportionalism, parliamentarianism, or federalism. These might influence the likelihood of conflict not because they make a country more inclusionary, but because they offer electoral and other incentives that steer the dynamics of political competition in a more peaceful direction. Many have argued that presidential democracies such as the United States increase the zero-sum character of political competition and thus the chances of violent conflict (Lijphart 1977; Linz 1990), while parliamentarian systems are more conducive to political compromise and negotiation. Others maintain the opposite: that dividing power between a strong president and a parliament helps to avoid such zero-sum competition (Saideman *et al.* 2002; Roeder 2005). Furthermore, elected presidents will be oriented toward the common good of the broader electorate rather than their narrow ethnic clienteles, and thus have reasons to avoid escalating ethnic claims or indulging in particularistic politics (Horowitz 2002; Reilly 2006).

The literature is equally divided when it comes to the peace-promoting effects of federalism. Nordlinger (1972) and Roeder (2007) argue that federalism provides a strong institutional platform from which regional elites can launch a violent secessionist project. Advocates of federalism (Lijphart 1977) have defended the opposite hypothesis: federalism often leads to ethnic self-rule at the regional level, thus decreasing the relevance of the power configuration at the center (in line with the theory of nationalist violence by Hechter 2004).

TABLE 6.2 *Political institutions and ethnic conflict (logit analyses)*

Model	1	2	3	4	5	6	7	8	9	10	11	12
Proportionalism												
Proportional systems, 1946–2002, GT	−0.0372 (0.396)											
Proportional systems, 1975–2005, WB		−0.0003 (0.000)										
Proportional systems, 1972–2005, IAEP			−0.3325 (0.332)									
Presidentialism												
Presidential systems, 1946–2002, GT				−0.6375 (0.327)								
Presidential systems, 1975–2005, WB					−0.0702 (0.288)							
Presidential systems, 1972–2005, IAEP						0.4115 (0.328)						
Federalism												
Federal systems, 1946–2002, GT							0.9364 (0.485)					
Federal systems, 1946–1994, Polity III								−0.1899 (0.354)				

TABLE 6.2 (cont.)

Model	1	2	3	4	5	6	7	8	9	10	11	12
Federal or federated systems, 1972–2005, IAEP									0.0554 (0.236)			
Autonomous provincial governments, 1972–2005, IAEP										−0.7074* (0.316)		
Locally elected governors of provinces, 1975–2005, WB											−0.0013 (0.001)	
Autonomous regions, 1975–2005, WB												−0.0006 (0.001)
Number of observations	3,369	4,049	3,729	3,366	4,185	4,032	3,366	5,123	4,502	4,408	2,914	3,987
	Without auto-cracies			Without auto-cracies			Without auto-cracies					

Note: Controls for GDP, population size, linguistic fractionalization, mountainous terrain, political instability, anocracy, oil production, ongoing war, calendar year, cubic splines, and constant not shown; robust standard errors in parentheses; * significant at 5%; ** significant at 1%

Finally, proponents of proportionalism argue that minorities are better represented in parliament if even small parties stand a chance of winning seats. Majoritarian rules, by contrast, tend to produce two-party systems in which minority candidates fare less well (Lijphart 1994, 1999).[10] Representation in the legislative branch of government could moderate minority demands and at the same time acquaint majority representatives with the perspectives and needs of minorities.[11] Both together might promote peace, even if proportionalism does not affect the power configuration in the executive branch of government, as we have seen above.

I will discuss the relation between these three institutional arrangements and armed conflict in two steps. In the first step, I seek to find out whether institutions affect ethnic armed conflicts in general. The second step proceeds to a more fine-grained analysis in which I again distinguish, as in the last chapter, between infighting and rebellion. This allows us to determine whether political institutions affect power-sharing partners in different ways than excluded groups. For both steps, I will use all the available datasets mentioned above: Gerring and Thacker's coding (GT for short) for non-autocratic countries since 1945, the World Bank dataset (WB for short), which starts in 1975, Polity III for federalism from 1946 to 1994, and the Institutions and Elections Project data (IAEP) that covers all countries since 1972. Both the IAEP and the WB data contain very fine-grained codings of electoral systems and federalism and for both variables I will use several measurements. The Polity III dataset has the advantage of the broadest coverage.

2.1 Ethnic armed conflict

Other researchers have already shown that proportional systems don't reduce the likelihood of armed conflict if we don't distinguish between ethnic and non-ethnic conflicts (Schneider and Wiesehomeier 2008; Gleditsch *et al.* 2009).[12] Using three different codings of proportionalism from the WB, IAEP, and GT datasets, I arrive at the same conclusion (results not shown). But maybe

[10] However, Reynolds (2011: 114–116) finds that majoritarian rules result in better minority representation in parliament. This finding is based on the election results in 50 countries.

[11] Reilly (2006) reviews the debate between "centripetalists," who advocate presidentialism, majoritarianism, and unitary systems, and "consociationalists," who favor parliamentarianism, proportionalism, and federalism. Centripetalists have proposed many other institutional features, such as demanding a trans-regional support basis for party registration or more complex electoral rules such as the alternative vote system (see Reilly 2011). The same goes for consociationalists, who also advocate mutual veto rights in a grand coalition of ethnic parties. These more detailed institutional arrangements are outside the purview of this chapter's analysis, either because global data is not available or because they have been applied too rarely to permit a statistical analysis.

[12] Other findings are conditional on ethnic demography, conflict intensity, or regime type (e.g. Schneider and Wiesehomeier 2008).

proportionalism affects specifically *ethnic* conflicts, as argued by consociational-ists? Table 6.2 evaluates this proposition. Models 1 to 3 use the same model spe-cification and independent variables as the analysis in the previous chapter plus one of the three available codings of proportionalism, based on the GT, WB, and IAEP datasets respectively. None of these variables produce statistically significant results, even though the coefficients at least all point into the same (negative) direction.[13]

Models 4 to 6 evaluate if presidential systems are more or less violence prone. Previous research has shown that presidential systems are neither associ-ated with full-scale civil war nor with lower-intensity armed conflict (Bates *et al.* 1998: 207; Gleditsch *et al.* 2009).[14] I confirm these findings for all three different codings of presidentialism (results not shown). But again, don't we need to focus exclusively on ethnic conflicts, since these are at the core of the debate among constitutional engineers? Models 4 to 6, however, don't show any significant association between presidentialism and ethnic conflict, whether using the GT, the WB, or the IAEP datasets.[15]

The final five models (7 to 12) explore a possible relationship between federal-ism and armed ethnic conflict. On the most general level, when not distinguish-ing between various types of armed conflict, Gleditsch *et al.* (2009) have already established that federalism is not associated with more or with less conflict in the post-1945 world.[16] Perhaps federalism prevents specifically *ethnic* conflict, as argued by consociationalists? Models 7 to 9 use different codings of how the constitution defines the division of power between different levels of govern-ment.[17] Models 10 to 12 evaluate variables that go beyond constitutional provi-sions and code in how far sub-national units do indeed wield political power: whether provinces have governments that are chosen independently of the cen-ter (Model 10), elect governors locally (Model 11), or are granted a special status as autonomous regions (Model 12).

---

[13] This seems to contrast with Reynal-Querol (2002), who reports that "inclusionary" political systems, defined as proportional and parliamentary systems, are less prone to ethnic civil war. It is difficult to determine, however, which political institutions produce which effect, since she codes a variable that cross-classifies various elements: 0 is defined as "unfree" political systems, 1 refers to "free," majoritarian, and parliamentary systems, 2 to free presidential systems, and 3 to free proportional and parliamentary systems.

[14] Other research offers some more conditional insights, with rather contradictory implications: presidentialism might increase the probability of armed conflict in ethnically *homogenous* democracies (Schneider and Wiesehomeier 2008), while it has no effect on very heterogeneous democratic polities.

[15] Both findings stand in opposition to those of Roeder (2005).

[16] Schneider and Wiesehomeier (2008) again offer a more nuanced assessment of the conditions under which federalism reduces conflict in democracies. Federalism is associated with peace in highly fractionalized societies, but *increases* conflict probability in societies with a demographically dominant majority.

[17] Gerring and Thacker, for example, code a state as federal if it has a bicameral legislature with one of the chambers composed of the delegates of the provinces.

Clearly, constitutional federalism has no effect whatsoever on conflict propensity (Models 7 to 9). But at least one of the de facto power variables does produce a significant result: autonomously chosen provincial governments, as coded by the IAEP, are associated with less ethnic conflict (Model 10). Unfortunately, however, this result is not upheld when using a similar WB coding of autonomous provincial government (Model 11). Furthermore, Model 10 relates to years after 1972 only, such that we cannot be entirely sure how much we should rely on this finding. This caution is reinforced by additional analysis (results not shown here): when using Fearon and Laitin's coding of ethnic civil war – relating to conflicts with at least 1,000 battle deaths – the finding reported in Model 10 disappears as well.

2.2 Infighting and rebellion

Maybe we arrive at a more positive conclusion regarding the peace-promoting effects of political institutions if we disaggregate the dependent variable? Isn't it likely that institutions affect members of a governing coalition differently from groups excluded from central government?[18] The picture that emerges is slightly more complex (see Table 6.3). Proportional systems don't influence the probability of either infighting or rebellions (see Models 1 to 3).[19] And for only one coding of presidentialism – the one based on the WB dataset shown in Model 5 – do we find a significant effect. Presidentialism is associated, in this model, with a lower likelihood of infighting between power-sharing partners, but not with rebellions.[20]

---

[18] In addition, shouldn't institutions also affect whether rebels and infighters seek to secede from a state or rather conquer the power center? I briefly evaluated this possibility by looking separately at secessionist conflicts, which are at the core of the debate about the peace-promoting effects of federalism. The results of this analysis can be found in Appendix Table 6.1. It contains six models, the first three again coding whether a country is constitutionally set up as a federal state, the second three relating to actually observed degrees of autonomy of sub-state entities. Only one of these variables is significantly (and negatively) associated with secession: states with provinces that have locally elected governors are less likely to see secessionist armed conflicts. This result is based on a relatively small number of observations (less than half of the full dataset used in the previous chapter). Still, it holds up even when controlling for the ethno-political power configuration by adding the share of the excluded population as well as the number of power-sharing partners to the equation, thus ruling out an indirect effect.

[19] Cohen (1997), however, reports that proportional systems decrease the likelihood of full-scale ethnic rebellion in democracies (though not the incidence of low-level violence). His analysis is based on the MAR dataset. If autocracies are excluded from consideration, I do find a negative significant association between rebellion and proportionalism for one of the three codings of the variable (the one provided by the WB dataset).

[20] This latter result is supported by Saideman *et al.* (2002), who report that neither presidentialism nor parliamentarianism have any effect on rebellion by politically marginalized ethnic groups (as defined by the MAR dataset).

TABLE 6.3 *Political institutions and infighting (Columns 1) and rebellion (Columns 2) (multinomial logit analyses)*

	Model 1		Model 2		Model 3		Model 4		Model 5		Model 6	
	1	2	1	2	1	2	1	2	1	2	1	2
Proportionalism												
Fully proportional systems, 1946–2002, GT	−1.3970 (1.144)	0.2523 (0.409)										
Proportional systems, 1975–2005, WB			0.0006 (0.001)	−0.0005 (0.000)								
Proportional systems, 1972–2005, IAEP					−0.8359 (1.164)	−0.2244 (0.353)						
Presidentialism												
Fully presidential systems, 1946–2002, GT							−1.0798 (0.675)	−0.5126 (0.352)				
Fully presidential systems, 1975–2005, WB									−1.5439** (0.595)	0.3651 (0.315)		
Presidential systems, 1972–2005, IAEP											0.4419 (0.991)	0.3909 (0.328)
Number of observations	3,369	3,369	4,049	4,049	3,729	3,729	3,366	3,366	4,185	4,185	4,032	4,032

Federalism

	Model 7		Model 8		Model 9		Model 10		Model 11		Model 12	
	1	2	1	2	1	2	1	2	1	2	1	2
Federal systems, 1946–1994, Polity III	2.6257** (0.666)	−0.9492** (0.324)										
Fully federal systems, 1946–2002, GT			1.4013 (0.886)	0.8757 (0.560)								
Federal or federated systems, 1972–2005, IAEP					0.4391 (0.520)	−0.0517 (0.261)						
Auton. provincial governments, 1972–2005, IAEP							−2.0082* (0.925)	−0.4914 (0.330)				
Locally elected provincial governors, 1975–2005, WB									−0.0023 (0.001)	−0.0008 (>.001)		
Autonomous regions, 1975–2005, WB											−0.0018 (0.002)	−0.0001 (0.001)
Number of observations	5,123	5,123	3,366	3,366	4,502	4,502	4,408	4,408	2,914	2,914	3,987	3,987

Notes: Controls for GDP, population size, linguistic fractionalization, mountainous terrain, political instability, anocracy, oil production, ongoing war, calendar year, cubic splines, and constant not shown; robust standard errors in parentheses; * significant at 5%; ** significant at 1%.

This is consistent with my analysis of infighting as a consequence of a commitment problem. A strong president might be better able to hold a fractious coalition together than a prime minister who dependends on parliamentary support. Further supporting this view with a relational analysis, Hale (2011) finds that in the post-Soviet world, presidentialism produces strongly integrated, hierarchical patronage networks focused on the president, while parliamentarianism tends to result in a more fragmented system of competing alliance networks. All of this would support those constitutional engineers who argue that strong presidents are less likely to cater to their own ethnic clientele and, if elected by popular vote, need to seek those votes across ethnic divides.

However, the association between infighting and presidentialism disappears once we take the ethno-political power configuration into account – albeit there is no association between presidentialism and the number of power-sharing partners (see Appendix Table 6.2), thus ruling out an indirect effect. Furthermore, the association again depends on a particular coding of presidentialism and does not show up with the other two codings (Models 4 and 6), thus raising doubts about its robustness.

In sum, neither proportionalism nor presidentialism has any significant effect on rebellions in the name of excluded populations. And there are only weak and not very robust signs that presidentialism might reduce the chances of infighting. This leaves us with federalism. The results are rather contradictory, in line with Horowitz's (1985) assessment of the qualitative evidence. In four of the six codings of federalism, no association whatsoever can be discerned (Models 8, 9, 11, and 12). But when using the Polity III data (Model 7), which covers all countries from 1946 to 1994, an interesting finding appears: federal states are significantly more likely to see infighting, but also experience significantly less rebellions in the name of excluded populations (in line with consociationalist arguments). However, the coding of federalism provided by the IAEP (Model 10) produces quite different results: autonomously chosen provincial governments are associated with *less* infighting (the opposite of Model 7) but not with rebellion. We already found a negative significant result for this coding of federalism when regressing on all ethnic conflict (Model 10 in Table 6.2). We can now add more precision to the analysis, since we now know that the effect is limited to conflicts between power-sharing partners.[21]

How to adjudicate between these two conflicting findings that we get from the Polity and IAEP codings of federalism? Much more detailed analysis of the actual coding rules and the case universes that they create would be needed to

---

[21] Equally contradictory are the findings of group-level analyses. When using the EPR dataset with ethnic groups as units of observations, I find that groups holding some sort of regional power are less likely to rebel than powerless or discriminated against groups (the effect is only marginally significant, however). This contrasts with the findings of Roeder (2007), which are based on his own dataset of 658 ethnic groups in 153 states from 1955 to 1999. He reports that political autonomy is associated with a heightened likelihood of violent ethno-political conflict.

answer this question. For the moment, it suffices to note that there are good reasons to trust the results based on the IAEP dataset more than those derived from the Polity data. First, the Polity III-based results disappear when India (a federal state with many infighting conflicts) is excluded from the analysis, or if linguistic fractionalization is not part of the equation, or if the ethno-political power configuration is taken into account by adding the number of power-sharing partners as well as the percentage of the excluded population to the regression model (results not shown). The IAEP results are more robust and hold up without India, without controlling for linguistic fractionalization, or with the ethno-political variables added.[22] In addition, a similar coding of provincial autonomy (based on whether or not provinces have locally elected governors) is associated with infighting in a similar way (Model 11) even though the effect misses standard levels of statistical significance.

One might object to this series of rather sobering results – from the point of view of constitutional engineers – that one needs to test whether presidentialism, federalism, and proportionalism have different effects in democracies and in autocracies. Electoral rules might only influence conflict processes when votes can indeed change who is in power; federalism could show its pacifying effects in autocratic regimes only, where conquering the center is unfeasible (as reported by Bermeo 2002; Saideman *et al.* 2002). To test for this possibility, I ran all models presented in Tables 6.2 and 6.3 for separate sub-samples of autocracies and non-autocratic regimes. The results remain substantially similar to those reported above, except that the findings regarding federalism are even more contradictory.[23]

But perhaps parliamentarianism shows its moderating effects on the dynamics of political competition and conflict only if combined with proportionalism – as argued by consociationalists? Indeed, for the GT as well as the IAEP datasets, a combination of proportionalism and parliamentarianism is associated with a significantly lower risk of infighting, while it does not affect rebellions. However, using the WB dataset produces the opposite result: infighting between power-sharing partners is significantly *more* likely in such consociational regimes, while again no associations with rebellions appears (results not shown). I conclude that there is no robust and consistent effect here.

---

[22] There is a positive association between the number of power-sharing partners and federalism according to Polity III data, but not when using the IAEP or the GT coding – indicating that the effect of autonomous provinces is not indirectly operating through the power configuration. No other political institution variable from the three datasets shows any association with the number of power-sharing partners (the results are reported in Appendix Table 6.2).

[23] In autocracies, federalism is associated with a decreased risk of infighting as well as rebellion when using the Polity coding, and with less infighting when using IAEP's coding of constitutional federalism. However, when considering de facto autonomy (coded either on the basis of the WB or the IAEP data), federalism *increases* the chances of infighting in autocracies.

2.3 Inclusion rather than institutional engineering

In sum, federalism or presidentialism might have an independent effect on the dynamic of political competition between power-sharing partners and reduce the chances of escalation into armed conflict. Autonomous provinces make it perhaps less urgent to fight for the spoils of government at the center; independent presidents might be in a better position to overcome commitment problems in a ruling coalition of ethnic elites than prime ministers responsible to the parliamentary representatives of these elites. The results reported above quite unequivocally indicate, however, that neither presidentialism, proportionalism, federalism, or a combination of such institutions have any effect on rebellions by excluded groups, the far more prevalent type of ethnic conflict: 90 out of the 110 ethnic conflicts in the dataset are fought in the name of such groups.

Peace therefore does not result from a specific institutional form of government, but from inclusive power configurations – whatever the institutional forms that sustain them. No institutional setup is universally suited to guarantee peace. Inclusive power structures can emerge in democratic or undemocratic polities, consociational[24] or centripetal regimes, federal or unitarian states, depending on context, historically established actor configurations, and institutional legacies (see the new realism among constitutional engineers: Ellis 2003; Horowitz 2004). No recipe of institutional reform – democratization, electoral systems engineering, or decentralization – will bring about political inclusion and sustainable peace.

The best strategy to avoid armed conflict and war is therefore to foster the political representation, at the highest level of government, of all politically relevant ethnic groups or to pursue a strategy of nation building that depoliticizes ethnicity over time. Effective and long-term prevention of ethnic conflicts might therefore need to touch the very fundamentals on which a nation-state is built: both the definition of the people in whose name a state is governed and the degree to and the ways in which ethnic background shapes access to central state power. If ethnic conflict is mostly the result of the capture of the state by specific ethnic elites and their constituencies, then nothing less than a lasting rearrangement of these power structures will suffice to bring durable peace.

Unfortunately and ironically, such exclusionary regimes can often only be overthrown through violence and war. The political elites in power and the

---

[24] The possible downsides of consociational regimes have been widely discussed: they perpetuate or even deepen ethnic dividing lines; they are inflexible and thus difficult to adapt to changing power relations and demographics; they invite outbidding by more radical ethno-nationalists; and they depend on a culture of consensus and accommodation that is rare to find (Rothchild and Roeder 2005). As noted above, consociationalism might be especially problematic if there is a high number of power-sharing partners such as in Lebanon. When a single, large ethnic group has been hitherto excluded from power, and ethnicity is thoroughly and irreversibly politicized, however, moving toward a consociational arrangement – as in Northern Ireland (O'Leary 1989) – might prove to be the only viable way to diffuse the potential for violence.

ethnic constituencies they privilege might not be willing to give up their monopoly over the state and its institutions. No prevention policy and no local "peace-building" initiative will convince them otherwise. It is unlikely, to illustrate, that Saddam Hussein would have opened up his tribalistic ethnocracy – under benevolent prodding by the "international community" – to include Kurdish and Shiite elite segments into the ruling coalition. Similarly, Rhodesia's white rulers showed little inclination, despite harsh international sanctions, to allow for an adequate political representation of the black majority. As neighboring South Africa shows, however, negotiated transitions away from ethnocracy are possible, if unfortunately rare. To increase the likelihood of such peaceful transitions, it may help to foster the willingness of ruling elites to share power, including by building up corresponding pressure from their constituencies, and to steer leaders of the excluded population toward moderation and away from maximalist claims or revanchist programs.

3 DOES MORE INCLUSION FOSTER INFIGHTING?

However, there is an obvious dilemma associated with this strategy of fostering inclusive government: exclusion and center segmentation are not independent from each other, and addressing one aspect of the overall power configuration might therefore adversely affect the other. More specifically, integrating hitherto marginalized ethnic groups into a power-sharing arrangement means that their leaders will now compete with existing elites for the distribution of state power. This will increase the commitment problems associated with a coalition of multiple players. Analysis of the EPR dataset on the group level (Cederman *et al.* 2010b) discovered an additional mechanism that makes power sharing with hitherto excluded groups problematic: ethnic elites who have lost relative power in the recent past are significantly more likely to engage in violent infighting (for further evidence, see Roessler 2011). Power sharing with hitherto excluded groups obviously implies such a relative loss of status for the exponents of the old regime.

To put this dilemma in the starkest possible terms: under which conditions will more inclusion *increase* the likelihood of violent conflict? All depends on the number of groups already sharing power and the size of the newly included population. The following four examples demonstrate this interrelationship between inclusion and center segmentation. In all these diverse ethno-political configurations, more inclusion ends up *decreasing* the overall likelihood of armed conflict despite increasing the number of power-sharing partners

We calculated expected war probabilities for Iraq, Mexico, Bosnia, and Myanmar based on Model 4 in Table 5.2. The average risk of armed conflict in the entire world sample is 1.5%. For Iraq, the regression model predicts that including Sunnis in the power-sharing arrangement between Shiite and Kurdish elites would halve the risk of violent conflict from the current 2.2% to

1.0%.[25] This is considerably lower than the predicted 3.1% risk of conflict for a Sunni-led ethnocratic regime as it existed under Saddam Hussein. Indeed, that era was characterized by an uninterrupted series of insurgencies by Kurdish nationalist and Shiite rebels. In Mexico, integrating the indigenous population into the power center would diminish an already low likelihood of armed conflict from 0.8% to 0.4%. Not surprisingly, the Zapatista uprising in Chiapas represented the only ethnic conflict in Mexico's postwar history. In Bosnia, finally, the current consociational arrangement between Bosniak, Serbians, and Croatians is associated with a risk of 2.2%, less than half the risk of any other possible configuration in that country. In Myanmar, however, including leaders of all ten politically relevant groups that fought separatist wars against the government or are otherwise politically marginalized, would decrease the risk of future conflict from the current level of 3.5% to only 3.3%.

Such calculations obviously don't represent "predictions" in any meaningful sense of the term – there are simply too many other influential factors not captured by our theory and data.[26] But they show that the benefits of more inclusion always outweigh the increased risks of infighting, if only marginally so in extreme cases with a very large number of politically relevant ethnic groups, such as Myanmar. The problems associated with balancing the interests of competing ethnic elites that share government power are less severe compared to the risks of rebellions incurred by exclusionary regimes.

4 POWER SHARING AFTER CONFLICT ENDS

This leads to the question of how to secure peace after violent conflict ends. Are power-sharing arrangements or democratization suitable tools to prevent the *recurrence* of violence? Perhaps democracy is better at post-conflict peace building than it is at preventing the outbreak of violence in the first place? A quantitative study of the durability of peace after civil war shows that holding elections, arguably the core democratic institution, has no overall effect on how long peace lasts. More disconcertingly, this study also shows that severe autocracies are the best guarantors of (cold) peace (Collier *et al.* 2008). This is in line with Paris' (1997) qualitative assessment that post-conflict democratization, contrary to a widely held belief in the Western policy-making community, might destabilize a country further, especially if it is pursued immediately and without mitigating its conflictual implications. On the other hand, however, Toft (2009) reports that she did not find any relationship between levels of democratization

---

[25] We used the beta coefficients derived from the full sample and then plugged in the values for all independent variables for the appropriate country in 2003, and varied only the size of the excluded population and the number of power-sharing partners.

[26] For a prominent attempt at forecasting civil war and state collapse, see Goldstone *et al.* (2010).

and the prospects of durable peace. And Mukherjee (2006) even finds that peace lasts longer the more democratic a state.

There is therefore no conclusive evidence on whether or not democratization can secure peace – mirroring the findings on democracy and armed conflict reported above. Perhaps power-sharing arrangements – whether democratic or not – are more effective. Many qualitative researchers are skeptical. Indeed, many post-conflict power sharing arrangements have fallen apart or were never implemented (Downes 2004), leading some to argue in favor of partition (Pounds 1964; Kaufmann 1998; Chapman and Roeder 2007) or of letting one side win, rather than intervening and forcing a power-sharing arrangement on opponents. This not only produces a more durable peace, so the argument goes, but also allows the victorious side to build an effective and autonomous state (Weinstein 2005). Others maintain that the international community's commitment to power sharing has produced a moral hazard problem and has led to many more armed rebellions in Africa, instigated by local leaders who hope to be integrated into a future power-sharing arrangement brokered by outside actors (Tull and Mehler 2005).

However, there is some quantitative evidence that power-sharing arrangements – and thus a more inclusive government – are an important, if difficult-to-implement ingredient of lasting peace. Perhaps this is true only if power sharing comes after a military victory by one side. This is the main finding of Mukherjee's (2006) comprehensive study of 111 post-conflict cases. The relationship is symmetric, however: victory without power sharing does not lead to lasting peace either.[27] Binningsbo's (2006) research also supports the political inclusion approach. Her analysis of 126 post-conflict periods reveals that a grand governing coalition and territorial autonomy prolong peace, independent of whether or not it is combined with victory.[28]

These certainly tentative findings are in line with the main argument outlined above. Ethnic dominance is a recipe for continued and repeated conflict, while moving toward a more inclusionary power structure helps to prevent a relapse into violence. In line with Mukherjee's study, I would argue that even a victory by one side needs to go hand in hand with the co-optation and integration of the ethnic constituencies of the losing side – not necessarily the leaders of the armed factions, to be sure. Otherwise, victory leads to the cold peace of an ethnocratic

---

[27] Power sharing combined with a military stalemate, however, makes it more likely that violence resumes.

[28] She also finds that a victory by government troops, but not by rebels, prevents a return to violence, while Toft (2009) arrives at the opposite conclusion. Licklider (1995) demonstrates that negotiated settlements – as opposed to victory – are only fragile if the war had been fought along ethnic lines. According to Hartzell and Hoddie (2003), who analyzed a much smaller sample of 38 negotiated peace settlements, those that include regional autonomy and rebel integration into the army prolong peace, while including political power or economic revenue sharing into a peace agreement has no effect on the likelihood that violence resumes. They unfortunately do not consider whether or not the peace agreements have actually been implemented.

regime that prepares the ground for future violence once the authoritarian grip on the political system loosens. Perhaps the current RPF-regime in Rwanda or Saddam Hussein's Iraq after the successful crushing of the Shiite uprising in the wake of the first Gulf War might serve as examples of cold peace.

5 NATION BUILDING OR SHARING SOVEREIGNTY?

So far, I have argued that inclusionary government should be the prime focus of prevention policies, while specific political institutions do not bring about more inclusive power structures, affect the conflict propensity of groups that are already part of the power structure at the margin only, and have no consequences for the likelihood of rebellions by excluded groups. It is now time to step back from this analysis a bit further and adopt a more long-term view on how peace could be secured. The preceding analyses of armed conflict has largely taken for granted that politics is a matter of ethnic power relations, and focused on the question of how far ethnically defined alliance networks are linked to or excluded from central government power.

As Chapter 2 demonstrated, however, power struggles can be decoupled from the question of ethnic self-rule; ethnicity does not need to be the prime focus of political loyalty and determine a person's relationship vis-à-vis the state. Encompassing relationships between state elites and the population can be established without including citizens as members of a particular ethnic community. This is, as I have shown elsewhere, the case in multiethnic Switzerland (Wimmer 2011), but also in countries such as Burkina Faso or Tanzania (Miguel 2004). In other words, nation building depoliticizes ethnicity and make sure that political contestation and competition don't end up in a struggle over which ethnic community "owns" the state.

This brings us to the "nation building" debate that has resurged over the past two decades in policy circles.[29] At the core of this debate is how to best enhance the loyalty of all citizens, independent of their ethnic background, toward the state. This allows the state to rely less on coercion and to secure compliance and provide security with the consent of the ruled. Chapter 2 suggested that the population will identify with and be loyal toward a state that offers a favorable exchange relationship. Conversely, a government that cannot deliver public goods and that cannot grant meaningful political participation should not expect the political loyalty and military support of its population, let alone that citizens identify with the nation and its state, rather than their ethnic community and its leadership. On the other hand, a population should not expect that state elites enter and maintain a national compact if the citizenry is not prepared to pay taxes and provide the state with soldiers. A mutually beneficial exchange relationship, in turn, needs to last over generations in order to routinize and

---

[29] For an overview, see Osler Hampson and Mendeloff (2007).

institutionalize such identification, loyalty, and support. Nation building takes generations, not years (for a similar argument, see Ayoob 2007; Darden and Mylonas 2011).

The historical development of France, discussed in Chapter 2, provides a good illustration. A full century had to elapse after the French revolutionaries had introduced the idea of the national community until the Third Republic realized and institutionalized the national compact – even though the French state was highly centralized and networks of voluntary organizations were well established – both together facilitating nation building and preventing the politicization of ethnic divides. Furthermore, Chapter 5 showed that secessions are more likely to haunt states with a long history of imperial rule. The peripheral population is only weakly integrated into the alliance networks stretching from the center of power and thus tends to disidentify with such a state and question its legitimacy and current territorial shape – independent of the power configuration at the center. As Chapter 2 suggests, citizens will shift their loyalty to and identify with the nation only if the exchange relationship with the state is favorable and if they can trust that this will remain so even if the ethnic background of those who reside in the government palace should change in the future.

The following example further illustrates the point: tribal villagers in Afghanistan need to know that the central authority is able to protect them from arbitrary violence and expropriation in the long run – and not just tomorrow with the help of foreign troops. Only then will they give up their Kalashnikovs as well as the system of self-defense based on honorable reputation that has served them well in the past, and send their sons to a national army, rather than under the command of a tribal leader. Similarly, they need to be certain that a state bureaucracy can credibly commit to provide public goods in an equitable way before they cease to rely on the mosque, village community, regional strongmen, or the help of international NGOs.

It is therefore unlikely that nation building can be achieved by outside actors who channel aid through local NGOs or their own on-the-ground agencies to avoid corruption and inefficiency. This undermines, rather than strengthens, the legitimacy of the state they are supposed to help build (Wimmer and Schetter 2003; Darden and Mylonas 2011).[30] Shifting political loyalty to and identifying with a state cannot be enforced from the outside, let alone over the course of a handful of years. Outside actors can merely strengthen a local government's capacity to provide public goods in an effective and equitable way, a project that is likely to take decades in the environment of a largely illiterate society such as Afghanistan.

The strategic orientation of outside assistance should therefore change: from a short-term to a generational perspective, best coordinated by international

---

[30] A survey shows that there is a negative correlation between trust in the central state and the amount of foreign aid received by Afghan villagers (Zürcher and Böhnke 2009).

organizations such as the UN or the World Bank that are independent of the electoral cycles of national governments and their security interests. Second, aid should primarily build the state's capacity to rule effectively, to provide public goods on a long-term basis, and to raise revenues though taxes (Fearon and Laitin 2004), rather than forever depending on foreign assistance or on corruption and bribery. This would allow a sustained state-building process to unfold and a new compact between the state and the population to eventually develop. Overall, then, the best strategy of conflict prevention for institutionally weak states is to encourage a gradual, endogenously sustained process of state formation and nation building that will allow political alliance networks to cut across ethnic divides and thus depoliticize ethnicity.

An alternative idea has recently been proposed: that sovereignty should be "shared" between such weak states and outside powers – regional hegemons, global powers, or international bodies. This might be an appropriate strategy for the short run (Krasner 2005). In the long run, however, such arrangements contradict the fundamental principles of legitimacy on which the modern world has come to rest: that states should be governed in the name of a nationally defined people by representatives of that people. A return to quasi-colonial government through ethnic others therefore lacks the basic legitimacy without which rule by consent cannot be established. Nation building, in other words, not only demands effective public goods provision, but also by the right people.[31] The spirit of nationalism, once released from its bottle and diffused across the globe, is difficult to tame.

---

[31] Hechter (2009a) found one single modern example for consensual "foreign rule": the Chinese Maritime Customs Administration.

7

Conclusions

I SUMMARY

We have now come to the end of a long journey across the history of the modern world, walking through different disciplinary landscapes, across forests of data, and underneath cascades of statistical models. The journey started with the Capetian kingdom of medieval France and showed how subsequent state centralization and the development of networks of voluntary organizations led state elites to extend alliance relationships – previously confined to other elite factions – to the rest of the population. Political identities and loyalties were restructured accordingly, and the first nation-states were born, based on the idea of popular sovereignty and national solidarity. The story then branched out and traced how the rest of the world gradually adopted this new template of political legitimacy, led by nationalists who dreamed of overcoming the hitherto taken-for-granted ethnic hierarchies of empire and achieving self-rule in a national state as powerful and legitimate as those first nation-states.

This dream became realized wherever the domestic and international power configuration allowed nationalists to overthrow or absorb the old regime, often helped by cascading creations of nation-states in the neighborhood or other parts of the empire (see the summary of the findings in Figure 7.1). Realizing these dreams often came at the price of war: many nationalists met stiff resistance from imperial or dynastic rulers who knew that there would be no place for them in the new national order based on the "like-over-like" principle.

In contrast to the first nations, these new states were often too weak to integrate the entire population into an encompassing network of exchange relationships within which the state's public goods and political influence would be traded against military loyalty and taxes. Lacking dense networks of voluntary organizations to establish and stabilize such encompassing networks further contributed to the politicization of ethnicity. Political alliances thus formed along ethnic divides, and nation building remained a rhetorical trope often evoked by the state's leaders but with little effect on the loyalties and identities

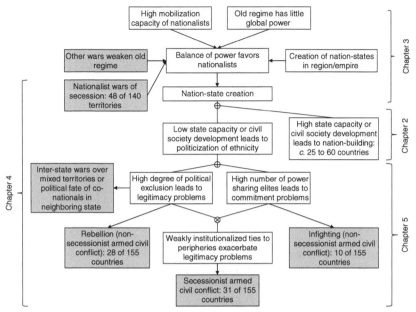

FIGURE 7.1 Synopsis: nation-state formation and war
Notes: ⊕ denotes an "or" relationship, while ⊗ refers to "and."

of the population at large. Many states with weak institutional capacity and civil societies were thus unable to overcome the ethno-political hierarchies inherited from the imperial past, or developed them anew. In extreme cases, the state apparatus – from the army to the presidency, the cabinet to high-ranking civil service posts – came to rest firmly in the hands of an ethnocratic minority elite.

However, such ethno-political inequality violates the very principles of legitimate rule according to which nation-states are supposed to be governed: that likes should rule over likes and that rulers should offer protection, public goods, and participation to "the nation" as a whole, rather than their own ethnic constituencies only. Various forms of violent conflict may ensue. First, a nationalizing state might interfere on behalf of co-nationals across the border who risk the fate of political domination by the majority in control of the neighboring state; or they might try to snatch away the territories inhabited by these co-nationals and bring them "Heim ins Reich," leading to wars between states. Second, domestic rebellions against domination by ethnic others have haunted many newly established nation-states. Third, competition between ethnically defined governing elites might escalate into violence, especially if a high number of power-sharing partners exacerbates the fear of losing out in the struggle over state power and risk "alien rule." Where the relationship between the peripheral population and the state hasn't yet been routinized and the new state therefore commands little political legitimacy, secessionist violence might challenge the territorial integrity of the new state.

This dynamic of rebellion and violent competition does not seem to be affected by the formal rules of the political game: it unfolds independently from whether a state is governed democratically or not, elects a strong president or lets its parliament choose a prime minister, has decentralized power to provinces or is set up as a unitarian state, and so forth. What matters for understanding peace and war is the power configuration at the center of government, rather than the institutional form it assumes.

To be sure, the story of this book is not entirely new. Some of its parts have been told in one form or another in existing literatures. And it certainly has its limitations: while the analysis does capture general patterns and trends in a probabilistic way, it is unsuited to explain the exact course that an individual case – an imperial province, an independent country – charts through the waters of possible histories. Furthermore, it brings into relief certain aspects of the history of the modern world and overlooks many others. It is a book about the political earthquakes and violent disruptions that the global rise of nationalism has brought about, not about modern history as a whole or every war that has ever been fought over the past 200 years. Important parts of this story – for example how strong states or civil societies emerge – remain outside the purview of this book (but see Wimmer, in preparation). And finally, some of the data analyzed in the various chapters remain sketchy and capture the relevant mechanisms in rather imprecise ways.

The advantage of the book, however, is that its narrative is based on systematic evidence gathered from the entire world and over long stretches of time. Its story therefore makes empirically more sense than other, perhaps equally plausible or appealing stories that have been told in the past. It thus offers lessons for a variety of other approaches. Much international relations scholarship neglects the power of nationalism in shaping the modern state system and the conflicts between its constituent units. Many important strands in comparative politics overlook how the lack of legitimacy and struggle over political power fuel the flames of civil war. As the previous chapters show, a substantial number of these wars are fought over the legitimate form of statehood and over who controls its government. The book also demonstrated how power configurations affect which templates of political legitimacy come to prevail – both during the emergence of the first nation-state and its subsequent diffusion across the world. By contrast, modernization theories rarely offer a specific analysis of what brought about the broad political transformations they seek to explain. Globalization theories and cultural approaches are often at a loss in understanding why particular institutional templates or cultural frameworks are adopted here but not there. Besides these substantial insights into a crucial, yet often-neglected aspect of modern history, the book offers new vistas on a variety of broader analytical issues to which they are more tangentially related. These will be briefly addressed now.

2 BEYOND IDENTITY VERSUS INTEREST, GREED VERSUS GRIEVANCE

The preceding analyses suggest that ethnicity and nationalism should not be associated exclusively with cultural "identity," and hence put in contrast to political and economic "interests," as in much of the political economy literature. Rather, ethnic and national identities result from and in turn influence the dynamics of political competition and alliance, and are inseparably interwoven with the struggle over state power and its principles of political legitimacy. Indeed, this book treats ethnic and national identities as equivalents to other political coalitions – as institutionalized, taken-for-granted bundles of alliances (in line with Bates 1974; Glazer and Moynihan 1975). Following this reasoning, ethnicity is not an aim in itself, but both the organizational means through which individuals struggle to gain power, as well as a perceptual framework through which they define their interests and identify the alliance partners they can take for granted. By implication, the analysis offered in Chapter 5 might be extended to other politically relevant social categories, such as regions, social classes, professional groups, and so on. These play important roles in some countries such as in ethnically homogenous Korea or where ethnicity is not politically relevant such as in Tanzania. The dynamics of political competition over who controls the nation-state unfold along similar lines as the ones I have analyzed for ethnically defined networks of alliances.

Highlighting the political and strategic nature of the ethnic phenomenon also avoids the popular distinction between "greed" and "grievance" introduced by Collier and Hoeffler (2004). The alliteration is certainly seductive and the dichotomy resonates well with Western traditions of opposing the material world to the domain of ideas. But it makes little empirical sense. Throughout the chapters, I have argued that ethnic politics simultaneously concerns "material" interests such as access to public goods, the political goal to gain power, and "idealist" motives such as striving for political legitimacy or the dignity and pride that comes with the recognition of one's ethnic heritage by the state. Because political domination by ethnic others affects one's economic, political, and symbolic standing alike, it is difficult to disentangle these intertwined and mutually reinforcing motives from each other.[1] The crucial question therefore is not whether rebels are coolly calculating materialists or hot-blooded idealists fighting for recognition of their "identity," but rather what causal dynamics will lead actors with complexly intertwined motives down the path toward violent conflict.

But aren't national and ethnic identities loaded with a special emotional charge that sets them apart from other political identities? To be sure, treating ethnicity and nationhood as bundles of taken-for-granted political alliances does not deny that ethnic and national identities are sometimes associated with

[1] See also Tarrow and Tilly (2006).

strong emotions and intense passions. But these are, as Petersen (2002) has shown, the outcome of certain power configurations and the political mobilizations and conflicts these produce. Emotions result from such configurations – such as the resentment of being governed by one's former subordinates – they don't produce them. Furthermore, these emotions and passions guide the actions of individuals during the "hot" phases of a conflict but may subside later on and no longer dominate individual's modes of reasoning and feeling.[2] Nor are intense emotions specific to ethnic identities and conflict. Similar fear, hatred, or resentment are associated with conflict and mobilization along other cleavage lines, as the cultural revolution in China or the overthrow of the Shah of Persia in the name of religious renewal illustrate. There is thus nothing specifically "deep" or "emotional" about ethnic and national identities per se.

3 WHY ETHNICITY?

The fact so many of today's conflicts are fought along ethnic and national lines has therefore little to do with the superior symbolic power or emotional depth of ethnicity and nationhood (*pace* Connor 1972). Rather, it is because ethnicity is so closely intertwined with the nationalist principles on which the modern state came to rest, thus granting a legitimacy to ethno-nationalist appeals and claims to power that surpasses that of other claims and appeals, making it more likely that ethno-political conflict escalates into violence and full-scale civil war (for empirical evidence, see Eck 2009).

To illustrate the point with a perhaps slightly overdrawn comparison, consider that old, male, upper middle-class lawyers have governed most Western states for decades, if not centuries, justifying their rule with their expertise in matters of the state acquired throughout long careers that led them through countless committees and councils. Political mobilization against the tyranny of the masters of the fine print, against patriarchy, or gerontocracy have remained rather muted, however. Imagine how unpopular and contested an equally unequal power configuration would be if aligned along an ethnic divide: if the American Senate and presidency were entirely controlled by the First Nations or by Mexicans who conquered the country after the Mexican-American war had ended in their favor. Political inequality needs to violate established principles of legitimacy to fuel popular dissatisfaction.

Other authors have offered different explanations of why ethnicity is often politicized and why many conflicts in the contemporary world are fought in the name of ethnic groups. The most prominent explanations in comparative politics point at the nature of ethnicity, which is supposed to provide an ideal basis for patronage politics. Fearon (1999) argues that the high "stickiness" of ethnic markers – a person born as a Tutsi will most likely die as a Tutsi – prevents

---

[2] See the analysis of the "rally-round-the-flag" phenomenon by Feinstein (2011).

too many individuals from joining a coalition and thus diluting the benefits of patronage.[3] Similarly, Chandra (2004) has argued with reference to India that the ethnic background of individuals is more "visible" and readily discernible than non-ethnic markers such as profession or class, which allows forming an ethnic clientele when information on politicians' future behavior is limited.

Both arguments seem to be plausible, but perhaps cannot be generalized easily. Many systems of ethnic classification are segmentally nested. To use a contemporary American example: a Hmong is a Vietnamese, is an Asian American, is an American (Wimmer 2008b). Such systems are especially widespread in Africa (Scarritt and Mozaffar 1999) where patronage politics is also common (Bratton and van de Walle 1994). Nested classifications, however, cannot offer firm boundaries to limit a patronage coalition (see Posner 2005). The visibility argument, on the other hand, makes less sense where ethnic membership is not easily read off the faces or names of politicians (former Yugoslavia is an example) or where patronage is not based on voting (see Rothchild 1986).

My own approach seeks to move away from the nature of ethnicity, as implied by the stickiness and visibility arguments, and toward a more institutionalist account. As I have argued in Chapter 2 and throughout the book, politicians rely on ethnic patronage networks when voluntary organizations to build and stabilize political coalitions are scarce and when the state's capacity is too limited to provide public goods equally across the entire citizenry. Politicians then use *ethnic* commonality – rather than other social categories and associated ties – to choose followers because the very principles of legitimacy of modern nation-states encourage them to favor co-ethnics over others, to "take care of their own people." Obviously, this hypothesis, while consistent with the data and analysis of the previous chapters, remains to be evaluated with an appropriate empirical research design.

4 GLOBALIZATION AND THE END OF HISTORY

Throughout the chapters, I have highlighted patterns that recur in various parts of the globe and throughout different historical epochs. Several such recurring patterns were discovered: the diffusion and balance-of-power effects that make nation-state creation more likely; how such nation-state creation is caused by secessionist wars and in turn causes irredentist wars between states and domestic ethnic conflict; that such domestic armed conflicts are most likely in ethnocracies, unstable multiethnic coalition regimes, or incohesive states with weakly institutionalized ties to their peripheries. The book thus revitalizes the search for regularities across time periods: the "big structures and large processes" that the late Charles Tilly (1989) sought to discover through "huge comparisons."

---

[3] For an agent-based model that supports this argument, see Laitin and van der Veen (forthcoming).

If causal patterns repeat over the long run, we ought to see the present through the eyes of the past, rather than to emphasize the disjuncture between today and yesterday, as in much of the globalization literature. Several authors have argued that the wave of civil wars that has swept over the globe since the 1970s must be related to increasing levels of globalization (Kaldor 1999; Chua 2004) or the end of the Cold War (Huntington 1993). By contrast, this book shows that events of recent decades may follow the script of an old story.

While history never repeats itself, to state the obvious, the same mechanisms may be operating at different times and in different historical contexts.[4] The dismemberment of empire and the formation of nation-states have followed a similar logic since the time of Napoleon. The armed conflicts in the Caucasus and in the Balkans during the 1990s resemble those on the Indian subcontinent in the 1940s, those of Eastern Europe during and after World War I, and so on. The return of the "Macedonian syndrome," as Myron Weiner (1971) has called the intermingling of ethnic conflict and irredentist wars, explains such recurrent patterns of nation-state formation and war much better than any variant of globalization theory. To see them as a fundamentally new phenomenon simply represents a good example of the widespread tendency to perceive one's own times as uniquely different from everything history has ever seen.[5]

But hasn't the era of the nation-state now come to an end? Haven't we crossed the threshold to the post-national, post-ethnic age in which the patterns of the past no longer provide clues for understanding the future? This book offers further reasons to be skeptical about the recent crescendo of such claims. Students of "global governance," for example, have emphasized the increasing power of a "transnational citizenship regime" embodied in a proliferating number of UN conventions (Soysal 1994), in transnational networks of human rights activists (Keck and Sikkink 1998), or in an emerging "global civil society" (Lipschutz 1992). Some political theorists passionately believe that these developments will eventually coalesce into a "cosmopolitan governance" structure thanks to which humanity will finally overcome its division into competing nations and start looking after the common good and the health of the planet (Held 1995; see also Beck and Cronin 2006).

There is no doubt that the twentieth century has seen a dramatic increase in global legal regimes, public spheres, and internationally networked actors. However, it is open to debate whether these will any time soon transcend and replace the nation-state and the dynamics of ethnic politics that it entails. The future of the nation-state is not so much guaranteed by our need to belong to historically meaningful and symbolically rich communities, as argued by Anthony Smith (1995). Rather, there seems to be no institutional form on the horizon of

---

[4] See the discussion of Collier and Mazzuca (2006).
[5] On "chronocentrism" see Fowles (1974).

history that could bind the interests of political elites and masses into as power-ful a contract as that provided by successful nation building.[6] None of the glo-bal institutions – from the UN to the WTO – enjoys any independent basis of popular support and legitimacy. None of the global civil society networks provides public goods or meaningful political participation beyond the confines of its own members.[7] If this book's analysis is correct, and collective identities and political loyalties need to rest on institutionalized exchange relationships and mutual trust, the nation-state will, for better or for worse, remain with us for some time to come.

The European Union seems to be the sole exception to that general state-ment, and many authors who write in the post-nationalist genre enthusiastically embrace it. Indeed, couldn't it represent the new institutional template that will diffuse over the world in the centuries to come – even if it is currently fraught with uncertainties and repeated crisis? A closer look at the Union reveals that its power and legitimacy remains dependent on component nation-states (Milward 2000). And even trans-nationally mobile, highly educated young Europeans identify more and more with their home country, the longer they have been living abroad (Favell 2008), not least because systems of social security remain firmly tied to long-term residence in individual member states. In order to replace nations as the focus of political loyalty and identity of the European population, the Union would need to transform itself from an alliance of states into a super-nation-state complete with welfare institutions, a tax regime, an army and so on, thus replacing the resource exchange between citizens and their respective national states. If this can be accomplished, it might lead to nation building writ large, and the population might finally adopt the European iden-tity that Brussels' bureaucrats work so hard to propagate.[8]

This book therefore does not anticipate the imminent end of the nation-state. On the other hand, however, it also does not suggest that the current world order of nation-states represents the end point of history, as plausible as this seems to be at first sight: it is indeed quite unlikely that many more existing states will fragment into a series of nation-states, as did the Soviet, British, or Ottoman empires. Some successful secession from already established nation-states will continue to occur, as the recent creations of Kosovo, East Timor, Montenegro, and Southern Sudan illustrate. And the few remaining pre-national, dynastic states in the Middle East might finally experience their own version of an "Arab spring" and be swept away by a constitutional revolution sometime in the future. Leaving aside such future creations of additional nation-states, the nationalist dream of organizing the world into a series of states each providing a roof for

---

[6] See also Calhoun (2007); from a normative point of view: Miller (1995).

[7] See the scathing criticism by Hansen (2009).

[8] While a possibility for Europe (Pierson 1996), the chances that a super-nation-state could be formed elsewhere are slim indeed (Mann 1993a).

a nationally defined people, to borrow one of Ernest Gellner's metaphors, has indeed come close to being realized. But history refuses to ever come to an end. It is a trail traversed in the past, not a compass to determine its future direction. Generations to come will most certainly imagine other communities than the nation, and reshape the world's political landscape according to tectonic principles that we cannot possibly imagine today.

Appendices

CONTENTS

Chapter 2

For the purpose of calibrating the model developed in Chapter 2, we need to estimate which actor controls how much of overall taxation capacity, political decision-making power, public service provision, and military support. We can provide estimates for three of the four resources. The difficulties were insurmountable, however, when trying to determine actors' control over political decision-making – an overview of the entire political edifice and the amount of power vested in the different offices and positions would be necessary to arrive at a reasonably accurate estimation. The estimations for the other three resources are explained in this appendix, while our assumptions regarding political decision-making are justified in the main text..

The first step is to define which periods correspond to a pre-modern, weakly centralized state and which ones to a centralized, modern territorial state. For France, we propose to look at three points in time. The "pre-modern" situation corresponds to the fourteenth century, i.e. after a state with the capacity for direct taxation and with a standing army had emerged under Charles V. The modern, territorial state in France arises with absolutism: tax rebellions (the "Fronde," 1648–1653) were successfully subdued, the collection of taxes became centralized (Kiser and Linton 2002), and the military revolution of the mid-sixteenth century institutionalized and strengthened a standing army under the command of the king. The seventeenth-century absolutist state, however, was still based on tax farming, and most offices (including in the army) were up for purchase. We thus take a third snapshot of the resource distribution in the late nineteenth century, i.e. after the Franco-Prussian war. Now tax farming has been abolished and universal conscription introduced. For the Ottoman empire, any data point after the establishment of the standing army in 1360 and before the beginning of the Tanzimat reforms in the early nineteenth century is adequate to represent the pre-modern situation. The late nineteenth century under Abdul Hamid stands as an example of a modern territorial state (with an army based on universal conscription, central taxation without tax farming, etc.).

I DISTRIBUTION OF CONTROL OVER TAXES

In contrast to the distribution of control over military support and public goods, we decided to empirically calibrate the post-exchange distribution, rather than the pre-exchange distribution of taxation. It is difficult to estimate how much the various actors contributed to the overall tax income of the state, while it is much easier to determine who receives how much of the revenues once they are collected and reappropriated.

I.I France

Even estimating the post-exchange tax distribution represents a steep challenge for pre-modern France, however, because of the sheer complexity of seignorial dues, local taxes, indirect taxes and an the even more complex set of exemptions, prerogatives and tax-sharing agreements, all of which varied from locality to locality depending on the balance of power between the king, the nobles, and the cities and peasant communities.

Fourteenth-/fifteenth-century France

The pre-modern situation corresponds to the tax regime between 1360 and 1450, or more precisely before the reforms of Charles VII (reigned 1422–1461), who abolished *tallages* (the seignorial dues to feudal elites) and monopolized direct taxation for the king,[1] and after King John introduced indirect taxes in 1360 (sales tax, wine tax, known together as *aides*, and a salt tax called *gabelles*, first established in 1341) and Charles V (reigned 1364–1380) established permanent taxes to the king, generalizing the previous system in which individuals would pay a sum instead of fulfilling their military obligations to the king, and from 1363 onward levied a hearth tax (*fouage*, later called *tailles*, from which nobles were exempt) on the inhabitants of crown lands. There existed municipal taxes as well (*socquet* and *barrage*, sometimes *tailles*) used for financing public infrastructure projects, most importantly fortification. On top of these regular taxes, the king from time to time imposed special taxes on his subjects (the *tailles générales*, e.g. to finance the marriage of the king's daughter or a crusade or a defensive war) or the clergy (the *décimes*). For the purpose of this analysis, however, we do not include one-time, special taxes such as the *tailles générales* and the *décimes*.

Besides these revenues that resemble taxes in the modern sense of the term, there were many seignorial prerogatives, dues, tributes, and duties, both for the domains of the king himself (considered his own seignorial property) as well as those of other nobles. The most important of these seignorial dues were the *cens* (an annual tax of vassals on leased land) and the *champart* (on average one-eighth of the cereal harvest paid to the owner of the land), as well as the *banalités* for using the lord's mills, wine press, etc.

We consider both the incomes derived from seignorial domains and from the *aides* as taxes. In order to calculate the share of the subordinate elite, we use information on the revenues that the royal domains produced and then assume that the other seignorial domains outside the control of the king yielded similar revenues. We know from Rey (1965: 45) that the royal domains contained roughly 33 percent of the territory of the kingdom during the reign of Charles VI (1388–1413).

To calculate royal domain income, we can rely on Rey (1965: 96ff.), who lists the income and expenses of the royal treasury over five years (based on the same source as Fawtier [1930]). The average annual income is 816,000 *livres*, of which on average (calculated on the basis of Rey 1965: 99) 52 percent was income from the royal domains and an additional 9 percent was mostly domain income owed from previous years (under the title of "recepte communes").[2] The average income from royal domains was therefore

---

[1] On the evolution of the French tax system, see Collins (1988); Wolfe (1972) details the late medieval system as well. Henneman (1971) writes about the situation before Charles V.

[2] Four percent were from coinage rights, 5 percent from "chancellerie" or in Latin "emulumentum" and "emende" (apparently a tax on royal seals on documents [Rey 1965: 155]), 10 percent from "compositions et amendes" ("financie et composiciones"), which were mostly pawns and penalties from litigated contributions from domain administrators (but included the *fouage* of certain localities and, until the end of the century the 6,000 *livres* paid by the Jewish community as a tax on usury), and finally 18 percent for the various "subsidies" paid to the king by his vassals but also transfers of income from the general sales tax to the royal treasury (see below).

500,000. We assume that the feudal nobility received, on the two-thirds of the kingdom's lands that were not part of the royal lands, a total of 1,000,000 (i.e. double the income of the king).

Rey (1965: 26off.) estimates the total income from the indirect taxes (the *aides*, a sales tax on all products, as well as the salt tax *gabelle*) to be 2,000,000 *francs*. This includes more than one-third, or 700,000 *francs*, that went to nobles, magistrates, and cities who were allowed to appropriate parts or all of these taxes. These 700,000 were not entering the royal accounts. We suggest splitting them between subordinate elites (350,000) and the cities representing the masses (125,000 each).

The remaining 1,300,000 *francs* were used to subsidize the royal treasury, to pay off the salaries of staff, to maintain the royal and princely households, for pensions and gifts to noblemen, and to finance wars. Two expense accounts of how the income of *aides* was used (one from 1398 and one from 1411, see Rey 1965: 266) allow us to estimate the share of dominant and subordinate elites: averaging over these two years and not taking "royal savings" into account, the king and his family received 271,000 *livres* while the nobility got 220,000. The treasurer of war received 365,000 on average – a sum that we attribute to the king since it helped to finance the war efforts that he commanded.

The municipalities were allowed to raise their own taxes, mostly in order to rebuild city walls and fortifications. It is difficult to know how much other taxes they were raising locally – but according to Rigaudière (1993: chapter 10), the fortifications were the major project for which the king allowed the towns to raise their own taxes. Using the estimates for fortification expenses that we discuss below (see "public goods and infrastructure"), we attribute an additional 160,000 *livres* to dominant and subordinate masses.

SUMMARY

Dominant elite: 816,000 from royal domain, 636,000 from the *aides*, total 1,452,000 (42%)

Subordinate elite: 1,000,000 from feudal domains, 570,000 from *aides*, total of 1,570,000 (46%)

Dominant mass: 125,000 from *aides*, 80,000 from special taxes, total of 205,000 (6%)

Subordinate mass: 125,000 from *aides*, 80,000 from special taxes, total of 205,000 (6%)

Total: 3,427,000

Late eighteenth-century France

By the late eighteenth century, the French state had dramatically increased its capacity to raise taxes, both direct and indirect. Among the former were property taxes (*vingtième*), income taxes (*taille*), and a general per person tax on all subjects ("poll tax"). The indirect taxes were basically sales taxes levied on a wide variety of goods. The state collected many of of these indirect taxes through its own administration, while others were raised through tax farmers (Matthews 1958: 3–33). Goldsmith (1832: 85) provides a detailed budget from 1785. The central state's tax revenues totaled 535.9 million *francs*.

In order to determine the subordinate elite's share of tax revenues, it is necessary to take into account the fact that there were two types of provinces under the Old Regime, and that these two types were subject to distinct systems of taxation. The *pays d'élection* had no power to tax, while the *pays d'état* did have this power (Matthews 1958: 23–24; Kwass

2000: 95). The *pays d'election*, however, did receive a share of the taxes collected in the provinces. As explained by Matthews (1958: 29), this amount appears as "charges" on the "general receipts" from the *pays d'election*. Because these monies do not go into the central treasury, they are not counted as receipts. Thus, they are not figured into the budget provided by Goldsmith (1832). However, Necker's (1781: 107) analysis of the 1780 budget fortunately provides this information. The "charges" made up 19.6 percent of the taxes collected in the *pays d'election*. We make the assumption that this was also true in 1785. However, in order to apply this assumption, it is first necessary to discern the amount of direct taxes paid by the *pays d'election* in 1785. Goldsmith (1832) does not provide this figure, but Necker does (1781: 123). In 1780, 94.8 percent of direct taxes were paid by the *pays d'election*. Assuming this was also true in 1785, 198.13 million of the 209 million in revenues from direct taxes came from the *pays d'election*. Because 198.13 million is 80.4 percent of 246.43 million, we surmise that the subordinate elites in the *pays d'election* received 48.30 million *francs* of tax revenue.

It is more difficult to determine the tax revenue of the subordinate elites in the *pays d'etat*. We make use of data from two of these provinces, Burgundy and Languedoc, *circa* 1700. Swann (2003: 179–184) provides information on Burgundy for 1689–1691 and 1706–1708. An average of 53.5 percent of expenditures went to the king, while 61 percent of the revenues came from taxes. Combining these figures, Burgundy retained 12.5 percent (i.e. [61–53.5]/61) of its tax revenues. Beik (1985: 262–263) contains information on the 1677 distribution of taxes in Languedoc. Seventy-five percent of the taxes collected went to the Crown, meaning that 25 percent was retained by the subordinate elite. Averaging these figures from Burgundy and Languedoc, we estimate that subordinate elites in the *pays d'etat* retained 18.7 percent of collected tax revenues. Assuming this share was constant across the eighteenth century makes it possible to apply this figure to the 1785 budget found in Goldsmith (1832: 85). Based on our earlier calculation, 10.87 million of the direct taxes came from the *pays d'etat*, which is 81.3 percent of 13.37 million. Thus, we estimate that subordinate elites in the *pays d'etat* retained 2.5 million in tax revenues. Combining this with the estimate from the *pays d'election* yields an overall estimate of 50.8 million *francs* revenue for the subordinate elite.

As for the masses, an array of indirect taxes (mainly sales taxes and tariffs) collectively known as the *octroi* were the primary source of financing municipal governments. Under a 1647 royal decree that remained in effect until the revolution, municipalities were required to give one-half of the *octroi* revenues to the central state (Matthews 1958: 166). According to Goldsmith (1832), 27 million *francs* of the central state's revenue in 1785 derived from the *octroi*. Thus, we estimate that the masses controlled 27 million *francs* in tax revenue.

SUMMARY

Dominant elites: 535.9 million (87.3%)
Subordinate elites: 50.8 million (8.3%)
Masses: 27 million (4.4%)
Total: 613.7 million

Late nineteenth-century France

To determine the distribution of tax revenues in the late nineteenth century, we associate three levels of government with the four actors: central state (dominant elite), departments (subordinate elites), and communes (dominant and subordinate masses). We do make one exception: we associate the dominant elite not only with the central state, but also the commune of Paris and the department (Seine) in which the capital city was located at this time.

The late nineteenth-century taxation system was even more centralized than that of the *ancien régime*.[3] The central state dictated the amount of taxes that each department owed. Each department in turn distributed its tax burden to its various communes. However, not all of the monies collected went to the central state. Additional taxes (the *centimes additionnels*) – also determined by the central state – were collected for the purpose of financing the departments and communes (Le Comte de Franqueville 1875: 299; Leacock 1906: 326). These "centimes" were the only source of financing for the departments (Scott 1871: 311). However, in addition to these direct taxes, communes were also allowed to collect a number of indirect taxes, such as tolls on roads and highways, as well as the *octroi*, a tax levied on various goods brought into the towns (Scott 1871: 311; Leacock 1906: 323). The central state also collected indirect taxes – indeed, a much wider range than the communes.

The central state budgets published by the Ministry of Public Instruction (1889) provide data on the apportionment of direct taxes to all actors as well as the indirect taxes collected by the central state, while Le Comte de Franqueville (1875) supplies data on the indirect taxes collected by the communes. Because the latter data are for 1871, that shall be the reference year for all other data as well. In 1871, the direct tax (i.e. *centimes*) share of departments and communes, respectively, was 193.9 million and 120.0 million (Ministry of Public Instruction 1889: 50). Given our adoption of the core–periphery model for identifying the different actors, it is necessary to deduce the 26.7 percent share of these numbers that went to the commune of Paris and the department of Seine. This leaves us with 88 million.[4] To this figure must be added all the *indirect taxes* collected by the communes. As mentioned, figures for 1871 are available from Le Comte De Franqueville (1875: 306–307). The *octroi* is the most important of indirect taxes (Scott 1871; Leacock 1906) and totaled 86.4 million. Adding tolls and duties (26.3 million) and the "dog tax" (4.7 million) yields 117.4 million. For the communes, which we associate with the masses, direct and indirect taxes together thus total 205.4 million.

A similar adjustment for the departmental *centimes* is necessary. At this time, Paris was located in the department of Seine. We make the same assumption as for the communes – i.e. that this department enjoyed a 26.7 percent share of all departmental *centimes*.

---

[3] The central state levied four direct types of taxes: *la contribution foncière* (real estate tax), *la contribution des portes et fênetres* (the "door and window tax"), *la contribution personnelle-mobilière* (personal tax), and *la contribution des patentes* (Scott 1871: 311; Le Comte de Franqueville 1875: 289; Ministry of Public Instruction 1889: 6–7; Leacock 1906: 324). The fourth tax is variously described as a "tax on business" (Leacock 1906: 324) and as a "tax levied on all trades and professions" (Scott 1871: 311).

[4] Thanks to Le Comte de Franqueville (1875: 307), we know the ratio of Paris expenditures to the expenditures of all other communes in 1871. Paris expenditures were about 200 million at this time, while all other communal expenditures were about 520 million. If we assume that Paris had a similar share of all communal *centimes*, then the communal figure identified above (i.e. 120 million) should be reduced by 26.7 percent (88.0 million).

This means a reduction of 51.8 million, leaving 142.1 million for the subordinate elite. As mentioned, departments were not allowed to collect indirect taxes.

The figures subtracted for the commune of Paris and the department of Seine are attributed to the dominant elite: 83.8 million. To this sum we add the central state's share of direct taxes, 323.2 million, yielding 407.0 million in direct taxes for the dominant elite in 1871. Most receipts of the central state derived from indirect taxes, however (Ministry of Public Instruction 1889: 8–19 and 22–30). These totaled 2,776,900,000 *francs.*[5] Adding these to the direct taxes yields 3,183,900,000 *francs* in taxes controlled by the dominant elite.

There is one more indirect tax that must be attributed to the dominant elite. As mentioned, the sum of indirect taxes collected by communes was 117.4 million in 1871. Consistent with the estimates discussed above, we assume that Paris' share of these taxes was 26.7 percent. However, this figure of 117.4 million is *not* the grand total, because Le Comte de Franqueville (1875: 307) excluded communal data from Seine. Because 117.4 million is 73.3 percent of 160,163,711, the difference (160,163,711 − 117,400,000) – i.e. 42,763,711 – is the estimated Parisian share of indirect taxes, which must be added to the grand running total of taxes controlled by the dominant elite. Doing so brings the total to 3,226,663,711 *francs.*[6]

SUMMARY

Dominant elites: 3,226,663,711 (90.3%)
Subordinate elites: 142,100,000 (4.0%)
Masses: 205,400,000 (5.7%), or 2.85%/2.85%
Total: 3,574,163,711

1.2 Ottoman empire

Sixteenth-century Ottoman empire

The Ottoman empire is an easier case since it never developed a feudal system comparable to Western Europe. The tax system was more centralized and uniform, though very important regional variations existed as well (and many parts of the empire remained outside the effective taxing capacity of the Sublime Porte). Cosgel and Miceli (2005: 815) contains a list that details, for the sixteenth century, the distribution of tax revenues between central government, provincial and district governments, fief holders and others. They list this distribution for five different regions of the empire and for one to three different years between 1521 and 1596. The share of the central government ranges from 0.26 to 0.5, with an average of 36%, that of provincial and district governments from 0.04 to 0.29, averaging 13%, fief holders got 29%, and "others" (private landholders, pious foundations, and tribal chiefs) received between 0.09 and 39% of the overall taxes (21% on

---

[5] This number was calculated by summing figures reproduced by the Ministry of Public Instruction (1889: 8–19 and 22–30). The following items were not included: all of pp. 20–21; columns 3 and 4 of p. 24 ("year" is the 0 column); and columns 2–4 of p. 25.

[6] To be sure, Paris was not the only commune in the department of Seine in the late nineteenth century. However, this city did account for practically the entire population – 2,226,023 out of a departmental population of 2,799,329 in the early 1880s (Ministry of Commerce and Industry 1968 [1886]: 31, 624, and 627).

average). Translated into our scheme of actors, dominant elites controlled 36% of overall taxes and subordinate elites 63%. We assume that tribal chiefs are part of the subordinate elite, but that private landholders and pious foundations represent non-elite, if affluent persons. We thus divide the 21% share of "others" into one-third for tribal leaders (adding 7% to the subordinate elite) and 14% to the masses.

SUMMARY

Dominant elites: 36%
Subordinate elites: 48%
Masses: 14%

Late nineteenth-century Ottoman empire

How did this distribution of tax income change after the Tanzimat reforms were completed? According to Stanford Shaw, all taxes and fees were collected directly by the central state treasury or specialized agencies by 1870, and tax farming had been entirely abolished (Shaw 1975). The only local revenues that were introduced are a small percentage of the taxes raised on property: "the municipalities … as they finally were organized, were allowed to keep small shares for themselves" (p. 427). Thus, at the end of the Tanzimat reforms, the center controlled almost all of the tax revenues. We estimate that the "small shares" controlled by municipalities amount to 5 percent for each of the masses and that the rest (90 percent) was entirely controlled by the dominant state elites.

SUMMARY

Dominant elites: 90%
Subordinate elites: 0%
Masses: 10%

2   CONTROL OVER MILITARY SUPPORT

In contrast to the tax distribution, we estimate how much capacity was distributed over actors before they exchanged resources with each other – because obviously, all post-exchange control over the army laid in the hands of the central elites (except during mutinies). We will look at the background of fighting troops to determine which of the four actors provided how many troops to the overall military machine. We thus assume that "control" does not refer to the line of commands on the battlefield, but rather to the provision of armed men. Correspondingly, we also include militias and other fighting units not integrated into the military command structure, but do not take into account police forces or the soldiers that were recruited for particular campaigns or during general mobilization.

2.1 France

The French military developed gradually. We again focus on three points in this development: (a) the pre-centralized army of the high middle ages (under Philippe Auguste and his successors, before the Hundred Years War), i.e. after the establishment of a group of permanent warriors in the service of the king, but while the army was still recruited mostly on the principle of feudal loyalty; (b) the army under the absolutist king Louis XIV; (c) the modern army as it had been reorganized after the Franco-Prussian war.

Twelfth- and thirteenth-century France

The fully mobilized army, such as engaged in the in the battles of 1285, 1327, 1329, and 1330, contained an average of 20,000 men. According to information found in Contamine (1992), it was composed of the following parts:

Provided by the king:
- The "house of the king," a small private army composed of the highest-ranking nobles closely related to the king through family ties and the "chevaliers de l'hotel," who were moving around with the king and formed a sort of royal guard. No figures for absolute size is available, we assume the same size as in the fifteenth century (see below): 200.
- Professional garrison soldiers, paid by the king: 1,250–1,450, average 1,350.
- *Arbatalières* (armbrusters), permanently employed by the king: 70–150, average 110.
- Militias of the cities that belonged to the royal domain: 2,040
- Total 3,700.

Provided by the nobility:
- The feudal army (or "l'arrière-ban"), levied in times of war through the principle of feudal loyalty. It comprised:
  - High-nobility chevaliers: total of 550.
  - The noble warriors mobilized by the chevaliers (on average each commanding his own troop of 50): 27,500.
- Total 28,050.

Provided by "the masses":
- *Roturiers*, i.e. non-armored and non-disciplined peasant militias: 300.
- Sergeants a cheval, i.e. mounted and fully armored warriors of lower-noble or commoner origin: 2,400.
- Total 2,700.

We assume that the difference between the theoretical strength of the army of 34,450 men, calculated on basis of the above information, and the average effective fighting strength in the various battles (20,000 men) is because not all of "l'arrière-ban" was actually mobilized for war, but only 13,600 (instead of the theoretical figure of 28,050). If we take effective war figures as a basis for calculating control over military support, we arrive at 18.5% share for the dominant elites, 68% for the subordinate elites, and 13.5% for the two masses.

SUMMARY

Dominante elite: 18.5%
Subordinate elite: 68%
Masses: 13.5%

Seventeenth-century France

According to Contamine (1992: 435, based on Belhomme), the regular and irregular troops that existed in 1690 (during the reign of Louis XIV) were the following:

- 342,000 regular troops, of which:
  - 277,000 infantry, including *c.* 37,000 officers.[7]
  - 65,000 mounted troops (including 10,000 members of the *maison militaire du roi*, which was now an elite troop, composed of the high nobility and the royal families, *c.* 3,000 Swiss guards, and 4,000 non-noble *gardes françaises*; see Rowlands [1999]), including 7,333 officers.
  - Of these 342,000 regular troops, 74,000 were mercenaries[8] (including some Frenchmen from Alsace and Roussillon), and 270,000 *régnicoles* (subjects of the king born in France).
- 92,000 *miliciens* (including 25,000 royal militiamen, the rest were local militias).
- *L'arrière-ban*, though the feudal army was abolished in 1694 and seems not to have been used anymore.
- 3,500–4,000 *archers de la maréchaussée*, a military police force under the command of the army marshals; the positions were sold to local citizens under Louis XIV.
- 70,000 members of the navy, since Colbert recruited through conscription (the first in military history, according to Contamine [1992: 504f.]) and commanded by 9,333 royal navy officers.
- 100,000 coastal guards, who were paid by the king (see Hippeau 1863: 148).

Including these militias, 678,000 were under arms. The problem is to determine the percentage of the regular army that was controlled by the feudal elite. Following Blaufarb (2002), we can assume that the entire officer corps of the army and navy was composed of nobles (with the exception of roughly 200 non-noble families who were ennobled through military service from 1750 onwards). We exclude, however, the *arrière-ban*. The nobility made up 53,666 officers, thus 8 percent of the total of armed men.

We can assume that the mercenaries as well as the royal guard (*la maison*) were directly controlled by the king, with the exception of the 4,000 *gardes francaises*, which were an elite infantry unit composed of commoners. The 74,000 mercenaries made 11% of the total of armed men, the 3,000 members of the royal guard that were neither mercenaries (the Swiss) nor *gardes francaises* represent another 0.5%. Thus, the royal elite controlled 11.5% of all armed men. The remaining 80% can be attributed to the masses.

SUMMARY

Dominante elite: 11.5%
Subordinate elite: 8.5%
Masses: 80%

Late nineteenth-century France

In 1870, the French army consisted of a total of 367,850 men, of which 16,869 or 4.6% were officers (Adriance 1987: 23). Officers belonged to either the dominant or subordinate elite. Serman (1979) provides the geographical origin of officers around this time. 8.6% hailed from the department of Seine. Thus, we associate 0.4% of the military with the

---

[7] The proportion of officers (sergeants, capitains, lieutnants, sous-lieutnants) per *compagnie* (of 50 soldiers) was five. Since five *compagnies* made a regiment, which had eight officers, the number of soldiers per officer was roughly 7.5.

[8] Lynn (1997) estimates the percentage of foreign mercenaries as 15–25 percent during Louis XIV's reign.

dominant elite and 4.2% with the subordinate elite. The remainder (95.4%) were split equally among the dominant and subordinate masses.

SUMMARY

Dominant elites: 0.4%
Subordinate elites: 4.2%
Masses: 95.4%

2.2 Ottoman empire

Sixteenth-century Ottoman empire
The fifteenth and sixteenth centuries again represent the "pre-modern" period. We have information on the composition of the army for two years and use these two data points to calculate an average figure. İnalcik (1994: 88ff.) provides detailed information for 1528. The army consisted of:

- Regular troops under direct control of the sultan (thus attributed to the dominant elite): the salaried soldiers such as the Janissaries (legally "slaves" of the sultan, recruited mostly among the Christian and other minorities of the empire), the fortress guards in the provinces, the cavalry of the Porte (*sipahis*), the inner palace servants, and the navy: 50,000.
- Beneficiaries of *hass*, *ziamet*, and *timar* grants in the provinces. These were given the right to tax the local population against military support of the sultan and represent the subordinate elite: 37,741.
- Auxiliary troops such as the *müsellems*, *canbaz*, *bazdars*, *yorüks*, and most importantly the *yayas*: groups of peasants who rotated the duty to serve among family members. Originally, the *yaya* were Turcoman tribal nomads who had fought with the sultan and were given lands in Central Anatolia after conquest. In political terms, these tribes saw themselves and were perceived as part of the imperial elite, because they had helped to found the empire and to defend it ever since. We thus count the *yayas* among the subordinate elites. These auxiliary troops were abolished in 1582: 15,180.
- Christian soldiers (representing the subordinate masses) who were recruited into a paid militia: 3,000.
- *Akincis*, i.e. frontier raiders who received a salary if registered and who were recruited among the population around a garrison (and whom we identify as representing the dominant masses): 12,000.

The information for 1473 is more sparse. According to İnalcik (*ibid.*), the army consisted of:
- Regular troops (Janissaries and *sipahis*): 19,500.
- Beneficiaries of *timar* grants: 64,000.
- *Azebs*, i.e. general army levied among the entire population (roughly half of them recruited in Christian Rumelia): 20,000.[9]

---

[9] Unfortunately, no figures for the recruits (*azebs*) are available for 1528. In 1389, 40,000 *azebs* fought in Kosova against the Serbs. In 1473, there were 18,000 in the army. In 1492, 9,000 were recruited in Rumelia, and Suleiman I recruited 20,000 also in Rumelia, most likely for a specific campaign.

We leave out *azebs* because these were recruited for specific campaigns. Divided up by the four actors and averaged between the 1473 and 1528 data, we arrive at the following figures for the early sixteenth-century empire (see Appendix Table 2.1).

Late nineteenth-century Ottoman empire

The army under the last sultan of the empire, Abdul Hamid, looked quite differ-ent. Universal conscription had already been introduced earlier (including *de iure* for Christian subjects), but actual service was still decided by the lot, and exemption through the payment of a fee (obligatory for Christians before the reforms, now for everybody) was still possible, while substitution through another person no longer represented an option for those who wanted to avoid serving. The feudal elements of the army had been abolished, and a new professional officer corps was trained in the military academies founded under Abdul Hamid's reign (Akmese 2005: 23).

Zürcher describes the army composition after the reforms of 1843 and 1869, which were largely inspired by the Prussian model: 210,000 regular troops (of which 60,000 active reserves), 190,000 reserve troops called *redif* (the Turkish version of *Landwehr*), as well as 300,000 non-combat reserves (the Ottoman *Landsturm*) (Zürcher 1998). This puts the number of fighting troops at 400,000. The only armed group of men outside of this system of mass recruitment was the Kurdish tribal regiments that Abdul Hamid institutionalized in 1892 (this time inspired by the Cossack militias of imperial Russia). By the end of the century, these tribal militias under the command of Kurdish *aghas* num-bered between 27,500 and 63,250 men (van Bruinessen 1999). Thus, the share of armed men under control of the subordinate elites (the tribal leaders) was somewhere between 6% and 14%, averaged to 10%.

How can we attribute the army officers and soldiers of the regular army to the various actors in our model environment? It is clear that all the rank and file seem to have been of Muslim peasant origin (Zürcher 1998) and can thus be attributed to the dominant mass. The new elementary and secondary schools established by and for the military all over the empire provided formidable avenues of upward mobility for provincial families that did not belong to the bureaucratic-military elites of the center (Hale 1994: 24). Based on a detailed study of the career paths of the students of one of these elite schools,[10] we can guess that of the 4% officers of the army in peacetime (Erickson 2000: 7), *c.* 1,920 (or 0.5% of the total number of fighters) were of dominant elite background and 9,600 (2.5%) came from families we could classify as members of the subordinate elite.

---

[10] The school in question (Mulkiye) was reformed by Abdul Hamid to train civil servants. Szyliowicz (1971) has studied a sample of 475 students. For the present purposes, we are only interested in those students whom he classifies as "successful," i.e. who later in their career reached the level of general director or higher (i.e. undersecretary, assistant undersecretary, ambassador, governor, and so forth), which was the case for 26% of all students. Of those 109 successful students, 13 had an "elite" background: their fathers bore the title pasha, effendi, or bey and occupied a high-level position (p. 396). Theses elite students therefore made up 9% of the entire student population, while 63% of the students came from an "official" background, i.e. from families belonging to the military-administrative caste, and 22% were not member of that group (p. 393). If we assume the same proportions for the "successful" non-central-elite students, we can estimate that 67 successful students were members of the subordinate elite, and 29 belonged to the dominant and subordinate masses. In percentage, 12% of the successful students had a dominant elite background, 61% a subordinate elite background, and 27% a non-elite background.

APPENDIX TABLE 2.1 *Ottoman army composition in 1473 and 1528*

	1528	%	1473	%	Average %
Dominant elite	50,000	42	19,500	23	32.5
Subordinate elite	52,921	45	64,000	77	61
Dominant mass	12,000	10	0	0	5
Subordinate mass	3,000	3	0	0	1.5
Total	117,921		83,500		

SUMMARY

Dominant elite: 0.5%
Subordinate elite: 12%
Masses: 87.5%

3 CONTROL OVER PUBLIC GOODS PROVISION

The public goods we are interested in here include welfare expenditures such as pensions (including those for soldiers and their families), unemployment benefits, etc., the provision of public security (excluding defense, but including infrastructure such as city walls), non-religious education in generic skills such as writing and math, and the maintenance of public infrastructure (such as city walls, public roads, fountains, etc.). How many of these public services were provided by central government elites (the dominant elite), by provincial elites in charge of regional, sub-state entities, and by municipalities, guilds, etc. (the masses)? By "control" we mean that the highest institutional level through which money circulates used for public service provision "controls" these resources. For example, if taxes are collected by the central state and then handed down to municipalities or religious fraternities to take care of the poor, we assume that the central state is "in control" of these resources. We also assume that if a higher level of government mandates public goods provision *and* exercises appointive power in those areas, then that higher level of government "controls" the resources. Perhaps not surprisingly, estimating who provides how much of the overall public services was even more difficult than for taxes and military support. Extensive historical research was necessary to come up with meaningful estimates.

3.1 France

Fourteenth-century France
In order to estimate the dominant elite's contribution to public goods provision in the first half of the fourteenth century, we make use of the royal accounts for 1322–1325 and 1349 reprinted by Fawtier (1930: LIX-LXI and LXIV). These accounts do not represent budgets of income or expenses, because both the costs of local administration and the costs of running the royal estates are not included. However, they do provide a picture

of what the king had at his disposal in terms of cash, as well as the uses to which he put this money. There are two relevant line items: *opera*, which pertain to public works such as roads and bridges, and *elemosine*, which refers to expenditures for housing, feeding, and clothing the poor. Based on the five accounts examined, the king's average annual expenditures on *opera* and *elemosine* was 14,930 *livres* (a little less than 3 percent of total royal expenditures).

The best data available for the subordinate elites and masses come from the city of Avignon in the first half of the fourteenth century. We exploit these data and then generalize to all of France. Since at this time Avignon was the seat of the antipope, an extraordinary system of services for the poor developed, which we do not consider here because it was quite exceptional. We do consider, however, expenditures on other items. The Papacy dispensed funds for various public construction projects such as bridges, granaries, and city gates (again called *opera*). Jean XXII's total expenditures were about 4.2 million *florins*, of which 2.9% (121,800 *florins*) went to such projects. Benoît XII allocated 18% of 730,000 *florins* for these purposes (thus, 131,400 *florins*). And 12.2% (207,400 *florins*) of Clément VI's 1.7 million *florins* of expenditures went to *opera* (Le Blévec 2000: 575 and 579). This yields a total of 460,600 *florins* for these 38 years, or about 12,100 *florins* per year. We also consider the services provided by four crusaders' orders in Avignon during the first half of the fourteenth century. One of these spent 38 *livres* on feeding the poor, housing pilgrims, and so on (Le Blévec 2000: 109). Assuming other crusaders' orders made comparable expenditures, this yields a total of 152 *livres* – or 150 for purposes of estimation. Second, as explained below in more detail, the subordinate elite controlled 330 *florins* per year in hospital funds. Adding together all these figures yields a total subordinate elite expenditure of 12,580 *livres*. This estimate can be generalized to France as a whole using Chevalier's (1982: 207) figure on the number of towns in fourteenth-century France – i.e. 226. Multiplying by this figure yields 2.73 million.

To estimate how much the masses spent on public services, we refer to hospitals, policing, and fortifications. Hospitals were a central institution of French society across the time periods we analyze. They cared for a broad range of needy individuals – not only the infirm (both physically and mentally) but also orphans and the poor. In some cases (especially the eighteenth century) "caring" for the poor amounted to confining them (McCloy 1946; Fairchilds 1976; Jones 1982; McHugh 2007). Hospitals were important enough that the Crown sought from the sixteenth century onward to gain control over them (Hickey 1997). After the revolution, the Convention alienated all hospital endowments (although the Directory later reversed course) (Ramsey 1988: 91).

To estimate the towns' contributions to hospital expenditures, we again make use of data from Avignon in the first half of the fourteenth century (Le Blévec 2000). By 1350 there were 22 hospitals in Avignon (Le Blévec 2000: 603). At this time, 20 *florins* were legally necessary to run a hospital (Le Blévec 2000: 683). Assuming that the average spent 30 *florins* annually, 660 *florins* per year went to hospitals in Avignon. Of all the hospitals for which there are records, 48 percent were run by aristocrats or members of the clergy (thus by the subordinate elite). Fifty-two percent were under the charge of municipalities or lay brotherhoods, or they had been founded by commoners. Thus, one-half of this money, or 330 *florins*, were controlled by the masses. Following the estimation method described above, we multiply this figure by the number of towns in fourteenth-century France (i.e. 226), yielding 74,580 *florins*.

To estimate the contributions that towns made to public safety and security, we first calculate the salaries of the *sergents* which became part of the newly professionalized municipal government. The *sergents* were, among other things, charged with policing the city at night, bringing criminals to court or prison, etc. In small cities such as Tours, four *sergents* were employed, while there were 24 in Bordeaux (Chevalier 1982: 207). They represented roughly 50 percent of all administrative personnel of these cities. The city of Provins, a small town, spent 8 percent of its 545 *livres* budget in 1451 on salaries for its officers (Chevalier 1982: 213). We can thus assume that half of this, or 22 *livres*, were necessary to support its *sergents*. How do we get at a national figure from these estimates? We know from the same source (Chevalier 1982: 41) that there were 226 towns in 1330. Of these, 21 were of comparable size to Bordeaux (i.e. they had four convents of the mendicant orders), while 13 were of medium and 192 of small size (one or two convents). If we assume that Provins is representative for these small towns, we can also assume that they each spent 22 *livres* on *sergents* (or 4,224 in total), while the big towns spent six times this figure, i.e. 132 *livres* each (or 2,727 in total). The medium-sized towns spent 77 each (or 1,001 in total). We thus arrive at 7,952 *livres*.

A much bigger investment in public security was the fortification of towns and villages. The efforts to rebuild city walls consumed large shares of municipal resources from the 1340s onwards (i.e. until the city walls lost their military function sometime in the fifteenth or sixteenth century). The collection of local taxes, administration of municipal bonds, and oversight of these works was one of the main tasks of the new local administrations, which had just recently emancipated themselves from seignorial rule. Rigaudière (1993: 488–496) provides detailed municipal budgets and lists how much the municipalities spent on fortifications. For Marseille, 15 budgets between 1361 and 1411 show an average expenditure of about 728 *livres*. For Saint-Flour, a small city in the Loire valley, 43 budgets between 1378 and 1467 allow us to calculate an average of 280 *livres* per year, while the 25 budgets between 1355 and 1380 of Dijon list 880 *livres* on average. Averaging the information on 11 budgets of Lisieux gives us an estimate of 945 *livres*. These figures are surprisingly consistent. Since it seems that small cities can invest as much in their city walls and towers as large ones, it's perhaps best to simply average over all these figures, arriving at 708 *livres* and thus 160,000 for all cities of fourteenth-century France. Summing the masses expenditures for poor relief, public safety, and fortifications results in a total estimate of roughly 242,530 *florins*.

SUMMARY

Dominant elite: 14,930 (0.5%)
Subordinate elite: 2,730,000 (91.4%)
Masses: 242,530 (8.1%)

Eighteenth-century France

Goldsmith (1832: 85) provides a detailed central budget for 1785, which gives us insight into how much the dominant elite invested in public service provision during the eighteenth century. Among such expenditures were funds for police, postal services, construction and repair projects, and education. These expenditures totaled 90.3 million *livres*.

Included among these central state expenditures were 26 million *livres* for hospitals (Goldsmith 1832). A government report of 1791 estimated total hospital receipts on the eve of the revolution at 29 million *livres* (McCloy 1946: 189). Thus, only three million of these funds are attributable to the subordinate elites and the masses. Carrying over the pre-modern estimate of proportional share, we thus estimate that the subordinate elites and the masses each controlled 1.5 million of these funds.

In order to estimate the value of additional service provision by the subordinate elite, we make use of budgetary data from two provinces in the late seventeenth century, Burgundy (Swann 2003) and Languedoc (Beik 1985). At this time, Burgundy spent 2.8 percent of its budget on public welfare (Swann 2003: 179–180), while Languedoc spent 1.4 percent (Beik 1985: 262–263), yielding an average of 2.1 percent. We estimate absolute figures for the provinces that were *pays d'etat*:[11] the late seventeenth-century Burgundy budgets indicate that an average of 58.5 percent of all expenditures were monies sent to the Crown. Assuming this was true in the eighteenth century as well, one can derive total provincial expenditures. According to earlier calculations (see "taxes") based on Necker (1781) and Goldsmith (1832), the *pays d'etat* sent 10.87 million *livres* to the Crown in 1785, which is 58.5 percent of an 18.6 million *livres* estimate for total provincial expenditures in the *pays d'etat*. Based on this information and the assumption that these provinces spent 2.1 percent on public welfare, we estimate that the subordinate elite spent about 400,000 of the *livres* on public services. Combining this figure with the hospital funds yields a total of 1.9 million *livres* attributable to the subordinate elites.

In order to calculate how much the masses spent on public service besides their contribution to hospitals, we use communal budget data. Pouchenot (1910: 55–93) provides detailed budgets for 1690, 1705, and 1710 for the commune of Besançon. This village of 11,500 (in 1708) spent money on road maintenance, water provision, aid to the poor, and other public services. On average, this accounted for 6.7 percent of total outlays, which is comparable to the village of Angers in the middle two quarters of the eighteenth century.[12] Averaging the three budgets, Besançon spent 6,867 *livres* per year for its 11,500 inhabitants. This amounts to a little less than 0.6 *livres* per person.[13] In order to generalize this figure across France, we make the assumption that such public service provision generally was not available to the masses of people who lived in rural areas. At the beginning of the eighteenth century, only 20 percent of France's population lived in towns of 2,000 or more.[14] Thus, we apply this per person expenditure of 0.6 *livres* to one-fifth of France's 1700 population of 19.3 million (Babuscio and Minta Dunn 1984: 335) – which yields a total public service expenditure of 2.316 million *livres*. However, this is an estimate for *c.* 1700,

---

[11] The *pays d'election* are inappropriate for generalization because they had no independent financing powers and received all funds for public service expenditures from the central state.

[12] In 1720, 1760, and 1780 respectively, public service expenditures accounted for 5.5%, 2.5%, and 9.2% of all spending in Angers (Maillard 2000: 175). Such variation was also evident in the Besançon budgets (9.5% in 1690; 3.4% in 1705; 5.9% in 1710).

[13] It should be noted that the 1690 budget entries are in *francs* rather than *livres* (Pouchenot 1910: 55–78). However, it is quite likely that these were actually *livres*: while *francs* went out of circulation in the seventeenth century, the term itself was typically a synonym for *livres*. See: www.britannica.com/EBchecked/topic/215751/franc (accessed May 6, 2008).

[14] These figures are available at http://chnm.gmu.edu/revolution/chap1a.html (accessed June 24, 2008). This website represents a collaborative effort between the Center for History and New Media at George Mason University and the American Social History Project at City University of New York, and it was made possible by grants from the Florence Gould Foundation and the National Endowment for the Humanities. A book version of the website's contents is available through Penn State University Press.

while other data cover the latter portion of the eighteenth century. Thus, we need to adjust this figure. We assume that central state receipts grew at the same rate as communal public service expenditures. Comparing 1695 to 1785, central state receipts were about 4.6 times higher in the later year.[15] Using this factor to estimate public service expenditures by the municipalities during the late eighteenth century, we arrive at a figure of 10.7 million *livres*. Combining this with the estimate for hospital funding made above yields 12.2 million *livres*.

SUMMARY

Dominant elite: 90.3 million (86.5%)
Subordinate elite: 1.9 million (1.8%)
Masses: 12.2 million (11.7%)
Total: 104.4 million

Late nineteenth-century France

We use the same strategy to identify actors as in the "control over taxes" section for late nineteenth-century France. The dominant elites are associated with the central state, the subordinate elite with departments, and the masses with communes. As with control over taxation, Paris and the department of Seine are considered to be part of the dominant elite. While most data refer to the early 1870s, we divide these between actors in view of the laws and regulations that existed during the 1890s.

Le Comte de Franqueville (1875: 298 and 307) provides comprehensive data on the public service expenditures of nearly all communes in 1871 and all departments in 1869. For communes, this included outlays for police, public worship, elementary education, streets and highways, and poor relief. These expenditures totaled 225.685 million *francs*. However, most of these expenditures can *not* be attributed to the masses. First, a significant share of these monies were collected by the central state and then redistributed to the communes. In 1871, the *centimes* (see "taxes") contributed 119.99 million *francs* of the financing of communes (Ministry of Public Instruction 1889: 50). Because we treat communes in the department of Seine differently, it is necessary to remove their estimated share of 26.7 percent (see discussion under "taxes") from this figure, which leaves 87.95 million *francs*. Communal expenditures (excluding department of Seine) totaled 401.38 million (excluding 123.81 million for war expenses; Le Comte de Franqueville 1875: 307). As the proportion of *centimes* (87.95 million) to total expenditures (396.69 million) is 22.2 percent, we subtract this proportion (50.768 million) from the total communal expenditures on public services, which leaves 174.917 million *francs*. This subtracted figure is then attributed to the central state because it is the ultimate source of this funding.

Other communal expenditures were "under control" of the dominant elite because the central state mandated them and appointed the civil servants working in these areas. This is true for the policing, highway construction, education, and caring for the poor and sick (Le Comte de Franqueville 1875: 305; Chapman 1955: 46; Imbert and Mollat 1982: 301 and 313). These expenditures totaled 162.38 million *francs* (after applying the 22.2 percent adjustment explained previously), which must be subtracted from the above total

---

[15] The 1785 receipts are available in Goldsmith (1832). Information on the 1695 central state income comes from European State Finance Database (n.d.).

and attributed to the dominant elite. This leaves 12.537 million *francs* under the control of the masses.

Departments spent on roads and highways, relief for the poor and mentally ill, public worship, education, and local railways. These expenditures totaled 96.207 million *francs*. However, departments no longer had any independent powers of taxation. Thus, all of these monies came from the central state and are attributed to the dominant elite.

To determine what the dominant elite spent on public services, it is first useful to tally what has already been attributed to them: i.e. 50.768 million in *centimes* to the communes; 162.380 million on mandated services provided by the communes but where the central state appointed the personnel of the corresponding agencies; and all spending (96.207 million) on public services by the departments, for a total of 309.355 million. Next, we estimate what the commune of Paris spent on public services, as this was not included in Le Comte de Franqueville (1875). We continue to assume (see "taxes") that Paris accounts for 26.7 percent of all communal expenditures. This allows us to calculate that the commune of Paris spent 82.208 million on public services, which we attribute to the dominant elite.

Finally, a very large portion of public service was directly provided by the central state. To maintain consistency with the data for departments and communes, we use the budget data of 1870 made available by the Ministry of Public Instruction (1889: 32–52). The central state spent large sums on a variety of public services including: pensions for civil and military employees, post and telegraph services, public worship, education, police, poor and emergency relief, roads and bridges, and subsidies to Paris. These expenditures totaled 301 million *francs* in 1870.

SUMMARY

Dominant elite: 50.768+162.380+96.207+82.208+301 = 692.563 million (98.2%)
Subordinate elite: 0 (0%)
Dominant and subordinate masses: 12.537 million (1.8%)
Total: 705.10 million

3.2 Ottoman empire

Seventeenth-century Ottoman empire

Faroqhi (1997: 541) provides detailed information on the 1669–1670 budget of the central government.[16] He writes that the sultan spent 189.2 million *akçes* on the upkeep of his palace, which represented 29.5% of his overall expenditures. From this we can infer that total expenditures were 641,355,932 *akçes*. Military activities consumed almost two thirds of his budget, leaving very little for other endeavors. Construction projects amounted to 2% of expenditures, while another 0.5% went to the *Hajj* and the inhabitants of Medina. Thus, public service cost the sultan 2.5% of his expenses, a total of 16,033,898 *akçes*. To this figure one must add (as explained below) the dominant elites' share of *waqf* expenditures – 4,629 *akçes* – to arrive at a rounded total of 16.039 million.

---

[16] Because of the accounting methods used by the Ottoman central government during this period, the only central budgets that contain unambiguous information on income and expenditures are those for 1527–1528, 1660–1661, and 1669–1670. However, none of these three budgets includes *timars* (Sahillioğlu 1999: 67, note 3).

Few details about provincial expenditures are known for this time period, which makes it difficult to estimate the contributions of the subordinate elite. However, thanks to the Herculean work of Stanford Shaw (1958), we have specific information on expenditures in Egypt, which was under Ottoman control at the time. Shaw provides both total expenditures (Shaw 1958: 399) and public service expenditures (Shaw 1958: 225–268) for decades before and after 1669–1670, the reference year for the central budget data analyzed above. We calculated an average based on the 40 years that straddle 1669–1670.[17] For most public service expenditures, data are available for all these years. The average total expenditure was calculated on the basis of the three years with corresponding data.[18] The average annual expenditures for public service (e.g. food and clothing for the poor; canal and mosque maintenance; water storage; pilgrimage; maintenance of holy cities) were 9,971,340 *paras*, or 13.8 percent of the total.[19]

Assuming that Egypt was representative of Ottoman provinces at the time, we could calculate how much public service was provided by the subordinate elite if we knew the total expenditures of all provinces. This total expenditure must be estimated, however. We do so by exploiting information on the relationship between provincial expenditures and central income in 1527–1528. Provincial expenditures amounted to about 75 percent of central state income at that time (İnalcik 1994: 82–83).[20] Assuming the same was true in 1669–1670, when central state income was 596,655,932 *akçes*, total provincial expenditures in that year could have been around 447,491,949 *akçes*.[21] Generalizing the Egyptian figure of 13.8 percent dedicated to public service provision, the subordinate elite across the Ottoman empire in the late seventeenth century contributed 61,753,889 *akçes* to public service provision.

The subordinate elite's contribution was not confined to those of the provincial governments it manned. Subordinate elites also controlled many *waqfs*, which for centuries have been important charitable institutions in Islamic society. Founders of *waqfs* set aside some revenue-producing resource (usually buildings or land) for specific purposes, which quite frequently were and are religious or charitable in character. Once a *waqf* is formed, it exists in perpetuity (it cannot be sold or alienated in any fashion), and its net revenues are distributed to "the object of endowment" (Barnes 1987: 1) – e.g. the charitable purpose. Over the centuries, *waqfs* have funded a variety of public services, including aid

---

[17] Most of Shaw's (1958) tables report many more years before and after 1669–1670. For example, many tables contain entries for 1020–1082 (i.e. 1611 to 1671 – see pp. xxvii–xxviii). However, because annual expenditures are constant across these time periods, it is possible to determine the average for the 20-year period with which we are concerned. That these entries relate to *annual* expenditures is not manifestly evident from examining the table, but Shaw (1958) indicates as much in a number of discussions in the text (see Shaw 1958: 90–91).

[18] During this time, 1 *para* = 1.2 *akçe* (İnalcik 1994: 87), on average. However, this conversion is unnecessary, as we make use of the *percentage* of expenditures devoted to public service provision and generalize this to the empire as whole.

[19] These were the input figures. All come from pp. 225–238, save for the last, which relates to spending on the pilgrimage and holy cities and comes from p. 268.

[20] 403.37 million out of 537.90 million.

[21] To calculate central state income, we substracted the 44.7 million *akçes* in deficit expenditures noted by Faroqhi (1997: 541) from the central state expenditure figure.

to the poor, public infrastructure projects, hospitals, and education (Barnes 1987; Hoexter 1998; Yüksel 1998; Leeuwen 1999).

Studies of more than 300 *waqfs* in the seventeenth century (Yüksel 1998: 220) and 6,000 in the eighteenth century (Yedıyıldiz 1975, cited in Barnes 1987: 43) confirm subordinate elites – e.g. the military caste officials of provincial governments, the religious class of *ulema* – founded the vast majority of these endowments (Yüksel estimates 89% and Yedıyıldiz 90%). On the other hand, Gerber (1983: 29) estimates that 2% of *waqfs* were controlled by the sultan and his family. Combining these two pieces of information, *waqf* public service expenditures can be attributed in the following fashion: 2% to the dominant elite, 89.5% to the subordinate elite, and the rest (8.5%) to the masses.[22]

To determine the portion of *waqf* expenditures that went to public service, we use Yüksel's (1998) major study of *waqf* budgets between 1585 and 1683 (993–1095 on the Muslim calendar). Across this century-long period, total *waqf* expenditures were 18,936,073 *akçes*, or about 186,000 per year (Yüksel 1998: 266). However, these figures come from the geographic expanse of modern-day Turkey, while the Ottoman empire was much larger. According to population figures for the year 1867 provided by Karpat (1985: 25), the region that is now Turkey contained about one-half of the empire's population. Assuming equal expenditures per person inside and outside geographic Turkey, we therefore double the per year expenditure to 372,000 *akçes*. A substantial portion of total expenditures, 63.5 percent, went to the provision of public services such as education, feeding and housing the poor, and maintaining an infrastructure for religious services (Yüksel 1998: 266). Thus, we estimate that in 1670, *waqf* expenditures devoted to public services totaled about 231,496 *akçes*. Adding the subordinate elite's share of this – 207,189 – to the figure calculated above yields a rounded total of 61.961 million.

The masses' share of *waqf* expenditures for public services totaled 19,677 *akçes*. Police protection was another public service provided by the masses (fortification, however, was never as important as in late medieval Europe). Emecen (1989: 339) provides detailed data on how much of Manisa, a city of average size (Emecen 1989: 54 n270; Erder and Faroqhi 1980: 273), spent on guards and night watchmen in 1572–1573. Each guard was responsible for collecting his salary directly from town citizens. As of 1575, the city had a population of 8,245 (Emecen 1989: 55). The guards collected 55,608 *akçes* in salaries from local citizens, yielding an average of 6.74 *akçes* per resident. How can this be generalized to the empire as a whole? The population of the Ottoman empire was about 15 million in the late sixteenth century (Kinross 1977: 206). However, we assume that this service was specific to the *urban* population of the Ottoman empire, as we did when calculating expenditures for *sergents* in France. According to Quaetaert (2001: 94), "[f]rom its inception until its demise" the Ottoman empire "was an agrarian empire and economy" in which "[t]hree quarters of the inhabitants lived in the countryside and drew their livings from the soil and agriculturally related activities." Thus, we estimate the urban population of the late sixteenth-century at 3.75 million and their expenditure for public security at 27,275,000 *akçes*. Combining this figure with the *waqf* estimate yields a rounded total value of public services provided by the masses of 27.295 million.

---

[22] The estimation of the masses' share is obviously residual, but it is also consistent with Yedıyıldiz (1975), who estimates that 10 percent of *waqfs* were founded by the *reaya* – i.e. peasants, artisans, or merchants. Yüksel (1998) attributes only 1 percent of the *waqfs* to the *reaya*, but 10 percent of his foundations have "unknown" founders.

SUMMARY

Dominant elites: 16.039 million *akçes* (15.2%)
Subordinate elites: 61.961 million *akçes* (58.8%)
Masses: 27.295 million *akçes* (26%)
Total: 105.295 million *akçes*

Nineteenth-century Ottoman empire

To calculate the dominant elite's contribution to public service provision, we used the central state budgets between 1874 and 1898 published by Shaw (1978). Compared to its pre-modern counterpart, the modern state had vastly wider concerns for public welfare. It invested in public works, provided for education, the administration of justice in both Muslim (through the Ilmiye Office) and non-Muslim areas (through the "Ministry of Justice and Sects"), policing, pensions for former government workers, postal and telegraph services, and funded the holy cities and a whole infrastructure set up for the pilgrims. Reported below are average annual figures for each of these services (in *kuruş*):

- Holy cities and pilgrimage:[23] 36.5 million
- Pensions:[24] 61.7 million
- Post Office and Telegraph Service:[25] 39.1 million
- Ministry of Police and Gendarmerie:[26] 120.2 million
- Ministry of Justice and Sects:[27] 40.1 million
- Ilmiye Office:[28] 21.4 million
- Education:[29] 13.2 million
- Public works:[30] 6.4 million

Total public service expenditures between 1874 and 1898 averaged 338.6 million *kuruş*. Adding to this figure the dominant elite's share of *waqf* expenditures for public services – 659,220 *kuruş* – yields 339.259 million *kuruş*. To this we need to add spending at the provincial level because since the nineteenth-century Tanzimat reforms, all tax money was collected in the name of the central state, went to the State Treasury, and returned to the provinces based on budgets approved by the central state (O'Meara 1894: 291; Shaw 1975). In order to determine how much of provincial spending needs to be attributed to the central elites we examined the expenditures of five provinces between 1874 and 1898. The following lists these provinces as well as the year of the budget data: Sivas (1898),

[23] Starting in 1868, this line item was moved to the Treasury of the Sultan. Thus, the 1874–1898 figure is based on an average of the years during which it appeared separately: 1860–1867.

[24] Because this line item was moved to the Ministry of Finance after 1881 and was no longer listed separately, the figure reported is an average of 1874–1881.

[25] This average is based on the following available years: 1874–1875, 1877–1878, and 1887–1898.

[26] This average is based on 1887–1898; most of the police funds were not listed separately from the general Ministry of Interior budget before that.

[27] This average is based on 1874–1875, 1877–1881, and 1887–1898.

[28] This averaged is based on 1887–1898.

[29] This ceases to be a separate line item after 1878 when it was moved to the Ministry of Interior. Thus, this average is based on two years, 1874–1875 and 1877–1878.

[30] This ceased to be a separate line item after 1878 when it was moved to the Ministry of Interior. This average is based on the available data from 1868–1878.

Hüdavendigar (1895), Ankara (1882), Syria (1878), and Halep (1874). Budgets for the first three provinces are from Kilia (2000), while the Halep provincial budget is provided by Akkuş (2008) and the one from Syria by Saliba (1978: 311). According to these budgets, provincial governments funded hospitals, police, education, courts, mail service, and infrastructure projects. These expenditures totaled 28.8 million *kuruş*. According to Karpat (1985: 160–161), the five provinces together accounted for 25 percent of the empire's population in 1897. Assuming equal per person spending across the empire (i.e. multiplying by four), public services provided by the provinces totaled 115.2 million *kuruş* on an average year between 1874 and 1898. Because the central state funded these activities, we attribute this sum to the dominant elite.

Most of the *waqf* money, on the other hand, can be attributed to the subordinate elites. Demirel (2000) provides total *waqf* expenditures for the province of Sivas in 1835. The portion going to such public services as education, libraries, mosque maintenance, and public fountains was 480,000 *kuruş*. According to Karpat (1985: 160–161), Sivas accounted for about 5 percent of the empire's total population in the nineteenth century. Assuming uniformity across the empire, *waqf* public service expenditures totaled 9.6 million *kuruş*.

A second data source allows us to avoid generalizing from a single province in the 1830s. Öztürk (1995: 49–56) provides data on 60 *waqfs* across the nineteenth century (technically: 1802–1911), 38 of these from 1868 or later (Öztürk 1995: 49). All of these *waqfs* were located in Anatolia. Average spending on the range of relevant services (religious, educational, and social, the latter of which included municipal services and welfare) totaled 8,046 *kuruş* per month for all 60 *waqfs*, or 96,552 *kuruş* per year. This yields 1,609.2 *kuruş* per *waqf* per year. We can now calculate the figure for the entire empire because Öztürk (1995: 56) provides the total number of *waqfs*: 35,000. *Waqf* expenditures on public services during a typical year in the nineteenth century therefore might have totaled 56,322,000 *kuruş*. Given that the two different data sources and methods of generalization produce very different estimates, we average the two to arrive at about 32.961 million *kuruş*. Assigning 89.5 percent of this to the subordinate elite – 29,500,092 – pushes the subordinate elite total to 144.7 million *kuruş*. The masses controlled 8.5 percent of total *waqf* expenditures or 2.802 million *kuruş*.

SUMMARY

Dominant elite: 454.459 million (93.4%)
Subordinate elite: 29.5 million (6.0%)
Masses: 2.802 million (0.6%)
Total: 486.761 million

Appendix Table 2.2 summarizes the estimates described in this appendix. It shows how, in both societies, the central elites were increasingly able to monopolize the provision of public services all the while siphoning off an increasing share of the taxes. The masses, on the other hand, replaced subordinate elites as the main source of military support.

APPENDIX 2.2 ACTOR ALLIANCES IN EMPIRES

To understand the various pathways of political modernization, it is useful to analyze the pre-modern equilibrium (or the "empire scenario" for short) in more detail. Appendix Table 2.3 summarizes the model assumptions and lists the empirical data on which actor

APPENDIX TABLE 2.2 *Summary of French and Ottoman data on actors' control over resources (percentages)*

	Taxes (post-exchange)					Military support (pre-exchange)					Public service provision (pre-exchange)				
	France, 1360–1380	Ottoman empire, 1521–1596	France, 1780s	Ottoman empire, 1870–1908	France, 1870–1900	France, 1180–1330	Ottoman empire, 1470–1530	France, 1690	Ottoman empire, 1870–1908	France, 1870–1900	France, 1322–1350	Ottoman empire, 1669/1670	France, 18th century	Ottoman Empire, 1870–1908	France, 1870–1900
dE	42	36	87.3	90	90.3	18.5	32.5	11.5	0.5	0.4	0.5	15.2	86.5	93.4	98.2
sE	46	49	8.3	0	4	68	61	8.5	12	4.2	91.4	58.8	1.8	6.0	0
dM	6	7	2.2	5	2.85	6.75	5	40	44	47.7	4.05	13	5.85	0.3	0.9
sM	6	7	2.2	5	2.85	6.75	1.5	40	43.5	47.7	4.05	13	5.85	0.3	0.9

APPENDIX TABLE 2.3 *Control and interest in empire*

Model assumptions

Control over:					Interest in:				
	Political decision-making	Public goods provision	Military support	Taxation		dE	sE	dM	sM
dE	0.6	0.05	0.20	0.42	Political decision-making	0.20	0.45	0	0
sE	0.4	0.85	0.70	0.48	Public goods provision	0.01	0.10	0.15	0.15
dM	0	0.05	0.05	0.05	Military support	0.20	0.15	0	0
sM	0	0.05	0.05	0.05	Taxation	0.59	0.30	0.85	0.85

Empirical data

France 1280–1350

	Political decision-making	Public goods provision	Military support	Taxation
dE	NA	0.005	0.185	0.42
sE	NA	0.915	0.68	0.46
dM	NA	0.04	0.0675	0.06
sM	NA	0.04	0.0675	0.06

Ottoman empire 1470–1670

dE	NA	0.152	0.325	0.36
sE	NA	0.588	0.61	0.49
dM	NA	0.13	0.05	0.07
sM	NA	0.13	0.015	0.07

Notes: The control matrix describes the pre-exchange distribution of control for each resource, while the interest matrix represents the distributions of interest for each actor. For control over taxation, however, we calculated post-exchange values.

controlled which resources in empires, based on the historical research summarized in Appendix 2.1. As can be seen, we model the "empire scenario" closer to the French data since the Ottoman sultan in the seventeenth century had more taxing capabilities and military power than the French king (cf. Barkey 1991: 704).

The historical data show, consistent with the historical sociology of empires (Eisenstadt 1963; Hechter 2000; Howe 2002; Barkey 2008), that the dominant elites of both societies relied on a system of indirect rule and taxation. They were only able to raise 10 percent of the taxes directly, while more than three-quarters of the overall tax volume (including income from seignorial domains in France) went to subordinate elites. The majority of public goods were also provided by subordinate elites, such as through the hospitals founded and funded by the nobility or Crusading Orders in France or the religious foundations in the Ottoman empire or the welfare expenditures of Ottoman provincial governors. The rest of public services was provided by the dominant elites on the one hand, who funded alimonies for the poor (in France), infrastructure and food for the pilgrims in Mecca (in the Ottoman empire), and the construction and maintenance of major roads. On the other hand, the masses provided public goods through the hospitals and religious foundations founded by townspeople, the police patrols paid for by local communities, or the town fortifications of Renaissance France.

Since in both empires the masses were excluded from supra-local politics, they had no control over political decision-making. Most political power lay with the dominant elites (0.6). However, before the advent of a centralized bureaucracy that replaced indirect rule, the subordinate elites held considerable power at the regional and local level (0.4) (on the political sociology of empires see again Eisenstadt 1963; Hechter 2000; Howe 2002; Barkey 2008). Military support was mostly provided by the subordinate elites (0.70), on whose troops the center depended to conduct large-scale war. In France, the king's army was mobilized through the principle of feudal fealty, while in the Ottoman empire the beneficiaries of the right to tax the local population owed the sultan military support. The center's own army was still very small in Renaissance France, just enough to guarantee the king's security (0.20). As mentioned before, it was considerably larger in the case of the Ottoman empire, where the famous *sipahi* cavalry and the palace guards formed a formidable fighting force. Before the advent of universal conscription, the masses only provided small, undisciplined militias or small contingents of mounted warriors in France, or the frontier raiders around garrison towns in the Ottoman empire (0.05 each).

We now turn to the interest distribution, for which we depend on plausibility arguments, as discussed in the main text, because it is not possible to estimate values based on quantitative empirical data. Since the masses were not organized beyond the local level and therefore rarely articulated political demands relevant for the entire polity (see "lateral insulation" in Gellner 1983: 9–11; Mann 1993: chapter 4), they were not interested in political decision-making at this level (0). Given that warfare was still very much an elite (and mercenary) affair that did not mobilize or involve the masses (Rogers 1995; on France, Lynn 1997), they were also not much interested in increasing their own command over military matters. Rather, their main interest was in taxation (0.85), i.e. to retain as much of their economic revenue as possible and thus ensure that they would not fall below what they considered a morally acceptable level of subsistence (Scott 1976). This is evidenced by the frequent tax rebellions characteristic of pre-modern and early modern polities (Mousnier 1970; Kiser and Linton 2002). We further assume that they were also interested in public service provision, but to a much lower degree (0.15) – since they relied on family, guild, village, or the local lord to provide for basic forms of social security, policing, and education (on rural life in medieval Europe, see Duby 1998 [1961]; on guilds in the Arab world, see Lewis 1937).

In systems of indirect rule, the greatest concern of the dominant elite was to increase their tax income (0.59) in order to finance their war enterprises, as a long line of research in comparative historical sociology has shown (from Tilly 1975 to Kiser and Linton 2001). Besides this, we assume they were interested in decision-making power and military support (0.20 each) as two important sources for expanding their domain and power. Since the center fought larger wars than did the subordinate elite, the latter were slightly less interested in military support by allies (0.15). We assume that they were mostly interested in taxes (0.30) and political power (0.45). This is plausible in view of the constant political rivalries and frequent wars between the French king and various factions of provincial nobles over taxation rights and access to political offices (Lachmann 1989); and the intense tug-of-war between the sultan and regional governors and military entrepreneurs (İnalcik 1980); and the frequent struggles between the Ottoman center and various victims of its centralization policies who then gathered under the mantle of Sufi Orders and called for religious renewal of the corrupt center (Barkey 2008: chapter 5). Being able to provide public services was also of some interest to the subordinate elites (0.10) since the stability of their rule depended on functioning patron–client relations with their dependents (in general, for peasant societies, see Scott 1976; for France, see the case study by Le Blévec 2000; on the *waqfs* in the Ottoman world, see Barnes 1987).

Given this specification of interests and control, and assuming that actors do not care about cultural traits or markers when forming alliances, the estate order constitutes the equilibrium. To make this result understandable, we describe why actors either have no incentive or are not able to unilaterally deviate from this equilibrium. In particular, we consider why the dominant and the subordinate elites do not exchange resources with the masses – as they will do in more centralized polities. We first note that the subordinate elite would do best if *all* actors exchanged resources with each other (nation building). The reason is that their taxation power (which they hold thanks to the principle of indirect rule) is highly demanded by all other actors. The masses would want the subordinate elites to rescind some of their coercive control over taxation. The dominant elite likewise demands a share of the subordinate elite.

The dominant elites therefore do much better if they do *not* have to compete with the masses for taxation. The dominant elite use their first-mover advantage to propose the estate order. The subordinate elite accept this proposal (rather than trying to align with the masses) because they in turn depend on an exchange relationship with the dominant elite to gain enough political decision-making power to stabilize their rule. Faced with the proposal of the dominant elite to form an alliance that excludes the masses, the subordinate elite has to agree if they want to end up in an alliance group that comprises the dominant elite. They do not even formulate a counter-proposal, and the estate order emerges as a stable status quo. Under this system, the dominant elite transfer certain political positions and rights to the subordinate elite and in return receive their military support and taxation.

Given the uncertainty of the model assumptions, we proceed in varying these assumptions systematically and see if the estate order still emerges as the equilibrium outcome. Similar to Figure 2.2 in the main text, Appendix Figure 2.1 depicts the equilibria resulting from various levels of state centralization and mass mobilization as well as from different modes of cultural differentiation. The empire scenario analyzed above corresponds to the center of the left-hand side graph. It shows the equilibrium classifications that result if there is no cultural differentiation – or if it is of no interest to the actors. The middle graph represents the outcome when cultural differentiation proceeds along status lines. The right-hand side graph depicts the equilibria for an ethnic trait distribution. As can be seen, the estate order emerges as the dominant equilibrium under all three different forms of cultural differentiation. When cultural traits align with class, it constitutes the equilibrium for all 25 model runs. Under an ethno-cultural differentiation, six of the model runs lead to an extended estate order as a second possible equilibrium. The extended estate order can be regarded a variant of the estate order: one of the masses is allowed into the existing elite coalition, which remains the defining

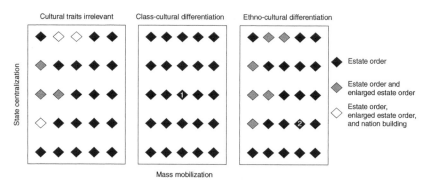

APPENDIX FIGURE 2.1 Equilibria in the "empire scenario" with different modes of cultural differentiation

feature of the alliance system (think of the constitutional monarchy in Great Britain in the early modern period or of France under Louis Philippe, when the royal house and the aristocratic elites granted limited voting rights to the bourgeois middle classes). If actors don't care about cultural similarity and difference, three outcomes will feature nation building as a third equilibrium. Note, however, that these nationalist equilibria are relatively far removed from the middle of the graph that corresponds to the actual assumptions for the empire scenario that we derived from the historical research documented in Appendix 2.1.

In any case, these empirical data put Renaissance France and the Ottoman empire of the classical age very squarely at the center of zones for which our model generates the estate order as equilibrium outcome. For historical reasons, discussed in the main text, it is safe to assume that a class-cultural differentiation was prevalent in Renaissance France, while the Ottoman "empire of difference" (Barkey 2008) institutionally supported cultural differentiations between ethno-religious communities. Appendix Figure 2.1 suggests that in these two societies the elite coalition and the exclusion of the masses was a rather stable outcome of the ongoing negotiation process that would survive considerable variation in the degree of state centralization (perhaps brought about by external wars) or the military mobilization of the population.

APPENDIX 2.3 SENSITIVITY ANALYSIS

This appendix describes a sensitivity analysis that we conducted in order to make sure that our inferences do not depend on fragile assumptions (Saltelli *et al.* 2008: 34). We concentrate on the main result, namely that a greater degree of state centralization leads to nation building and makes ethnic closure or populist nationalism less likely. This result was derived assuming specific distributions of interests and control. Where available, we used historical data to empirically ground the assumptions about which actor controlled how much of which resource. However, the exact parameter values necessarily entail some degree of arbitrariness, given the abstractness of our model. This holds even more true with regard to actors' interests, since these assumptions had to be based on historical plausibility alone.

The sensitivity analysis randomly varies the exact specification of the control and interest matrices that describe the shift from weak to strong state centralization. We then record whether the resulting equilibria are in line with our main expectation.[31] Whenever more state centralization *leads away* from nation building and toward ethnic closure or populist nationalism, we would have to be concerned about the robustness of our main findings. We assume a strongly developed network of voluntary associations ($U^{meaning} = 0$) since the impact of this one-dimensional factor is already well understood. We also set mass mobilization at medium or strong levels (varying the exact values randomly). Based on the results discussed in the main text, we know that this factor exerts only a weak influence on the outcome.

The independent variables are the parameters that define weak and strong state centralization. For each of these parameters in the control and interest matrices, we define an interval Δ of possible values (which includes the one used in the main analysis). These intervals define a multidimensional space of input parameters. Since the number of parameters is high, it is impossible to derive the complete multidimensional "response surface," i.e. a full picture of how the dependent variable changes as a function of the input parameters (Oliver 1993; Oliver and Myers 2002). The most widely used strategies in such complex situations are to either focus on specific combinations of parameter values or vary one factor at a time (OAT) (Saltelli *et al.* 2006). However, both approaches are clearly insufficient as they cannot account for non-linear effects and interactions (Oliver 1993; Oliver and Myers 2002). We therefore use the Elementary Effect Test developed by Morris (1991) and extended by Campolongo *et al.* (2007), which can deal with a large number of input factors in a computationally efficient way all the while paying attention to possible non-linearities and interactions (Saltelli *et al.* 2008).

In the Elementary Effect Test, each of k independent input factors X_i ($i = 1,...,k$) is allowed to vary across p selected levels. For a given vector $\mathbf{X} = (X_1, X_2,...,X_k)$, the elementary effect of the *i*th input factor is defined as

$$EE_i(\mathbf{X}) = \frac{\left[Y(X_1, X_2,...,X_{i-1}, X_i + \Delta,...X_k) - Y(\mathbf{X})\right]}{\Delta},$$

where Δ is the size of the sampling step in the scale $[0,1]$ after the range of each factor has been rescaled on this interval (Saltelli *et al.* 2008: 110, 120).[32] Although this method also varies one factor at a time, it computes several elementary effects for each variable at different points of the input space. Averaging over these elementary effects allows us to arrive at a sensitivity measure that is increasingly independent of the specific points at which the elementary effects were computed (Saltelli *et al.* 2004: 92–93). It is thus a global method in the sense of exploring several regions of the input space. This also ensures that possible interactions among input factors can be detected.

---

[31] Note that our focus is on how shifts in the configurations of interests and control impact the resulting alliance system instead of exploring the sensitivity of point predictions, as we did with the graphs.

[32] More precisely, Δ is a value in $\{1/(p-1),...,1-1/(p-1)\}$, since the sampling steps occur on the *p*-level grid Ω into which the input space has been discretized. Also, the point that one arrives at when in- or decrementing a factor in $(X_1, X_2,...,X_k)$ by Δ has still to lie in Ω (Saltelli *et al.* 2008: 110, 120).

Since it is impossible to compute all elementary effects, special techniques have been developed that lead to an efficient sampling of such effects (Morris 1991; Campolongo *et al.* 2007). Denoting the number of input factors by k, the idea is to build "r trajectories of (k+1) points in the input space, each providing k elementary effects, one per input factor, for a total of r(k+1) sample points" (Saltelli *et al.* 2008: 110, 120). Thus, a trajectory constitutes a particular path through the multidimensional input space that varies one factor at a time. Following the sampling strategy developed by Campolongo *et al.* (2007), we select the *r* trajectories in a way that maximizes their spread in the input space (Saltelli *et al.* 2008: 110, 120). Following recommendations in the literature, we select a set of 10 (out of 500 randomly generated) trajectories that satisfies this criterion.

In order to apply the Elementary Effect method to our model results, two features have to be taken into account. First, the control and interest matrices (each containing 4x4 cells) for weak and strong state centralization amount to 64 input parameters. The effective number is smaller, however, since parameters that do not vary with state centralization need to be held constant. These are the dominant elite's interests, the subordinate elite's interest in taxation, the masses' interest in military support, and the masses' control over political decision-making and over provision of public goods. Subject to the sensitivity analysis are the specific values at which these parameters are held constant. We also retain our simplifying assumption that both masses have identical shares of control and interest.

Second, the general properties of Coleman's exchange model demand that relative interests of each actor sum up to 1, as do relative shares of control over each resource. Both kinds of restrictions mean that one cannot vary each parameter independently. Rather, parameters are varied by groups so that all restrictions are met when randomly drawing parameter values. This produces eight groups of parameters. In Appendix Table 2.4, parameters belonging to the same group are enclosed by bold rectangles. The table lists the intervals of the input parameters used in the sensitivity analysis. The intervals are generally of size 0.10 and centered at the value that underlies the analysis in the main text. The random draws can select one of three levels: the mean value or the lower or upper bound of the intervals. Whenever a group moves within a trajectory, a set of parameter values that satisfies its internal restrictions is drawn randomly. Together, this implies that individual parameters shift either by 0.05, 0.10, or not at all. The few exceptions to these rules concern parameter values that are already close to the extremes. For example, where relative interest is assumed to be zero, it seems sufficient to investigate whether assuming an interest of 0.05 leads to the same result.

Since there are eight groups of parameters, a trajectory in which each group moves once encompasses nine different parameter lists. Each parameter list corresponds to a different specification of weak and strong state centralization (within the intervals given in Appendix Table 2.4). As in the main text (see Figure 2.2), six model evaluations are used to analyze the shift from one scenario to the next. Thus, in total, the sensitivity analysis is based on 90 parameter lists (10 maximally spreading trajectories, each comprising nine parameter lists) and 540 model evaluations.

None of them resulted in an alliance system that contradicted the argument that more state centralization leads to nation building and away from ethnic closure and populist nationalism. The sensitivity analysis therefore establishes the robustness of this result, at least within the intervals presented in Appendix Table 2.4. Trivially, if we increased the intervals further, we would ultimately run into equilibria that contradicted our result.

APPENDIX TABLE 2.4 *Parameter intervals for sensitivity analysis and for which the impact of state centralization was confirmed*

	Political decision-making				Public goods provision				Military support[a]				Taxation			
	dE	sE	dM	sM	dE	sE	dM	sM	dE	sE	dM	sM	dE	sE	dM	sM
C_weak	[.7 .8] (.75)	[.2 .3] (.25)	[0 .05] (0)	identical values as dM	[.5 .6] (.56)	[.35 .45] (.38)	[0 .05] (.03)	identical values as dM	[.05 .15] (.13)	[.05 .15] (.38)	[.35 .45] (.25)	identical values as dM	[.15 .25] (1.20)	[.15 .25] (.20)	[.25 .35] (.30)	as dM
C_strong	[.85 .95] (.90)	[.05 .15] (.10) as C_weak	as C_weak	as dM	[.85 .95] (.91)	[0 .1] (.03)	as C_weak	as dM	held constant (.05)	held constant (.05)	held constant (.45)	as dM	[1.45 .55] (.50)	[.05 .15] (.10)	[.15 .25] (.20)	as dM

	dE				sE				dM				sM			
	Decision	Public	Military	Taxes	Decision	Public	Military	Taxes	Decision[a]	Public	Military	Tax	Decision[a]	Public	Military	Taxes
X_weak	[.15 .25] (.20)	[0 .05] (.01)	[.15 .25] (.20) as X_weak	[.55 .65] (.59)	[.05 .15] (.10)	[.1 .2][a] (.15)	[.4 .5] (.50)	[.2 .3] (.25)	[.45 .55] (.20)	[.15 .25] (.20)	[0 .05] (0)	[.15 .4][b] (.60)	identical values as dM			
X_strong					[.25 .35] (.30)	[.15 .25][a] (.20)	[.2 .3] (.25)	as C_weak (.25)	held cons. (.50)	[.35 .45] (.40)	as C_weak	[0 .2][b] (.10)				

Notes: Parameter values used in the main text are given in parentheses below the intervals used in the sensitivity analysis. *Indicators of mass mobilization are varied together and held constant within each trajectory. [a] Restriction: Subordinate elite's interest in public goods provision under strong state centralization is at least as high as under weak state centralization. [b] Masses' relative interest in taxation is set equal to the remaining share after the other three interest parameters have been drawn.

However, our goal was to show that results remain stable even if we vary the values of the model parameters by 0.10 around those used for the analysis in the main text. Differences of 0.10 are substantial, given that parameters range from 0 to 1 and constitute *relative* interests or shares of control so that a shift by 0.10 implies an equally sized shift with respect to the other interests or control shares by other actors.

Chapter 3

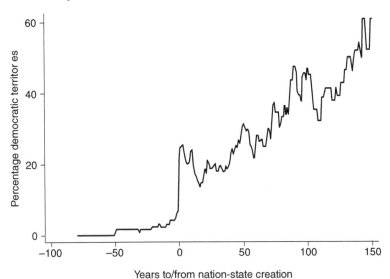

APPENDIX FIGURE 3.1 Nation-state formation and democracy

APPENDIX 3.2 YEARS OF NATION-STATE CREATION

Territory	1st NSC	2nd NSC	3rd NSC
Afghanistan	1964		
Algeria	1963		
Angola	1975		
Argentina	1824		
Armenia	1918	1991	
Australia	1948		
Austria	1918		
Azerbaijan	1917	1991	
Bahrain			
Bangladesh	1972		
Belarus	1991		
Belgium	1831		
Benin	1960		
Bhutan	1998		
Bolivia	1825		

APPENDIX 3.2 (*cont.*)

Territory	1st NSC	2nd NSC	3rd NSC
Bosnia and Herzegovina	1921	1992	
Botswana	1966		
Brazil	1889		
Bulgaria	1879		
Burkina Faso	1960		
Burundi	1962		
Cambodia	1953		
Cameroon	1960		
Canada	1867		
Central African Republic	1960		
Chad	1960		
Chile	1828		
China	1911		
Colombia	1821	1831	
Congo, Dem. Republic	1960		
Congo, Rep.	1960		
Costa Rica	1823	1839	
Croatia	1921	1991	
Cuba	1902		
Cyprus	1960		
Czech Republic	1918	1993	
Denmark	1849		
Dominican Republic	1844		
Ecuador	1821	1830	
Egypt	1923		
El Salvador	1823	1841	
Eritrea	1993		
Estonia	1918	1991	
Ethiopia	1974		
Finland	1917		
Gabon	1960		
Gambia	1965		
Georgia	1918	1991	
Germany	1871		
Ghana	1957		
Greece	1844		
Guatemala	1823	1839	
Guinea	1958		

Territory	1st NSC	2nd NSC	3rd NSC
Guinea-Bissau	1974		
Guyana	1970		
Honduras	1823	1839	
Hungary	1918		
India	1947		
Indonesia	1950		
Iran	1906		
Iraq	1932		
Ireland	1931		
Israel	1948		
Italy	1861		
Ivory Coast	1960		
Japan	1868		
Jordan	1946		
Kazakhstan	1991		
Kenya	1963		
Kuwait			
Kyrgyzstan	1991		
Laos	1954		
Latvia	1918	1991	
Lesotho	1966		
Liberia	1944		
Libya			
Lithuania	1918	1991	
Macedonia	1921	1991	
Madagascar	1960		
Malawi	1964		
Malaysia	1957		
Mali	1960		
Mauritania	1960		
Mauritius	1968		
Mexico	1824		
Moldova	1991		
Mongolia	1924		
Morocco	1996		
Mozambique	1975		
Myanmar	1948		
Nepal	1990		
Netherlands	1848		

APPENDIX 3.2 *(cont.)*

Territory	1st NSC	2nd NSC	3rd NSC
New Zealand	1907		
Nicaragua	1823	1839	
Niger	1960		
Nigeria	1960		
North Korea	1948		
Norway	1905		
Oman			
Pakistan	1947		
Panama	1821	1831	1903
Papua New Guinea	1975		
Peru	1824		
Philippines	1946		
Poland	1921		
Portugal	1822		
Qatar	1971		
Romania	1878		
Russia	1905		
Rwanda	1962		
Saudi Arabia			
Senegal	1960		
Sierra Leone	1961		
Slovakia	1918	1993	
Slovenia	1921	1991	
Somalia	1960		
South Africa	1994		
South Korea	1948		
Spain	1820		
Sri Lanka	1948		
Sudan	1956		
Suriname	1975		
Sweden	1866		
Switzerland	1848		
Syria	1946		
Taiwan	1949		
Tajikistan	1991		
Tanzania	1961		
Thailand	1932		

Territory	1st NSC	2nd NSC	3rd NSC
Togo	1960		
Tunisia	1956		
Turkey	1924		
Turkmenistan	1992		
Uganda	1962		
Ukraine	1918	1991	
United Arab Emirates			
Uruguay	1830		
USA	1868		
Uzbekistan	1991		
Venezuela	1821	1829	
Vietnam	1954		
Yemen	1962	1967	1990
Yugoslavia	1878	1921	
Zambia	1964		
Zimbabwe	1980		

APPENDIX 3.3 SOURCES FOR LITERACY ESTIMATES

Same source for multiple territories across continents

Banks, Arthur. 1976. *Cross-National Time Series, 1815–1973.* Ann Arbor: Inter-University Consortium for Political and Social Research.
(Algeria 1963, Bangladesh 1972, Benin 1960, Burkina Faso 1960, Cambodia 1953, Cameroon 1960 and 1962, Chad 1960, Congo, Dem. Republic 1960, Congo, Rep. 1960, Cyprus 1960, Ethiopia 1960, Gabon 1960, Gambia 1965, Guinea 1958, Guyana 1970, India 1947, Jordan 1946, Kenya 1963, Kuwait 1961, Laos 1954, Liberia 1946, Libya 1952, Malawi 1964, Mauritania 1960, Mexico 1858, Morocco 1956, Niger 1960, Nigeria 1960, Pakistan 1947, Poland 1919 and 1921, Qatar 1971, Russia 1879 and 1905, Saudi Arabia 1946 and 1954, Senegal 1960, Sierra Leone 1961, Somalia 1960, Swaziland 1968, Sweden 1866 and 1867, Taiwan 1949, Tanzania 1961, Thailand 1936 and 1946, Tunisia 1956, Uganda 1962, United Arab Emirates 1971, Yemen 1962, Zambia 1964)
Darden, Keith and Anna Grzymala-Busse. 2006. "The great divide: literacy, nationalism, and the communist collapse," *World Politics* 59 (1): 83–115.
(Armenia 1920, Azerbaijan 1918, Bosnia and Herzegovina 1920, Croatia 1920, Czech Republic, Estonia 1918, Latvia 1918)
Meyers Konversationslexikon 1885–1892. Vienna and Leipzig: Verlag des Bibliographischen Instituts.
(USA 1880, Serbia 1874, Portugal 1878)
UNESCO. 1977. *Statistics of Educational Attainment and Illiteracy 1945–1974.* Paris: UNESCO.

(Bahrain 1971, Bangladesh 1961, Botswana 1964, Burundi 1962, Cyprus 1964, Guinea-Bissau 1962, Guyana 1946, Ivory Coast 1962, Kenya 1962, Mali 1960, Mauritania 1965, Sudan 1956)

2005. *Education for All, Literacy for Life*. Paris: UNESCO. Available online at: http://portal.unesco.org/education/en/ev.php-URL_ID=43283&URL_DO=DO_TOPIC&URL_SECTION=201.html.

(Indonesia 1950, Malawi 1950, Mozambique 1950, Nigeria 1950, Sri Lanka 1920, Uganda 1950)

UNESCO Institute for Statistics. 2002. *Literacy and Non Formal Education Sector: Estimates and Projections of Adult Illiteracy for Population Aged 15 Years and Above, by Country and by Gender, 1970–2015*. Available online at: www.uis.unesco.org/en/stats/statistics/literacy2000.htm.

(Belarus 1990, Kazakhstan 1990, Moldova 1990, Mozambique 1975, Oman 1970, Tajikistan 1990, Turkmenistan 1995, Uzbekistan 1990, Zimbabwe 1980)

Vanhanen, Tatu. 2000. "A new dataset for measuring democracy, 1810–1998," *Journal of Peace Research* 37 (2): 251–265.

(Afghanistan 1928, Argentina 1858, Austria 1928, Bolivia 1858 and 1878, Brazil 1858 and 1888, Chile 1858, Colombia 1858, Costa Rica 1858 and 1888, Czech Republic 1998, Denmark 1858, Djibouti 1988, Dominican Republic 1858 and 1868, Ecuador 1858, El Salvador 1868 and 1918, Ethiopia 1978, Guatemala 1868, Guinea-Bissau 1988, Honduras 1858 and 1888, Iran 1908, Iraq 1938, Ireland 1938, Israel 1948, Kuwait 1968, Kyrgyzstan 1998, Liberia 1908, Mongolia 1928, Nepal 1938, Netherlands 1858, Nicaragua 1858 and 1898, Norway 1888 and 1908, Panama 1908 and 1928, Paraguay 1858 and 1878, Peru 1858, South Africa 1918 and 1998, Suriname 1988, Switzerland 1858, Uruguay 1858, Venezuela 1858)

Ottoman provinces

Behar, Cem. 1986. Review of *Ottoman Population, 1830–1914* by Kemal H. Karpat, in *Population Studies* 40 (2): 322–323

(Istanbul 1904 with 40 percent literate males, supports Findley's estimates and refutes Kemal Karpat's census figures)

Bergaoui, Sami. 1996. "Distribution des notaires dans la régence de Tunis en 1874," *Arabica* 43 (3): 422–436.

(Tunisia, Libya, Algeria, Morocco, Malaysia 1816. In Tunisia in 1874, all males that were minimally literate could register as a notary, and many did in villages, among tribes, and in the cities. Most of the Ulema, Bergaoui maintains, were registered as notaries as well. He arrives at a total number of 0.4 of the male population, which is very low; we estimate a 1 percent literacy rate, assuming that all women were illiterate but 2 percent of men could read and write. We use this figure for Libya, Algeria, Morocco, and Malaysia for 1816.)

Cole, Juan Ricardo. 2000. *Colonialism and Revolution in the Middle East: Social and Cultural Origins of Egypt's 'Urabi Movement*. American University in Cairo Press.

(p. 114 estimates readership of newspapers in Cairo at 1 percent in 1800 and 4.5 percent in 1880; supports Findley)

Daskalova, Krassimira. 1997. *Literacy and Reading in Nineteenth-Century Bulgaria*. University of Washington.

(Bulgaria 1887 and later)

Findley, Carter W. 1989. *Ottoman Civil Officialdom*. Princeton University Press.

(Ottoman empire 1800 and 1900)

Gordon, Jr., Raymond. 2005. *Ethnologue: Languages of the World, 15th Edition.* Dallas: SIL International.

(Oman 1993)

Hanna, Nelly. 2007. "Literacy and the 'great divide' in the Islamic world, 1300–1800," *Journal of Global History* 2: 175–193.

(One-third of the male population in Cairo in the late eighteenth century had gone to elementary schools; Damascus early eighteenth century: 20 percent of households had books; figures not used, but support low literacy rates in peripheries of Ottoman empire at the beginning of nineteenth century)

Khalidi, Rashid. 2006. *The Iron Cage: The Story of the Palestinian Struggle for Statehood.* Boston: Beacon Press.

(p. 14, separate literacy figures for Jews and Arabs in Palestine; combined with population statistics from McCarthy to calculate overall literacy rate)

McCarthy, Justin. 1988. *The Population of Palestine: Population History and Statistics of the Late Ottoman Period and the Mandate.* New York: Columbia University Press.

(p. 31, population figures for Israel)

Roudometof, Victor. 2000. "The social origins of Balkan politics: nationalism, under-development, and the nation-state in Greece, Serbia, and Bulgaria, 1880–1920," *Mediterranean Quarterly* 11 (3): 144–163.

(Greece 1840)

Simon, Reeva. 1986. *Iraq Between the Two World Wars: The Implementation of Nationalist Ideology.* New York: Columbia University Press.

(Iraq 1918 on p. 81; supports Findley's estimates)

Somel, Selcuk Aksin. 2001. *The Modernization of Public Education in the Ottoman Empire: 1839–1908.* Leiden: Brill.

(p. 19 states, on the basis of traveler reports about the number of Quran schools in the sixteenth and seventeenth centuries, that "at least" one-fourth of the urban population could read and write in Turkish; we assume he meant males only; supports Findley)

South and Southeast Asia

Basu, Aparna. 1981. *Essays in the History of Indian Education.* New Delhi: Concept Publishers.

(Bombay, Gujarat, Bengal 1821; used to calculate India overall).

Bayly, C. A. 2008. "Indigenous and colonial origins of comparative economic development: The case of colonial India and Africa," *BMPI Working Paper 59.*

(India 1800; confirms the calculations based on Basu)

Cheesman, Nick. 2003. "State and Sangha in Burma," *Comparative Education* 39 (1): 45–63.

(Burma 1872; 32 percent male literacy according to British census; older adult male prison population had literacy rate of 60 percent, which we use to estimate pre-colonial literacy rate in Burma)

Myrdal, Gunnar. 1968. *Asian Drama: An Inquiry into the Poverty of Nations, Volume III.* New York: Pantheon.

(Burma, Sri Lanka, Malaysia, Philippines 1901 and 1931; India, Burma, and Sri Lanka based on UNESCO, *Progress of Literacy in Various Countries;* Philippines from *Human Relations Area Files,* Malaysia from UNESCO, *World Illiteracy at Mid-Century*).

Nederlandsch-Indie. 1922. *Uitkomsten der in de Maand November 1920 Gehouden Volkstelling.* Batavia: Drukkerijen Ruygrok.

(Indonesia 1920)

Reid, Anthony. 1990. *Southeast Asia in the Age of Commerce, 1450–1680: Volume One: The Lands below the Winds.* New Haven: Yale University Press.

(For interpretation of 1920 Indonesian data; with regard to Siam during the second half of nineteenth century, French missionaries report that only 10 percent of boys who went to school could read *and* write; short characterization of educational system in Malaysia that was geared toward literacy in Arabic by elites, not mass literacy in vernaculars, which justifies giving it the 1800 figures of Maghreb countries)

Statesman's Year-Book. 1885. Entry for "India." Basingstoke: Palgrave.

(India 1881)

Tambiah, Stanley. 1975. "Literacy in a Buddhist village in north-east Thailand," in Jack Goody, ed., *Literacy in Traditional Societies.* Cambridge University Press. 85–131.

(Thailand, Cambodia, Laos 1800; estimates pre-modern peripheral village literacy based on Buddhist schools in Thailand; arrives at 20 percent literacy for males, of which, however, some lost capacity to read after school, as Reid's missionaries stated in the second half of nineteenth century; 10 percent literacy is thus assumed for Thailand, Cambodia, and Laos in 1800)

Europe

Crafts, N. 2002. "The human development index, 1870–1999: some revised estimates," *European Review of Economic History* 6: 395–405.

(Australia, Belgium, Canada, Denmark, Finland, Norway, Spain, Sweden, Switzerland 1870)

Grunder, Hans-Ulrich. 1998. "Alphabetisierung," in *Historisches Lexikon der Schweiz.* Bern: Swiss Academy of Humanities and Social Sciences.

(Additional data on late eighteenth-century Switzerland)

Johansson, Egil. 1988. "Literacy campaigns in Sweden," *Interchange* 19 (3): 135–162.

(Finland 1880 and 1920)

Markussen, Ingrid. 1990. "The development of writing ability in the Nordic countries in the eighteenth and nineteenth century," *Scandinavian Journal of History* 15: 37–63.

(For estimation of growth rate of full literacy among Danes, based on growth of signing ability of peasants and reading ability of prison inmates, used to extrapolate Danish census data back)

Messerli, Alfred. 2002. *Lesen un Schreiben 1700 bis 1900.* Tübingen: Niemeyer.

(Switzerland, eighteenth century)

Myers, Martha. 1977. *The Early Development of the Serbian and Romanian National Movements: 1800–1866.* Paper given at the Department of History and the Honors College at the University of Oregon.

(Serbia 1866)

Reis, Jaime. 2005. "Economic growth, human capital formation and consumption in Western Europe before 1800," in Robert C. Allen, Tommy Bengtsson, and Martin Dribe, eds., *Living Standards in the Past.* Oxford University Press. 195–225.

(Belgium, Hungary, Netherlands, Norway, Portugal, Sweden 1800)

Soubeyroux, Jacques. 1985. "Niveles de alfabetización en la España del siglo XVIII. Primeros resultados de una encuesta en curso," *Revista de Historia Moderna* 5: 159–172.

(Spain, late eighteenth century)

Statesman's Year-Book. 1885. Entry for "Serbia." Basingstoke: Palgrave.

(Serbia 1884)

Tortella, Gabriel. 1994. "Patterns of economic retardation and recovery in south-western Europe in the nineteenth and twentieth centuries," *The Economic History Review* 47 (1): 1–21.

(Belgium, Portugal, Spain 1860)

Toth, Istvan György. 1996. *Literacy and Written Culture in Early Modern Central Europe.* Budapest: CEU Press.

(p. 53 for Hungarian lands in the first half of nineteenth century, confirms Reis' figure, based on ability to sign, not full literacy)

Habsburg domains

Hickman, Anton. 1909. *Geographisch-statistischer Taschen-Atlas von Oesterreich-Ungarn.* Wien: Freytag & Berndt.

(Austrian successor states in 1880, Austrian parts of Croatia)

Toth, Istvan György. 1996. *Literacy and Written Culture in Early Modern Central Europe.* Budapest: CEU Press.

(pp. 36–46 for the parallels in effective implementation of school reforms in Prussia and Austria, and the comparable rates of primary school attendance in the early nineteenth century; p. 196 for 1870 and 1890 literacy rates among Hungarians, Slovaks, Croatians, Romanians in the Hungarian kingdom, based on census data; the Croatian data were combined with those reported by Hickman for the Austrian part)

van Horn Melton, James. 1988. *Absolutism and Eighteenth-Century Origins of Compulsory Schooling in Prussia and Austria.* Cambridge: Cambridge University Press.

(For the parallel efforts at developing an "enlightened" school system in Prussia and Austria in the late eighteenth century)

Vardy, Bela. 2001. "Image and self-image among Hungarian Americans," *East Europe Quarterly* 35 (3): 309–345.

(Slovakia 1910)

Winnige, Norbert. 2001. "Alphabetisierung in Brandenbug-Preussen 1600–1850. Zu den Grundlagen von Kommunikation und Rezeption," in Ralf Pröve and Norbert Winnige, eds., *Wissen ist Macht. Herrschaft und Kommunikation in Brandenburg-Preussen 1600–1850.* Berlin: Spitz. 49–67.

(Data for Prussian provinces, based on recruitment data and signatures of marrying couples; we use the Westphalian couple signature data (45 percent) in 1800–1814 for getting a starting point for the Austrian, Slovenian, and Czech data-series; the Westphalian provinces were, as recruitment data show, closer in degrees of alphabetization to Prussia-Brandenburg than for example Saxony or the Rhineland.)

Russian empire

Bogdanov, Ivan Mikhailovich. 1964. *Gramotnost I obrazovanie v dorevoliutsionnoi Rossii I v USSR; Istoriko-statisticheskii ocherki.* Moscow: Statistika.

(Bessarabia 1883 and 1897, which we took to be representative of Moldova)

Cipolla, Carlo M. 1969. *Literacy and Development in the West.* Baltimore: Pelican.

(Prussia, Posnaia, and Pomerania 1871, which were combined with data on European Russia from 1897, based on Obshtii Svod, to calculate Poland)

Dickens, Mark. 1988. *Soviet Language Policy in Central Asia*. Available online at: www.oxus-com.com/lang-policy.htm.

(Central Asian republics 1897)

Hughes, Lindsey. 2006. "Russian culture in the eighteenth century," in Maureen Perrie, ed., *The Cambridge History of Russia: Imperial Russia, 1691–1917*. Cambridge University Press. 67–91.

(Russia 1797)

Liber, George. 1982. "Language, literacy, and book publishing in the Ukrainian SSR, 1923–1928," *Slavic Review* 41 (4): 673–685.

(Ukraine 1897)

Raun, Toivo U. 1979. "The development of Estonian literacy in the 18th and 19th centuries," *Journal of Baltic Studies* 10 (2): 115–126.

(Baltic states 1816, calculated on the basis of older age cohorts in later censuses, plus Estonian and Livland literacy in 1881 census data)

StateUniversity.com. 2009. *Belarus – History and Background*. Available online at: http://education.stateuniversity.com/pages/139/Belarus-HISTORY-BACKGROUND.html.

(Belarus 1894, Lithuania 1894)

Troinitskii, N. A. 1905. *Obshtii Svod po Imperii Rezultatov Razrabotki Dannuih Pervoi Vseobshtei Perepisi Nasalenia, Proizvedennoi 28 Yanvarya 1897 Goda*. Saint Petersburg: Tsentralny statisticheskii komitet.

(Caucasian republics 1897; data on European Russia used to calculate Poland; unfortunately these figures seem to be referring to reading, not reading and writing, according to Raun)

Yudina, P. F. and F. N. Petrova. 1946. *Strany Mira*. Moscow: Gosudarstvenii Nauchnii Institute "Sovetskaya Entsiklopediya".

(Russia, Ukraine, Belarus, Azerbaijan, Georgia, Armenia, Turkmenistan, Uzbekistan, Tadjikistan, Kazakstan, Kyrgyzistan 1926 and 1939)

The Americas and Pacific settler societies

Commonwealth Bureau of Census and Statistics and Chas H. Wickens. 1921. *Census of the Commonwealth of Australia, Taken for the Night between the 3rd and 4th April, 1921*. Melbourne: H. J. Green, Government Printer.

(Australia 1901, 1911, 1921; excludes Aborigines)

Korotayev, Andrey, Artemy Malkov and Daria Khaltourina. 2006. *Introduction to Social Macrodynamics. Compact Macro-models of the World System Growth*. Moscow: Editorial URSS.

(Mexico 1800, pp. 87ff.)

Leigh, Edwin. 1870. "Illiteracy in the United States," *American Journal of Education* 19: 801–835.

(United States 1850 and 1860)

Lloyd Prichard, Muriel F. 1970. *An Economic History of New Zealand to 1939*. Auckland: Collins.

(New Zealand 1896 and 1911)

Seecharan, Clem. 1997. *Tiger in the Stars: The Anatomy of Indian Achievement in British Guiana 1919–1929*. London: Macmillan.
(Guyana 1931)

Sinclair, Keith. 1990. *The Oxford Illustrated History of New Zealand*. Auckland: Oxford University Press.
(New Zealand 1871 and 1886)

Soltow, Lee. 1981. *The Rise of Literacy and the Common School in the United States: A Socioeconomic Analysis to 1870*. University of Chicago Press.
(Figures for whites in 1800 are used to calculate an overall 1800 figure, using the ratio of white to non-white literacy from Leigh)

Africa

Campbell, Gwyn. 1991. "The state and pre-colonial demographic history: the case of nineteenth-century Madagascar," *The Journal of African History* 32 (3): 415–445.
(Nineteenth-century Madagascar population figures)

Census Office of the Cape of Good Hope. 1875. *Census of the Colony of the Cape of Good Hope*. Cape Town: Saul Solomon and Company.
(Lesotho/Basutoland 1875)

Central Intelligence Agency. 2009. "Eritrea," in *World Factbook*. Available online at: www.cia.gov/library/publications/the-world-factbook/print/er.html.
(Eritrea 2003)

Gogue, Anne Marie. 2006. *Aux origins du mai malgache: désir d'école et competition sociale, 1951–1972*. Paris: Karthala.
(Madagascar, pre-colonial period)

Hizen, H. and V. H. Hundsdörfer. 1979. *The Tanzanian Experience: Education for Liberation and Development*. Hamburg: UNESCO Institute for Education.
(Tanzania 1967)

Lange, Matthew. 2003. "Embedding the colonial state: a comparative analysis of state building and broad-based development in Mauritius," *Social Science History* 27 (3): 397–423.
(Mauritius 1931, 1944, 1952, and an estimate for 1830, assuming that all slaves and former slaves of mixed descent were illiterate, and 50 percent whites and frees literate, i.e. to the same degree as in France of 1830 according to Cipolla)

Moradi, A. n.d. *Men under Arms in Colonial Africa: Gold Coast Regiment*. University of Sussex, Department of Economics, unpublished manuscript.
(Ghana 1916 and 1942; based on literacy tests for world war army recruits, used to calculate increase between these data points in other British colonies in Africa)

Smith, Michael G. 1975. *Corporations and Society: On the Social Anthropology of Collective Action*. New Brunswick: Aldine.
(Guyana 1946)

Snelson, Peter. 1974. *Educational Development in Northern Rhodesia, 1883–1945*. Lusaka: National Educational Company of Zambia.
(Zambia 1945)

StateUniversity.com. *Angola – Constitutional and Legal Foundations*. Available online at: http://education.stateuniversity.com/pages/33/Angola-CONSTITUTIONAL-LEGAL-FOUNDATIONS.html.

(Angola 1975)
UNESCO. 1957. *World Illiteracy at Mid-Century: A Statistical Study*. Paris: UNESCO.
(Eritrea 1950, Gambia 1950)

East Asia

Cooke, Nola. 1995. "The composition of the nineteenth-century political elite of pre-colonial Nguyen Vietnam (1802–1883)," *Modern Asian Studies* 29 (4): 741–764.
(p. 201 supports idea of widespread minimal literacy in pre-colonial Vietnam, even though the Confucian examination system was highly elitist)
Dore, Ronald P. 1992. *Education in Tokugawa Japan*. Berkeley: University of California Press.
(Estimates in Appendix 1 that 26.5 percent of school-aged children had attended three to four years of writing school in 1868; our data rely on Taira's interpretation of Dore's data)
Kim, Chong-Soi. 2001. *Hane’guk munhae kyoyuk yoine'gu*. Seoul: Kyoyuk Kwahaksa.
(Korea 1930, based on census: 15.5% read Korean script; 7.6% both Korean and Japanese; and 0.03% Japanese scripts only, average 22.3% in either Korean or Japanese)
Rawski, Evelyn S. 1979. *Education and Popular Literacy in Ch'ing China*. Ann Arbor: University of Michigan Press.
(China 1850-1900, based on chapter 7; also used for pre-colonial Vietnam and Korea)
Rubinger, Richard. 2007. *Popular Literacy in Early Modern Japan*. Honolulu: University of Hawaii Press.
(Full literacy in remote rural village in 1881: 8.2% of males, largely stable over generations; 20-year-old military recruits in 1899 [able to sign plus more than "some education"]: 53%; gender gap in ability to sign one's name in three prefectures from 1876 to 1885: 34%; combining gender gap and military recruits data, one arrives at estimate for 1889 for 20-years-olds of 36%; all these data not used, we relied on Taira instead)
Simpson, Andrew. 2007. *Language and National Identity in Asia*. Oxford University Press.
(p. 210 mentions that literacy in Korean in pre-colonial Korea was not higher than during colonial times; which confirms taking the Chinese figures for pre-colonial Korea)
Taira, Koji. 1971. "Education and literacy in Meiji Japan: an interpretation," *Explorations in Economic History* 8 (4): 371–394.
(Japan 1816, 1868, 1910; the first two estimates are based on Dore, the third on school enrollment rates, made plausible by data from military recruits plus factory surveys)
Woodside, Alexander. 1983. "The triumphs and failures of mass education in Vietnam," *Pacific Affairs* 56 (3): 401–427.
(Criticizes the Viet Kong's assertion, repeated in UNESCO documents, that 95 percent of the population were illiterate in 1945; supports idea of widespread literacy)

APPENDIX 3.4 CORRELATION MATRIX, MEANS, AND STANDARD DEVIATIONS

APPENDIX TABLE 3.1 *Means, standard deviations, and correlations among variables*

	R	L	Y	E	S_1	S_2	I	NS_W	NS_E	NS_N	P	W_E	W_T
R: Length of railway tracks per km²		0.514	0.553	0.025	0.346	0.273	0.229	0.279	−0.005	0.065	0.085	0.057	−0.001
L: Percent literates among adults			0.711	0.292	0.563	0.588	0.336	0.597	0.012	0.088	0.267	0.017	0.002
Y: Years since first national organization founded				0.218	0.602	0.667	0.445	0.654	0.071	0.118	0.141	0.011	0.068
E: Central government expenditure for territory					0.419	0.494	0.299	0.502	0.064	0.053	−0.005	0.011	0.041
S_1: 1st cubic spline on year						0.912	0.810	0.911	0.244	0.167	0.053	0.129	0.049
S_2: 2nd cubic spline on year							0.786	0.960	0.240	0.145	0.029	0.060	0.048
I: Center's membership in IGOs								0.713	0.443	0.150	0.025	0.227	0.066
NS_W: Total no. of nations-states in world									0.208	0.143	0.044	0.004	0.033
NS_E: No. of nation-states created in the empire past five years										0.264	−0.040	0.180	0.088
NS_N: No. of nation-states created in neighborhood past five years											−0.053	0.074	0.179
P: Center's share of global power												0.244	0.028
W_E: Number of wars fought in the empire													0.165
W_T: Number of wars fought in the territory													
Mean	5.671	20.563	11.655	.447	1888.442	21.581	15.202	40.360	0.252	0.087	0.074	0.539	0.056
Standard deviation	16.044	27.161	24.185	1.249	46.625	30.221	20.805	26.898	1.075	0.361	0.080	1.134	0.252
N	17,500	17,667	17,667	9,821	17,667	17,667	17,518	17,667	17,667	17,667	16,488	17,522	17,522

Chapter 4

The Wimmer/Min dataset of world conflict is a territory–year dataset spanning 150 territories over the 186 periods between 1816 and 2001. It contains 28,162 territory–year observations, including a large number of observations in periods prior to nation-statehood.[33] The unit of observation is territory, a geographic unit distinct from the state or government ruling over that territory at any point in time. We used the division of the world's states in 2001 as a territorial grid, extending these fixed geographic units back to the beginning of our dataset in 1816. The dataset includes coding on 484 distinct wars fought across 619 territories. These 484 wars include 77 wars of conquest, 111 inter-state wars, 187 non-secessionist civil wars, and 109 secessionist civil wars. To code when wars break out and how long they last, we first reviewed the widely used Correlates of War (COW) list of wars and then modified and extended this list substantially. We describe these extensions in detail here.

Adding wars

The COW dataset only includes states with diplomatic relationships with Britain or France prior to 1920, or members of the League of Nations or the United Nations thereafter. To overcome this Western bias in the COW dataset, we added wars in territories controlled by states not recognized by the Western powers. This expands the horizon to include Latin America in the nineteenth century and Asian and African territories in years prior to COW recognition as colonies or as independent states. A second bias is introduced because in colonial territories, only wars that involved the colonial power are included in the COW dataset. This colonial center bias was overcome by specifically looking for civil wars that happened during periods of colonial rule.

To code additional wars and territories, we turned to the original sources of COW and other quantitative studies that have appeared over the past decades. We added nine wars based on Richardson's *Statistics of Deadly Quarrels* (Richardson 1960). Twenty-four additional wars were found in Clodfelter's (2002) monumental *Warfare and Armed Conflict*. We also reviewed OnWar.com, an amateur online website that lists a large number of wars with unsystematic but sometimes preciously rich information. We went through this list and added 18 new wars after verifying date and battle death information from at least one additional independent source (usually found on the Internet). Finally, we also updated the list to 2001 adding seven wars, relying on Gleditsch *et al.* (2002) and adopting some of the revisions proposed by Gleditsch (2004). A total of 58 new wars were added from these various sources.

To decide whether or not to include a war from these various sources, we used COW's battle death threshold of 1,000 per year. All newly identified wars for which this death toll could not be confirmed were ultimately excluded from our list (a considerable number, especially in Richardson's [1960] list). We also cross-checked our list against additional

---

[33] We include 262 additional territory–year observations beyond the 150×186 standard observations to account for years during which more than one war onset occurs.

sources including *World Military and Social Expenditures* (1987: 29–31), Butterworth's (1976) list of wars in the post-World War II era, as well as a handful of less extensive lists (Miall 1992; Licklider 1995), none of which provided new information.

While we have made every attempt to develop the most comprehensive list of conflicts possible, there remain potential gaps in our coverage. Of most concern are wars in pre-colonial eras. Due to a lack of written historical sources and/or historical research our dataset likely misassesses the frequency of warfare in pre-colonial Africa and parts of Asia. We guess that some of the following wars may have reached the 1,000 battle death threshold but were unable to confirm this through multiple sources: the wars among Yoruba states in pre-colonial Nigeria; the civil wars in Ethiopia and Afghanistan during the middle of the nineteenth century; the wars connected to Buganda's expansion in Uganda in the pre-colonial era; and the wars between the khanates of Central Asia before Russian conquest.

Some wars of conquest may also have been missed because counts of the casualties suffered by anticolonial forces are rare. In the first versions of COW, only the casualties of imperial forces were taken into consideration. Later versions included the death toll of local fighters but it is unclear whether previously excluded wars were added retrospectively (Sambanis 2004). Our impression is that this was not done systematically, and we have added a handful of such wars where we came across well-documented cases.

New coding for the location of wars

The COW dataset provides information on the states involved in a war but not on its location. In order to produce a war list compatible with the territory–year design of our dataset, we added locational codes for all wars, taking the current division of the globe into states as a constant territorial grid. The OnWar.com database and Clodfelter's (2002) list were our main sources for determining battlefield locations; where necessary, we did additional internet searches to find information on the geographical locations of major battles. If battlefields were located on more than one territory (such as during the Russian revolution), we coded multiple locations. Following the coding rules that COW used for determining who counts as a war participant, we coded as a war location each territory on which at least 100 died in battle or 1,000 troops were actively engaged.

There were a few cases where we diverted from these coding rules: in some civil wars, the forces that aim at overthrowing the government may set up a base of operation outside the territory of the country. These bases may come under attack by cross-border operations of government forces. We decided that such cross-border pursuits did not justify adding a second location to the war (this was relevant for the civil wars in Nicaragua, Angola, Zimbabwe, and Turkey).

The locational coding produced some oddities, mainly in cases where expanding empires meet outside of their core territories, vying for control over a region without local force strong enough to participate in battle. According to the territorial logic, this war is then related not to the two empires, but to the territory on which the battles took place. The cases are the Russo-Japanese war of 1904, which is attributed to China (and not to Russia or Japan), the Russo-Persian war of 1826, which is coded as relating to Armenia, Afghanistan, and Turkey (but neither Russia nor Persia), the Italo-Ethiopian war of 1887, which is related to Eritrea (not to Ethiopia), Russia vs. Central Asian Rebels of 1931, which is coded as a war in China. We retained this strictly territorial coding for the sake of consistency.

A new war typology

The COW dataset classifies wars based on the type of actors involved rather than their political goals. An inter-state war involves two sovereign state actors while a civil war is fought between a sovereign state and a domestic non-state actor. If one of the two state actors is located outside of the system of internationally recognized states, the war is coded as an imperial war. When the state actor in a civil war is not an internationally recognized independent state, but a dependency of such a state, the war is termed "colonial." For the purposes of our project, we are less interested in the status war participants hold in the international system and more in the political goals they seek to achieve: building a nation-state, enlarging the domain of an empire, gaining power in an existing state, etc.

In the new typology we developed, inter-polity wars are divided into wars of conquest and inter-state wars. Civil wars can be either non-secessionist or secessionist. Secessionist wars are further subdivided into non-nationalist and nationalist, while non-secessionist civil wars split into ethnic and non-ethnic subtypes, using the same criterion as Fearon and Laitin (2003). In Chapter 4, we do not make use of the distinction between ethnic and non-ethnic civil wars and I will therefore not elaborate upon the underlying coding rules here.

Appendix Table 4.1 shows how the new typology of wars relates to the old COW war types. Most of the wars in the COW dataset had to be reclassified according to the following coding principles. First, we treated non-colonial empires (the Ottoman, Habsburg, Chinese, Romanov, Abyssinian empires) and communist empires (the Soviet Union), in the same way as colonial empires (French, Portuguese, British, Dutch). Therefore, rebellions against Ottoman rule, e.g. in the Balkans (the Greek, Serbian, etc. "wars of liberation"), were classified in the same category as the anticolonial wars in Algeria or Angola. By contrast, COW classifies the Cretan uprisings against the Ottomans as civil wars and the Algerian wars of national liberation as wars.

Second, we replaced COW's distinction between colonial and imperial wars with a distinction between nationalist and non-nationalist wars of secession, based on the different political projects pursued by actors. "Nationalist wars of secession" were defined as rebellions against the political center (an imperial center or an already established nation-state) with the explicit aim of establishing a separate state representing a nationally defined people, thus conforming to the modern ideal of the nation-state. If the breakaway movement was not motivated by nationalist ideology, but rather by pre-modern principles of political legitimacy, we classified this as a non-nationalist war of secession. If, however, a rebellion against the political center was directed against laws that infringed on traditional rights, or new taxes, or direct administration by the center, without challenging the borders of the existing state, we classified this as a non-secessionist civil war.

There is obviously a fine line between secessionist and non-secessionist civil wars, since many tax rebellions turned into nationalist wars of liberation, and many anti-imperial movements were composed of groups with different motives. The Druze rebellions against the French in Lebanon from 1925 to 1927 are a case in point. They were initiated by Druze mountain tribes resisting direct administration and later joined by Arab Syrian nationalists. Similarly, it may be difficult to determine whether the demand for a new state is nationalist or non-nationalist. Was the semi-independent Bosnian province under a Bosnian vizier that Christian rebels demanded from the Ottoman sultan in 1836 a modern nation-state? Did the independent khanate that Muslim rebels envisioned in 1863 China or bringing the Mogul back to nineteenth-century India represent nationalist ideals? We decided on the basis of more in-depth historical ana-lysis whether or not the nationalist elements were dominant among the most important actors involved in these and some other borderline cases. We also had to distinguish between cases where the demand for independence was of a tactical nature (the Karen's threat to establish an independent state) or represented a long-term strategic objective (such as when a coalition of leaders from various ethnic groups headed by Uyghurs established the short-lived "Islamic Republic of Eastern Turkistan" in what is today western China).

Third, we distinguished between wars of conquest and inter-state wars. States fight wars of conquest to permanently incorporate a territory as a dependent entity into its domain. Attempts at "pacifying" the hinterland (such as the wars in Libya against the Sanusi tribes in the 1920s) are also coded as wars of imperial conquest. Fifty-four wars that COW defines as extra-state wars were included in this new category of wars of imperial conquest. We also added nine wars that COW had categorized as inter-state wars, since these wars were fought against imperial encroachments and ended, in all but a handful of cases such as in Afghanistan, with the defeat of independent kingdoms or tribal confederacies and their permanent incorporation into an imperial domain. Note that since our units of observation are territories, the two world wars are treated as a series of different war episodes, and we determined for each of them the most appro-priate classification. The wars connected to Hitler's occupation of Eastern Europe, to give an example, were coded as wars of conquest, while the battles in England were coded as inter-state war, since there was no plan in the German *Generalstab* to conquer and permanently incorporate the British state into the domains of the new Reich. All of the above reclassifications and additions resulted in a total of 484 wars including 77 wars of conquest, 111 inter-state wars, 187 non-secessionist civil wars, and 109 secessionist civil wars.

War rate calculation

We assigned a 1 in the year of war onset and a 0 in all other years. In addition, we coded an ongoing war variable to equal 1 in all years in which a war was fought and a 0 for all years of peace. All of the analysis in Chapter 4 focuses on the war onset variable rather than the ongoing war variable. In order to calculate the war onset rates of Figures 1.4, 4.2, and 4.3, all onsets needed to be related to a unique episode of imperial incorp-oration or nation-state creation. For example, Algeria is incorporated into the French empire in 1848 and becomes an independent nation-state in 1963. The Franco-Algerian war of 1954 was thus identified to occur nine years before nation-state creation and 106 years after imperial incorporation. In some cases, however, territories experienced more than one instance of imperial incorporation or nation-state creation. For example, the

APPENDIX TABLE 4.1 *War typology*

Main types		Inter-polity wars
Subtypes	**Wars of conquest**	**Inter-state wars**
Definition of subtypes	Expansion of state territory, permanent incorporation of new territories and populations; resistance against such expansion	Fight between states over borders and territory, regional hegemony (but without aim of permanent incorporation)
Sub-subtypes		
Definition of sub-subtypes		
COW category that corresponds most closely	Imperial wars	Inter-state wars, but with some reclassifications into wars of conquest if war goal is permanent absorption of enemy territory into empire

Iraqi-Kurdish war of 1961 occurs both after Iraq's absorption into the British empire from 1914–1932 and after its incorporation into the Ottoman domain from 1531–1913. In this case and as a general rule, the war is related to the closest episode of institutional transformation, and is thus coded as occurring 47 years after imperial incorporation. Exceptions were made only if a war was causally responsible for bringing about a transition, in which case we assigned the war to the latter even if another transition had occurred within fewer years. This was the case for some wars of conquest, which led to imperial incorporation, and a number of nationalist wars of liberation, which helped to establish nation-states.

Civil wars			
Secessionist civil wars		**Non-secessionist civil wars**	
Fight against the political center with the aim to establish an independent state		Fight between groups, at least one of which represents the central government, over domestic power relations, degree of autonomy of provinces or ethnic groups, tax burden, dynastic succession etc.	
Non-nationalist wars of secession	**Nationalist wars of secession**	**Ethnic civil wars**	**Non-ethnic civil wars**
Fight for a separate, non-modern state (an independent khanate, sultanate, kingdom, tribal confederacy)	Fight for a separate, modern nation-state	Lines of conflict defined in ethnic terms and/ or significant recruitment on the basis of ethnic networks	Lines of conflict not defined in ethnic terms and no recruitment on the basis of ethnic networks
Colonial wars, if aim is founding of a pre-modern state; some wars from civil war category added	Colonial wars, if aim is founding of an independent national state as opposed to less taxes, changes in administrative structures, reinstallation of privileges etc. Some wars added from civil war category if goal is independent national state	Civil wars but with some wars added from colonial war category, if war goal is reduction of taxes, changes in administrative principles, reinstallation of privileges etc.	

APPENDIX 4.2 THE INSTITUTIONAL RULE DATASET AND OTHER
INDEPENDENT VARIABLES

Date of imperial incorporation and nation-state creation

In order to understand how different types of wars relate to the two major institutional transformations in the model – imperial expansion and nation-state formation – we need to know the precise dates of both the incorporation into empire and of the creation of a nation-state (as sometimes different from the juridical date of independence). Of the 156 territories in the dataset, 140 territories were incorporated into an empire (92 during the temporal range of the dataset, 1816–2001), and 150 experienced at least one nation-state creation.

In order to determine the year in which a territory became part of a larger political entity (usually an empire), we searched for evidence of one of the following and coded the year of incorporation to whichever came first:

- the territory is effectively administered by an occupying force;
- a garrison is established that aims at expanding military control over the territory;
- the territory becomes a protectorate or colony.

The establishment of military posts that only provide military protection to foreign traders, however, was not treated as a case of imperial incorporation. Temporary military occupation that lasted three or fewer years and that was not intended to permanently "absorb" the occupied territory into the state was also not coded as a case of imperial incorporation but coded separately as "military occupation." Some territories have been conquered by multiple empires; some were governed by several empires contemporaneously. These complexities had to be recorded in the institutional history data set.

Nation-state creation is coded as the year in which an independent state begins to be self-governed in the name of a nationally defined people and no longer according to dynastic or religious principles. More precisely, (1) a nation-state has a written constitution that (a) defines the nation as the sovereign, (b) introduces equality before the law for all members of the nation, and (c) provides for some institutional representation of the nation (e.g. an elected body); (2) a nation-state has de facto control over its foreign policy. Both criteria had to be fulfilled in order to define a polity as a modern nation-state.

Since this definition has already been discussed extensively in Chapter 2 section 2, I will merely add some coding details here. The "control-over-foreign-policy" criterion proved to be the most problematic. It is a matter of historical judgment and definitional precision to decide how much control a state must have over its foreign policy to be classified as sovereign, given various forms of shared sovereignty across history, such as Canada's dominion status in the British empire, the quasi-dominion status of Zimbabwe, or the almost-independent foreign policy of Egypt when formally still part of the Ottoman empire but de facto under the tutelage of Britain. Many decolonizing states also shared sovereignty during the transition period, introducing further ambiguity: was Cambodia's "50 percent independence" that the French granted from 1950 onward enough to classify it as a sovereign state or should the year of nation-state creation be 1953 when legal independence was reached? We decided to regard dominion status (or quasi-dominion status) as providing "enough" control over foreign policy, but think that full independence in situations of decolonization is necessary to consider a state as fully sovereign.

As discussed in the main text, some states have experienced several episodes of nation-state formation, interrupted by new episodes of colonization (e.g. Haiti, the Dominican Republic, and the Baltic and Caucasian states). If a modern nation-state split into two or more separate nation-states (Czechoslovakia, Pakistan, the Central American Republic), we coded a new episode of nation-state formation for both territories if the split-away territory comprised at least one-third of the entire population. A reunification with a population increase of at least one-third was also considered as a new episode of nation-state creation (Yemen, Germany, and Vietnam). We coded only successful nation-states, i.e. states that survived for more than three years and achieved international recognition by at least two states, thus excluding short-lived states such as the West Ukrainian National Republic, the Kurdish republic of Mahabad in Iran, or the Republic of Uyghurstan in China. This is a reasonable selection principle, since we would otherwise face the difficult problem of dealing with states that were declared independent by politically marginal movements that never achieved de facto control over any territory.

Types of institutional rule over a territory

We complemented coding of imperial incorporation and nation-state creation with that of some additional types of political rule in order to reconstruct the full institutional history of each territory from 1816 to 2001. This institutional history file is used in Chapter 4 and to draw Figure 1.1, which shows the portion of the world's surface governed by different types of polities. The institutional history dataset offers a more fine-grained classificatory scheme than the one used for Figure 1.1. We cross-tabulate types of institutional rule over a territory (nation-state, empire, military occupation, "other") with the political status of a territory, i.e. whether it is governed autonomously or whether it is ruled as a dependency. The distinction between imperial, nation-state, and "other" principles of governing a territory has been discussed in the main text. Sufficient is to remind the reader here that "other" polities include absolutist kingdoms, city-states, tribal confederacies, patrimonial empires, etc. As Appendix Table 4.2 shows, only seven out of the 16 possible categories established by the cross-tabulation were used. There were no (or only very few) empirical constellations that would have fit into the other nine types.

Types of political regimes (democracy versus autocracy)

The dataset contains four regime type variables: democracy, autocracy, anocracy, and anarchy. We relied primarily upon the 20-point scores from the Polity IV project, using the standard +6 and −6 cutoffs to distinguish between democracies and autocracies. In order to identify the regime type of pre-independent territories, we diverted from Fearon and Laitin's (2003) procedure and coded all colonial dependencies as autocracies. Following the Polity IV coding rules, we discovered after a series of test coding, colonies would never be coded as democracies or anocracies. The imperial dependencies of the land-based classical empires of the Habsburgs, Ottomans, etc. received the same regime classification as the imperial center. We also followed this coding rule for the settler colonies of Canada, New Zealand, and Australia as soon as these became part of the British empire.

All territories that were neither part of an empire nor independent nation-states were coded individually, choosing between democracy, anarchy (no central government or no statehood at all, i.e. the −77 polity code), autocracy (traditional states such as khanates, emirates, etc.), or anocracy (e.g. the elite democracies of the Swiss kantons before 1848). For pre-colonial African territories, we relied on Müller's (1999) atlas of pre-colonial cultures, which aggregates ethnographic data on pre-colonial political systems at the country level. All "simple states without social classes," "feudal states," and "complex states" were classified as autocracies, while territories with lower levels of political centralization

APPENDIX TABLE 4.2 *Types of institutional rule*

Political status	Institutional principle	Nation-state	Empire	Other	Military occupation
Autonomous		*Autonomous nation-states* (e.g. France)	*Imperial centers* (e.g. Turkey under the Ottomans)	*Other autonomous states* (e.g. Bhutan, Saudi Arabia)	--
Dependent	… on a nation-state center	*"Internal colonies"* (e.g. Georgia under Soviet rule)	*Colonial dependency* (e.g. Algeria under the French)	--[a]	*Militarily occupied territories*
	… on an imperial center	--[b]	*Imperial dependency* (e.g. Bosnia under Ottoman rule)		
	… on a center governed by "other principles"		--[c]		

Notes: [a] In this category we would subsume traditional client states of nation-states, empires, or other traditional polities. We avoided using this category since it is difficult to determine at which point a political alliance between a stronger and a weaker state makes such states dependent territories (e.g. Korea and China).

[b] Would be a dependent part of an empire that is governed like a nation-state, perhaps Hong Kong under China, if we would code China as an empire.

[c] Would be a dependent part of an "other" type of center, which rules the territory according to nation-state principles, imperial principles, or "other" principles (Central Asia under the Mongols; Crete under Venetian rule).

were defined as anarchies. We defined years of military occupation (Polity code −66) as autocracy, consistent with our way of coding colonial dependencies. For years of transition (Polity code −88), we interpolated Polity scores.

Change in military personnel

The Military Personnel Change variable calculates how much (in percentage) the number of military personnel in a given year deviated from the average of the previous five years. We relied on COW's National Material Capabilities dataset to develop this measurement. Unfortunately, COW's data do not include colonial armies such as the British Indian army but count only soldiers under the direct command of the motherland's government. Still, it is a good enough measurement of the capacity of an imperial center to suppress rebellions in its dependent territories. For independent nation-states, this variable measures the change in the state's domestic military strength. For colonies and imperial dependencies, we calculated the change in military strength of that territory's imperial center.

GDP and population size

The most extensive and reliable historical data on income and population come from Maddison (2003). For the Soviet and Yugoslav successor states, the Czech Republic and Slovakia, and Pakistan and Bangladesh we took the earliest available data, calculated their shares of the undivided countries' GDPs and populations, and then extrapolated back into the past based on data for the undivided countries. We excluded GDP data for Turkey up to 1923 because they seemed to relate to the entire empire. Germany's data reflect various borders over time; no consistent data series for Germany in its post-1990 borders are available.

Chapter 5

APPENDIX 5.1 THE ETHNIC POWER RELATIONS DATASET

The EPR dataset is based on the information provided by nearly 100 experts on ethnic politics who assessed formal and informal degrees of political participation and exclusion along ethnic lines in all countries of the world since 1945.[34] Apart from being relatively inexpensive and feasible, expert surveys have the advantage of providing contextual knowledge about underlying ethno-political power structures beyond the reach of more mechanistic approaches such as determining the ethnic background of leading politicians.[35] This method has been applied to a wide variety of topics in the social sciences, most prominently the characterization of party platforms (Benoit and Laver 2006).

Politically relevant ethnic groups

Following the Weberian tradition, we define ethnicity as subjectively perceived membership in a community based on the belief in common ancestry and shared culture. Different markers may be used to indicate such shared ancestry and culture: common language, similar phenotypical features, adherence to the same faith, and so on. Our definition of ethnicity thus includes ethno-linguistic, ethno-somatic (or "racial"), and ethno-religious groups, but not tribes and clans that define ancestral relations in genealogical terms, nor regional identities not based on the idea of shared ancestry. Ethnic categories may be hierarchically nested and comprise several levels of differentiation, not all of which are politically relevant (see Wimmer 2008).

An ethnic category is politically relevant if at least one significant political actor claims to represent the interests of that group in the national political arena, or if members of an ethnic category are systematically and intentionally discriminated against in the domain of public politics. By "significant" political actor we mean a political organization (not necessarily a party) that is active and known in the national political arena. We define discrimination as political exclusion directly targeted at members of an ethnic community – thus disregarding indirect discrimination based, for example, on educational disadvantage or discrimination in the labor or credit markets. The coding scheme allows us to identify countries or specific periods in which political objectives, alliances, or disputes were never framed in ethnic terms, thus avoiding using an ethnic lens for countries not characterized by ethnic politics, such as Tanzania and Korea. The coding rules mirror the

---

[34] The process of contacting and interacting with country experts took almost two years. Once reasonably adequate country codings were available, we held workshops with regional experts to take final decisions. We discussed each coding in light of the experts' comments, as well as additional data sources and the accumulating comparative knowledge of the project team itself. In many cases, we returned to the initial coders or invited additional experts to help decide between different options.

[35] See Fearon *et al.* (2007), who coded the ethnic background of heads of state. While certainly more traceable and less ambiguous, this approach overlooks the possibility of "token" representatives (such as a Muslim president of India); and it cannot grasp more complex configurations such as power-sharing arrangements.

MAR dataset's definition of political relevance but do not restrict the universe of cases to politically excluded minorities but include majority and dominant groups as well.

We do not distinguish between degrees of representativity of political actors who claim to speak for an ethnic group, nor do we take into account that the political positions voiced by leaders claiming to represent the same community may differ very substantially from each other (Bowen 1996; Brubaker 2004; Zartman 2004). Such detail is beyond the scope of the EPR project and would require a coding scheme in which political organizations form the units of observation. We thus assume that ethnic categories become politically relevant as soon as there is a minimal degree of political mobilization or intentional political discrimination along ethnic lines. This happens regardless of the level of support for an ethno-political project and whatever the heterogeneity of positions voiced in the name of a group. Our dataset does not provide information on how such ethnic mobilization occurs but only records its effect – that a particular ethnic category has become a meaningful point of reference in national politics.

If politically relevant categories and access to political power change over time, country experts divided the 1946 to 2005 period and provided separate coding for each sub-period. This was also necessary when the list of politically relevant categories changed from one year to the next. In a second step, we coded the degree of access to power enjoyed by political leaders who claim to represent these various groups.

Coding access to power

We focused on executive-level power, that is, representation in the presidency, cabinet, and senior posts in the administration, including the army. The weight given to these institutions depended on the de facto power constellations of the country in question. In a military dictatorship, we determined the ethno-political power configuration in the army; in presidential systems, the focus was on the senior cabinet. We were primarily interested in major power shifts, rather than day-to-day reorganizations of cabinets or the promotion of officers in the army. Experts were told to code absolute access to power irrespective of the question of under- or overrepresentation relative to the demographic size of an ethnic category.

We used a series of ordered categories to code the degree of access to central state power. Some representatives of an ethnic community held full control of the executive branch with no meaningful participation by members of any other group, some shared power with others, and some were excluded altogether from decision-making authority. Within each of these three major categories, we differentiated between further subtypes, giving rise to the following coding scheme.

ABSOLUTE POWER. The political elites who claim to represent an ethnic group do not significantly share power with other political leaders. There are two subtypes monopoly and dominant.

Monopoly: elite members of an ethnic community hold monopoly power in the executive level at the exclusion of all other ethnic groups. The Ladino community in Guatemala is a good example. They ruled without any significant participation from the indigenous population until the end of the civil war.

Dominant: elite members of the group hold dominant power in the executive level but there is some limited representation of members of other groups. This includes token members of the cabinet with a different ethnic background, such as Saddam Hussein's minister of foreign affairs, who was Christian rather than Sunni Arab. Token members do not effectively act as representatives of the non-dominant group, nor do they advocate for policies that would correspond to demands voiced by other leaders of that group.

POWER-SHARING REGIMES. By power sharing, we mean any arrangement that divides executive power among leaders who claim to represent different ethnic groups. Such an arrangement can be either formal, as in Lebanon, or informal, as in Switzerland. Although consociationalism illustrates this type of power structure, we do not limit our definition of power sharing to consociational regimes. The representatives of an ethnic category can play either the role of a junior or senior partner in power-sharing governments.

Senior partner: representatives are the more powerful partner in a formal or informal power-sharing arrangement.

Junior partner: representatives are the less powerful partners in government.[36]

EXCLUSION FROM CENTRAL POWER. When political leaders who claim to represent a particular ethnic category are excluded from participation in central government, we distinguish between those with local autonomy and those who are powerless or discriminated against.

Regional autonomy: elite members of the group have no central power but wield some influence at the sub-national level (by controlling a provincial or district level government).[37] Local governments controlled by secessionist groups, such as Abkhazians in independent Georgia, are a special case. We mark such situations with an additional coding as "secessionist autonomy."[38]

Powerless: elite representatives hold no political power at the national or regional levels without being explicitly discriminated against.

Discriminated: group members are subjected to active, intentional, and targeted discrimination with the intent of excluding them from both regional and national power. Examples include African Americans until the civil rights movement and Guatemaltecan Indians until the end of the civil war. Such active discrimination can be either formal or informal. Formal discrimination legally limits access to government positions to citizens

---

[36] The choice between senior and junior depends on the number and relative importance of the positions controlled by group members. For example, in ethnic party systems such as that of Malaysia, the Malay governing party is the senior partner, while the Chinese party is a junior partner. In countries without ethnic party systems, such as Switzerland, it may be meaningful to identify senior partners (the Swiss Germans) and junior partners (the French and Italian speakers), based on the informally set distribution of cabinet seats between members of the main ethno-linguistic groups.

[37] We do not consider local power at the municipal level. By control, we mean that group members occupy a leading position or are coalition partners in a regional government (where such governments exist); or that they participate significantly in the executive branch on the regional level (e.g. where regional governors are appointed by the central government); or that they profit from ethnic quotas in the regional or local administration (such as in India or the FSU).

[38] We code regional autonomy exclusively for politically relevant groups. We therefore do not consider ethnic communities whose representatives control municipal governments because of a high local population share but never appear in the national political arena (e.g. Albanian speakers in Italy). We exclude such groups from the data and consider them politically irrelevant.

who speak a certain mother tongue, display certain phenotypical features, or adhere to certain faiths. Informal discrimination actively and intentionally inhibits individuals of certain ethnic backgrounds from rising within the ranks of government.[39]

Descriptive statistics[40]

The EPR dataset identifies 733 unique politically relevant ethnic groups in 155 sovereign states from 1946 to 2005 (see Appendix Table 5.1). An average country counts between five and six politically relevant ethnic groups. The most frequent configuration of political power is one in which a single majority group holds either a Monopoly or Dominant position in a country's executive branch, with one to three groups excluded from power, typically representing between 10% and 20% of the population. This configuration describes about half of the 7,155 country–year observations in the dataset. Some 340 of these country–years reflect extreme cases of ethnocratic rule, in which a single group representing less than 20% of the population controls the executive branch.[41]

Power-sharing arrangements exist in a third of all country–years. In these cases, an average of three to four groups share executive power, representing 80% of the population. Power-sharing arrangements have become slightly more common over time, occurring in 40% of the world's countries today compared with around 30% in the 1960s and 1970s. Some rare cases of minoritarian power-sharing regimes exist (66 country–years), in which power-sharing partners represent less than 20% of the population.[42]

Ethnic power relations in most countries are far from stable. On average, we identify about three distinct periods per country reflecting changes in the set of politically relevant groups or the distribution of access to power. Some 21 countries have as many as six periods, while six countries have eight or more (Benin, Chad, Congo, Indonesia, Nigeria, and Thailand).

Appendix Table 5.1 also provides descriptive statistics at the group, rather than at the country level, revealing substantial variation in the distribution of political power across groups around the world. Ethnic elites that enjoy a "monopoly" or "dominant" hold on executive branch power typically represent large majorities in Western democracies, Eastern Europe, Latin America, and to a lesser extent, in Asia. But in Africa and the Middle East, political elites holding absolute power often represent less than half the population. Power-sharing arrangements between senior and junior partners are prevalent in Africa, the Middle East, and the West but rare in Latin America and Eastern

---

[39] We do not include in this category (1) groups suffering from *indirect* political discrimination because they are disadvantaged in the economic sphere or the educational system and thus are unlikely to successfully compete in the political arena; (2) general social discrimination (e.g. on the labor or marriage markets); and (3) the exclusion of non-citizens from power, as long as they hold passports of other states and can effectively return there. This notion of discrimination does not refer to representation relative to population size. A large group may be underrepresented in government without being actively and intentionally discriminated against.

[40] This section is adapted from Min *et al.* (2010).

[41] Countries with ethnocratic rule for 30 years or more are Sudan, South Africa, Liberia, Iraq, Syria, and Burundi.

[42] Minority rule by a group of power-sharing partners existed in the Dem. Rep. of Congo, Central African Republic, Congo, and Liberia.

APPENDIX TABLE 5.1 *Descriptive statistics on politically relevant ethnic groups*

	West and Japan	East. Europe	Asia	N. Africa and ME	Sub-Sah. Africa	Latin Am. and Carib.	WORLD
No. of countries	22	29	22	19	41	22	155
No. of groups	50	177	171	59	221	55	733
Groups/country	2.3	6.1	7.8	3.1	5.4	2.5	4.7
Avg. no. of periods	1.8	1.7	3.8	2.0	3.8	1.9	2.7

Observations by group status (% of group–country–year observations)

	West and Japan	East. Europe	Asia	N. Africa and ME	Sub-Sah. Africa	Latin Am. and Carib.	WORLD
Included Groups	*51.3*	*20.0*	*30.4*	*49.1*	*56.3*	*39.5*	*39.3*
Monopoly	13.2	4.1	1.2	6.2	2.5	21.8	5.7
Dominant	3.9	4.2	5.9	5.8	5.2	12.0	5.8
Senior Partner	16.2	6.7	5.5	15.2	15.0	2.8	9.7
Junior Partner	18.0	5.0	17.8	21.9	33.6	2.8	18.1
Excluded Groups	*48.7*	*80.0*	*69.6*	*50.9*	*43.7*	*60.5*	*60.7*
Regional Autonomy	8.9	37.6	25.1	2.4	2.7	26.8	18.6
Separatist Autonomy	0.0	1.3	4.7	1.1	0.1	0.0	1.6
Powerless	29.6	23.2	28.6	27.7	27.3	9.2	25.3
Discriminated	10.1	18.0	11.2	19.7	13.7	24.5	15.2
TOTAL	*100*	*100*	*100*	*100*	*100*	*100*	*100*
	(n=2,585)	(n=6,051)	(n=7,783)	(n=2,882)	(n=7,422)	(n=2,856)	(N=29,579)

Average size of groups by status (% of total population)

	West and Japan	East. Europe	Asia	N. Africa and ME	Sub-Sah. Africa	Latin Am. and Carib.	WORLD
Included Groups							
Monopoly	88.9	90.0	60.5	50.3	37.3	81.0	74.6
Dominant	78.0	81.2	67.7	60.1	21.7	63.8	58.5
Senior Partner	70.2	42.2	47.6	30.0	22.1	71.5	38.3
Junior Partner	13.6	15.2	10.7	19.2	15.6	26.3	14.7
Excluded Groups							
Regional Autonomy	4.1	0.8	2.2	5.0	7.4	9.1	2.9
Separatist Autonomy	–	6.0	4.0	17.0	7.0	–	5.2
Powerless	3.7	2.1	2.6	12.3	12.5	22.0	7.0
Discriminated	2.2	3.2	5.2	16.5	17.7	8.7	9.3
All groups	*30.3*	*12.1*	*11.3*	*22.3*	*16.6*	*34.7*	*17.8*

Europe. Globally, nearly a third of all groups are powerless, lacking representation at the executive branch. In Latin America, however, there are relatively few powerless but many discriminated against groups including the large indigenous groups across the highlands. Contrary to conventional wisdom, the share of groups that are discriminated in sub-Saharan Africa is low compared to much of the world. However, whereas discriminated groups are typically small in size, those in Africa and the Middle East are much larger than elsewhere, representing on average one-sixth of the national population.

War coding

Our coding of civil conflicts is based on the UCDP/PRIO Armed Conflicts Dataset (ACD) (Gleditsch *et al.* 2002). ACD defines conflict as any armed and organized confrontation either between government troops and rebel organizations or between army factions, that reaches an annual battle-death threshold of 25 individuals. Massacres and genocides are not included because the victims are neither organized nor armed; communal riots and pogroms are excluded because the government is not directly involved. We drew primarily on version 3–2005b of the ACD, which provides two levels of conflict identification, a more general war ID number and a disaggregated sub-ID that identifies whenever the constellation of rebel organizations changes completely or when more than 10 years elapse between episodes of violence.[43] We relied on these sub-IDs to construct our own conflict list because we are interested in a disaggregated dependent variable that would allow us to differentiate between conflicts fought by actors claiming to represent different ethnic communities. As a result, we code a larger number of armed conflict onsets than does the original ACD. To preserve comparability with other studies of civil war, we identify high-intensity conflicts as those that reach the standard threshold of 1,000 battle deaths in at least one year. For each conflict, we coded whether actors pursued ethno-nationalist aims and/or secessionist objectives.

Ethnic conflicts are distinguished from other conflicts depending on the aims of the armed organizations and their recruitment and alliance strategies, in line with other ongoing coding projects (Sambanis 2009). Ethnic wars involve conflicts over ethno-national self-determination, the ethnic balance of power in government, ethno-regional autonomy, ethnic and racial discrimination (whether alleged or real), and language and other cultural rights. We define all other war aims as non-ethnic. Examples of non-ethnic conflicts include the various military coups staged in Argentina and the civil wars in China, Greece, and Algeria. Ethnic rebels recruit fighters predominantly among their own ethnic group and forge alliances with other organizations on the basis of ethnic affinity. For a conflict to be classified as ethnic, armed organizations have to both explicitly pursue ethno-nationalist aims, motivations, and interests, *and* follow an ethnic logic of recruiting fighters and forging alliances. We looked at the aims and recruitment patterns of each armed organization separately. In some complex cases (e.g. Afghanistan, Burma, Chad, Uganda, Angola, and Zaire), we disaggregated a conflict into several war fronts with different claims made by different organizations, such that one of those fronts would be

---

[43] The ACD appears to be more consistent with regard to sub-IDs from 1989 onward. We split or merged some older conflicts following ACD's rules. We also fused sub-IDs that were based on a change in the type of civil war (e.g. internationalized versus non-internationalized conflicts). A list of our conflicts and how they relate to the ACD war IDs is available online.

associated with an ethnic conflict, while others would represent non-ethnic conflicts. This was sometimes also necessary when the constellation of rebel organizations changed over time.

Separatist conflicts are fought by armed organizations that aim at establishing a separate, independent, internationally recognized state or that want to join another existing state (irredentism). We assessed the intentions of armed organizations immediately before the outbreak of war because our analysis takes war onset as the dependent variable. We also distinguished between cases where the demand for independence was tactical (the Karen's threat to establish an independent state) or represented a long-term strategic objective (as in Southern Sudan).

APPENDIX 5.2 SUMMARY STATISTICS FOR CORE VARIABLES

Appendix Table 5.2 provides summary statistics for the core variables in the dataset. It includes 7,155 observations covering 156 sovereign states in all years after independence from 1946–2005.

APPENDIX TABLE 5.2 *Summary of statistics of core variables*

Variable	Observations	Mean	Standard deviation	Minimum	Maximum
% excluded population (logged)	7,138	1.864	1.589	0	4.595
Number of power-sharing partners	7,138	1.638	1.856	0	14
Duration of imperial past	7,155	0.475	0.314	0	1
Linguistic fractionalization	7,151	0.381	0.284	0.001	0.925
GDP per capita (in 1,000 USD)	6,990	5.968	7.292	0.028	110.315
Population (logged)	7,060	9.188	1.390	5.581	14.076
Mountainous terrain (logged)	7,155	2.204	1.391	0	4.421
Soldiers per capita	6,489	7.719	9.432	0	211.297
Political instability	7,155	0.122	0.327	0	1
Anocracy	6,986	0.224	0.417	0	1
Oil production per capita (in barrels)	7,060	2.072	13.087	0	272.403

APPENDIX 5.3 ADDITIONAL TABLES

APPENDIX TABLE 5.3A *Robustness checks and additional models for Models 1–3 in Table 5.2 (comparing models with ongoing war years included or dropped)*

	Ongoing war years included						Ongoing war years dropped			
	(replicates Models 1–3 in Table 5.2, adds additional models)									
	1	2	3	4	5	6	7	8	9	10
	ACD	ACD	ACD High intensity	Fearon and Laitin	Sambanis	ACD	ACD	ACD High intensity	Fearon and Laitin	Sambanis
Ethnic politics variables										
% excluded population	0.1887**	0.1291*	0.2859**	0.2564**	0.2792**	0.1880**	0.1441*	0.3348**	0.2774**	0.3213**
	(0.0513)	(0.0558)	(0.0834)	(0.0779)	(0.0808)	(0.0569)	(0.0666)	(0.0893)	(0.0805)	(0.0807)
No. of power-sharing partners	0.0862**	0.0587	0.0562	0.0771	0.0177	0.0567	0.0296	0.0735	0.1172	0.0068
	(0.0295)	(0.0389)	(0.0455)	(0.0586)	(0.0491)	(0.0380)	(0.0513)	(0.0605)	(0.0888)	(0.0500)
Duration of imperial past	0.2075	0.4579	0.7285	0.7899*	0.5932	0.2104	0.4321	0.6893	0.6799	0.6890
	(0.2614)	(0.2886)	(0.4441)	(0.3568)	(0.3307)	(0.2910)	(0.3244)	(0.4958)	(0.3550)	(0.3637)
Other variables										
Linguistic fractionalization		0.6298	0.1244	−0.0283	0.0261		0.5650	−0.1778	−0.0685	−0.2278
		(0.3227)	(0.4597)	(0.4274)	(0.3989)		(0.3891)	(0.5401)	(0.4736)	(0.4893)
GDP per capita	−0.1239**	−0.1093**	−0.1902**	−0.1267**	−0.1750**	−0.1203**	−0.1044**	−0.1640**	−0.1245**	−0.1598**
	(0.0271)	(0.0276)	(0.0546)	(0.0374)	(0.0472)	(0.0277)	(0.0275)	(0.0539)	(0.0372)	(0.0492)
Population size	0.1556**	0.1397**	0.0865	0.2354**	0.2135**	0.1278*	0.0884	0.0504	0.2541**	0.1400*
	(0.0559)	(0.0532)	(0.0636)	(0.0672)	(0.0616)	(0.0573)	(0.0631)	(0.0801)	(0.0781)	(0.0702)

APPENDIX TABLE 5.3A (*cont.*)

| | Ongoing war years included (replicates Models 1–3 in Table 5.2, adds additional models) | | | | | Ongoing war years dropped | | | | |
| | 1 | 2 | 3 | 4 | 5 | 6 | 7 | 8 | 9 | 10 |
	ACD	ACD	ACD High intensity	Fearon and Laitin	Sambanis	ACD	ACD	ACD High intensity	Fearon and Laitin	Sambanis
Mountainous terrain		0.1241*	0.1901	0.1581*	0.1320		0.0926	0.1796	0.1662*	0.1391
		(0.0601)	(0.1117)	(0.0794)	(0.0765)		(0.0630)	(0.1086)	(0.0799)	(0.0871)
Political instability		0.3454	0.4555	0.2693	0.2655		0.4846*	0.5714	0.1866	0.2420
		(0.1764)	(0.2852)	(0.2754)	(0.2412)		(0.1951)	(0.2972)	(0.2944)	(0.2598)
Anocracy		0.4292**	0.4014	0.7218**	0.6478**		0.4527*	0.2991	0.6474**	0.6810**
		(0.1625)	(0.2511)	(0.2369)	(0.1863)		(0.1760)	(0.2987)	(0.2485)	(0.2196)
Oil production per capita		0.0171**	0.0051	0.0056	0.0176*		0.0158*	0.0062	0.0042	0.0101
		(0.0063)	(0.0162)	(0.0165)	(0.0078)		(0.0063)	(0.0137)	(0.0183)	(0.0134)
Ongoing war	-0.9832**	-0.9678**	-1.2732**	-2.1655**	-1.4045**					
	(0.3620)	(0.3733)	(0.4690)	(0.4777)	(0.4435)					
Observations	6,938	6,865	6,865	6,934	5,818	5,980	5,923	6,204	5,268	5,076

Notes: Calendar year, peace years since last conflict, cubic splines and constant not shown.
Robust standard errors in parentheses; ** $p < 0.01$; * $p < 0.05$.

APPENDIX TABLE 5.3B *Robustness checks for Models 1–3 in Table 5.2 (with continental dummies)*

	Ongoing war years included						Ongoing war years dropped			
	11	12	13	14	15	16	17	18	19	20
	ACD	ACD	ACD High intensity	FL	Sambanis	ACD	ACD	ACD High intensity	FL	Sambanis
% excluded population	0.1724**	0.1076	0.2896**	0.2402**	0.2538**	0.1696**	0.1164	0.3119**	0.2662**	0.2870**
	(0.0531)	(0.0590)	(0.0924)	(0.0784)	(0.0769)	(0.0560)	(0.0618)	(0.0944)	(0.0795)	(0.0758)
No. of power-sharing partners	0.0837**	0.0505	0.0549	0.0731	0.0158	0.0570	0.0240	0.0692	0.1145	−0.0021
	(0.0267)	(0.0342)	(0.0449)	(0.0549)	(0.0504)	(0.0355)	(0.0479)	(0.0598)	(0.0849)	(0.0484)
Duration of imperial past	0.1782	0.4881	0.4724	0.9134*	0.4749	0.3755	0.6485	0.5558	0.8809	0.7226
	(0.2935)	(0.3310)	(0.5174)	(0.4482)	(0.3948)	(0.3423)	(0.3754)	(0.6665)	(0.4865)	(0.4310)
Linguistic fractionalization		0.8174*	0.2142	0.0241	−0.2251		0.7798	−0.0085	−0.0424	−0.4585
		(0.3638)	(0.5042)	(0.5441)	(0.4564)		(0.4532)	(0.5916)	(0.5874)	(0.5574)
GDP per capita	−0.0776*	−0.0784*	−0.1555*	−0.0793	−0.0994*	−0.0768*	−0.0769*	−0.1450*	−0.0653	−0.0784
	(0.0310)	(0.0325)	(0.0718)	(0.0503)	(0.0503)	(0.0316)	(0.0332)	(0.0724)	(0.0482)	(0.0581)
Population size	0.1557	0.1440*	0.0507	0.2424**	0.2232**	0.1511*	0.1167	0.0377	0.2549**	0.1802*
	(0.0604)	(0.0574)	(0.0746)	(0.0723)	(0.0642)	(0.0640)	(0.0672)	(0.0871)	(0.0810)	(0.0760)
Mountainous terrain		0.0966	0.1318	0.1481	0.1489		0.0792	0.1475	0.1544	0.1751
		(0.0682)	(0.1197)	(0.0900)	(0.0788)		(0.0774)	(0.1249)	(0.0908)	(0.0912)
Political instability		0.3328	0.4734	0.2533	0.2626		0.4590*	0.5651	0.1381	0.2271
		(0.1740)	(0.2803)	(0.2733)	(0.2387)		(0.1937)	(0.2903)	(0.2954)	(0.2596)
Anocracy		0.3945*	0.3983	0.6712**	0.6558**		0.3961*	0.2855	0.6059*	0.6938**

APPENDIX TABLE 5.3B (cont.)

	Ongoing war years included					Ongoing war years dropped				
	11	12	13	14	15	16	17	18	19	20
	ACD	ACD	ACD High intensity	FL	Sambanis	ACD	ACD	ACD High intensity	FL	Sambanis
		(0.1578)	(0.2326)	(0.2393)	(0.1873)		(0.1709)	(0.2940)	(0.2565)	(0.2217)
Oil production per capita		0.0119	-0.0074	-0.0102	0.0085		0.0106	-0.0023	-0.0167	-0.0097
		(0.0066)	(0.0285)	(0.0296)	(0.0111)		(0.0069)	(0.0239)	(0.0338)	(0.0340)
Ongoing war	-1.0293**	-0.9995**	-1.3561**	-2.2937**	-1.5312**					
	(0.3621)	(0.3711)	(0.4675)	(0.4192)	(0.4493)					
Latin America	2.0041**	1.8174**	14.3871	1.6200	1.4301	1.6782**	1.4593*	0.7262	1.7340	1.5872
	(0.6828)	(0.6946)	(14.2780)	(1.0741)	(1.0801)	(0.6066)	(0.6078)	(1.1743)	(1.0875)	(1.1256)
Eastern Europe	1.6963*	1.4976*	14.4878	0.8710	0.5810	0.9840	0.7939	0.5752	0.7169	0.5771
	(0.7367)	(0.7470)	(14.2882)	(1.1423)	(1.2443)	(0.6826)	(0.6904)	(1.2016)	(1.1757)	(1.2782)
North Africa and Middle East	1.9146**	1.7064*	14.5809	1.4877	1.8034	1.4899*	1.2792*	0.9573	1.5172	1.8219
	(0.6995)	(0.7046)	(14.2685)	(1.1048)	(1.0867)	(0.6475)	(0.6506)	(1.2057)	(1.1303)	(1.1324)
Sub-Saharan Africa	1.8850**	1.5021	14.3026	1.4148	1.9804	1.4588**	1.0645	0.5693	1.4805	2.1008
	(0.7296)	(0.7673)	(14.3189)	(1.1803)	(1.1563)	(0.6694)	(0.7018)	(1.2611)	(1.1917)	(1.2242)
Asia	2.0290**	1.6564*	14.7869	1.4627	1.7612	1.4545*	1.0524	0.8708	1.5818	1.6105
	(0.7185)	(0.7444)	(14.2329)	(1.1637)	(1.1266)	(0.6709)	(0.6889)	(1.3111)	(1.1962)	(1.2060)
Observations	6,938	6,865	6,865	6,034	5,818	5,980	5,923	6,204	5,268	5,076

Robust standard errors in parentheses; ** $p<0.01$; * $p<0.05$.

Notes: Calendar year, peace years since last conflict, cubic splines and constant not shown.

APPENDIX TABLE 5.3C *Robustness checks for Models 1–3 in Table 5.2 (including number of past conflicts)*

| | Ongoing war years included | | | | | Ongoing war years dropped | | | | |
| | 21 | 22 | 23 | 24 | 25 | 26 | 27 | 28 | 29 | 30 |
	ACD	ACD	ACD High intensity	Fearon and Laitin	Sambanis	ACD	ACD	ACD High intensity	Fearon and Laitin	Sambanis
Ethnic politics variables										
% excluded population	0.1898**	0.1261*	0.2842**	0.2464**	0.2734**	0.1838**	0.1369*	0.3166**	0.2507**	0.3091**
	(0.0510)	(0.0551)	(0.0831)	(0.0773)	(0.0771)	(0.0551)	(0.0594)	(0.0898)	(0.0821)	(0.0799)
No. of power-sharing partners	0.0832*	0.0505	0.0488	0.0479	−0.0231	0.0523	0.0237	0.0578	0.0915	−0.0237
	(0.0334)	(0.0386)	(0.0462)	(0.0552)	(0.0424)	(0.0371)	(0.0492)	(0.0605)	(0.0808)	(0.0476)
Duration of imperial past	0.2178	0.4864	0.7564	0.8878*	0.7341*	0.2413	0.4716	0.7596	0.8049*	0.8278*
	(0.2658)	(0.2851)	(0.4591)	(0.3599)	(0.3307)	(0.2934)	(0.3210)	(0.4824)	(0.3529)	(0.3524)
Other variables										
Number of past conflicts	0.0184	0.0501	0.0460	0.1793*	0.2288**	0.0745	0.0910	0.1353	0.2809**	0.2782**
	(0.0621)	(0.0630)	(0.1035)	(0.0843)	(0.0831)	(0.0977)	(0.0987)	(0.1221)	(0.0940)	(0.1012)
Linguistic fractionalization		0.6404*	0.1193	−0.0384	−0.0212		0.5984	−0.1656	−0.0590	−0.2299
		(0.3153)	(0.4582)	(0.4168)	(0.3736)		(0.3875)	(0.5313)	(0.4620)	(0.4908)
GDP per capita	−0.1232**	−0.1075**	−0.1878**	−0.1154**	−0.1604**	−0.1184**	−0.1021**	−0.1597**	−0.1059**	−0.1453**
	(0.0271)	(0.0274)	(0.0558)	(0.0375)	(0.0471)	(0.0274)	(0.0272)	(0.0539)	(0.0372)	(0.0501)
Population size	0.1478*	0.1186*	0.0657	0.1577*	0.1088	0.1049	0.0613	−0.0004	0.1379	0.0288
	(0.0603)	(0.0588)	(0.0772)	(0.0728)	(0.0610)	(0.0622)	(0.0716)	(0.0887)	(0.0790)	(0.0822)
Mountainous terrain		0.1242*	0.1923	0.1674*	0.1316		0.0941	0.1824	0.1858*	0.1470
		(0.0595)	(0.1122)	(0.0809)	(0.0792)		(0.0623)	(0.1085)	(0.0832)	(0.0920)
Political instability		0.3556*	0.4639	0.2947	0.3115		0.4879*	0.5745	0.1972	0.2571
		(0.1772)	(0.2889)	(0.2752)	(0.2432)		(0.1948)	(0.2960)	(0.2903)	(0.2644)

APPENDIX TABLE 5.3C (*cont.*)

	Ongoing war years included						Ongoing war years dropped			
	21	22	23	24	25	26	27	28	29	30
	ACD	ACD	ACD High intensity	Fearon and Laitin	Sambanis	ACD	ACD	ACD High intensity	Fearon and Laitin	Sambanis
Anocracy		0.4357**	0.4035	0.7271**	0.6801**		0.4507*	0.2849	0.6374*	0.6901**
		(0.1621)	(0.2512)	(0.2388)	(0.1900)		(0.1773)	(0.3001)	(0.2541)	(0.2240)
Oil production per capita		0.0167**	0.0044	-0.0004	0.0148		0.0154*	0.0050	-0.0088	0.0052
		(0.0063)	(0.0167)	(0.0231)	(0.0081)		(0.0063)	(0.0143)	(0.0323)	(0.0170)
Ongoing war	-1.0004**	-1.0144**	-1.3326**	-2.3266**	-1.5263**					
	(0.3767)	(0.3845)	(0.5062)	(0.4452)	(0.4565)					
Calendar year	0.0054	0.0030	0.0002	0.0152	0.0121	0.0068	0.0047	-0.0011	0.0154	0.0105
	(0.0058)	(0.0059)	(0.0085)	(0.0082)	(0.0083)	(0.0056)	(0.0060)	(0.0091)	(0.0083)	(0.0089)
Peace years since last conflict	-0.2430	-0.2169	-0.3379**	-0.2868*	-0.2474	-0.1894	-0.1514	-0.3462*	-0.3497**	-0.0799
	(0.1423)	(0.1430)	(0.1210)	(0.1407)	(0.1306)	(0.1155)	(0.1112)	(0.0994)	(0.0993)	(0.1040)
Spline 1 for peace years	-0.0057	-0.0033	-0.0025	-0.0037	-0.0030	-0.0024	-0.0017	-0.0025*	-0.0046*	-0.0003
	(0.0040)	(0.0041)	(0.0014)	(0.0025)	(0.0025)	(0.0034)	(0.0033)	(0.0012)	(0.0019)	(0.0021)
Spline 2 for peace years	0.0004	0.0003	0.0007	0.0009	0.0006	0.0001	-0.0001	0.0007	0.0012	-0.0002
	(0.0010)	(0.0010)	(0.0007)	(0.0009)	(0.0009)	(0.0009)	(0.0008)	(0.0007)	(0.0007)	(0.0008)
Spline 3 for peace years	0.0002	0.0002	0.0002	-0.0000	0.0001	0.0002	0.0002	0.0002	-0.0001	0.0002
	(0.0002)	(0.0002)	(0.0002)	(0.0002)	(0.0002)	(0.0002)	(0.0002)	(0.0002)	(0.0002)	(0.0002)
Constant	-14.8530	-10.8694	-5.5443	-35.9657*	-29.0679	-17.3455	-13.7013	-2.3564	-36.0454*	-25.9568
	(11.5312)	(11.8701)	(16.9660)	(16.1619)	(16.3615)	(11.1654)	(11.9571)	(18.0679)	(16.2469)	(17.4632)
Observations	6,938	6,865	6,865	6,934	5,818	5,980	5,923	6,204	5,268	5,076

Robust standard errors in parentheses; ** $p<0.01$; * $p<0.05$.

APPENDIX TABLE 5.3D *Robustness checks for Models 1–3 in Table 5.2 (using rare events logit)*

	Ongoing war years included						Ongoing war years dropped			
	31	32	33	34	35	36	37	38	39	40
	ACD	ACD	ACD High intensity	Fearon and Laitin	Sambanis	ACD	ACD	ACD High intensity	Fearon and Laitin	Sambanis
Ethnic politics variables										
% excluded population	0.1876**	0.1275*	0.2705**	0.2459**	0.2734**	0.1865**	0.1420*	0.3143**	0.2654**	0.3119**
	(0.0513)	(0.0556)	(0.0832)	(0.0777)	(0.0806)	(0.0567)	(0.0604)	(0.0891)	(0.0803)	(0.0804)
No. of power-sharing partners	0.0873**	0.0600	0.0636	0.0817	0.0231	0.0594	0.0322	0.0825	0.1183	0.0147
	(0.0295)	(0.0388)	(0.0454)	(0.0584)	(0.0489)	(0.0379)	(0.0511)	(0.0603)	(0.0885)	(0.0498)
Duration of imperial past	0.2079	0.4540	0.6916	0.7594*	0.5821	0.2098	0.4269	0.6444	0.6531	0.6654
	(0.2609)	(0.2898)	(0.4430)	(0.3558)	(0.3298)	(0.2905)	(0.3235)	(0.4945)	(0.3540)	(0.3625)
Other variables										
Linguistic fractionalization		0.6241	0.1225	-0.0309	0.0179		0.5618	-0.1965	-0.0649	-0.2311
		(0.3220)	(0.4586)	(0.4262)	(0.3977)		(0.3880)	(0.5387)	(0.4721)	(0.4878)
GDP per capita	-0.1213**	-0.1081*	-0.1998**	-0.1324**	-0.1729**	-0.1175**	-0.1032*	-0.1714**	-0.1314**	-0.1623**
	(0.0271)	(0.0276)	(0.0545)	(0.0373)	(0.0470)	(0.0277)	(0.0274)	(0.0557)	(0.0371)	(0.0491)
Population size	0.1561**	0.1406**	0.0909	0.2372**	0.2156**	0.1290*	0.0901	0.0550	0.2525**	0.1434*
	(0.0558)	(0.0530)	(0.0635)	(0.0670)	(0.0614)	(0.0572)	(0.0629)	(0.0799)	(0.0778)	(0.0700)
Mountainous terrain		0.1230*	0.1958	0.1574*	0.1304		0.0920	0.1777	0.1661*	0.1385
		(0.0600)	(0.1114)	(0.0791)	(0.0763)		(0.0629)	(0.1083)	(0.0797)	(0.0868)
Political instability		0.3303	0.4737	0.2817	0.2728		0.4876**	0.5802	0.2006	0.2542
		(0.1760)	(0.2845)	(0.2746)	(0.2405)		(0.1946)	(0.2565)	(0.2935)	(0.2590)
Anocracy		0.4301**	0.3989	0.7230**	0.6464**		0.4535**	0.2969	0.6510**	0.6816**
		(0.1621)	(0.2505)	(0.2362)	(0.1857)		(0.1756)	(0.2579)	(0.2477)	(0.2189)

APPENDIX TABLE 5.3D (*cont.*)

	Ongoing war years included						Ongoing war years dropped			
	31	32	33	34	35	36	37	38	39	40
	ACD	ACD	ACD High intensity	Fearon and Laitin	Sambanis	ACD	ACD	ACD High intensity	Fearon and Laitin	Sambanis
Oil production per capita		0.0226**	0.1132**	0.0671**	0.0355**		0.0214**	0.0965**	0.0719**	0.0513**
		(0.0063)	(0.0162)	(0.0164)	(0.0078)		(0.0063)	(0.0156)	(0.0183)	(0.0134)
Ongoing war	−0.9989**	−0.9847**	−1.3247**	−2.1652**	−1.4157**					
	(0.3613)	(0.3724)	(0.4673)	(0.4265)	(0.4422)					
Calendar year	0.0059	0.0046	0.0019	0.0215**	0.0202**	0.0091	0.0075	0.0039	0.0254**	0.0202**
	(0.0052)	(0.0053)	(0.0068)	(0.0075)	(0.0075)	(0.0051)	(0.0052)	(0.0069)	(0.0068)	(0.0076)
Peace years since last conflict	−0.2504	−0.2270	−0.3432**	−0.2976*	−0.2679*	−0.2026	−0.1674	−0.3570*	−0.3771**	−0.1076
	(0.1422)	(0.1431)	(0.1207)	(0.1396)	(0.1270)	(0.1128)	(0.1102)	(0.1000)	(0.0976)	(0.0972)
Spline 1 for peace years	−0.0039	−0.0035	−0.0025	−0.0038	−0.0032	−0.0027	−0.0020	−0.0026*	−0.0050**	−0.0006
	(0.0040)	(0.0041)	(0.0014)	(0.0025)	(0.0025)	(0.0033)	(0.0033)	(0.0012)	(0.0019)	(0.0020)
Spline 2 for peace years	0.0004	0.0004	0.0007	0.0010	0.0006	0.0002	0.0000	0.0008	0.0013	−0.0001
	(0.0010)	(0.0010)	(0.0007)	(0.0009)	(0.0009)	(0.0008)	(0.0008)	(0.0007)	(0.0007)	(0.0008)
Spline 3 for peace years	0.0002	0.0002	0.0001	−0.0001	0.0001	0.0002	0.0002	0.0001	−0.0001	0.0002
	(0.0002)	(0.0002)	(0.0002)	(0.0003)	(0.0002)	(0.0002)	(0.0002)	(0.0002)	(0.0002)	(0.0002)
Constant	−16.0138	−14.1499	−8.7728	−48.8662**	−45.6975**	−22.0351*	−19.2989	−12.4807	−56.3906**	−45.6418**
	(10.2469)	(10.4900)	(13.5100)	(14.6386)	(14.7698)	(10.1250)	(10.2884)	(13.4507)	(13.3841)	(14.8690)
Observations	6,938	6,865	6,865	6,034	5,818	5,980	5,923	6,204	5,268	5,076

Robust standard errors in parentheses; ** p<0.01; * p<0.05.

APPENDIX TABLE 5.3E *Robustness checks and additional models for Models 4 and 5 in Table 5.2 (comparing models with ongoing war years included or dropped)*

	Ongoing war years included				Ongoing war years dropped			
	1	2	3	4	5	6	7	8
	ACD	ACD	ACD High intensity	Fearon and Laitin	ACD	ACD	ACD High intensity	Fearon and Laitin
Ethnic politics variables								
% excluded population	0.4192**	0.3191**	0.5347**	0.3667**	0.4559**	0.3810**	0.6809**	0.3482**
	(0.0862)	(0.0875)	(0.1351)	(0.1214)	(0.0994)	(0.0994)	(0.1525)	(0.1143)
No. of power-sharing partners	0.1554**	0.1120**	0.1272*	0.0969	0.1852**	0.1498**	0.2047**	0.0682
	(0.0312)	(0.0370)	(0.0530)	(0.0747)	(0.0411)	(0.0571)	(0.0713)	(0.0645)
Duration of imperial past	0.6401	0.9301*	1.1793	1.5761**	1.1480	1.3016*	1.4439	1.6206**
	(0.4477)	(0.4426)	(0.6304)	(0.4244)	(0.6012)	(0.5921)	(0.7797)	(0.4262)
Other variables								
Linguistic fractionalization		1.2800**	0.2563	0.5990		1.0111	−0.4869	0.5614
		(0.3997)	(0.4974)	(0.6656)		(0.6003)	(0.6621)	(0.5661)
GDP per capita	−0.1446**	−0.1256**	−0.1921**	−0.1554**	−0.1089**	−0.0930*	−0.1494*	−0.1529*
	(0.0415)	(0.0448)	(0.0746)	(0.0585)	(0.0400)	(0.0422)	(0.0711)	(0.0611)
Population size	0.2171**	0.2102**	0.1884*	0.3609**	0.1710*	0.1740*	0.1561	0.3461**
	(0.0714)	(0.0656)	(0.0757)	(0.0894)	(0.0863)	(0.0876)	(0.1040)	(0.0887)
Mountainous terrain		0.1749	0.3258*	0.0701		0.0765	0.2289	0.0695
		(0.0984)	(0.1483)	(0.1090)		(0.1108)	(0.1634)	(0.1104)
Political instability		0.1544	0.2979	−0.0441		0.3313	0.4556	−0.0702
		(0.2726)	(0.3958)	(0.3549)		(0.2825)	(0.4152)	(0.3359)
Anocracy		0.4469*	0.5681	0.9738**		0.5720*	0.5640	1.0183**

APPENDIX TABLE 5.3E (cont.)

	Ongoing war years included				Ongoing war years dropped			
	1	2	3	4	5	6	7	8
	ACD	ACD	ACD High intensity	Fearon and Laitin	ACD	ACD	ACD High intensity	Fearon and Laitin
		(0.2263)	(0.2929)	(0.2614)	(0.2614)	(0.2869)	(0.4232)	(0.2614)
Oil production per capita	0.0359 (0.6123)	0.0180* (0.0091)	0.0277** (0.0083)	0.0064 (0.0284)	0.0231** (0.0070)	0.0169 (0.0097)	0.0272** (0.0093)	0.0098 (0.0381)
Ongoing war		−0.0697 (0.6666)	−0.7636 (0.6271)	−2.2861** (0.5551)				
Calendar year	0.0150* (0.0073)	0.0122 (0.0077)	0.0091 (0.0091)	0.0365** (0.0090)		0.0199* (0.0078)	0.0117 (0.0104)	0.0307** (0.0100)
Peace years since last conflict	0.0761 (0.2299)	0.0553 (0.2357)	−0.1467 (0.1685)	−0.2426 (0.1825)	0.1372 (0.1497)	0.1563 (0.1422)	0.0137 (0.1186)	0.2664* (0.1153)
Spline 1 for peace years	0.0051 (0.0065)	0.0046 (0.0067)	0.0004 (0.0019)	−0.0031 (0.0032)	0.0066 (0.0046)	0.0070 (0.0044)	0.0019 (0.0016)	0.0043 (0.0024)
Spline 2 for peace years	−0.0017 (0.0016)	−0.0016 (0.0016)	−0.0008 (0.0010)	0.0008 (0.0011)	−0.0020 (0.0012)	−0.0021 (0.0012)	−0.0015 (0.0009)	−0.0013 (0.0009)
Spline 3 for peace years	0.0004 (0.0003)	0.0004 (0.0003)	0.0005 (0.0003)	−0.0001 (0.0003)	0.0005* (0.0002)	0.0005* (0.0002)	0.0007 (0.0003)	0.0003 (0.0003)
Constant	−37.1296* (14.6291)	−32.6393* (15.1798)	−26.7855 (17.9573)	−80.7809** (17.4279)	−53.4462** (13.9033)	−48.1186** (15.2944)	−32.6002 (20.2037)	−71.1914** (19.3289)
Observations	6,938	6,865	6,865	6,934	6,262	6,191	6,415	6,934

Robust standard errors in parentheses; ** $p<0.01$; * $p<0.05$.

APPENDIX TABLE 5.3F *Robustness checks for Models 4 and 5 in Table 5.2 (including continental dummies)*

	Ongoing war years included					Ongoing war years dropped		
	9	10	11	12	13	14	15	16
	ACD	ACD	ACD High intensity	Fearon and Laitin	ACD	ACD	ACD High intensity	Fearon and Laitin
Ethnic politics variables								
% excluded population	0.4283**	0.3430**	0.5443**	0.3612**	0.4266**	0.3663**	0.6486**	0.3337**
	(0.0976)	(0.0980)	(0.1528)	(0.1122)	(0.1013)	(0.1032)	(0.1629)	(0.1080)
No. of power-sharing partners	0.1564**	0.1153**	0.1292*	0.1086	0.1722**	0.1450*	0.1944*	0.0866
	(0.0297)	(0.0370)	(0.0564)	(0.0799)	(0.0428)	(0.0571)	(0.0772)	(0.0691)
Duration of imperial past	0.2540	0.5864	0.5892	1.2252*	1.0968	1.3199	0.9802	1.1801*
	(0.5287)	(0.5492)	(0.7351)	(0.5067)	(0.8228)	(0.7949)	(0.9364)	(0.4766)
Other variables								
Linguistic fractionalization		1.820*	0.2249	−0.0644		1.1612	−0.5631	−0.0294
		(0.5595)	(0.5533)	(0.7673)		(0.9248)	(0.7805)	(0.7280)
GDP per capita	−0.1295***	−0.1375**	−0.1691*	−0.0960	−0.1107**	−0.186**	−0.1394	−0.1061
	(0.0404)	(0.0433)	(0.0862)	(0.0565)	(0.0423)	(0.0457)	(0.0774)	(0.0606)
Population size	0.1913*	0.1867*	0.1938*	0.3717**	0.2339**	0.2144*	0.2250*	0.3674**
	(0.0767)	(0.0727)	(0.0865)	(0.0903)	(0.0854)	(0.0886)	(0.1058)	(0.0872)
Mountainous terrain		0.1417	0.2812	0.1213		0.1110	0.2502	0.1186
		(0.1072)	(0.1450)	(0.1061)		(0.1460)	(0.1818)	(0.1094)
Political instability		0.1726	0.3343	−0.0398		0.3342	0.4842	−0.0665
		(0.2676)	(0.3871)	(0.3585)		(0.2831)	(0.4124)	(0.3360)

APPENDIX TABLE 5.3F (cont.)

| | Ongoing war years included | | | | | Ongoing war years dropped | | |
| | 9 | 10 | 11 | 12 | 13 | 14 | 15 | 16 |
	ACD	ACD	ACD High intensity	Fearon and Laitin	ACD	ACD	ACD High intensity	Fearon and Laitin
Anocracy		0.4768*	0.6075*	1.0339**		0.5656	0.5764	1.0768**
		(0.2224)	(0.3047)	(0.2618)		(0.2892)	(0.4480)	(0.2635)
Oil production per capita		0.0172*	0.0230*	0.0082		0.0178*	0.0245*	0.0087
		(0.0080)	(0.0092)	(0.0188)		(0.0088)	(0.0111)	(0.0236)
Ongoing war	0.0370	−0.0553	−0.7255	−2.3414**				
	(0.6070)	(0.6140)	(0.6367)	(0.5411)				
Calendar year	0.0133	0.0115	0.0045	0.0323**	0.0205**	0.0187*	0.0046	0.0246**
	(0.0074)	(0.0076)	(0.0099)	(0.0090)	(0.0076)	(0.0082)	(0.0103)	(0.0092)
Peace years since last conflict	0.0716	0.0504	−0.1513	−0.2617	0.1187	0.1421	−0.0244	0.2487*
	(0.2314)	(0.2369)	(0.1682)	(0.1809)	(0.1521)	(0.1470)	(0.1201)	(0.1194)
Spline 1 for peace years	0.0050	0.0045	0.0002	−0.0034	0.0062	0.0067	0.0014	0.0040
	(0.0066)	(0.0067)	(0.0019)	(0.0032)	(0.0047)	(0.0046)	(0.0017)	(0.0025)
Spline 2 for peace years	−0.0017	−0.0016	−0.0007	0.0010	−0.0019	−0.0021	−0.0013	−0.0012
	(0.0016)	(0.0016)	(0.0010)	(0.0011)	(0.0012)	(0.0012)	(0.0009)	(0.0009)
Spline 3 for peace years	0.0004	0.0004	0.0005	−0.0002	0.0005*	0.0005*	0.0006	0.0002
	(0.0003)	(0.0003)	(0.0003)	(0.0003)	(0.0002)	(0.0002)	(0.0003)	(0.0003)

Latin America	−0.7122	−1.0462	12.5662**	−1.4217	−0.5368	−0.8514	12.9563	−1.4840
	(0.7677)	(0.7862)	(0.7963)	(1.3654)	(0.8468)	(0.8604)	(20.0662)	(1.3508)
Eastern Europe	0.3578	0.0117	14.1140	0.0269	−0.1368	−0.4613	14.3146	0.2705
	(0.7703)	(0.7777)	(0.0000)	(1.1615)	(0.9856)	(1.0027)	(20.1085)	(1.1467)
North Africa and Middle East	0.0902	−0.1814	13.8881**	0.1045	0.0552	−0.2561	14.0842	0.1343
	(0.8176)	(0.7576)	(0.4101)	(1.1333)	(1.0560)	(1.0288)	(20.0526)	(1.1167)
Sub-Saharan Africa	0.1165	−0.4849	13.6138***	0.8051	0.0346	−0.5833	14.0484	0.7713
	(0.7649)	(0.8347)	(0.4854)	(1.2644)	(0.9330)	(1.0552)	(20.0567)	(1.2763)
Asia	0.2857	−0.2242	13.6988***	0.3514	−0.5327	−1.0071	13.4720	0.2805
	(0.7766)	(0.8061)	(0.4624)	(1.1890)	(0.9743)	(0.9777)	(19.9451)	(1.1722)
Constant	−33.5183*	−30.4891*	−31.0531	−73.0238***	−48.4899***	−45.5171***	−32.5058	−59.2994**
	(14.6755)	(14.9511)	(19.4908)	(17.4297)	(14.7184)	(15.9651)	(0.0000)	(17.8704)
Observations	6,938	6,865	6,865	6,034	6,262	6,191	6,415	6,034

Robust standard errors in parentheses; ** $p<0.01$; * $p<0.05$.

APPENDIX TABLE 5.3G *Robustness checks for Models 4 and 5 in Table 5.2: (including number of past conflicts)*

	Ongoing war years included				Ongoing war years dropped			
	17	18	19	20	21	22	23	24
	ACD	ACD	ACD High intensity	Fearon and Laitin	ACD	ACD	ACD High intensity	Fearon and Laitin
Ethnic politics variables								
% excluded population	0.4432**	0.3217**	0.5364**	0.3575**	0.4613**	0.3857**	0.6801**	0.3449**
	(0.0872)	(0.0891)	(0.1354)	(0.1205)	(0.0982)	(0.1008)	(0.1524)	(0.1134)
No. of power-sharing partners	0.1631**	0.1166**	0.1328*	0.0759	0.1908**	0.1544*	0.2037**	0.0563
	(0.0397)	(0.0441)	(0.0583)	(0.0782)	(0.0441)	(0.0617)	(0.0755)	(0.0678)
Duration of imperial past	0.6142	0.9125*	1.1589	1.6567**	1.1241	1.2798*	1.4474	1.6698**
	(0.4582)	(0.4505)	(0.6597)	(0.4450)	(0.6136)	(0.6680)	(0.7757)	(0.4429)
Other variables								
Number of past conflicts	-0.0356	-0.0231	-0.0268	0.1027	-0.0516	-0.0423	0.0069	0.0599
	(0.0830)	(0.0872)	(0.1314)	(0.1060)	(0.1570)	(0.1656)	(0.1639)	(0.0997)
Linguistic fractionalization		1.2770**	0.2613	0.5893		0.9988	-0.4866	0.5458
		(0.3993)	(0.5021)	(0.6030)		(0.6163)	(0.6628)	(0.5578)
GDP per capita	-0.1463**	-0.1266**	-0.1940*	-0.1471*	-0.1112**	-0.0949*	-0.1489*	-0.1481*
	(0.0412)	(0.0446)	(0.0771)	(0.0582)	(0.0398)	(0.0423)	(0.0729)	(0.0604)
Population size	0.2353**	0.2222**	0.2022**	0.3084**	0.1913	0.1911	0.1533	0.3166**
	(0.0777)	(0.0814)	(0.0952)	(0.1046)	(0.1067)	(0.1198)	(0.1146)	(0.1013)
Mountainous terrain		0.1740	0.3224*	0.0785		0.0739	0.2294	0.0733
		(0.0981)	(0.1453)	(0.1130)		(0.1126)	(0.1635)	(0.1132)

Political instability	0.1483	0.2901	−0.0227		0.3239	0.4572	−0.0568
	(0.2723)	(0.4046)	(0.3585)		(0.2338)	(0.4153)	(0.3405)
Anocracy	0.4423*	0.5655	0.9771**		0.5747*	0.5630	1.0233**
	(0.2212)	(0.2928)	(0.2611)		(0.2896)	(0.4236)	(0.2609)
Oil production per capita	0.0183*	0.0280**	−0.0002		0.0174	0.0271**	−0.0002
	(0.0091)	(0.0084)	(0.0400)		(0.0094)	(0.0092)	(0.0436)
Ongoing war	0.0640	−0.0503	−0.7368	−2.3635**			
	(0.6232)	(0.6252)	(0.6555)	(0.5598)			
Calendar year	0.0165	0.0102	0.0322**	0.0247**	0.0212**	0.0115	0.0283*
	(0.0087)	(0.0119)	(0.0100)	(0.0074)	(0.0081)	(0.0138)	(0.0010)
Peace years since last conflict	0.0731	−0.1479	−0.2365	0.1301	0.4481	0.0144	0.2797*
	(0.2347)	(0.1685)	(0.1829)	(0.1535)	(0.1475)	(0.1181)	(0.1163)
Spline 1 for peace years	0.0046	0.0003	−0.0030	0.0065	0.0069	0.0019	0.0045
	(0.0067)	(0.0019)	(0.0032)	(0.0047)	(0.0045)	(0.0016)	(0.0024)
Spline 2 for peace years	−0.0016	−0.0008	0.0008	−0.0020	−0.0021	−0.0015	−0.0014
	(0.0016)	(0.0010)	(0.0011)	(0.0012)	(0.0012)	(0.0009)	(0.0009)
Spline 3 for peace years	0.0004	0.0005	−0.0001	0.0005*	0.0005*	0.0007	0.0003
	(0.0003)	(0.0003)	(0.0003)	(0.0002)	(0.0002)	(0.0003)	(0.0003)
Constant	−34.5333	−29.0721	−72.2836**	−56.7649**	−50.6848**	−32.0663	−66.2468**
	(17.5709)	(23.6087)	(19.5818)	(14.7511)	(16.0926)	(27.1872)	(21.4979)
Observations	6,938	6,865	6,034	6,262	5,191	6,415	6,034

Robust standard errors in parentheses; ** p<0.01; * p<0.05.

APPENDIX TABLE 5.3H Robustness checks for Models 4 and 5 in Table 5.2 (using rare events logit)

	Ongoing war years included				Ongoing war years dropped			
	25	26	27	28	29	30	31	32
	ACD	ACD	ACD High intensity	Fearon and Laitin	ACD	ACD	ACD High intensity	Fearon and Laitin
Ethnic politics variables								
% excluded population	0.4142**	0.3082**	0.5108**	0.3376**	0.4494**	0.3672**	0.6500**	0.3224**
	(0.0861)	(0.0873)	(0.1348)	(0.1211)	(0.0992)	(0.0992)	(0.1521)	(0.1140)
No. of power-sharing partners	0.1556**	0.1113**	0.1321*	0.0990	0.1881**	0.1489**	0.2107**	0.0708
	(0.0311)	(0.0369)	(0.0529)	(0.0745)	(0.0410)	(0.0569)	(0.0711)	(0.0644)
Duration of imperial past	0.6352	0.9113*	1.1454	1.5112**	1.1295	1.2722*	1.3711	1.5545**
	(0.4469)	(0.4415)	(0.6289)	(0.4232)	(0.6001)	(0.5906)	(0.7778)	(0.4251)
Other variables								
Linguistic fractionalization		1.2730**	0.2332	0.6223		1.0139	−0.5010	0.5656
		(0.3987)	(0.4962)	(0.6139)		(0.5988)	(0.6605)	(0.5646)
GDP per capita	−0.1382**	−0.1290**	−0.1883*	−0.1714**	−0.1021*	−0.0989*	−0.1495*	−0.1623**
	(0.0415)	(0.0447)	(0.0744)	(0.0584)	(0.0399)	(0.0421)	(0.0709)	(0.0609)
Population size	0.2171**	0.2113**	0.1909*	0.3587**	0.1731*	0.1778*	0.1623	0.3463**
	(0.0713)	(0.0654)	(0.0755)	(0.0892)	(0.0862)	(0.0874)	(0.1038)	(0.0885)
Mountainous terrain		0.1758	0.3226*	0.0787		0.0789	0.2199	0.0757
		(0.0982)	(0.1479)	(0.1087)		(0.1105)	(0.1630)	(0.1101)

	(1)	(2)	(3)	(4)	(5)	(6)	(7)	(8)
Political instability		0.1696	0.3206	−0.0239		0.3391	0.4686	−0.0501
		(0.2720)	(0.3949)	(0.3539)		(0.2818)	(0.4142)	(0.3350)
Anocracy		0.4515*	0.5690	0.9773**		0.5748*	0.5621	1.0183**
		(0.2257)	(0.2921)	(0.2607)		(0.2852)	(0.4221)	(0.2607)
Oil production per capita		0.0620**	0.0771**	0.1712**		0.0555**	0.0830**	0.1398**
		(0.0090)	(0.0082)	(0.0283)		(0.0097)	(0.0092)	(0.0380)
Ongoing war	−0.0333	−0.1550	−0.8374	−2.2987**				
	(0.6113)	(0.6151)	(0.6255)	(0.5536)				
Calendar year	0.0148*	0.0119	0.0089	0.0351**	0.0226**	0.0193*	0.0111	0.0296**
	(0.0073)	(0.0076)	(0.0091)	(0.0090)	(0.0070)	(0.0078)	(0.0104)	(0.0099)
Peace years since last conflict	0.0535	0.0329	−0.1604	−0.2534	0.1263	0.1488	0.0049	0.2621*
	(0.2295)	(0.2351)	(0.1681)	(0.1820)	(0.1495)	(0.1418)	(0.1183)	(0.1150)
Spline 1 for peace years	0.0044	0.0040	0.0001	−0.0033	0.0061	0.0067	0.0017	0.0042
	(0.0065)	(0.0067)	(0.0019)	(0.0032)	(0.0046)	(0.0044)	(0.0016)	(0.0024)
Spline 2 for peace years	−0.0015	−0.0014	−0.0006	0.0009	−0.0019	−0.0020	−0.0013	−0.0013
	(0.0016)	(0.0016)	(0.0010)	(0.0011)	(0.0012)	(0.0012)	(0.0009)	(0.0009)
Spline 3 for peace years	0.0004	0.0004	0.0004	−0.0001	0.0004	0.0004	0.0006	0.0002
	(0.0003)	(0.0003)	(0.0003)	(0.0003)	(0.0002)	(0.0002)	(0.0003)	(0.0003)
Constant	−36.4818*	−31.8726*	−26.1246	−78.1012**	−52.4697**	−46.7584**	−31.1435	−68.8738**
	(14.6039)	(15.1423)	(17.9129)	(17.3789)	(13.8789)	(15.2550)	(20.1535)	(19.2778)
Observations	6,938	6,865	6,865	6,034	6,262	6,191	6,415	6,034

Robust standard errors in parentheses; ** $p<0.01$; * $p<0.05$.

APPENDIX TABLE 5.4A *Robustness checks for Table 5.3 (comparing models with ongoing war years included or dropped)*

	Ongoing war years included							
	1				2 (replicates Table 5.3)			
	Secession by power holders	Secession by excluded	Infighting by power holders	Rebellion by excluded	Secession by power holders	Secession by excluded	Infighting by power holders	Rebellion by excluded
Ethnic politics variables								
% excluded population	0.2576	0.3136**	−0.1541	0.7207**	−0.2032	0.2554*	−0.4504	0.7501**
	(0.3100)	(0.1119)	(0.2217)	(0.1303)	(0.3306)	(0.1109)	(0.3156)	(0.1277)
No. of power-sharing partners	0.5745**	−0.0120	0.3129**	0.0526	0.4956**	0.0008	0.3176**	0.0689
	(0.1386)	(0.0364)	(0.0958)	(0.0962)	(0.1164)	(0.0417)	(0.0960)	(0.1001)
Duration of imperial past	13.2111**	1.5563	0.6913	−0.6137	14.6269**	1.9524*	1.1870	−0.8041
	(3.8934)	(0.9976)	(1.2838)	(0.7215)	(2.8503)	(0.8152)	(1.6311)	(0.7777)
Other variables								
Linguistic fractionalization	−0.8256	1.7657**	−1.0875	1.2688	1.4433	1.9997**	0.9991	0.9796
	(1.8082)	(0.6791)	(1.6961)	(0.8772)	(1.2707)	(0.6431)	(1.6116)	(0.8709)
GDP per capita	−0.4672*	−0.0334	−0.2832	−0.1705*	−0.6017	−0.0226	−0.1914	−0.1833*
	(0.2151)	(0.0474)	(0.2490)	(0.0815)	(0.3302)	(0.0584)	(0.1750)	(0.0814)
Population size	−0.2108	0.5483**	−0.4306*	0.1937	−0.1882	0.4835**	−0.7321**	0.2498
	(0.1746)	(0.1144)	(0.1848)	(0.1173)	(0.1925)	(0.1256)	(0.1841)	(0.1329)
Mountainous terrain					0.6948	0.3943	0.5656*	−0.0913
					(0.3751)	(0.2211)	(0.2815)	(0.1608)
Political instability					−35.2497**	0.3655	1.0312	0.0291
					(0.6728)	(0.5128)	(0.7487)	(0.4485)
Anocracy					1.4050	0.2931	0.0115	0.6333
					(0.9854)	(0.3892)	(0.7129)	(0.3639)
Oil production per capita					−0.3692	0.0016	0.0126	0.0296**
					(0.4031)	(0.0452)	(0.0088)	(0.0085)
Ongoing war	3.1974	−0.1486	−0.4537	−0.0672	2.6879	−0.1664	−0.5972	−0.0502
	(2.6581)	(1.0980)	(1.6849)	(0.8797)	(2.9776)	(1.0923)	(1.7814)	(0.9068)
Calendar year	0.1228**	−0.0011	0.0193	0.0210*	0.1347**	0.0012	−0.0072	0.0181
	(0.0198)	(0.0120)	(0.0294)	(0.0107)	(0.0196)	(0.0113)	(0.0347)	(0.0119)
Peace years since last conflict	1.0337	−0.1104	0.1950	0.1562	0.9721	−0.1063	−0.1573	0.1953
	(0.8278)	(0.4496)	(0.4550)	(0.3274)	(1.0367)	(0.4530)	(0.4326)	(0.3263)
Spline 1 for peace years	0.0230	−0.0003	0.0092	0.0080	0.0202	−0.0002	−0.0004	0.0091
	(0.0229)	(0.0121)	(0.0137)	(0.0095)	(0.0299)	(0.0123)	(0.0145)	(0.0094)
Spline 2 for peace years	−0.0052	−0.0003	−0.0031	−0.0024	−0.0045	−0.0004	−0.0010	−0.0027
	(0.0057)	(0.0029)	(0.0036)	(0.0024)	(0.0073)	(0.0029)	(0.0039)	(0.0023)
Spline 3 for peace years	0.0006	0.0002	0.0008	0.0005	0.0005	0.0003	0.0007	0.0005
	(0.0009)	(0.0004)	(0.0008)	(0.0004)	(0.0010)	(0.0004)	(0.0008)	(0.0004)
Constant	−263.53**	−10.26	−40.61	−50.42*	−290.34**	−15.66	12.10	−45.22
	(42.96)	(23.64)	(58.49)	(20.84)	(41.44)	(22.44)	(68.21)	(23.18)
Observations	6,935	6,935	6,935	6,935	6,865	6,865	6,865	6,865

Robust standard errors in parentheses; ** p<0.01; * p<0.05.

	Ongoing war years dropped							
	3				4			
	Secession by power holders	Secession by excluded	Infighting by power holders	Rebellion by excluded	Secession by power holders	Secession by excluded	Infighting by power holders	Rebellion by excluded
Ethnic politics variables								
% excluded population	0.2338	0.3358**	−0.2010	0.7080**	0.0155	0.3481*	−0.5585	0.7665**
	(0.3181)	(0.1270)	(0.2551)	(0.1413)	(0.2716)	(0.1392)	(0.4325)	(0.1441)
No. of power-sharing partners	0.5150**	0.0141	0.3612**	0.1238	0.4470**	0.0568	0.3787**	0.1662
	(0.1694)	(0.0919)	(0.1039)	(0.1233)	(0.1536)	(0.1023)	(0.1154)	(0.1290)
Duration of imperial past	11.0713**	3.3782**	1.0747	−0.7222	11.4021**	3.3013**	1.9873	−0.8254
	(3.7842)	(1.0901)	(1.5393)	(0.8939)	(2.8605)	(1.0548)	(2.1680)	(0.9633)
Other variables								
Linguistic fractionalization	−1.1127	1.7289	−1.4383	1.4368	0.2196	1.2332	0.5250	1.1602
	(1.8391)	(0.8958)	(1.8308)	(1.2007)	(1.1450)	(0.9264)	(2.0738)	(1.2722)
GDP per capita	−0.3894*	0.0018	−0.2457	−0.1175	−0.4634	0.0068	−0.1430	−0.1228
	(0.1777)	(0.0414)	(0.2162)	(0.0680)	(0.3248)	(0.0629)	(0.1331)	(0.0661)
Population size	−0.2503	0.5710**	−0.4646*	0.1452	−0.3360	0.5571**	−0.8134**	0.1600
	(0.1991)	(0.1255)	(0.2128)	(0.1454)	(0.2411)	(0.1329)	(0.2094)	(0.1632)
Mountainous terrain					0.4004	0.0433	0.5907	−0.0245
					(0.4421)	(0.2051)	(0.3085)	(0.1852)
Political instability					−41.995**	0.5009	1.1665	0.2621
					(0.7458)	(0.6352)	(0.7871)	(0.5056)
Anocracy					1.4103	0.5680	0.3403	0.6308
					(1.2166)	(0.5431)	(0.7058)	(0.4734)
Oil production per capita					−0.2362	−0.0020	0.0114	0.0267**
					(0.4535)	(0.0369)	(0.0090)	(0.0078)
Ongoing war								
Calendar year	0.1231**	0.0103	0.0402*	0.0282**	0.1300**	0.0110	0.0184	0.0270*
	(0.0257)	(0.0131)	(0.0197)	(0.0092)	(0.0385)	(0.0132)	(0.0202)	(0.0107)
Peace years since last conflict	1.0057	−0.2603	0.3608	−0.0669	1.0015	−0.2174	0.0563	−0.0097
	(0.7114)	(0.3010)	(0.3873)	(0.2133)	(0.7972)	(0.2850)	(0.3877)	(0.2217)
Spline 1 for peace years	0.0230	−0.0046	0.0133	0.0024	0.0229	−0.0035	0.0050	0.0040
	(0.0205)	(0.0085)	(0.0126)	(0.0066)	(0.0251)	(0.0083)	(0.0140)	(0.0065)
Spline 2 for peace years	−0.0053	0.0007	−0.0040	−0.0012	−0.0053	0.0005	−0.0022	−0.0015
	(0.0051)	(0.0021)	(0.0034)	(0.0017)	(0.0063)	(0.0021)	(0.0039)	(0.0017)
Spline 3 for peace years	0.0006	0.0001	0.0010	0.0004	0.0006	0.0001	0.0008	0.0004
	(0.0008)	(0.0004)	(0.0008)	(0.0003)	(0.0009)	(0.0004)	(0.0009)	(0.0003)
Constant	−261.47**	−34.25	−82.46*	−64.01**	−275.91**	−35.69	−39.15	−62.05**
	(55.31)	(25.91)	(39.70)	(17.75)	(78.41)	(26.02)	(38.89)	(20.71)
Observations	5,977	5,977	5,977	5,977	5,923	5,923	5,923	5,923

APPENDIX TABLE 5.4B *Robustness checks for Table 5.3 (including continental dummies)*

	Ongoing war years included							
	5				6			
	Secession by power holders	Secession by excluded	Infighting by power holders	Rebellion by excluded	Secession by power holders	Secession by excluded	Infighting by power holders	Rebellion by excluded
Ethnic politics variables								
% excluded population	0.1127	0.4841**	−0.2129	0.6851**	−0.2877	0.3884**	−0.4013	0.7216**
	(0.2925)	(0.1380)	(0.2031)	(0.1322)	(0.3482)	(0.1311)	(0.2861)	(0.1340)
No. of power-sharing partners	0.4805**	0.0024	0.2584**	0.0442	0.3738**	0.0167	0.3114**	0.0611
	(0.1332)	(0.0417)	(0.0952)	(0.0865)	(0.1055)	(0.0433)	(0.1148)	(0.0905)
Duration of imperial past	12.5040**	1.0057	0.5106	−0.7772	12.6420**	1.2581	2.1259	−0.9783
	(3.6411)	(1.0961)	(2.5142)	(0.8137)	(3.4492)	(0.9156)	(3.3801)	(0.8806)
Other variables								
Linguistic fractionalization	3.7002*	2.6055**	−0.3659	1.2100	7.3669**	2.3896**	0.7300	0.9469
	(1.8334)	(0.8758)	(3.7189)	(1.0549)	(2.0976)	(0.8023)	(3.1086)	(1.0121)
GDP per capita	−0.8568	−0.1110*	−0.2204	−0.0869	−0.7278	−0.1111*	−0.0856	−0.0967
	(0.4851)	(0.0547)	(0.1728)	(0.0560)	(0.3847)	(0.0567)	(0.1320)	(0.0560)
Population size	−0.4322*	0.4393**	−0.3438	0.1625	−0.5158*	0.4381**	−0.5589*	0.1999
	(0.2060)	(0.1445)	(0.2239)	(0.1241)	(0.2372)	(0.1447)	(0.2663)	(0.1400)
Mountainous terrain					0.1717	0.2777	0.6326	−0.0718
					(0.3963)	(0.2488)	(0.3249)	(0.1910)
Political instability					−43.93	0.4097	1.0487	0.0582
					(0.00)	(0.5102)	(0.7507)	(0.4514)
Anocracy					1.2268	0.3601	−0.1140	0.6633
					(1.0315)	(0.3857)	(0.7760)	(0.3527)
Oil production per capita					−0.3634	0.0278*	0.0069	0.0120
					(0.5075)	(0.0115)	(0.0214)	(0.0173)
Ongoing war	2.7449	−0.0805	−0.4461	−0.1394	2.0217	−0.0490	−0.5512	−0.1136
	(2.4303)	(1.0764)	(1.5866)	(0.8912)	(2.8838)	(1.0788)	(1.9959)	(0.9248)
Latin America	−21.652	−34.084**	17.692	17.450	−33.252	−46.343	18.954	17.182
	(50.486)	(0.781)	(74.769)	(24.927)	(0.000)	(0.000)	(107.074)	(26.035)
Eastern Europe	8.8132	−0.1213	−15.8749	−15.4252	8.5695	−0.3817	−26.0411	−27.5109
	(50.9486)	(0.9965)	(75.9011)	(24.9522)	(48.6357)	(0.9572)	(0.0000)	(0.0000)
North Africa and Middle East	10.4999	−1.7024	18.7770	18.3964	11.3842	−1.9644*	18.5846	18.2280
	(50.3101)	(0.9105)	(75.3341)	(24.8718)	(47.7777)	(0.8927)	(107.7832)	(26.0022)
Sub-Saharan Africa	4.7977	−2.2204	17.8491	18.1472	3.8840	−2.1174	19.2555	17.9200
	(51.3631)	(1.2810)	(76.5624)	(24.9761)	(48.4543)	(1.2944)	(108.8119)	(26.0597)
Asia	8.3008	−1.0384	17.5022	18.2555	8.4783	−1.3495	17.8774	18.1197
	(51.0437)	(1.0737)	(76.4715)	(24.6985)	(48.4585)	(1.1094)	(108.8568)	(25.8820)
Observations	6,935	6,935	6,935	6,935	6,865	6,865	6,865	6,865

Robust standard errors in parentheses; ** p<0.01; * p<0.05.

	Ongoing war years dropped							
	7				8			
	Secession by power holders	Secession by excluded	Infighting by power holders	Rebellion by excluded	Secession by power holders	Secession by excluded	Infighting by power holders	Rebellion by excluded
Ethnic politics variables								
% excluded population	0.0210	0.4238*	−0.2230	0.6378**	−0.1791	0.4448*	−0.5168	0.6887**
	(0.2790)	(0.1654)	(0.2264)	(0.1123)	(0.3294)	(0.1828)	(0.3715)	(0.1199)
No. of power-sharing partners	0.4407**	−0.0262	0.2858**	0.1011	0.4144**	0.0315	0.3734*	0.1386
	(0.1320)	(0.0884)	(0.1078)	(0.1087)	(0.1528)	(0.1093)	(0.1551)	(0.1218)
Duration of imperial past	12.1933**	3.9814**	1.5290	−0.7871	12.3838**	3.8943**	4.2394	−0.9237
	(3.9701)	(1.2982)	(2.3417)	(1.0587)	(4.5130)	(1.3505)	(3.1811)	(1.1794)
Other variables								
Linguistic fractionalization	2.9526	3.7990**	−0.2925	1.3513	6.1424**	3.0331*	1.1404	1.0640
	(1.9239)	(0.9998)	(4.9072)	(1.4891)	(2.2755)	(1.2056)	(4.4380)	(1.3694)
GDP per capita	−0.5509	−0.1599*	−0.1945	−0.0458	−0.5672	−0.1674*	−0.0561	−0.0251
	(0.2972)	(0.0791)	(0.1534)	(0.0442)	(0.3749)	(0.0738)	(0.1281)	(0.0816)
Population size	−0.4816*	0.6003**	−0.2883	0.1580	−0.7179*	0.6235**	−0.5455	0.1414
	(0.2412)	(0.1069)	(0.3064)	(0.1351)	(0.3362)	(0.1165)	(0.4788)	(0.1618)
Mountainous terrain					0.1230	−0.0510	0.8028	0.0476
					(0.5026)	(0.2116)	(0.4132)	(0.2432)
Political instability					−33.49**	0.5719	1.2708	0.3235
					(0.91)	(0.6630)	(0.7830)	(0.5292)
Anocracy					1.4137	0.6490	0.1659	0.6257
					(1.2668)	(0.5951)	(0.9058)	(0.4486)
Oil production per capita					−0.5442	0.0316*	0.0107	−0.0107
					(0.5401)	(0.0124)	(0.0271)	(0.0429)
Ongoing war								
Latin America	−29.006	−43.464**	18.009	18.423	−20.485	−34.754**	20.655	18.293
	(50.056)	(0.986)	(64.332)	(20.336)	(105.426)	(0.932)	(83.582)	(22.971)
Eastern Europe	11.9135	−2.2506	−25.3591	−24.1080	10.3555	−2.4484*	−14.6393	−15.0571
	(50.2593)	(1.2322)	(65.5984)	(20.3976)	(105.0863)	(1.2305)	(83.6162)	(23.1771)
North Africa and Middle East	14.0720	−2.3769*	18.7070	19.3434	13.4881	−2.7130*	19.3258	19.4017
	(49.8387)	(1.2008)	(64.5442)	(20.2838)	(104.0344)	(1.1830)	(82.7956)	(22.9627)
Sub-Saharan Africa	9.1365	−4.3191**	17.6996	19.0024	6.3236	−4.4963**	19.9123	19.1169
	(50.4536)	(1.5204)	(66.6451)	(20.3727)	(105.0645)	(1.5228)	(85.0442)	(22.9483)
Asia	12.2908	−3.4391*	−25.1013	18.7419	10.9633	−3.8060*	−15.0224	18.7529
	(50.3345)	(1.4613)	(65.5614)	(20.1923)	(105.4128)	(1.5101)	(84.0301)	(22.9813)
Observations	5,977	5,977	5,977	5,977	5,923	5,923	5,923	5,923

Chapter 6

APPENDIX TABLE 6.1 *Federalism and secessionist armed conflict*

Model	1	2	3	4	5	6
Federal systems, 1946–2002, GT	0.5888 (0.698)					
Federal systems, 1946–1994, Polity III		−0.0131 (0.412)				
Federal or federated systems, 1972–2005, IAEP			0.6773 (0.352)			
Auton. provincial governments, 1972–2005, IAEP				−0.2012 (0.418)		
Locally elected provincial governors, 1975–2005, WB					−0.0037** (0.001)	
Autonomous regions, 1975–2005, WB						−0.0015 (0.001)
Number of observations	3,366	5,123	4,502	4,408	2,914	3,987

Notes: Controls for GDP, population size, linguistic fractionalization, mountainous terrain, political instability, anocracy, oil production, ongoing war, calendar year, cubic splines, and constant not shown; robust standard errors in parentheses; *significant at 5%; **significant at 1%.

APPENDIX TABLE 6.2 *Number of power-sharing partners and political institutions (negative binomial regression models)*

	Coefficient	(Std. error)
Democracy, lagged, Polity IV	0.0996	(0.171)
Presidential systems, 1972–2005, IAEP	−0.1296	(0.124)
Fully presidential systems, 1972–2005, WB	−0.1211	(0.127)
Fully presidential systems, 1946–2002, GT	−0.3289	(0.201)
Fully parliamentary systems, 1946–2002, GT	−0.0631	(0.209)
Parliamentary systems, 1972–2005, IAEP	0.2541	(0.154)
Fully parliamentary systems, 1975–2005, WB	0.0420	(0.186)
Proportional systems, 1975–2005, WB	0.0001	(0.000)
Proportional systems, 1972–2005, IAEP	−0.0863	(0.130)
Fully proportional systems, 1946–2002, GT	−0.3627	(0.192)
Semi-federal systems, 1946–2002, GT	0.0039	(0.158)
Fully federal systems, 1946–2002, GT	0.4731	(0.243)

APPENDIX TABLE 6.2 (cont.)

Federal or federated systems, 1972–2005, IAEP												0.0377 (0.141)				
Federal systems, 1972–2005, IAEP													0.0192 (0.140)			
Federal systems, 1946–1994, Polity III														0.4542* (0.225)		
Auton. chosen provincial gov., 1972–2005, IAEP															−0.0289 (0.128)	
Locally elected governors of provinces, 1975–2005, WB																0.0005 (0.000)
Number of observations	6,956	4,049	4,211	3,396	4,049	4,211	4,080	3,752	3,399	3,396	3,396	4,530	4,530	5,174	4,443	2,945

Notes: Controls for GDP, population size, linguistic fractionalization, calendar year, cubic splines, and constant not shown; robust standard errors in parentheses; * significant at 5%; ** significant at 1%.

APPENDIX BIBLIOGRAPHY (EXCLUDING THE LITERACY DATA
SOURCES OF APPENDIX 3.3)

Adriance, Thomas J. 1987. *The Last Gaiter Button: A Study of the Mobilization and Concentration of the French Army in the War of 1870*. New York: Greenwood Press.

Akkuş, Yakup. 2008. *Vilayet Bütçeleri Çerçevesinde Tanzimat Sonrası Osmanlı Taşra Maliyesi (1860–1913)*. Dissertation. Istanbul, Istanbul University.

Akmese, Handan Nezir. 2005. *The Birth of Modern Turkey: The Ottoman Military and the March to World War I.* London: Tauris.

Babuscio, Jack and Richard Minta Dunn. 1984. *European Political Facts, 1648–1789*. New York: Facts on File Publications.

Barkey, Karen. 1991. "Rebellious alliances: the state and peasant unrest in early seventeenth-century France and the Ottoman empire," *American Sociological Review* 56: 699–715.

2008. *Empire of Difference: The Ottomans in Comparative Perspective*. Cambridge University Press.

Barnes, John Robert. 1987. *An Introduction to Religious Foundations in the Ottoman Empire*. Leiden: Brill.

Beik, William. 1985. *Absolutism and Society in Seventeenth-Century France. State Power and Provincial Aristocracy in Languedoc*. Cambridge University Press.

Benoit, Kenneth and Michael Laver. 2006. *Party Politics in Modern Democracies*. New York: Routledge.

Blaufarb, Rafe. 2002. *The French Army, 1750–1820: Careers, Talent, Merit*. Manchester University Press.

Bowen, John R. 1996. "The myth of global ethnic conflict," *Journal of Democracy* 7 (4): 3–14.

Brubaker, Rogers. 2004. "Ethnicity without groups," in Andreas Wimmer, Donald Horowitz, Richard Goldstone, Ulrike Joras, and Conrad Schetter, eds., *Facing Ethnic Conflicts: Toward a New Realism*. Lanham: Rowman & Littlefield. 34–52.

Buhaug, Halvard, Lars-Erik Cederman, and Jan Ketil Rød. 2008. "Disaggregating ethnic conflict: a dyadic model of exclusion theory," *International Organization* 62: 531–551.

Butterworth, Robert Lyle. 1976. *Managing Interstate Conflict, 1945–1974*. Pittsburg: University Center for International Studies.

Campolongo, Francesca, Jessica Cariboni, and Andrea Saltelli. 2007. "An effective screening design for sensitivity analysis of large models," *Environmental Modelling and Software* 22: 1509–1518.

Cederman, Lars-Erik and Luc Girardin. 2007. "Beyond fractionalization: mapping ethnicity onto nationalist insurgencies," *American Political Science Review* 101: 173–185.

Chapman, Brian. 1955. *The Prefects and Provincial France*. London: George Allen & Unwin Ltd.

Chevalier, Bernard. 1982. *Les bonnes villes de France XIVe au XVIe*. Paris: Aubier Montaigne.

Clodfelter, Michael. 2002. *Warfare and Armed Conflicts: A Statistical Reference to Casualty and Other Figures, 1500–2000*. Jefferson: McFarland.

Contamine, Philippe. 1992. *Histoire militaire de la France. Des origins à 1715*. Paris: PUF.

Cosgel, Metin M. and Thomas J. Miceli. 2005. "Risk, transaction costs, and tax assignment: government finance in the Ottoman empire," *The Journal of Economic History* 65 (3): 806–821.

Demirel, Ömer. 2000. *Osmanli Vakif-Şehir İliskisine Bir Örnek: Sivas Şehir Hayatında Vakiflarin Rolü.* Ankara: Türk Tarih Kurumu Basimevi.

Duby, Georges. 1998 [1961]. *Rural Economy and Country Life in the Medieval West.* Philadelphia: University of Pennsylvania Press.

Eisenstadt, Samuel N. 1963. *The Political Systems of Empires.* New York: Free Press.

Emecen, Feridun. 1989. *XVI. Asırda Manisa Kazâsi.* Ankara: Türk Tarih Kurumu Basimevi.

Erder, Leila T. and Suraiya Faroqhi. 1980. "The development of the Anatolian urban network during the sixteenth century," *Journal of the Economic and Social History of the Orient* 23 (3): 265–303.

Erickson, Edward. 2000. *Ordered to Die: A History of the Ottoman Army in the First World War.* Westport: Greenwood.

European State Finance Database. n.d. "Seventeenth-century French revenues and expenditures."

Fairchilds, Cissie C. 1976. *Poverty and Charity in Aix-en-Provence, 1640–1789.* Baltimore and London: The Johns Hopkins University Press.

Faroqhi, Suraiya. 1997. "Part II crisis and change, 1590–1699," in Halil İnalcik and Donald Quaetaert, eds., *An Economic and Social History of the Ottoman Empire, Volume 2: 1600–1914.* Cambridge University Press. 411–636.

Fawtier, Robert. 1930. *Comptes du trésor.* Paris: Imprimerie Nationale.

Fearon, James D. and David D. Laitin. 2003. "Ethnicity, insurgency, and civil war," *American Political Science Review* 97 (1): 1–16.

Fearon, James D., Kimuli Kasara, and David D. Laitin. 2007. "Ethnic minority rule and civil war onset," *American Political Science Review* 101 (1): 187–193.

Gellner, Ernest. 1983. *Nations and Nationalism.* Ithaca: Cornell University Press.

Gerber, Haim. 1983. "The Waqf institution in early Ottoman Erdine," *Asian and African Studies* 17: 29–45.

Gleditsch, Kristian Skrede. 2004. "A revised list of wars between and within independent states, 1816–2002," *International Interactions* 30 (3): 231–262.

Gleditsch, Nils Petter, Peter Wallensteen, Mikael Erikson, Margareta Sollenberg, and Håvard Strand. 2002. "Armed conflict 1946–2001: a new dataset," *Journal of Peace Research* 39 (5): 615–637.

Goldsmith, Lewis. 1832. *Statistics of France.* London: Gale, Cengage Learning.

Hale, William M. 1994. *Turkish Politics and the Military.* London: Routledge.

Hardt, Michael and Antonio Negri. 2000. *Empire.* Cambridge, MA: Harvard University Press.

Hechter, Michael. 2000. *Containing Nationalism.* Oxford University Press.

Henneman, John Bell. 1971. *Royal Taxation in Fourteenth Century France: The Development of War Financing 1322–1356.* Princeton University Press.

Hickey, Daniel. 1997. *Local Hospitals in Ancien Régime France: Rationalization, Resistance, Renewal 1530–1789.* Montreal and Kingston: McGill-Queen's University Press.

Hippeau, M.C. 1863. *Le gouvernement de Normandie au XVIIe et au XVIIIe siècle.* Caen: Goussiaume de la Porte.

Hoexter, Miriam. 1998. *Endowments, Rulers and Community: Waqf al-Haramayn in Ottoman Algiers.* Leiden and Boston: Brill.

Howe, Stephen. 2002. *Empire: A Very Short Introduction.* Oxford University Press.

Imbert, Jean and Michel Mollat. 1982. *Histoire des hôpitaux en France.* Toulouse: Privat.

İnalcik, Halil. 1973. *The Ottoman Empire: The Classical Age, 1300–1600.* London: Weidenfeld & Nicolson.

1980. "Military and fiscal transformation in the Ottoman empire, 1600–1700," *Archivum Ottomanicum* 6: 283–337.

1994. *An Economic and Social History of the Ottoman Empire, 1300–1914.* Cambridge University Press.

Jones, Colin. 1982. *Charity and Bienfaisance: The Treatment of the Poor in the Montpellier Region, 1740–1815.* Cambridge University Press.

Karpat, Kemal H. 1985. *Ottoman Population, 1830–1914: Demographic and Social Characteristics.* Madison: University of Wisconsin Press.

Kilia, S. 2000. "Tanzimat sonrasi osmanli vilayet bütçeleri," *Tarih Arastirmalari Dergisi* 20 (3): 196–206.

Kinross, Patrick Balfour. 1977. *The Ottoman Centuries: The Rise and Fall of the Turkish Empire.* New York: Morrow.

Kiser, Edgar and April Linton. 2001. "Determinants of the growth of the state: war and taxation in early modern France and England," *Social Forces* 80 (2): 411–448.

2002. "The hinges of history: state-making and revolt in early modern France," *American Sociological Review* 67: 889–910.

Kwass, Michael. 2000. *Privilege and the Politics of Taxation in Eighteenth-Century France.* Cambidge University Press.

Lachmann, Richard. 1989. "Elite conflict and state formation in 16th- and 17th-century England and France," *American Sociological Review* 54: 141–162.

Le Blévec, Daniel. 2000. *La part du pauvre: L'assistance dans les pays du bas-Rhône du XIIe siècle. Volumes 1 and 2.* Rome: École française de Rome.

Le Comte de Franqueville, M. 1875. "Local government in France," in J.W. Probyn, ed., *Local Government and Taxation.* New York and London: Cassell, Petter, and Galpin. 283–308.

Leacock, Stephen. 1906. *Elements of Political Science.* New York: Houghton Mifflin.

Leeuwen, Richard van. 1999. *Waqfs and Urban Structues: The Case of Ottoman Damascus.* Leiden and Boston: Brill.

Lewis, Bernard. 1937. "The Islamic guilds," *The Economic History Review* 8 (1): 20–37.

Licklider, Roy. 1995. "The consequences of negotiated settlements in civil wars, 1945–1993," *American Political Science Review* 89 (3): 681–690.

Lynn, John Albert. 1997. *Giant of the Grand Siècle: The French Army, 1610–1715.* Cambridge University Press.

Maddison, Angus. 2003. *The World Economy: Historical Statistics.* Paris: OECD.

Maillard, Jacques. 2000. "Les resources de la ville d'Angers au XVIIIe siécle," in Françoise Bayard, ed., *Les finances en province sous l'ancien Régime: Journée d'études tenue à Bercy le 3 décembre 1998.* Paris: Ministére de l'économie, des finances et de l'industrie, Comité pour l'histoire économique et financiére de la France. 167–177.

Mann, Michael. 1993. *The Sources of Social Power, Vol. 2: The Rise of Classes and Nation States, 1760–1914.* Cambridge: Cambridge University Press.

2006. *American Empire: Past and Present.* Paper given at the Comparative Social Analysis Workshop, Department of Sociology, UCLA.

Matthews, George T. 1958. *The Royal General Farms in Eighteenth-Century France.* New York: Columbia University Press.

McCloy, Shelby T. 1946. *Government Assistance in Eighteenth-Century France.* Durham, NC: Duke University Press.

McHugh, Tim. 2007. *Hospital Politics in Seventeenth-Century France: The Crown, Urban Elites, and the Poor.* Aldershot: Ashgate.

Miall, Hugh. 1992. *The Peacemakers: Peaceful Settlement of Disputes since 1945.* New York: St. Martin's Press.

Min, Brian, Lars-Erik Cederman, and Andreas Wimmer. 2010. *Ethnic Exclusion, Economic Growth, and Civil War.* Manuscript, University of California Los Angeles.

Ministry of Commerce and Industry. 1968 [1886]. *Annuaire statistique de la France: neuvième année, 1886.* Nendeln, Liechtenstein: Kraus Reprint Ltd. (originally published in Paris by Imprimerie Nationale).

Ministry of Public Instruction. 1889. *Les recettes et les dépenses de la république Française de 1870 a 1889. Facsimile No. 96.* Paris: Imprimerie Alcide Picard et Kaan.

Morris, Max D. 1991. "Factorial sampling plans for preliminary computational experiments," *Technometrics* 33: 161–174.

Mousnier, Roland. 1970. *Peasant Uprisings in Seventeenth-Century France, Russia, and China.* New York: Harper Torchbooks.

Müller, Hans-Peter. 1999. *Atlas vorkolonialer Gesellschaften. Sozialstrukturen und kulturelles Erbe der Staaten Afrikas, Asiens und Melanesiens. Ein ethnologisches Kartenwerk für 95 Länder mit Texten, Datenbanken und Dokumentationen auf CD-ROM.* Berlin: Reimer.

Necker, Jacques. 1781. *State of the Finances of France, laid before the King, by Mr. Necker, Director-General of the finances, in the month of January, 1781.* London: G. Kearsley and Associates.

Oliver, Pamela E. 1993. "Formal models of collective action," *Annual Review of Sociology* 19: 271–300.

Oliver, Pamela E. and Daniel J. Myers. 2002. "Formal models in the study of social movements," in Bert Klandermans and Suzanne Staggenborg, eds., *Methods of Research in Social Movements.* Minneapolis: University of Minnesota Press. 32–61.

O'Meara, John J. 1894. *Municipal Taxation at Home and Abroad: Local Government – Indebtedness and Valuation.* London, Paris, and Melbourne: Cassell and Company, Limited.

Öztürk, Nazif. 1995. *Türk Yenilesme Tarihi Çerçevesinde Vakif Müessesesi.* Ankara: Türkiye Diyanet Vakfi.

Pouchenot, Marius. 1910. *Le budget communal de Besançon au début du XVIIIe siècle.* Paris: Librairie Honoré Champion.

Quaetaert, Donald. 2001. "Labor history in the Ottoman Middle East, 1700–1922," *International Labor and Working-Class History* 60: 93–109.

Ramsey, Matthew. 1988. *Professional and Popular Medicine in France, 1770–1830: The Social World of Medical Practice.* Cambridge and New York: Cambridge University Press.

Rey, Maurice. 1965. *Le domaine du roi et les finances extraordinaires sous Charles VI, 1388–1413.* Paris: S.E.V.P.E.N.

Richardson, Lewis Frey. 1960. *Statistics of Deadly Quarrels.* Quincy Wright and C.C. Lienau, eds. Pittsburgh: Boxwood Press.

Rigaudière, Albert. 1993. *Gouverner la ville au Moyen Age.* Paris: Anthropos.

Rogers, Clifford J. 1995. *The Military Revolution Debate.* Boulder: Westview Press.

Rowlands, Guy. 1999. "Louis XIV, aristocratic power and the elite units of the French army," *French History* 13 (3): 303–331.

Sahillioğlu, Halil. 1999. *Studies on Ottoman Economic and Social History.* Istanbul: Research Centre for Islamic History, Art and Culture.

Saliba, Najib E. 1978. "The achievements of Midhat Pasha as governor of the province of Syria, 1878–1880," *International Journal of Middle East Studies* 9 (3): 307–323.

Saltelli, Andrea, Stefano Tarantola, Francesca Campolongo, and Marco Ratto. 2004. *Sensitivity Analysis in Practice: A Guide to Assessing Scientific Models.* New York: Wiley.

Saltelli, Andrea, Marco Ratto, Stefano Tarantola, and Francesca Campolongo. 2006. "Sensitivity analysis practices: strategies for model-based inference," *Reliability Engineering and System Safety* 91: 1109–1125.

Saltelli, Andrea, Marco Ratto, Terry Andres, Francesca Campolongo, Jessica Cariboni, Debora Gatelli, Michaela Saisana, and Stefano Tarantola. 2008. *Global Sensitivity Analysis: The Primer.* New York: Wiley.

Sambanis, Nicholas. 2004. "What is civil war? Conceptual and empirical complexities of an operational definition," *Journal of Conflict Resolution* 48 (6): 814–858.

2009. *What is an Ethnic War? Organization and Interests in Insurgencies.* New Haven: Department of Political Science, Yale University.

Scott, James C. 1976. *The Moral Economy of the Peasant: Rebellion and Subsistence in South-East Asia.* New Haven: Yale University Press.

Scott, John. 1871. "On local taxation," *Journal of the Statistical Society of London* 34 (3): 281–333.

Serman, William. 1979. *Les origines des officiers Francais, 1848–1870.* Paris: Publications de la Sorbonne.

Shaw, Stanford J. 1958. *The Financial and Administrative Organization and Development of Ottoman Egypt 1517–1798.* Princeton University Press.

1975. "The nineteenth-century Ottoman tax reforms and revenue systems," *International Journal of Middle East Studies* 6 (4): 421–459.

1978. "Ottoman expenditures and budgets in the late nineteenth and early twentieth centuries," *International Journal of Middle East Studies* 9: 373–378.

Swann, Julian. 2003. *Provincial Power and Absolute Monarchy: The Estates General of Burgundy, 1661–1790.* Cambridge University Press.

Szyliowicz, Joseph S. 1971. "Elite recruitment in Turkey: the role of the Mulkiye," *World Politics* 23 (3): 371–398.

Tilly, Charles. 1975. "Western state-making and theories of political transformation," in Charles Tilly, *The Formation of National States in Western Europe.* Princeton University Press. 601–638.

van Bruinessen, Martin. 1999. *Kurds, States, and Tribes.* Paper given at the Tribes and Powers in the Middle East Conference, London, January 23–24.

Wimmer, Andreas. 2008. "The making and unmaking of ethnic boundaries. A multi-level process theory," *American Journal of Sociology* 113 (4): 970–1022.

World Military and Social Expenditures. 1987. *World Military and Social Expenditures, vol. 11.* Leesburg: WMSE Publications.

Yedıyıldiz, B. 1975. *L'institution du vaqf au XVIIIe siècle en Turquie; étude socio-historique.* Dissertation. Sorbonne, University of Paris.

Yüksel, Hasan. 1998. *Osmanli Sosyal Ve Ekonomik Hayatında Vakıflarin Rolü (1585–1683).* Sivas: Dilek Matbaasi.

Zartman, William. 2004. "Sources and settlements of ethnic conflicts," in Andreas
    Wimmer, Donald Horowitz, Richard Goldstone, Ulrike Joras, and Conrad Schetter,
    eds., *Facing Ethnic Conflicts: Toward a New Realism*. Lanham: Rowman & Littlefield.
    141–159.
Zürcher, Eric-Jan. 1998. "The Ottoman conscription system in theory and practice, 1844–
    1918," *International Review of Social History* 43 (3): 437–449.

Bibliography

Aas Rustad, Siri Camilla, Halvard Buhaug, Ashild Falch, and Scott Gates. 2010. "All conflict is local: modeling sub-national variation in civil conflict risk," *Conflict Management and Peace Science* 28 (1): 15–40.

Abbott, Andrew. 1998. "Transcending general linear reality," *Sociological Theory* 6: 169–186.

Akar, Şevket K. 1999. "Osmanlı maliyesinde bütçe uygulaması," in G. Eren, ed., *Osmanlı, Vol. 3.* Ankara: Yeni Türkiye Yayınları. 565–570.

Akerlof, George A. and Rachel E. Kranton. 2000. "Economics and identity," *The Quarterly Journal of Economics* 115 (3): 715–753.

Anderson, Benedict. 1991. *Imagined Communities: Reflections on the Origin and Spread of Nationalism.* London: Verso.

Anonymous. 1989. "Ethnicity and pseudo-ethnicity in the Ciskei," in Leroy Vail, ed., *The Creation of Tribalism in Southern Africa.* London: James Currey. 395–413.

Axelrod, Robert. 1997. "Promoting norms: an evolutionary approach to norms," in Robert Axelrod, *The Complexity of Co-operation: Agent-Based Models of Competition and Collaboration.* Princeton University Press. 44–68.

Ayoob, Mohammed. 2007. "State making, state-breaking, and state failure," in Chester A. Crocker, Fen Osler Hampson, and Pamela Aall, eds., *Leashing the Dogs of War. Conflict Management in a Divided World.* Washington, DC: USIP Press. 95–114.

Badie, Bertrand. 2000. *The Imported State: The Westernization of the Political Order.* Stanford University Press.

Bardon, Jonathan. 2001. *A History of Ulster.* London: Blackstaff.

Barkey, Karen. 1991. "Rebellious alliances: the state and peasant unrest in early seventeenth-century France and the Ottoman empire," *American Sociological Review* 56: 699–715.

2008. *Empire of Difference: The Ottomans in Comparative Perspective.* Cambridge University Press.

Barkey, Karen and Mark von Hagen. 1997. *After Empire: Multiethnic Societies and Nation-Building. The Soviet Union and the Russian, Ottoman, and Habsburg Empires.* Colorado: Westview.

Barrett, David. 2001. *World Christian Encyclopedia: A Comparative Study of Churches and Religions in the Modern World, 1900–2000.* Oxford University Press.

Barth, Fredrik. 1969. "Introduction," in Frederik Barth, ed., *Ethnic Groups and Boundaries: The Social Organization of Culture Difference.* London: Allen & Unwin. 1–38.

Bates, Robert. 1974. "Ethnic competition and modernization in contemporary Africa," *Comparative Political Studies* 6: 457–484.

Bates, Robert H., Avner Greif, Margaret Levi, Jean-Laurent Rosenthal, and Barry Weingast. 1998. *Analytical Narratives.* Princeton University Press.

  2000. "The analytical narrative project," *American Political Science Review* 94 (3): 696–702.

Beck, Nathaniel, Jonathan N. Katz, and Richard Tucker. 1998. "Taking time seriously: time-series-cross-section analysis with a binary dependent variable," *Journal of Political Science* 42 (4): 1260–1288.

Beck, Ulrich and Ciaran Cronin. 2006. *Cosmopolitan Vision.* Cambridge: Polity Press.

Beissinger, Mark. 2002. *Nationalist Mobilization and the Collapse of the Soviet State.* Cambridge University Press.

Bendix, Reinhard. 1964. *Nation-building and Citizenship: Studies in Our Changing Social Order.* New York: John Wiley.

Bengio, Ofra. 2004. "The new Iraq: challenges for state building," in Christian-Peter Henelt, Giacomo Luciani, and Felix Neugart, eds., *Regime Change in Iraq: The Transatlantic and Regional Dimensions.* Florence: European University Institute. 45–63.

Bengtsson, Tommy, Cameron Campbell, and James Lee. 2004. *Life Under Pressure: Mortality and Living Standards in Europe and Asia, 1700–1900.* Cambridge, MA: MIT Press.

Bennett, D. Scott and Allan C. Stam. 2004. *The Behavioral Origins of War.* Ann Arbor: University of Michigan Press.

Ben-Yehuda, Hemda and Meirav Mishali-Ram. 2006. "Ethnic actors and international crisis: theory and findings, 1918–2001," *International Interactions* 32 (1): 49–78.

Bermeo, Nancy. 2002. "A new look at federalism. The import of institutions," *Journal of Democracy* 13 (2): 96–110.

Bhaskar, Roy. 1979. *A Realist Theory of Science.* Brighton: Harvester.

Binningsbo, Helga Malmin. 2006. *Power-sharing and Postconflict Peace Periods.* Paper given at Power-sharing and Democratic Governance in Divided Societies, Oslo, August 21.

Blalock, Hubert M. 1982. *Race and Ethnic Relations.* Englewood Cliffs: Prentice-Hall.

Blau, Peter. 1986 [1964]. *Exchange and Power in Social Life.* New Brunswick: Transactions.

Boix, Charles. 2003. *Democracy and Redistribution.* Cambridge University Press.

  2011. "Democracy, development, and the international system," *American Political Science Review* 105 (4): 809–828.

Boix, Charles and Susan C. Stokes. 2003. "Endogenous democratization," *World Politics* 55 (4): 517–549.

Bonacich, Edna. 1974. "A theory of ethnic antagonism: the split labor market," *American Sociological Review* 37: 547–559.

Bonine, Michael E. 1998. "The introduction of railroads in the Eastern Mediterranean: economic and social impacts," in Thomas Philipp and Brigit Schaebler, eds., *The Syrian Land: Processes of Integration and Fragmentation.* Stuttgart: Franz Steiner. 53–78.

Brass, Paul. 1979. "Elite groups, symbol manipulation and ethnic identity among the Muslims of South Asia," in David Taylor and Malcolm Yapp, eds., *Political Identity in South Asia.* London: Curzon Press. 35–77.

Bratton, Michael and Nicolas van de Walle. 1994. "Neopatrimonial regimes and political transitions in Africa," *World Politics* 46: 453–489.

Breuilly, John. 2005. "Dating the nation: how old is an old nation?" in Atsuko Ichijo and Gordana Uzelac, eds., *When is a Nation? Towards an Understanding of Theories of Nationalism.* London: Routledge. 15–39.

Brinton, Mary C. and Victor Nee. 2001. *The New Institutionalism in Sociology.* Stanford University Press.

Brooks, Stephen. 2005. *Producing Security: Multinational Corporations, Globalization, and the Changing Calculus of Conflict.* Princeton University Press.

Brubaker, Rogers. 1992. *Citizenship and Nationhood in France and Germany.* Cambridge, MA: Harvard University Press.

   1996. *Nationalism Reframed: Nationhood and the National Question in the New Europe.* Cambridge University Press.

   2004. "Ethnicity without groups," in Andreas Wimmer, Donald Horowitz, Richard Goldstone, Ulrike Joras, and Conrad Schetter, eds., *Facing Ethnic Conflicts: Toward a New Realism.* Lanham: Rowman & Littlefield. 34–52.

Bueno de Mesquita, Bruce, James D. Morrow, Randolph M. Siverson, and Alastair Smith. 1999. "An institutional explanation of the democratic peace," *American Political Science Review* 93 (4): 791–807.

Buhaug, Halvard. 2006. "Relative capability and rebel objective in civil war," *Journal of Peace Research* 43 (6): 691–708.

Buhaug, Halvard and Jan Ketil Rød. 2005. *Local Determinants of African Civil Wars, 1970–2001.* Paper given at Disaggregating the Study of Civil War and Transnational Violence, San Diego: University of California Institute of Global Conflict and Cooperation. March 7–8.

Buhaug, Halvard, Lars-Erik Cederman, and Jan Ketil Rød. 2008. "Disaggregating ethnic conflict: a dyadic model of exclusion theory," *International Organization* 62: 531–551.

Burbank, Jane and Frederick Cooper. 2010. *Empires in World History: Power and the Politics of Difference.* Princeton University Press.

Burg, Steven L. and Paul S. Shoup. 1999. *The War in Bosnia-Herzegovina: Ethnic Conflict and International Intervention.* New York: Sharpe.

Calhoun, Craig. 2007. *Nations Matter: Culture, History, and the Cosmopolitan Dream.* London: Routledge.

Campolongo, Francesca, Jessica Cariboni, and Andrea Saltelli. 2007. "An effective screening design for sensitivity analysis of large models," *Environmental Modelling and Software* 22: 1509–1518.

Cardoso, Eliana and Ann Helwege. 1991. "Populism, profligacy, and redistribution," in Rudiger Dornbusch and Sebastian Edwards, eds., *The Macroeconomics of Populism in Latin America.* University of Chicago Press. 45–74.

Carment, David and Patrick James. 1995. "Internal constraints and interstate ethnic conflict," *Journal of Conflict Resolution* 39 (1): 82–109.

Carpenter, Daniel. 2000. "What is the marginal value of Analytical Narratives?" *Social Science History* 24 (4): 655–667.

Cederman, Lars-Erik. 1996. *Emergent Actors in World Politics: How States and Nations Develop and Dissolve.* Princeton University Press.

   2002. "Endogenizing geopolitical boundaries with agent-based modeling," *Proceedings of the National Academy of Sciences of the United States of America* 99: 7296–7303.

Cederman, Lars-Erik and Luc Girardin. 2007. "Beyond fractionalization: mapping ethnicity onto nationalist insurgencies," *American Political Science Review* 101: 173–185.

Cederman, Lars-Erik, Luc Girardin, and Kristian Skrede Gleditsch. 2009. "Ethnonationalist triads. Assessing the influence of kin groups on civil wars," *World Politics* 61 (3): 403–437.

Cederman, Lars-Erik, Simon Hug, and Lutz Krebs. 2010a. "Democratization and civil war: empirical evidence," *Journal of Peace Research* 47 (4): 377–394.

Cederman, Lars-Erik, Andreas Wimmer, and Brian Min. 2010b. "Why do ethnic groups rebel? New data and analysis," *World Politics* 62 (1): 87–119.

Cederman, Lars-Erik, Nils B. Weidmann, and Kristian Skrede Gleditsch. 2011. "Horizontal inequalities and ethnonationalist civil war: a global comparison," *American Political Science Review* 105 (3): 478–495.

Cem Behar, Osmanlı. 1996. *İmparatorluğu'nun ve Türkiye'nin Nüfusu, 1500–1927*. Ankara: DİE.

Centeno, Miguel Angel. 2003. *Blood and Debt: War and the Nation-State in Latin America*. Pittsburg: Pennsylvania State University Press.

Central Statistical Administration, Council of Ministers USSR. 1957. *USSR Transport and Communication: A Statistical Compilation*. Moscow: State Statistical Publishing House.

Chafer, Tony. 2002. *The End of Empire in French West Africa: France's Successful Decolonization?* Oxford: Berg.

Chai, Sun-Ki. 2005. "Predicting ethnic boundaries," *European Sociological Review* 21 (4): 375–391.

Chandra, Kanchan. 2004. *Why Ethnic Parties Succeed: Patronage and Ethnic Head Counts in India*. Cambridge University Press.

   Forthcoming. *Constructivist Theories of Ethnic Politics*. Oxford University Press.

Chandra, Kanchan and Cilanne Boulet. 2005. *Ethnic Cleavage Structures, Permanent Exclusion and Democratic Stability*. Paper given at the Alien Rule and its Discontents Conference, University of Washington.

Chandra, Kanchan and Steven Wilkinson. 2008. "Measuring the effect of 'ethnicity'," *Comparative Political Studies* 41 (4/5): 515–563.

Chapman, Thomas and Philip G. Roeder. 2007. "Partition as a solution to wars of nationalism: the importance of institutions," *American Political Science Review* 101 (4): 677–691.

Christin, Thomas and Simon Hug. 2009. *Federalism, the Geographic Location of Groups, and Conflict*. Geneva: University of Geneva, unpublished manuscript.

Chua, Amy. 2004. *World on Fire: How Exporting Free Market Democracy Breeds Ethnic Hatred and Global Instability*. New York: Anchor Books.

Cipolla, Carlo M. 1969. *Literacy and Development in the West*. Baltimore: Pelican.

Clapham, Christopher. 1982. *Private Patronage and Public Power: Political Clientelism in the Modern State*. Basingstoke: Palgrave.

Clodfelter, Michael. 2002. *Warfare and Armed Conflicts: A Statistical Reference to Casualty and Other Figures, 1500–2000*. Jefferson: McFarland.

Cohen, Frank. 1997. "Proportional versus majoritarian ethnic conflict management in democracies," *Comparative Political Studies* 30 (5): 607–630.

Cohen, Ronald. 1978. "Ethnicity: problem and focus in anthropology," *Annual Review of Anthropology* 7: 397–403.

Cole, Juan. 2003. "The United States and Shi'ite religious factions in post-Ba'thist Iraq," *The Middle East Journal* 57 (4): 543–566.

Coleman, James S. 1990. *Foundations of Social Theory*. Cambridge, MA: Belknap Press.

Collier, George and Elisabeth Lowery Quaratiello. 1994. *Basta! Land and the Zapatista Rebellion in Chiapas.* Oakland: Institute for Food and Development Policy.

Collier, Paul and Anke Hoeffler. 2000. *Greed and Grievance in Civil War.* Washington, DC: World Bank Development Research Group.

2004. "Greed and grievance in civil war," *Oxford Economic Papers* 56 (4): 563–595.

Collier, Paul, Anke Hoeffler, and Dominic Rohner. 2006. "Beyond greed and grievance: feasibility and civil war," *Center for the Study of African Economics Working Paper* 10.

Collier, Paul, Anke Hoeffler, and Mans Söderbom. 2008. "Post-conflict risks," *Journal of Peace Research* 45 (4): 461–478.

Collier, Ruth Berins and Sebastián Mazzuca. 2006. "Does history repeat?" in Robert E. Goodin and Charles Tilly, eds., *The Oxford Handbook of Contextual Political Analysis.* Oxford University Press. 472–489.

Congleton, Roger D. 1995. "Ethnic clubs, ethnic conflict, and the rise of ethnic nationalism," in Albert Breton, Gianluigi Galeotti, Pierre Salmon, and Ronald Wintrobe, eds., *Nationalism and Rationality.* Cambridge University Press. 71–97.

Connor, Walker. 1972. "Nation-building or nation-destroying?" *World Politics* 24: 319–355.

Cornell, Stephen. 1996. "The variable ties that bind: content and circumstance in ethnic processes," *Ethnic and Racial Studies* 19 (2): 265–289.

COW. 2008. *Direct Contiguity Data, 1816–2006. Version 3.1.*

Cunningham, David E. 2011. *Barriers to Peace in Civil Wars.* Cambridge University Press.

Darden, Keith. 2011. *Resisting Occupation: Mass Schooling and the Creation of Durable National Loyalties.* Cambridge University Press.

Darden, Keith and Harris Mylonas. 2011. "The Promethean dilemma: third-party state-building in occupied territories," *Ethnopolitics* 11 (1): 85–93.

Davies, Graeme A. M. 2002. "Domestic strife and the initiation of international conflicts: a directed dyad analysis, 1950–1982," *Journal of Conflict Resolution* 46 (5): 672–692.

Davis, David R. and Will H. Moore. 1997. "Ethnicity matters: transnational ethnic alliances and foreign policy behaviour," *International Studies Quarterly* 41: 171–184.

Davison, Roderic H. 1954. "Turkish attitude concerning Christian–Muslim equality in the nineteenth century," *American Historical Review* 59 (4): 844–864.

1963. *Reform in the Ottoman Empire, 1856–1876.* Princeton University Press.

Despres, Leo A. 1968. "Anthropological theory, cultural pluralism, and the study of complex societies," *Current Anthropology* 9 (1): 3–26.

Deutsch, Karl W. 1953. *Nationalism and Social Communication: An Inquiry into the Foundations of Nationality.* Cambridge, MA: MIT Press.

Dickson, Eric and Kenneth Scheve. 2006. "Social identity, political speech, and electoral competition," *Journal of Theoretical Politics* 18 (1): 5–39.

Diehl, Paul F. and Gary Goertz. 1988. "Territorial changes and militarized conflict," *Journal of Conflict Resolution* 32 (1): 103–122.

1991. "Entering international society: military conflict and national independence, 1816–1980," *Comparative Political Studies* 23 (4): 497–518.

2000. *War and Peace in International Rivalry.* Ann Arbor: University of Michigan Press.

diMaggio, Paul and Walter W. Powell. 1991. *The New Institutionalism in Organizational Analysis.* University of Chicago Press.

Dobbin, Frank, Beth Simmons, and Geoffrey Garrett. 2007. "The global diffusion of public policies: social construction, coercion, competition, or learning?" *Annual Review of Sociology* 33 (1): 449–472.

Downes, Alexander B. 2004. "The problem with negotiated settlements to ethnic civil wars," *Security Studies* 13 (4): 230–279.

Easterly, William and Ross Levine. 1997. "Africa's growth tragedy: policies and ethnic divisions," *The Quarterly Journal of Economics* (November): 1203–1250.

Eck, Kristine. 2009. "From armed conflict to war: ethnic mobilization and conflict intensification," *International Studies Quarterly* 53 (2): 369–388.

Eifert, Benn, Edward Miguel, and Daniel N. Posner. 2010. "Political competition and ethnic identification in Africa," *American Journal of Political Science* 52 (2): 494–510.

Eisenstadt, Samuel N. 1963. *The Political Systems of Empires*. New York: Free Press.

Elbadawi, Nicholas and Nicholas Sambanis. 2000. "Why are there so many civil wars in Africa? Understanding and preventing violent conflict," *Journal of African Economics* 9 (3): 244–269.

Elkins, Zachary and John Sides. 2007. "Can institutions build unity in multi-ethnic states?" *American Political Science Review* 101 (4): 693–708.

Ellingsen, Tanja. 2000. "Colorful community or ethnic witches' brew? Multiethnicity and domestic conflict during and after the Cold War," *Journal of Conflict Resolution* 44 (2): 228–249.

Ellis, Andrew. 2003. "The politics of electoral systems in transition," in Andreas Wimmer, Donald Horowitz, Richard Goldstone, Ulrike Joras, and Conrad Schetter, eds., *Facing Ethnic Conflicts: Toward a New Realism*. Boulder: Rowman & Littlefield. 258–273.

Elster, Jon. 2000. "Rational choice history: a case of excessive ambition," *American Political Science Review* 94 (3): 685–702.

Esherick, Joseph W., Hasan Kayali, and Eric van Young. 2006. *Empire to Nation: Historical Perspectives on the Making of the Modern World*. Lanham: Rowman & Littlefield.

Esman, Milton. 1994. *Ethnic Politics*. Ithaca: Cornell University Press.

Favell, Adrian. 2008. *Eurostars and Eurocities: Free Movement and Mobility in an Integrating Europe*. Oxford: Blackwell.

Fearon, James D. 1995. "Rationalist explanations of war," *International Organization* 49 (3): 379–414.

    1998. "Commitment problems and the spread of ethnic conflict," in David A. Lake and Donald Rothchild, eds., *The International Spread of Ethnic Conflict*. Princeton University Press. 107–126.

    1999. *Why Ethnic Politics and "Pork" Tend to go Together*. Stanford: Department of Political Science, unpublished manuscript.

    2003. "Ethnic and cultural diversity by country," *Journal of Economic Growth* 8 (2): 195–222.

Fearon, James D. and David Laitin. n.d. *Civil War Narratives*. Stanford: Department of Political Science.

    1996. "Explaining interethnic cooperation," *American Political Science Review* 90 (4): 715–735.

    2003. "Ethnicity, insurgency, and civil war," *American Political Science Review* 97 (1): 1–16.

    2004. "Neotrusteeship and the problem of weak states," *International Security* 28 (4): 5–43.

Fearon, James D., Kimuli Kasara, and David D. Laitin. 2007. "Ethnic minority rule and civil war onset," *American Political Science Review* 101 (1): 187–193.

Feinstein, Yuval. 2011. *Rallying around the Flag: Nationalist Emotions in American Mass Politics.* University of California Los Angeles.

Fieldhouse, David Kenneth. 1966. *The Colonial Empires.* New York: Dell.

Fjelde, Hanne and Indra de Soysa. 2009. "Coercion, co-optation, or cooperation? State capacity and the risk of civil war, 1961–2004," *Conflict Management and Peace Science* 26 (5): 5–25.

Flint, John. 1983. "Planned decolonization and its failure in British Africa," *African Affairs* 82: 389–411.

Forsberg, Erika. 2008. "Polarization and ethnic conflict in a widening strategic setting," *Journal of Peace Research* 45 (2): 283–300.

Fowles, Jib. 1974. "Chronocentrism," *Futures* 6 (1): 65–68.

Fox, Jonathan. 1994. "The diffiult transition from clientelism to citizenship: lessons from Mexico," *World Politics* 46 (2): 151–184.

2000. "The effects of religious discrimination on ethno-religious protest and rebellion," *Journal of Conflict Studies* 20 (2): 16–43.

Furnivall, John S. 1939. *Netherlands India: A Study of Plural Economy.* Cambridge University Press.

Gagnon, Valère Philip. 2006. *The Myth of Ethnic War: Serbia and Croatia in the 1990s.* Ithaca: Cornell University Press.

Geertz, Clifford. 1963. "The integrative revolution. Primordial sentiments and civil politics in the new states," in Clifford Geertz, *Old Societies and New States: The Quest for Modernity in Asia and Africa.* New York: The Free Press. 105–157.

Gehlbach, Scott. 2006. "A formal model of exit and voice," *Rationality and Society* 18: 395–418.

Gellner, Ernest. 1983. *Nations and Nationalism.* Ithaca: Cornell University Press.

1991. "Nationalism and politics in Eastern Europe," *New Left Review* 189: 127–143.

Gerring, John and Strom Thacker. 2008. *A Centripetal Theory of Democratic Governance.* Cambridge University Press.

Ghai, Yash. 1998. "The structure of the state: federalism and autonomy," in Benjamin Reilly and Peter Harris, eds., *Democracy and Deep-Rooted Conflict: Options for Negotiators.* Stockholm: International IDEA. 155–168.

Gilley, Bruce. 2009. *The Right to Rule.* New York: Columbia University Press.

Gilpin, Robert. 1981. *War and Change in World Politics.* Cambridge University Press.

Glaser, Charles L. 1997. "The security dilemma revisited," *World Politics* 50 (1): 171–201.

Glazer, Nathan and Daniel Patrick Moynihan. 1975. "Introduction," in Nathan Glazer and Daniel Patrick Moynihan, eds., *Ethnicity: Theory and Experience.* Cambridge, MA: Harvard University Press. 1–11.

Gleditsch, Kristian Skrede. 2003. *Transnational Dimensions of Civil War.* University of California, San Diego.

2004. "A revised list of wars between and within independent states, 1816–2002," *International Interactions* 30 (3): 231–262.

2007. "Transnational dimensions of civil war," *Journal of Peace Research* 44 (3): 293–330.

Gleditsch, Kristian Skrede and Michael D. Ward. 2006. "Diffusion and the international context of democratization," *International Organization* 60: 911–933.

Gleditsch, Kristian Skrede, Idean Salehyan and Kenneth Schultz. 2008. "Fighting at home, fighting abroad. How civil wars lead to international disputes," in *Journal of Conflict Resolution* 52 (4):479–506.

Gleditsch, Nils Petter, Peter Wallensteen, Mikael Erikson, Margareta Sollenberg, and Håvard Strand. 2002. "Armed conflict 1946–2001: a new dataset," *Journal of Peace Research* 39 (5): 615–637.

Gleditsch, Nils Petter, Håvard Hegre, and Håvard Strand. 2009. "Democracy and civil war," in Manus I. Midlarsky, ed., *Handbook of War Studies III: The Intrastate Dimension.* Ann Arbor: University of Michigan Press. 155–192.

Goldstein, Joshua S. 1991. "A war-economy theory of the long wave," in N. Thygesen, K. Velupillai, and S. Zambelli, eds., *Business Cycles: Theories, Evidence and Analysis.* New York University Press. 303–325.

Goldstone, Jack A., Robert H. Bates, David L. Epstein, Ted Robert Gurr, Michael B. Lustik, Monty G. Marshall, Jay Ulfelder, and Mark Woodward. 2010. "A global model for forecasting political instability," *American Journal of Political Science* 54 (1): 190–208.

Goodwin, Jeff. 2001. *No Other Way Out: States and Revolutionary Movements, 1945–1991.* Cambridge University Press.

Gould, Roger V. 1995. *Insurgent Identities: Class, Community, and Protest in Paris from 1848 to the Commune.* University of Chicago Press.

1996. "Patron–client ties, state centralization, and the Whiskey rebellion," *American Journal of Sociology* 102 (2): 400–429.

Greenfeld, Liah. 1992. *Nationalism: Five Roads to Modernity.* Cambridge, MA: Harvard University Press.

Greif, Avner and David Laitin. 2004. "A theory of endogenous institutional change," *American Political Science Review* 98: 633–652.

Grillo, Ralph. 1998. *Pluralism and the Politics of Difference: State, Culture, and Ethnicity in Comparative Perspective.* Oxford University Press.

Gurr, Ted R. 1993a. *Minorities at Risk: A Global View of Ethnopolitical Conflict.* Washington, DC: United States Institute of Peace Press.

1993b. "Why minorities rebel: a global analysis of communal mobilization and conflict since 1945," *International Political Science Review* 14 (2): 161–201.

Habermas, Jürgen. 1989. *The Structural Transformation of the Public Sphere: An Inquiry into a Category of Bourgeois Society.* Cambridge, MA: MIT Press.

Habyarimana, James, Macartan Humphreys, Daniel N. Posner, and Jeremy M. Weinstein. 2007. "Why does ethnic diversity undermine public goods provision?" *American Political Science Review* 101 (4): 709–725.

Hale, Henry. 2000. "The parade of sovereignties: testing theories of secession in the Soviet setting," *British Journal of Political Science* 30: 31–56.

2004. "Explaining ethnicity," *Comparative Political Studies* 37 (4): 458–485.

2011. "Formal constitutions in informal politics: institutions and democratization in post-Soviet Eurasia," *World Politics* 63 (4): 581–617.

Haller, William, Alejandro Portes, and Scott M. Lynch. 2011. "Dreams fulfilled, dreams shattered: determinants of segmented assimilation in the second generation," *Social Forces* 89 (3): 733–762.

Hansen, Randall. 2009. "The poverty of postnationalism: citizenship, immigration, and the new Europe," *Theory and Society* 38: 1–24.

Harding, Robert R. 1978. *Anatomy of a Power Elite: The Provincial Governors of Early Modern France*. New Haven: Yale University Press.

Hardt, Michael and Antonio Negri. 2000. *Empire*. Cambridge, MA: Harvard University Press.

Hart, Sergiu and Mordecai Kurz. 1983. "Endogenous formation of coalitions," *Econometrica* 51: 1047–1064.

Hartzell, Caroline and Matthew Hoddie. 2003. "Institutionalizing peace: power sharing and post-civil war conflict management," *American Journal of Political Science* 47 (2): 318–332.

Hechter, Michael. 1975. *Internal Colonialism: The Celtic Fringe in British National Development, 1536–1966*. Berkeley: University of California Press.

   2000. *Containing Nationalism*. Oxford University Press.

   2004. "Containing nationalist violence," in Andreas Wimmer, Donald Horowitz, Richard Goldstone, Ulrike Joras, and Conrad Schetter, eds., *Facing Ethnic Conflicts: Toward a New Realism*. Boulder: Rowman & Littlefield. 283–300.

   2009a. "Alien rule and its discontent," *American Behavioral Scientist* 53 (3): 289–310.

   2009b. "Legitimacy in the modern world," *American Behavioral Scientist* 53 (3): 279–288.

Hechter, Michael and Margaret Levi. 1979. "The comparative analysis of ethnoregional movements," *Ethnic and Racial Studies* 2 (3): 260–274.

Hedström, Peter and Peter Bearman. 2009. *The Oxford Handbook of Analytical Sociology*. Oxford University Press.

Hegre, Håvard and Nicholas Sambanis. 2006. "Sensitivity analysis of empirical results on civil war onset," *Journal of Conflict Resolution* 50 (4): 508–535.

Hegre, Håvard, Tanja Ellingsen, Scott Gates, and Nils Petter Gleditsch. 2001. "Toward a democratic civil peace? Democracy, political change, and civil war, 1816–1992," *American Political Science Review* 95 (1): 33–48.

Heinersdoff, Richard. 1975. *Die K.U.K. privilegierten Eisenbahnen der österreichisch-ungarischen Monarchie, 1828–1918*. Vienna: Molden.

Held, David. 1995. *Democracy and the Global Order: From the Modern State to Cosmopolitan Governance*. Stanford University Press.

Heper, Metin, Ali Kazancigil, and Bert Rockman. 1997. *Institutions and Democratic Statecraft*. Boulder: Westview Press.

Herbst, Jeffrey. 2000. *States and Power in Africa: Comparative Lessons in Authority and Control*. Princeton University Press.

Hiers, Wesley and Andreas Wimmer. In press. "Is nationalism the cause or consequence of imperial breakdown?" in John Hall and Sinisa Malesevic, eds., *Nationalism and War*. Cambridge University Press.

Hintze, Otto. 1975. "Military organization and the organization of the state," in Felix Gilbert, ed., *The Historical Essays of Otto Hintze*. New York: Oxford University Press. 178–215.

Hironaka, Ann. 2005. *Neverending Wars: The International Community, Weak States, and the Perpetuation of Civil War*. Cambridge University Press.

Hobsbawm, Eric and Terence Ranger. 1983. *The Invention of Tradition*. Cambridge University Press.

Hobson, John M. 2000. *The State and International Relations*. Cambridge University Press.

Holsti, Kalevi J. 1991. *Peace and War: Armed Conflicts and International Order, 1648–1989*. Cambridge University Press.

Horn Melton, James van. 2001. *The Rise of the Public in Enlightenment Europe*. Cambridge University Press.

Horowitz, Donald. 1985. *Ethnic Groups in Conflict*. Berkeley: University of California Press.

    2002. "Constitutional design: proposals vs. process," in Andrew Reynolds, ed., *The Architecture of Democracy: Constitutional Design, Conflict Management, and Democracy*. Oxford: Oxford University Press. 15–36.

    2004. "Some realism about constitutional engineering," in Andreas Wimmer, Donald Horowitz, Richard Goldstone, Ulrike Joras, and Conrad Schetter, eds., *Facing Ethnic Conflicts. Toward a New Realism*. Boulder: Rowman & Littlefield. 245–257

Houle, Christian. 2009. "Inequality and democracy. Why inequality harms consolidation but does not affect democratization," *World Politics* 61 (4): 589–622.

Howe, Stephen. 2002. *Empire: A Very Short Introduction*. Oxford University Press.

Hroch, Miroslav. 2000 [1969]. *Social Preconditions of Patriotic Groups Among the Smaller European Nations*. New York: Columbia University Press.

Humphreys, Macartan. 2005. "Natural resources, conflict, and conflict resolution. Uncovering the mechanisms," *Journal of Conflict Resolution* 49 (4): 508–537.

Huntington, Samuel. 1993. "The clash of civilizations?" *Foreign Affairs* 72: 22–49.

Hutchings, Raymond. 1983. *The Soviet Budget*. Albany: SUNY Press.

Huth, P. K. 1996. "Enduring rivalries and territorial disputes, 1950–1990," *Conflict Management and Peace Science* 15: 7–41.

Ikegami, Eiko. 2005. *Bonds of Civility: Aesthetic Networks and the Political Origins of Japanese Culture*. Cambridge University Press.

Isaac, Larry W. and Larry J. Griffin. 1989. "Ahistoricism in time-series analyses of historical process: critique, redirection, and illustration from US labor history," *American Sociological Review* 54 (6): 873–890.

Jackson, Robert H. 1990. *Quasi-States: Sovereignty, International Relations, and the Third World*. New York: Cambridge University Press.

Jansen, Robert. 2011. "Populist mobilization: a new theoretical approach to populism," *Sociological Theory* 29 (2): 75–96.

Jenne, Erin K., Stephen M. Saideman, and Will Lowe. 2007. "Separatism as a bargaining posture: the role of leverage in minority radicalization," *Journal of Peace Research* 44 (5): 539–558.

Kaestle, Carl F. 1985. "The history of literacy and the history of readers," *Review of Research in Education* 12 (1): 11–53.

Kahler, Miles. 2002. "The state of the state in world politics," in Ira Kathnelson and Helen V. Milner, eds., *Political Science: State of the Discipline*. New York: Norton. 56–83.

Kaldor, Mary. 1999. *New and Old Wars: Organized Violence in a Global Era*. Cambridge: Polity Press.

Kalter, Frank. 2000. "Structural conditions of preferences for segregation," *Rationality and Society* 12: 425–448.

Karkar, Yaqub N. 1972. *Railway Development in the Ottoman Empire, 1856–1914*. New York: Vantage Press.

Karpat, Kemal. 1973. *An Inquiry into the Social Foundations of Nationalism in the Ottoman State: From Social Estates to Classes, from Millets to Nations*. Princeton: Center of International Studies.

    1985. *Ottoman Population, 1830 1914: Demographic and Social Characteristics*. Madison: University of Wisconsin Press.

    2002. *The Politicization of Islam: Reconstructing Identity, State, Faith, and Community in the Late Ottoman State*. Oxford University Press.

Kaufmann, Chaim. 1998. "When all else fails: separation as a remedy for ethnic conflicts, ethnic partitions and population transfers in the twentieth century," *International Security* 23 (2): 120–156.

Keck, Margaret and Kathryn Sikkink. 1998. *Activists Beyond Borders: Advocacy Networks in International Politics*. Ithaca: Cornell University Press.

Keohane, Robert. 1984. *After Hegemony: Cooperation and Discord in the World Political Economy.* Princeton University Press.

King, Gary, Robert Keohane, and Sidney Verba. 1994. *Designing Social Inquiry: Scientific Inference in Qualitative Research.* Princeton University Press.

Kirschbaum, Stanislav J. 1993. "Czechoslovakia: the creation, federalization and dissolution of a nation-state," *Regional Politics and Policy* 3 (1): 69–95.

Kiser, Edgar and Michael Hechter. 1998. "The debate on historical sociology: rational choice theory and its critics," *American Journal of Sociology* 104 (3): 785–816.

Kiser, Edgar and Joshua Kane. 2001. "Revolution and state structure: the bureaucratization of tax administration in early modern England and France," *American Journal of Sociology* 107 (1): 183–223.

Kiser, Edgar and April Linton. 2001. "Determinants of the growth of the state: war and taxation in early modern France and England," *Social Forces* 80 (2): 411–448.

2002. "The hinges of history: state-making and revolt in early modern France," *American Sociological Review* 67: 889–910.

Kitschelt, Herbert and Steven I. Wilkinson. 2007. *Patrons, Clients and Politics: Patterns of Democratic Accountability and Political Competition.* Cambridge University Press.

Klein, Herbert. 1998. *The American Finances of the Spanish Empire: Royal Income and Expenditures in Colonial Mexico, Peru, and Bolivia, 1680–1809.* Albuquerque: University of New Mexico Press.

Kohn, Hans. 1944. *The Idea of Nationalism.* New York: Collier.

Koopmans, Ruud, Paul Statham, Marco Giugni, and Florence Passy. 2005. *Contested Citizenship: Immigration and Cultural Diversity in Europe.* Minneapolis: University of Minnesota Press.

Kozlov, Victor. 1988. *The Peoples of the Soviet Union.* Hutchinson: Indiana University Press.

Krasner, Steven. 2005. "The case for shared sovereignty," *Journal of Democracy* 16 (1): 69–83.

Kuran, Timur. 1998. "Ethnic norms and their transformation through reputational cascades," *Journal of Legal Studies* 27: 623–659.

Kurzban, Robert, John Tooby, and Leda Cosmides. 2001. "Can race be erased? Coalitional computation and social categorization," *Proceedings of the National Academy of Sciences of the United States of America* 98 (26): 15398–15392.

Kymlicka, Will. 2007. *Multicultural Odysseys: Navigating the New International Politics of Diversity.* Oxford University Press.

Lachmann, Richard. 2011. *Mercenary, Citizen, Victim: The Evolution of the Western Soldier.* Paper given at the Nationalism and War Workshop, McGill University. March 24–26.

Laitin, David. 1986. *Hegemony and Culture: Politics and Religious Change Among the Yoruba.* University of Chicago Press.

1995. "National revivals and violence," *Archives Européennes de Sociologie* 36 (1): 3–43.

2007. *Nations, States, and Violence.* Oxford University Press.

Laitin, David and Maurits van der Veen. Forthcoming. "Ethnicity and pork: a virtual test of causal mechanisms," in Kanchan Chandra, ed., *Constructivist Theories of Ethnic Politics.* Oxford University Press.

Lake, David A. and Donald Rothchild (eds.) 1998. *The International Spread of Ethnic Conflict.* Princeton University Press.

Lange, Matthew. 2005. "British colonial state legacies and development trajectories: a statistical analysis of direct and indirect rule," in Matthew Lange and Dietrich Rueschemeyer, eds., *States and Development: Historical Antecedents of Stagnation and Advance.* Palgrave: Macmillan. 117–140.

Lapid, Yosef and Friedrich Kratochwil. 1996. "Revisiting the 'national': toward an identity agenda in neorealism?" in Yosef Lapid and Friedrich Kratochwil, eds., *The Return of Culture and Identity in International Relations Theory.* Boulder: Rienner. 105–127.

Lemarchand, Rene and Keith Legg. 1972. "Political clientelism and development: a preliminary analysis," *Comparative Politics* 4 (2): 149–178.

Levi, Margaret. 1988. *Of Rule and Revenue.* Berkeley: University of California Press.
  1997. *Consent, Dissent, and Patriotism: Political Economy of Institutions and Decisions.* Cambridge University Press.

Levi Martin, John. 2009. *Social Structures.* Princeton University Press.

Levy, Jack S. 1998. "The causes of war and the conditions of peace," *Annual Review of Political Science* 1: 39–65.

Levy, Jack S. and William R. Thompson. 2010. *Causes of War.* Chichester: Wiley-Blackwell.
  2011. *The Arc of War: Origins, Escalation, and Transformation.* University of Chicago Press.

Lewis, Bernard. 1962. *The Emergence of Modern Turkey.* London: Oxford University Press.

Licklider, Roy. 1995. "The consequences of negotiated settlements in civil wars, 1945–1993," *American Political Science Review* 89 (3): 681–690.

Lieberman, Evan S. 2005. "Nested analysis as a mixed-method strategy for comparative research," *American Political Science Review* 99 (3): 435–452.

Lieberman, Evan S. and Prerna Singh. Forthcoming. "The institutional origins of ethnic violence," *Comparative Politics.*

Lieberson, Stanley. 1991. "Small N's and big conclusion: an examination of the reasoning in comparative studies based on a small number of cases," *Social Forces* 70 (2): 307–320.

Lieven, Dominic. 2000. *Empire: The Russian Empire and its Rivals.* New Haven: Yale University Press.

Lijphart, Arend. 1977. *Democracy in Plural Societies: A Comparative Exploration.* New Haven: Yale University Press.
  1994. *Electoral Systems and Party Systems: A Study of Twenty-Seven Democracies, 1945–1990.* Oxford University Press.
  1999. *Patterns of Democracy: Government Forms and Performance in Thirty-Six Countries.* New Haven: Yale University Press.

Linz, Juan J. 1990. "The perils of presidentialism," *Journal of Democracy* 1 (1): 51–60.

Lipschutz, Ronnie D. 1992. "Reconstructing world politics: the emergence of global civil society," *Journal of International Studies* 21 (3): 389–420.

Lodge, R. Anthony. 1993. *French: From Dialect to Standard.* London: Routledge.

Luard, Evan. 1986. *War in International Society: A Study in International Sociology.* New Haven: Yale University Press.

Lustick, Ian. 1979. "Stability in deeply divided societies: consociationalism versus control," *World Politics* 31 (3): 325–344.
  2000. "Agent-based modelling of collective identity: testing constructivist theory," *Journal of Artificial Societies and Social Simulation* 3 (1). Available online at: http://jasss.soc.surrey.ac.uk/3/1/1.html.

Maddison, Angus. 2003. *The World Economy: Historical Statistics.* Paris: OECD.

Mahoney, James and Kathleen Thelen. 2010. "A theory of gradual institutional change," in James Mahoney and Kathleen Thelen, *Explaining Institutional Change: Ambiguity, Agency, and Power.* Cambridge University Press. 1–37.

Mann, Michael. 1993a. "Nation-states in Europe and other continents: diversifying, developing, not dying," *Daedalus* 112 (3): 115–140.

1993b. *The Sources of Social Power, Vol. 2: The Rise of Classes and Nation States, 1760–1914.* Cambridge University Press.

1995. "A political theory of nationalism and its excesses," in Sukumar Periwal, ed., *Notions of Nationalism.* Budapest: Central European University. 44–64.

2006. *American Empire: Past and Present.* Paper given at the Comparative Social Analysis Workshop, Department of Sociology, UCLA.

Mansfield, Edward D. and Jack Snyder. 1995. "Democratization and the danger of war," *International Security* 20 (1): 5–38.

2005a. *Electing to Fight: Why Emerging Democracies Go To War.* Cambridge, MA: MIT Press.

2005b. "Prone to violence: the paradox of democratic peace," *The National Interest,* December 22.

Maoz, Zeev. 1989. "Joining the club of nations: political development and international conflict, 1816–1976," *International Studies Quarterly* 33 (2): 199–231.

Marshall, Thomas H. 1950. *Citizenship and Social Class.* Cambridge University Press.

McElreath, Richard, Robert Boyd, and Peter J. Richerson. 2003. "Shared norms and the evolution of ethnic markers," *Current Anthropology* 44 (1): 122–130.

McGarry, John and Brendan O'Leary. 1993. "Introduction: the macro-political regulation of ethnic conflict," in John McGarry and Brendan O'Leary, *The Politics of Ethnic Conflict Regulation: Case Studies in Protracted Ethnic Conflicts.* London: Routledge.

McKelvey, Richard D., Andrew M. McLennan, and Theodore L. Turocy. 2007. *Gambit: Software Tools for Game Theory. Version 0.2007.01.30.* Available online at: http:/gambit.sourceforge.net.

Mearsheimer, John J. 1990. "Back to the future: instability in Europe after the Cold War," *International Security* 15: 5–56.

2001. *The Tragedy of Great Power Politics.* New York: Norton.

Meyer, John, John Boli, George M. Thomas, and Francisco O. Ramirez. 1997. "World society and the nation-state," *American Journal of Sociology* 103 (1): 144–181.

Midgal, Joel S. 2001. *State in Society: Studying How States and Societies Transform and Constitute One Another.* Cambridge University Press.

Miguel, Edward. 2004. "Tribe or nation? Nation building and public goods in Kenya versus Tanzania," *World Politics* 56 (3): 327–362.

Miller, Benjamin. 2007. *States, Nations, and the Great Powers: The Sources of Regional War and Peace.* Cambridge University Press.

Miller, David. 1995. *On Nationality.* Oxford University Press.

Milward, Alan. 2000. *The European Rescue of the Nation State.* London: Routledge.

Mishali-Ram, Meirav. 2006. "Ethnic diversity, issues, and international crisis dynamics, 1918–2002," *Journal of Peace Research* 43 (5): 583–600.

Mitchell, Brian R. Various years. *International Historical Statistics.* New York: Palgrave.

Modelski, George and Patrick Morgan. 1985. "Understanding global war," *Journal of Conflict Resolution* 29 (3): 391–417.

Montalvo, José G. and Marta Reynal-Querol. 2005. "Ethnic polarization, potential conflict and civil wars," *American Economic Review* 95 (3): 796–816.

Moravcsik, Andrew. 1997. "Taking preferences seriously: a liberal theory of international politics," *International Organization* 51 (4): 513–553.

Mufti, Malik. 1996. *Sovereign Creations: Pan-Arabism and Political Order in Syria and Iraq.* Ithaca: Cornell University Press.

Mukherjee, Bumba. 2006. "Why political power-sharing agreements lead to enduring peaceful resolution of some civil wars, but not others," *International Studies Quarterly* 50: 479–504.

Müller, Edward N. and Erich Weede. 1990. "Cross-national variation in political violence: a rational action approach," *Journal of Conflict Resolution* 34 (4): 624–651.

Mylonas, Harris. Forthcoming. *The Politics of Nation-Building: The Making of Co-Nationals, Refugees, and Minorities.* Cambridge University Press.

Nairn, Tim. 1993. "All Bosnians now?" *Dissent* (Fall): 403–410.

Narang, Vipin and Rebecca Nelson. 2009. "Who are these belligerent democracies? Reassessing the impact of democratization on war," *International Organization* 63 (2): 357–379.

New World Demographics. 1992. *The Firstbook of Demographics for the Republics of the Former Soviet Union, 1951–1990.* Shady Side: New World Demographics.

Nodia, Ghia. 1992. "Nationalism and democracy," *Journal of Democracy* 3 (4): 3–22.

Nordlinger, Eric A. 1972. *Conflict Regulation in Divided Societies.* Cambridge, MA: Center for International Affairs, Harvard University.

Nunn, Nathan. 2009. "The importance of history for economic development," *Annual Review of Economics* 1 (1): 65–92.

Oberegger, Elmar. 2008. *Zur Eisenbahngeschichte des Alpen-Donau-Adria Raumes.* Available online at: http://member.a1.net/edze/enzyklopaedie/bihb.htm.

O'Leary, Brendan. 1989. "The limits of coercive consociationalism in Northern Ireland," *Political Studies* 37: 562–588.

Olzak, Susan. 2006. *The Global Dynamics of Race and Ethnic Mobilization.* Stanford University Press.

Olzak, Susan and Joane Nagel. 1986. *Competitive Ethnic Relations.* New York: Academic Press.

Organski, A. F. K. and Jacek Kugler. 1980. *The War Ledger.* University of Chicago Press.

Osborne, Martin J. and Ariel Rubinstein. 1994. *A Course in Game Theory.* Cambridge, MA: MIT Press.

Osler Hampson, Fen and David Mendeloff. 2007. "Intervention and the nation-building debate," in Chester A. Crocker, Fen Osler Hampson, and Pamela Aall, eds, *Leashing the Dogs of War: Conflict Management in a Divided World.* Washington, DC: USIP Press. 679–700.

Parikh, Sunita. 2000. "The strategic value of Analytic Narratives," *Social Science History* 24 (4): 677–684.

Paris, Roland. 1997. "Peacebuilding and the limits of liberal internationalism," *International Security* 22 (2): 54–89.

Penn, Elizabeth Maggie. 2008. "Citizenship versus ethnicity: the role of institutions in shaping identity choice," *Journal of Politics* 70 (4): 956–973.

Perl, Louis. 1872. *Die russischen Eisenbahnen im Jahre 1970–1971.* St. Petersburg: Kaiserliche Hofbuchhandlung.

Petersen, Roger D. 2002. *Understanding Ethnic Violence: Fear, Hatred, and Resentment in Twentieth-Century Eastern Europe*. Cambridge University Press.

Pierson, Paul. 1996. "The path to European integration. A historical institutionalist analysis," *Comparative Political Studies* 29 (2): 123–163.

2003. "Big, slow-moving, and … invisible. Macrosocial processes in the study of comparative politics," in James Mahoney and Dietrich Rueschemeyer, eds., *Comparative Historical Analysis in the Social Sciences*. Cambridge University Press. 177–207.

Pierson, Paul and Theda Skocpol. 2002. "Historical institutionalism in contemporary political science," in Ira Kathnelson and Helen V. Milner, eds., *Political Science: State of the Discipline*. New York: Norton. 693–721.

Pinard, Maurice. 2011. *Motivational Dimensions of Social Movements and Contentious Collective Action*. Montreal: McGill-Queen's University Press.

Plotnikov, Kirill Nikanarovich. 1948/1954. *Ocherki istorii biudzheta Sovetskogo gosudarstva*. Moscow: Gosfinizdat.

Polachek, Solomon W. 1980. "Conflict and trade," *Journal of Conflict Resolution* 24 (1): 55–78.

Pollins, Brian M. 1996. "Global political order, economic change, and armed conflict: coevolving systems and the use of force," *American Political Science Review* 90 (1): 103–117.

Portes, Alejandro and Lori D. Smith. 2010. "Institutions and national development in Latin America: a comparative study," *Socio-Economic Review* 8 (4): 1–37.

Posen, Barry. 1993a. "The security dilemma and ethnic conflict," in Michael E. Brown, ed., *Ethnic Conflict and International Security*. Princeton University Press. 103–124.

1993b. "Nationalism, the mass army, and military power," *International Security* 18 (2): 80–124.

Posner, Daniel. 2004. "Measuring ethnic fractionalization in Africa," *American Journal of Political Science* 48 (4): 849–863.

2005. *Institutions and Ethnic Politics in Africa*. New York: Cambridge University Press.

Pounds, Norman. 1964. "History and geography: a perspective on partition," *Journal of International Affairs* 18 (2): 172.

Ragin, Charles. 1989. *The Comparative Method: Moving Beyond Qualitative and Quantitative Strategies*. Berkeley: University of California Press.

Raleigh, Clionadh and Håvard Hegre. 2005. *Introducing ACLED: An Armed Conflict Location and Event Dataset*. Paper given at Disaggregating the Study of Civil War and Transnational Violence, San Diego: University of California Institute of Global Conflict and Cooperation. March 7–8.

Rautavuiori, Mauri. 2008. *Russian Railways*. Available online at: http://personal.inet.fi/private/raumarail/russia/main.htm.

Regan, Patrick and David Clark. 2011. *Institutions and Elections Project*.

Regan, Patrick and Daniel Norton. 2005. "Greed, grievance, and mobilization in civil wars," *Journal of Conflict Resolution* 49 (3): 319–336.

Reilly, Benjamin. 2006. *Democracy and Diversity: Political Engineering in the Asia-Pacific*. Oxford University Press.

2011. "Centripetalism: cooperation, accommodation, and integration," in Stefan Wolff and Christalla Yakinthou, eds., *Conflict Management in Divided Societies: Theories and Practice*. London: Routledge. 57–64.

Reis, Jaime. 2005. "Economic growth, human capital formation and consumption in Western Europe before 1800," in Robert C. Allen, Tommy Bengtsson, and Martin Dribe, eds., *Living Standards in the Past*. Oxford University Press. 195–225.

Reynal-Querol, Marta. 2002. "Ethnicity, political systems, and civil wars," *Journal of Conflict Resolution* 46 (1): 29–54.

Reynolds, Andrew. 2011. *Designing Democracy in a Dangerous World*. Oxford University Press.

Richardson, Lewis Frey. 1960. *Statistics of Deadly Quarrels*. Quincy Wright and C.C. Lienau, eds. Pittsburgh: Boxwood Press.

Riker, William H. 1962. *The Theory of Political Coalitions*. New Haven: Yale University Press.

Risse-Kappen, Thomas. 1996. "Collective identity in a democratic community: the case of NATO," in Peter Katzenstein, ed., *The Culture of National Security: Norms and Identity in World Politics*. New York: Columbia University Press. 357–399.

Roberts, Kenneth M. 1996. "Neoliberalism and the transformation of populism in Latin America: the Peruvian case," *World Politics* 48 (1): 82–116.

Roeder, Philip G. 2005. "Power dividing as an alternative to ethnic power sharing," in Philip G. Roeder and Donald Rothchild, eds., *Sustainable Peace: Power and Democracy after Civil Wars*. Ithaca: Cornell University Press. 51–82.

2007. *Where Nation-States Come From: Institutional Change in the Age of Nationalism*. Princeton: Princeton University Press.

Roessler, Philip G. 2011. "The enemy from within. Personal rule, coups, and civil wars in Africa," *World Politics* 63 (2): 399–346.

Roll, Freiherr von. 1915. *Enzyklopädie des Eisenbahnwesens*. Vienna: Urban & Schwarzenberg.

Roshwald, Aviel. 2001. *Ethnic Nationalism and the Fall of Empires: Central Europe, Russia and the Middle East, 1914–1923*. London: Routledge.

Ross, Michael. 2003. "Oil, drugs, and diamonds. The varying roles of natural resources in civil war" in Karen Ballentine and Jake Sherman, eds., *Beyond Greed and Grievance: The Political Economy of Armed Conflict*. Boulder: Lynne Rienner. 47–70.

2004. "What do we know about natural resources and civil war?" *Journal of Peace Research* 41: 337–356.

2012. *The Oil Curse: How Petroleum Wealth Shapes the Development of Nations*. Princeton University Press.

Rothchild, Donald. 1986. "Hegemonial exchange: an alternative model for managing conflict in Middle Africa," in Dennis Thompson and Dov Ronen, eds., *Ethnicity, Politics, and Development*. Boulder: Lynne Rienner. 65–104.

2004. "Liberalism, democracy and conflict management: the African experience," in Andreas Wimmer, Donald Horowitz, Richard Goldstone, Ulrike Joras, and Conrad Schetter, eds., *Facing Ethnic Conflicts: Toward a New Realism*. Boulder: Rowman & Littlefield. 226–244.

Rothchild, Donald and Philip G. Roeder. 2005. "Power sharing as an impediment to peace and democracy," in Philip G. Roeder and Donald Rothchild, eds., *Sustainable Peace: Power and Democracy after Civil Wars*. Ithaca: Cornell University Press. 29–50.

Rothschild, Joseph. 1981. *Ethnopolitics: A Conceptual Framework*. New York: Columbia.

Russet, Bruce M. 1993. *Grasping the Democratic Peace: Principles for a Post-Cold War Period*. Princeton University Press.

Saideman, Stephen M. and R. William Ayres. 2000. "Determining the causes of irredentism: logit analyses of minorities at risk data from the 1980s and 1990s," *Journal of
Politics* 62 (4): 1126–1144.

2008. *For Kin and Country: Xenophobia, Nationalism, and War.* New York: Columbia
University Press.

Saideman, Stephen M., David J. Lanoue, Michael Campenni, and Samuel Stanton. 2002.
"Democratization, political institutions, and ethnic conflict. A pooled time-series
analysis, 1985–1998," *Comparative Political Studies* 35 (1): 103–129.

Sakari, Salo and Hovi Likka. 2003. *Estonian Railways Today.* Available online at: www.rrdc.
com/article_05_2003_evr_todays_rwys.pdf.

Saltelli, Andrea, Stefano Tarantola, Francesca Campolongo, and Marco Ratto. 2004.
Sensitivity Analysis in Practice: A Guide to Assessing Scientific Models. New York:
Wiley.

Saltelli, Andrea, Marco Ratto, Terry Andres, Francesca Campolongo, Jessica Cariboni,
Debora Gatelli, Michaela Saisana, and Stefano Tarantola. 2008. *Global Sensitivity
Analysis: The Primer.* New York: Wiley.

Sambanis, Nicholas. 2001. "Do ethnic and nonethnic civil wars have the same causes?"
Journal of Conflict Resolution 45 (3): 259–282.

2004. "What is civil war? Conceptual and empirical complexities of an operational definition," *Journal of Conflict Resolution* 48 (6): 814–858.

2009. *What is an Ethnic War? Organization and Interests in Insurgencies.* New Haven:
Department of Political Science, Yale University.

Sambanis, Nicholas and Annalisa Zinn. 2006. *From Protest to Violence: Conflict Escalation
in Self-determination Movements.* New Haven: Department of Political Science, Yale
University.

Scarritt, James R. and Shaheen Mozaffar. 1999. "The specification of ethnic cleavages and
ethnopolitical groups for the analysis of democratic competition in contemporary
Africa," *Nationalism and Ethnic Politics* 5 (1): 82–117.

Schermerhorn, Richard A. 1970. *Comparative Ethnic Relations: A Framework for Theory and
Research.* New York: Random House.

Schmitter, Philippe C. 1974. "Still the century of corporatism?" *Review of Politics* 36 (1):
85–131.

Schneider, Gerald and Nina Wiesehomeier. 2008. "Rules that matter: political institutions
and the diversity conflict nexus," *Journal of Peace Research* 45 (2): 183–203.

Scott, James C. 1972. "Patron–client politics and political change in Southeast Asia," *The
American Political Science Review* 66 (1): 91–113.

Senese, Paul D. and John A. Vasquez. 2008. *Steps to War: An Empirical Study.* Princeton
University Press.

Sewell, William H. 1996. "Three temporalities: toward an eventful sociology," in Terence
J. McDonald, ed., *The Historic Turn in the Human Sciences.* Ann Arbor: University of
Michigan Press. 245–280.

Shaw, Stanford J. 1975. "The nineteenth-century Ottoman tax reforms and revenue systems," *International Journal of Middle East Studies* 6 (4): 421–459.

1976. *History of the Ottoman Empire and Modern Turkey, Vol. 1: Empire of the Gazis, the Rise and
Decline of the Ottoman Empire, 1280–1808.* Cambridge University Press.

1978. "Ottoman expenditures and budgets in the late nineteenth and early twentieth
centuries," *International Journal of Middle East Studies* 9: 373–378.

Shayo, Moses. 2009. "A model of social identity with an application to political economy: nation, class and redistribution," *American Political Science Review* 103 (2): 147–174.

Simpson, Jacqueline C. 1995. "Pluralism. The evolution of a nebulous concept," *American Behavioral Scientist* 38 (3): 459–477.

Singer, J. David. 1987. "Reconstructing the Correlates of War Dataset on material capabilities of states, 1816–1985," *International Interactions* 14: 115–132.

Skocpol, Theda. 1979. *States and Social Revolutions: A Comparative Analysis of France, Russia and China.* Cambridge University Press.

    1994. "Reflections on recent scholarship about social revolutions and how to study them," in Theda Skocpol, *Social Revolutions in the Modern World.* New York: Cambridge University Press. 301–343.

    2000. "Theory tackles history," *Social Science History* 24 (4): 669–676.

Smith, Anthony D. 1986. *The Ethnic Origins of Nations.* Oxford: Blackwell.

    1990. "The supersession of nationalism?" *International Journal of Comparative Sociology* 31 (1–2): 1–31.

    1995. *Nations and Nationalism in a Global Era.* Cambridge: Polity Press.

    2003. *Chosen Peoples: Sacred Sources of National Identity.* Oxford University Press.

Smith, Carol A. 1990. "Failed nationalist movements in 19th-century Guatemala: a parable for the Third World," in Richard G. Fox, ed., *Nationalist Ideologies and the Production of National Cultures.* Washington, DC: American Anthropological Association. 148–177.

Smith, Michael G. 1969. "Institutional and political conditions of pluralism," in Leo Kuper and Michael G. Smith, eds., *Pluralism in Africa.* Berkeley: University of California Press. 27–66.

Snow, David, E. Burke Rochford, Steven K. Worden, and Robert D. Benford. 1986. "Frame alignment processes, micromobilization, and movement participation," *American Sociological Review* 51: 464–481.

Snyder, Jack. 1991. *Myths of Empire: Domestic Politics and International Ambition.* Ithaca: Cornell University Press.

    2000. *From Voting to Violence: Democratization and Nationalist Violence.* New York: Norton.

Somers, Margaret R. 1998. "'We're no angels': realism, rational choice, and relationality in social science," *American Journal of Sociology* 104 (3): 722–784.

Soysal, Yasemin Nuhoglu. 1994. *Limits of Citizenship: Migrants and Postnational Membership in Europe.* University of Chicago Press.

Spruyt, Hendrik. 1996. *The Sovereign State and Its Competitors.* Princeton University Press.

    2005. *Ending Empire: Contested Sovereignty and Territorial Partition.* Ithaca: Cornell University Press.

Stares, Paul B. and Micah Zenko. 2009. *Enhancing U.S. Preventive Action.* New York: Council on Foreign Relations.

Steinmo, Sven, Kathleen Thelen, and Frank Longstreth. 1992. *Structuring Politics: Historical Institutionalism in Comparative Analysis.* Cambridge University Press.

Stewart, Frances. 2008. *Horizontal Inequalities and Conflict: Understanding Group Violence in Multiethnic Societies.* Houndsmills: Palgrave.

Strach, Hermann. 1906. *Geschichte der Eisenbahnen der österreichisch-ungarischen Monarchie,* various volumes. Vienna: Karl Prochaska.

Strang, David. 1990. "From dependency to sovereignty: an event history analysis of decolonization 1879–1987," *American Sociological Review* 55: 846–860.

1991a. "Anomaly and commonplace in European political expansion: realist and institutional accounts," *International Organization* 45 (2): 143–162.

1991b. "Global patterns of decolonization, 1500–1987," *International Studies Quarterly* 35: 429–454.

Streeck, Wolfgang and Kathleen Thelen. 2005a. *Beyond Continuity: Institutional Change in Advanced Political Economies*. Oxford University Press.

2005b. "Introduction: institutional change in advanced political economies," in Wolfgang Streeck and Kathleen Thelen, *Beyond Continuity: Institutional Change in Advanced Political Economies*. Oxford University Press. 1–39.

Stryker, Sheldon and Peter J. Burke. 2000. "The past, present, and future of an identity theory," *Social Psychology Quarterly* 63: 284–297.

Svodnii otdel gosudarstvennogo byudzheta. Various years. *Gosudarstvennyi byudzhet SSSR: Statisticheskii Sbornik*. Moscow: Finansy i statistika.

Tajfel, Henri. 1981. *Human Groups and Social Categories: Studies in the Social Psychology*. Cambridge University Press.

Taliaferro, Jeffrey W. 2009. "Neoclassical realism and resource extraction: state building for future war," in Steven E. Lobell, Norrin M. Ripsman, and Jeffrey W. Taliaferro, eds., *Neoclassical Realism, the State, and Foreign Policy*. Cambridge: Cambridge University Press. 194–226.

Tarrow, Sidney and Charles Tilly. 2006. *Contentious Politics*. Cambridge University Press.

Thies, Cameron G. 2010. "Of rulers, rebels, and revenue: state capacity, civil war onset, and primary commodities," *Journal of Peace Research* 47 (3): 321–332.

Thompson, William R. 1988. *On Global War: Historical-Structural Approaches to World Politics*. Columbia: University of South Carolina Press.

Thorsten Beck, George Clarke, Alberto Groff, Philip Keefer, and Patrick Walsh. 2001. "New tools in comparative political economy: the Database of Political Institutions," *World Bank Economic Review* 15 (1): 165–176.

Tilly, Charles. 1975. "Western state-making and theories of political transformation," in Charles Tilly, *The Formation of National States in Western Europe*. Princeton University Press. 601–638.

1978. *From Mobilization To Revolution*. Reading: Addison-Wesley.

1989. *Big Structures, Large Processes, Huge Comparisons*. New York: Russel Sage Foundation.

1994. "States and nationalism in Europe, 1492–1992," *Theory and Society* 23 (1): 131–146.

2000. "Processes and mechanisms of democratization," *Sociological Theory* 18 (1): 1–16.

2005. *Trust and Rule*. Cambridge University Press.

2006. *Identities, Boundaries, and Social Ties*. Boulder: Paradigm Press.

Toft, Monica. 2003. *The Geography of Ethnic Violence: Identity, Interests, and the Indivisibility of Territory*. Princeton University Press.

2009. *Securing the Peace: The Durable Settlement of Civil Wars*. Princeton University Press.

Torfason, Magnus Thor and Paul Ingram. 2010. "The global rise of democracy: a network account," *American Sociological Review* 75 (3): 355–377.

Tsebelis, George. 2002. *Veto Players: How Political Institutions Work*. New York: Russel Sage.

Tull, Denis M. and Andreas Mehler. 2005. "The hidden costs of power sharing: reproducing insurgent violence in Africa," *African Affairs* 104/416: 375–398.

Turchin, Peter. 2003. *Historical Dynamics: Why States Rise and Fall*. Princeton University Press.

Van Evera, Stephen. 1999. *Causes of War: Power and the Roots of Conflict.* Ithaca: Cornell University Press.

Vanhanen, Tatu. 1999. "Domestic ethnic conflict and ethnic nepotism: a comparative analysis," *Journal of Peace Research* 36 (1): 55–73.

2000. "A new dataset for measuring democracy, 1810–1998," *Journal of Peace Research* 37 (2): 251–265.

Varshney, Ashutosh. 2003. *Ethnic Conflict and Civil Life.* New Haven: Yale University Press.

Vasquez, John A. 2009. *The War Puzzle Revisited.* Cambridge University Press.

Vasquez, John and Christopher S. Leskiw. 2001. "The origins and war proneness of interstate rivalries," *Annual Review of Political Science* 4: 295–316.

Vreeland, James Raymond. 2008. "The effect of political regime on civil war: unpacking anocracy," *Journal of Conflict Resolution* 52 (3): 401–425.

Vu, Tuong. 2009. "Studying the state through state formation," *World Politics* 62 (1): 148–175.

Wacquant, Loïc. 1997. "Towards an analytic of racial domination," *Political Power and Social Theory* 11: 221–234.

Wagner-Pacifici, Robin. 2010. "Theorizing the restlessness of events," *American Journal of Sociology* 115 (5): 1351–1386.

Walter, Barbara. 2006. "Information, uncertainty, and the decision to secede," *International Organization* 60: 105–135.

2009. "Bargaining failures and civil war," *Annual Review of Political Science* 12: 243–261.

Waltz, Kenneth N. 1979. *Theory of International Politics.* Boston: McGraw-Hill.

Weber, Eugen. 1979. *Peasants into Frenchmen: The Modernisation of Rural France, 1870–1914.* London: Chatto & Windus.

Weber, Max. 1968 [1922]. *Economy and Society: An Outline of Interpretive Sociology.* New York: Bedminster Press.

Weiner, Myron. 1971. "The Macedonian syndrome: an historical model of international relations and political development," *World Politics* 23 (4): 665–683.

Weinstein, Jeremy M. 2005. *Autonomous Recovery and International Intervention in Comparative Perspective.* Washington, DC: Center for Global Development.

Weyland, Kurt. 1996. "Neopopulism and neoliberalism in Latin America: unexpected affinities," *Studies in Comparative International Development* 31: 3–31.

Wimmer, Andreas. 1995a. "Die erneute Rebellion der Gehenkten, Chiapas 1994," *Zeitschrift für Sozialgeschichte des 20. und 21. Jahrhunderts* 3: 59–68.

1995b. *Die komplexe Gesellschaft. Eine Theorienkritik am Beispiel des indianischen Bauerntums.* Berlin: Reimer.

1995c. *Transformationen. Sozialer Wandel im indianischen Mittelamerika.* Berlin: Reimer.

1997. "Who owns the state? Understanding ethnic conflict in post-colonial societies," *Nations and Nationalism* 3 (4): 631–665.

2002. *Nationalist Exclusion and Ethnic Conflicts: Shadows of Modernity.* Cambridge University Press.

2003. "Democracy and ethno-religious conflict in Iraq," *Survival: The International Institute for Strategic Studies Quarterly* 45 (4): 111–134.

2008a. "How to modernize ethnosymbolism," *Nations and Nationalism* 14 (1): 9–14.

2008b. "The making and unmaking of ethnic boundaries. A multi-level process theory," *American Journal of Sociology* 113 (4): 970–1022.

2011. "A Swiss anomaly? A relational account of national boundary making," *Nations and Nationalism* 17 (4): 718–737.

In preparation. *Nation Building or Ethnic Exclusion? A Global Analysis.* Los Angeles: UCLA.

Wimmer, Andreas and Yuval Feinstein. 2010. "The rise of the nation-state across the world, 1816 to 2001," *American Sociological Review* 75 (5): 764–790.

Wimmer, Andreas and Nina Glick Schiller. 2002. "Methodological nationalism and beyond. Nation-state formation, migration and the social sciences," *Global Networks* 2 (4): 301–334.

Wimmer, Andreas and Brian Min. 2006. "From empire to nation-state. Explaining wars in the modern world, 1816–2001," *American Sociological Review* 71 (6): 867–897.

2009. "The location and purpose of wars around the world. A new global dataset, 1816–2001," *International Interactions* 35 (4): 390–417.

Wimmer, Andreas and Conrad Schetter. 2003. "Putting state-formation first. Some recommendations for reconstruction and peace-making in Afghanistan," *Journal of International Development* 15: 1–15.

Winnifrith, Tony. 1993. "The Vlachs of the Balkans: a rural minority which never achieved ethnic identity," in David Howell, ed., *Roots of Rural Ethnic Mobilisation: Comparative Studies on Governments and Non-Dominant Ethnic Groups in Europe, 1850–1940.* Aldershot: Dartmouth. 277–303.

Woocher, Lawrence. 2009. *Preventing Violent Conflict: Assessing Progress, Meeting Challenges.* Washington, DC: USIP.

Woodwell, Douglas. 2004. "Unwelcome neighbors: shared ethnicity and international conflict during the Cold War," *International Studies Quarterly* 48: 197–223.

2007. *Nationalism in International Relations.* Houndsmill: Palgrave.

Woronoff, Jon. Various years. *Historical Dictionaries (Various Volumes).* Lanham: Scarecrow Press.

Wucherpfennig, Julian, Nils B. Weidmann, Luc Girardin, Lars-Erik Cederman, and Andreas Wimmer. 2011. "Politically relevant ethnic groups across space and time: introducing the GeoEPR dataset," *Conflict Management and Peace Science* 20 (10): 1–15.

Yi, Sang-Seung and Hyukseung Shin. 2000. "Endogenous formation of research coalitions with spillovers," *International Journal of Industrial Organization* 18: 229–256.

Young, Crawford. 1976. *The Politics of Cultural Pluralism.* Madison: University of Wisconsin Press.

Young, Cristobal. 2009. "Model uncertainty in sociological research: an application to religion and economic growth," *American Sociological Review* 74: 380–397.

Young, H. Peyton. 1998. *Individual Strategy and Social Structure: An Evolutionary Theory of Institutions.* Princeton University Press.

Zürcher, Christoph and Jan R. Böhnke. 2009. *Aid, Minds, and Hearts: The Impact of Aid in Conflict Zones.* Paper given at the GROW-Net Conference, Zürich, September 18–20.

Index

Cambridge Studies in Comparative Politics

Other Books in the Series (continued from page iii)

Timothy Frye, *Building States and Markets After Communism: The Perils of Polarized Democracy*

Geoffrey Garrett, *Partisan Politics in the Global Economy*

Scott Gehlbach, *Representation through Taxation: Revenue, Politics, and Development in Postcommunist States*

Jane R. Gingrich, *Making Markets in the Welfare State: The Politics of Varying Market Reforms*

Miriam Golden, *Heroic Defeats: The Politics of Job Loss*

Jeff Goodwin, *No Other Way Out: States and Revolutionary Movements*

Merilee Serrill Grindle, *Changing the State*

Anna Grzymala-Busse, *Rebuilding Leviathan: Party Competition and State Exploitation in Post-Communist Democracies*

Anna Grzymala-Busse, *Redeeming the Communist Past: The Regeneration of Communist Parties in East Central Europe*

Frances Hagopian, *Traditional Politics and Regime Change in Brazil*

Mark Hallerberg, Rolf Ranier Strauch, Jürgen von Hagen, *Fiscal Governance in Europe*

Henry E. Hale, *The Foundations of Ethnic Politics: Separatism of States and Nations in Eurasia and the World*

Stephen E. Hanson, *Post-Imperial Democracies: Ideology and Party Formation in Third Republic France, Weimar Germany, and Post-Soviet Russia*

Gretchen Helmke, *Courts Under Constraints: Judges, Generals, and Presidents in Argentina*

Yoshiko Herrera, *Imagined Economies: The Sources of Russian Regionalism*

J. Rogers Hollingsworth and Robert Boyer, eds., *Contemporary Capitalism: The Embeddedness of Institutions*

John D. Huber and Charles R. Shipan, *Deliberate Discretion? The Institutional Foundations of Bureaucratic Autonomy*

Ellen Immergut, *Health Politics: Interests and Institutions in Western Europe*

Torben Iversen, *Capitalism, Democracy, and Welfare*

Torben Iversen, *Contested Economic Institutions*

Torben Iversen, Jonas Pontussen, and David Soskice, eds., *Union, Employers, and Central Banks: Macroeconomic Coordination and Institutional Change in Social Market Economics*

Thomas Janoski and Alexander M. Hicks, eds., *The Comparative Political Economy of the Welfare State*

Joseph Jupille, *Procedural Politics: Issues, Influence, and Institutional Choice in the European Union*

Stathis Kalyvas, *The Logic of Violence in Civil War*

David C. Kang, *Crony Capitalism: Corruption and Capitalism in South Korea and the Philippines*

Junko Kato, *Regressive Taxation and the Welfare State*

Orit Kedar, *Voting for Policy, Not Parties: How Voters Compensate for Power Sharing*

Robert O. Keohane and Helen B. Milner, eds., *Internationalization and Domestic Politics*

Herbert Kitschelt, *The Transformation of European Social Democracy*

Herbert Kitschelt, Kirk A. Hawkins, Juan Pablo Luna, Guillermo Rosas, and Elizabeth J. Zechmeister, *Latin American Party Systems*

Herbert Kitschelt, Peter Lange, Gary Marks, and John D. Stephens, eds., *Continuity and Change in Contemporary Capitalism*

Herbert Kitschelt, Zdenka Mansfeldova, Radek Markowski, and Gabor Toka, *Post-Communist Party Systems*

David Knoke, Franz Urban Pappi, Jeffrey Broadbent, and Yutaka Tsujinaka, eds., *Comparing Policy Networks*

Allan Kornberg and Harold D. Clarke, *Citizens and Community: Political Support in a Representative Democracy*

Amie Kreppel, *The European Parliament and the Supranational Party System*

David D. Laitin, *Language Repertoires and State Construction in Africa*

Fabrice E. Lehoucq and Ivan Molina, *Stuffing the Ballot Box: Fraud, Electoral Reform, and Democratization in Costa Rica*

Mark Irving Lichbach and Alan S. Zuckerman, eds., *Comparative Politics: Rationality, Culture, and Structure, 2nd edition*

Evan Lieberman, *Race and Regionalism in the Politics of Taxation in Brazil and South Africa*

Julia Lynch, *Age in the Welfare State: The Origins of Social Spending on Pensioner's Workers and Children*

Pauline Jones Luong, *Institutional Change and Political Continuity in Post-Soviet Central Asia*

Pauline Jones Luong and Erika Weinthal, *Oil is Not a Curse: Ownership Structure and Institutions in Soviet Successor States*

Doug McAdam, John McCarthy, and Mayer Zald, eds., *Comparative Perspectives on Social Movements*

Lauren M. MacLean, *Informal Institutions and Citizenship in Rural Africa: Risk and Reciprocity in Ghana and Côte d'Ivoire*

Beatriz Magaloni, *Voting for Autocracy: Hegemonic Party Survival and its Demise in Mexico*

James Mahoney, *Colonialism and Postcolonial Development: Spanish America in Comparative Perspective*

James Mahoney and Dietrich Rueschemeyer, eds., *Historical Analysis and the Social Sciences*

Scott Mainwaring and Matthew Soberg Shugart, eds., *Presidentialism and Democracy in Latin America*

Isabela Mares, *The Politics of Social Risk: Business and Welfare State Development*

Isabela Mares, *Taxation, Wage Bargaining, and Unemployment*

Cathie Jo Martin and Duane Swank, *The Political Construction of Business Interests: Coordination, Growth, and Equality*

Anthony W. Marx, *Making Race, Making Nations: A Comparison of South Africa, the United States, and Brazil*

Bonnie M. Meguid, *Party Competition between Unequals: Strategies and Electoral Fortunes in Western Europe*

Joel S. Migdal, *State in Society: Studying How States and Societies Constitute One Another*

Joel S. Migdal, Atul Kohli, and Vivienne Shue, eds., *State Power and Social Forces: Domination and Transformation in the Third World*

Scott Morgenstern and Benito Nacif, eds., *Legislative Politics in Latin America*

Layna Mosley, *Global Capital and National Governments*

Layna Mosley, *Labor Rights and Multinational Production*

Wolfgang C. Müller and Kaare Strøm, *Policy, Office, or Votes?*

Maria Victoria Murillo, *Political Competition, Partisanship, and Policy Making in Latin American Public Utilities*

Maria Victoria Murillo, *Labor Unions, Partisan Coalitions, and Market Reforms in Latin America*

Monika Nalepa, *Skeletons in the Closet: Transitional Justice in Post-Communist Europe*

Ton Notermans, *Money, Markets, and the State: Social Democratic Economic Policies since 1918*

Aníbal Pérez-Liñán, *Presidential Impeachment and the New Political Instability in Latin America*